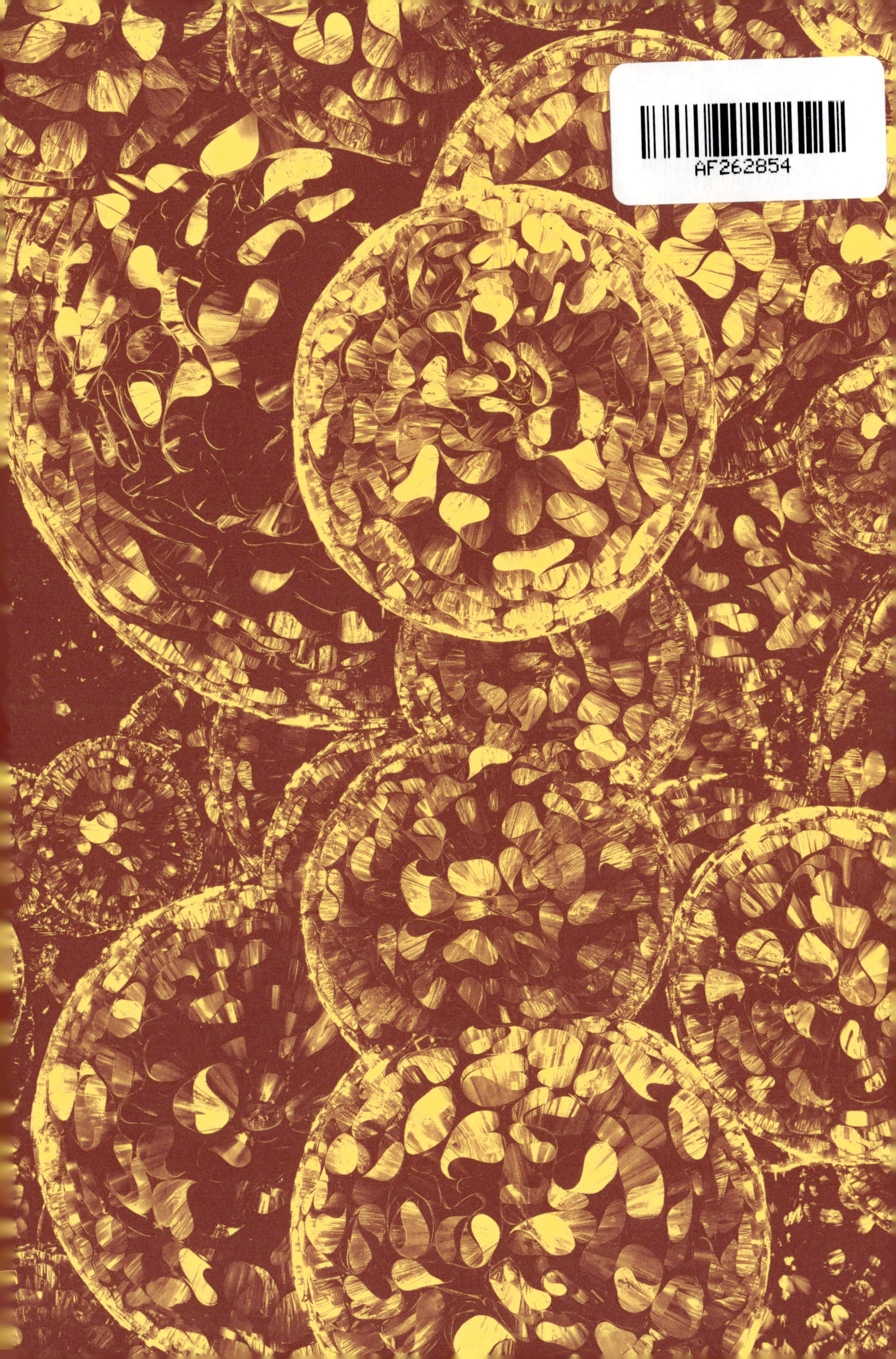
AF262854

When Forms Come Alive

Sixty Years of Restless Sculpture

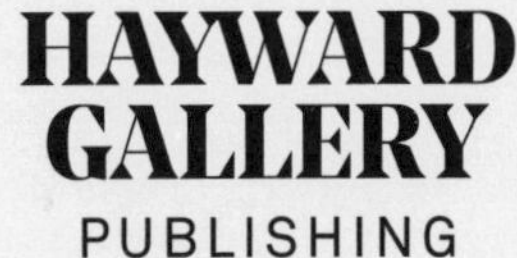

HAYWARD
GALLERY
PUBLISHING

When

Forms

Come

Alive

Foreword 6

Ralph Rugoff
Restless Sculpture 9

Natalie Rudd
**Going with the Flow:
Ways of Bringing Sculpture to Life** 25

Artists
Ruth Asawa 42, 194
Nairy Baghramian 50, 196
Phyllida Barlow 58, 198
Lynda Benglis 64, 200
Michel Blazy 70, 202
Paloma Bosquê 76, 204
Olaf Brzeski 82, 206
Choi Jeong Hwa 88, 208
Tara Donovan 96, 210
DRIFT 104, 212
Eva Fàbregas 112, 214
Holly Hendry 120, 216
EJ Hill 128, 218
Marguerite Humeau 134, 220
Jean-Luc Moulène 142, 222
Senga Nengudi 150, 224
Ernesto Neto 156, 226
Martin Puryear 164, 228
Matthew Ronay 170, 230
Teresa Solar Abboud 178, 232
Franz West 186, 234

Exhibited Works 236
Photographic Credits 238
Acknowledgements 239

FOREWORD

Spanning several generations, *When Forms Come Alive* highlights a lineage of contemporary sculpture that reflects on and explores aspects of movement, flux and organic growth. Beginning with key works by a pioneering group of women artists – Ruth Asawa, Lynda Benglis and Senga Nengudi – the exhibition traces an aesthetic evolution that has taken place over the past 60 years, up through the work of a younger generation that has developed these concerns in highly compelling and inventive new directions. Referencing organic topographies and often embodying qualities of liquidity and buoyancy, the artworks featured in *When Forms Come Alive* issue a playful rebuke to rigid geometries. Often taking on ambiguous or uncanny forms, they evince a compelling corporeality, actively engaging our sense of touch as well as sight. In an era when our social encounters increasingly take place in the digital ether, the work of these artists urges us to rediscover the pleasures of spontaneous gesture and movement, the poetics of gravity and the experience of sensation itself.

To some extent, this exhibition adds another chapter to a sculptural history examined in an earlier Hayward Gallery show, *Move: Choreographing You* (2010–11), which looked at the fertile cross-talk between the visual arts, dance and performance. *When Forms Come Alive* examines the relationship of sculpture and movement from a very different perspective, yet similarly reflects the Hayward's focus on opening up new narratives in the recent history of art, especially those that address salient aspects of contemporary experience.

Organising an exhibition of this complexity and ambition involves innumerable challenges and requires the help of a great many people. This exhibition could not have been realised without the generous support of the *When Forms Come Alive* Exhibition Supporters Group: Bianca and Stuart Roden, Simon Morris and Annalisa Burello, White Cube, Sarah Cannon, Thomas Dane Gallery, Gagosian, Sprüth Magers and David Zwirner Gallery. Additional support has also kindly been provided by the Henry Moore Foundation, Hauser & Wirth and Fluxus Art Projects. I also wish to acknowledge the generosity of the many lenders involved. We extend to them our deepest gratitude and appreciation for making these artworks available to the public.

Hayward Publisher Mary Richards, working with the innovative design team Sophie Demay and Maël Fournier-Comte at In the Shade of a Tree, ensured that this book matches the adventurous spirit of the art that it chronicles. Natalie Rudd deserves our thanks for her insightful historical essay, and for their excellent short texts our gratitude goes to contributing authors James Attlee, Helen Luckett and Lorena Muñoz-Alonso.

Assistant Curator Katie Guggenheim, along with Curatorial Assistant Anusha Mistry, did a superb job in all aspects of researching and organising the exhibition, and contributing texts to this book. Hayward Senior Technician Archie Bell successfully led a very challenging planning process and skillfully led the technical team during the installation. Hayward Senior Registrar Charlotte Pearson expertly oversaw transport and conservation for the many sculptures in the exhibition. Many other people on the Hayward team and at Southbank Centre have contributed to realising this exhibition – their names appear on page 239.

As always, I am grateful for the support of Southbank Centre CEO Elaine Bedell and Artistic Director Mark Ball, as well as Southbank Centre's Board of Trustees and Arts Council England. Finally, I wish to express our enormous appreciation and admiration to all of the participating artists in *When Forms Come Alive* for making such brilliant and engaging work, and for profoundly enhancing and energising our curiosity about our ever-changing world.

Ralph Rugoff
Director, Hayward Gallery

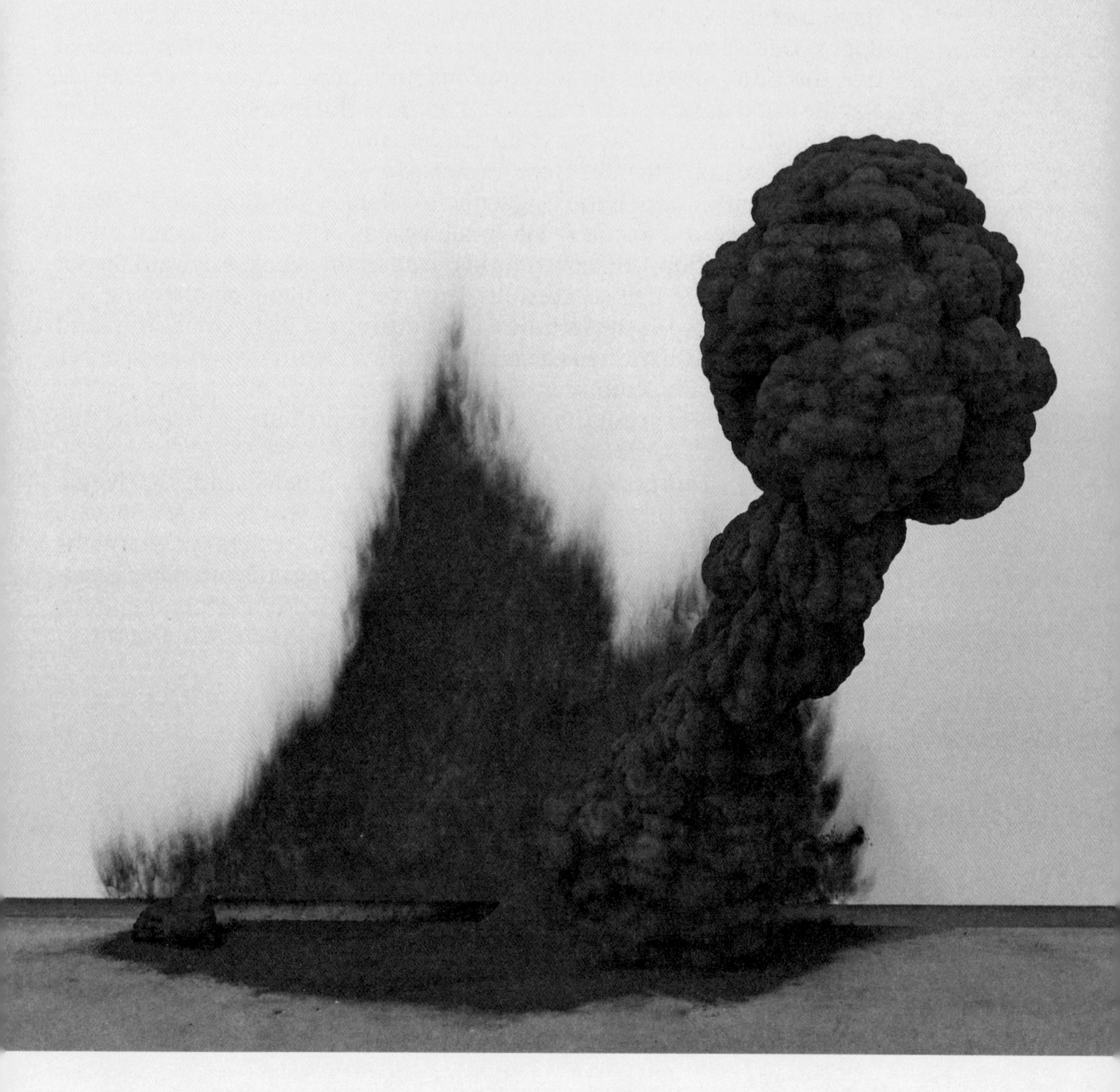

Olaf Brzeski, *Dream – Spontaneous Combustion*, 2008

RALPH RUGOFF

Restless Sculpture

*My work belongs to the realm of the somatic, the experiential,
the guttural and the unnameable.* — EVA FÀBREGAS [1]

Across the span of societal activity from work to leisure, consumption to reproduction, every object with a defined purpose has a particular name, a designated word to describe it. Our vocabularies are geared to refer to a world of manufactured things, predictable architectures, standardised shapes and gestures. But as a culture, we suffer from a kind of linguistic impoverishment when it comes to talking about 'organic' or 'irregular' forms. And typically, when we encounter things that have no place in our language and so prove difficult to speak of, we feel anxious or unsettled. Unnameable forms issue a disconcerting challenge to our tacitly assumed, know-it-all sovereignty.

Many of the artists featured in *When Forms Come Alive* engage us in this kind of disarming (and enlivening) encounter. We have no precise labels for the ambiguous and unsettled forms with which their sculptures confront us. Their uncertain topographical provenance can leave us baffled, so that we end up trying to describe them in terms that refer only to characteristics that they seem to lack: we call them 'formless' or 'shapeless', or comment on the absence of any discernible formal organisation in a particular sculpture. But how does one precisely describe, for instance, the abstract coagulation of Olaf Brzeski's *Dream – Spontaneous Combustion* (2008, p. 83), a frozen cloud of charred ash that seems to erupt in the gallery's hygienic confines like a projectile vomiting of black filth? We recognise it as a form linked to explosions or fires, but our lack of any terms to precisely delineate its specific shape and volume contributes to our feeling of being somehow muted and mesmerised before this uncanny apparition.

Spanning a period of more than 60 years, *When Forms Come Alive* highlights the ways in which recent sculpture has drawn on references to mobility, flux and organic growth to conjure realms of fluid and shifting experience. In the process, the 21 artists presented here have introduced into the medium's vocabulary an extraordinary range of indefinable shapes, irregular surfaces and precarious protuberances, including complex aggregations of forms that depart from conventional geometries. Whether they appear to be oozing, undulating, cascading, coagulating or promiscuously proliferating, these artists' sculptures evince an almost palpable vitality. No matter how abstract they might be, each conveys an impression of being uncannily animated: their unexpected curves or knot-like structures evoking circuits of flow and transformation. As artist Holly Hendry has aptly described her own work, these sculptures appear to be 'twitching with life'.[2]

With the exception of a few kinetic installations, the 'liveliness' of these artworks springs from an implied mobility rather than literal movement. In other words, it is largely through perceptual and conceptual means that such works convey a sense of motion. They remind us that forms cannot be neatly demarcated and isolated, because they engage in continual conversation with other forms (as well as with the space around them), transforming one another in the process. Reflecting on this unending back-and-forth dialogue in his book *The Life of Forms in Art* (1934), art historian Henri Focillon (1881–1943) characterised forms as 'alive' precisely because they are never immobile – not only in terms of how we perceive their shifting visual relationships, but also because of the endless associations and allusions that forms generate, enabled by the correspondences that exist between the shapes and contours of so many diverse things.[3]

The artists discussed here generally traffic in non-Euclidean geometries. They deal in asymmetrical forms that are conventionally referred to as 'organic', and which may be reminiscent of biology or botany, naturally occurring patterns and topographies. Several of their sculptures might bring to mind the 'biomorphic' profile associated with the work of twentieth-century artists such as Hans Arp (1886–1966), Henry Moore (1898–1986) or Barbara Hepworth (1903–75). Still, as a group, these works stand apart from that earlier tradition through their dynamic evocation of the flux and flow of lived experience, including the transience and mutability of matter, and natural systems of growth and entropy. Rather than anatomical allusions, many of these artists invoke references linked to an array of material processes, from the interlacing of a spider's web to the viscous dribble of molten metal.

Whether inspiring thoughts of fungal blooms, mushroom clouds or the diurnal choreography of flowers, these artworks prompt us to consider anew the 'life of forms'. Given the conceptual bias of so much contemporary art, this may seem like an anachronistic and irrelevant concern. But as the work featured here makes evident, the material and conceptual fluidity of form is what drives and facilitates sculpture's provocatively restless identity, and enables it to continue to resonate with key aspects of contemporary life and thought.

The relationship between sculptural form and notions of movement and growth became a focus for a number of pioneering artists in the 1960s and 1970s, including Ruth Asawa, Lynda Benglis and Senga Nengudi. Their work departed not only from the clean geometries of minimalism, but also from the monumental character of much large-scale work made of traditional sculptural media such as bronze, steel and stone. In contrast to the monolithic or industrially fabricated structures created by many male artists of the time, sculptures by Asawa, Benglis and Nengudi conveyed a sense of contingency and impermanence. Asawa's metal wire sculptures, which she first began making in the mid-1950s, nested spherical forms inside hourglass shapes, elaborating multi-layered and translucent sculptural volumes through which air could freely pass. Hung from the ceiling to enable a subtle swaying motion, these intricate and buoyant forms would cast billowing shadows across the walls and floor of the gallery, adding another suggestion of flux to their ephemeral presence.

Asawa's sculpture stood in sharp counterpoint to standard notions of sculptural mass and solidity. Equally subversive of the medium's norms, Benglis's late 1960s sculptures, made by pouring latex or polyurethane foam onto the floor, resembled oozing landscapes or psychedelic industrial spills that spread across flat surfaces or piled up in corners. By foregrounding a tactile sense of material malleability and change, these sculptures dramatically departed from the 'rational' rectilinearity favoured across much modernist design and epitomised by the 'white cube' art gallery spaces then coming into fashion. 'The pouring of the material was very much about wanting to create undulating surfaces and complex planes that resist geometry,' Benglis explained. 'I like things to flow.'[4]

An implicit political stance was embedded in this embrace of mobile form. Rejecting tropes of stability, the work of these artists articulated a distinctly non-monumental approach to sculpture; as if reflecting some of the ethos of the period's counterculture, their work gave value to fleeting states of being, temporary situations and fluctuating relationships. Rather than permanence, an artist like Senga Nengudi focused on sculptural values that could convey the energy and tension of everyday existence in a physical body. Her 1970s installations featuring nylon stockings that stretched across the floors and walls of an exhibition space, often knotted and weighted with sand, alluded to the elasticity and flexibility of the human body, its shape-shifting character and mobility. Further underscoring this engagement with movement, Nengudi often used performers to activate and interact with these sculptures in choreographies that highlighted the push-and-pull of gravity.

A similarly non-hierarchical dynamic is evident in many of the aggregate sculptures created by Phyllida Barlow, who from the late 1980s developed an improvisational approach to working with common and recycled materials. Works such as *untitled: modernsculpture; 2022* (2022, p. 63) – a densely clustered, forest-like grouping of vertical forms – evince an anarchic, decentred energy that springs from the lively and open-ended conversations that develop between its many constituent parts. In describing her sculptures as 'nonmonumental', owing to their rejection of rigidly unified compositions, Barlow underscored her commitment to making art that was too fluid to be easily pinned down or pigeonholed. 'I want the work to change depending on where it is viewed from so its image and pictorial identity are constantly dissolved', she noted.[5]

That ethos of perpetual transformation and dissolution also animates the work of Michel Blazy. Over the past three decades, Blazy has frequently made sculptures incorporating ephemeral materials that change over time, including plants, food and microorganisms. *Bouquet Final* (2012, pp. 71–73) is a kind of multi-tiered fountain constructed with industrial scaffolding;

in place of water, however, it features a slow-motion, shape-shifting cascade of thick white foam that spills out from holding trays in which scented bubble bath has been whipped up by aerator pumps. Making use of gravity as a force of composition as well as decomposition, *Bouquet Final* suggests a bricoleur's homage to entropy's relentless drift. More sombrely, it also brings to mind spectacles of runaway industrial waste and consumer pollution.

In different ways, the work of all of these artists insinuates that nothing stays the same, that everything changes – including our ways of seeing and the myriad assumptions that buttress the reigning cultural status quo. It comprises an aesthetic that conspicuously deviates from the general principles of public order, which rely on regulation and control. The power of the State comes with an unspoken, coercive injunction: follow the rules and live in a well-regulated society, or else descend into disorder. Artworks that activate the fluidity of forms, on the other hand, remind us that these ostensibly opposed conditions are never really separate – that chaos has its own alternative geometries, and order is always already in the process of becoming something else.

Bodies in Motion

Form is not primarily line and color, it is a dynamic organization. — HENRI FOCILLON[6]

While they avoid directly representing the human body, most of the artworks in this survey display a distinctive corporeality. Their lively forms and tactile surfaces invite a haptic gaze. Playing on the infinite diversity of gesture and movement, and drawing on an understanding of how bodies change shape when in motion or repose, these sculptures trigger a range of visceral responses. Some of them, through the buoyant interplay of their forms and materials, beckon us with the immediacy of a live event or performance. Commenting on her early performer-activated installations, Nengudi observed: 'In a literal sense, the sculpture is a dance partner.'[7] This relationship can exist even when the work does not itself include a performative dimension: the writer Hilton Als describes witnessing a pair of young museum visitors who spontaneously burst into dance in front of a sculpture by Martin Puryear. 'They wanted their bodies to be "like" the work: joyous, free, disciplined, exact.'[8] Without ever directly alluding to anatomical forms, the sensuous, slinky curves and tactile surfaces of Puryear's sculpture – like the work of many other artists in this exhibition – solicit a distinctly somatic response. They activate our bodily sense of rhythm.

The allure of lilting, dance-like movement animates DRIFT's 2006–14 *Shylight* installation (pp. 105–9). Suspended from the ceiling, luminous organic forms made of silk and steel continually mimic the folding and unfolding of flowers that close at night. Lonneke Gordijn, one of DRIFT's two co-founders (with Ralph Nauta), has described this synchronised choreography as 'a performative sculpture: when you enter the space, it becomes a kind of dance that is performed in front of you'.[9] Just as we can connect with others through rhythmic movement and music, *Shylight* offers a vision for 'aligning the frequency of our heartbeat, or our breath, to the movements that are always present in nature'.[10]

12

Sinuously fluttering overhead, *Shylight* evokes a sensation of weightlessness, as if these glowing kinetic sculptures, through their mesmerising motion, had somehow neutralised the pull of gravity. Alluding to a very different kind of dialogue between gravity and weightlessness, EJ Hill's light installation *A Subsequent Offering* (2017, p. 130) presents a neon track that outlines the familiar trajectory of a rollercoaster as it rises and falls across a low, twisting, attenuated wooden scaffold. Displayed in an unlit gallery, Hill's installation radiates a muted, memorial-tinged elegance even as it quietly triggers memories of thrillingly antic motion. Proposing that we regard rollercoasters as public monuments to the possibility of experiencing joy – which Hill considers to be 'a critical component of social equity' – the artist has said that he employs their familiar serpentine form as a means to 'communicate ideas that I have about struggle and mortality and the impulse to go higher and faster and test our physical and mental limits'.[11]

Eva Fàbregas's sprawling installations of inflatable sculptures – some of which call to mind enormous, pastel-coloured intestinal worms – owe part of their animated character to sound. *Pumping* (2019, pp. 113–17), which features a tangled mass of long mesh tubes stuffed with knobby massage balls, literally vibrates with the heavy basslines of its electronic soundtrack. Viewers are free to touch the resonating, membrane-like surfaces of the sculpture, allowing the low-frequency audio to pulsate like a foreign heartbeat inside their own skins. *Pumping* provokes thoughts of internal bodily landscapes, digestive processes and swarming cellular metamorphoses; at the same time, when presented in a dark room illuminated by changing coloured lights, it might also conjure a nightclub where our dance partners are chilled-out alien organisms. 'I see my work as creatures that can help us imagine other possible bodies,' the artist has remarked, 'other ways of living, and new forms of desire and affect.'[12]

Architectures of Growth

*If you study the principles of nature, then the answers
are all there.* — RUTH ASAWA[13]

Structures of organic life comprise a key departure point for many of the artists featured here. Ruth Asawa, for instance, remarked that her sculptures were inspired by her observation of forms in nature, including 'plants, the spiral shell of a snail, seeing light through insect wings, watching spiders repair their webs in the early morning'.[14] Tara Donovan deploys material aggregation as a means of suggesting processes of growth: the artist employs tens of thousands of tiny, mass-produced items to compose sprawling sculptures that evoke phenomena ranging from complex molecular constellations to otherworldly cloud formations. Noting that 'the idea of growth is central to my understanding of how I work',[15] Donovan has explained that in her sculpture she is not 'trying to simulate nature. It's more of a mimicking of the way of nature, the way things actually grow.'[16]

Repetition of form as a metaphor for organic growth is also a primary driver of Choi Jeong Hwa's extensive sculptural series *Blooming matrix* (2018, pp. 89–95). Choi combines identical, cheaply made objects into densely clustered stacks that resemble botanical forms or crystalline geological structures.

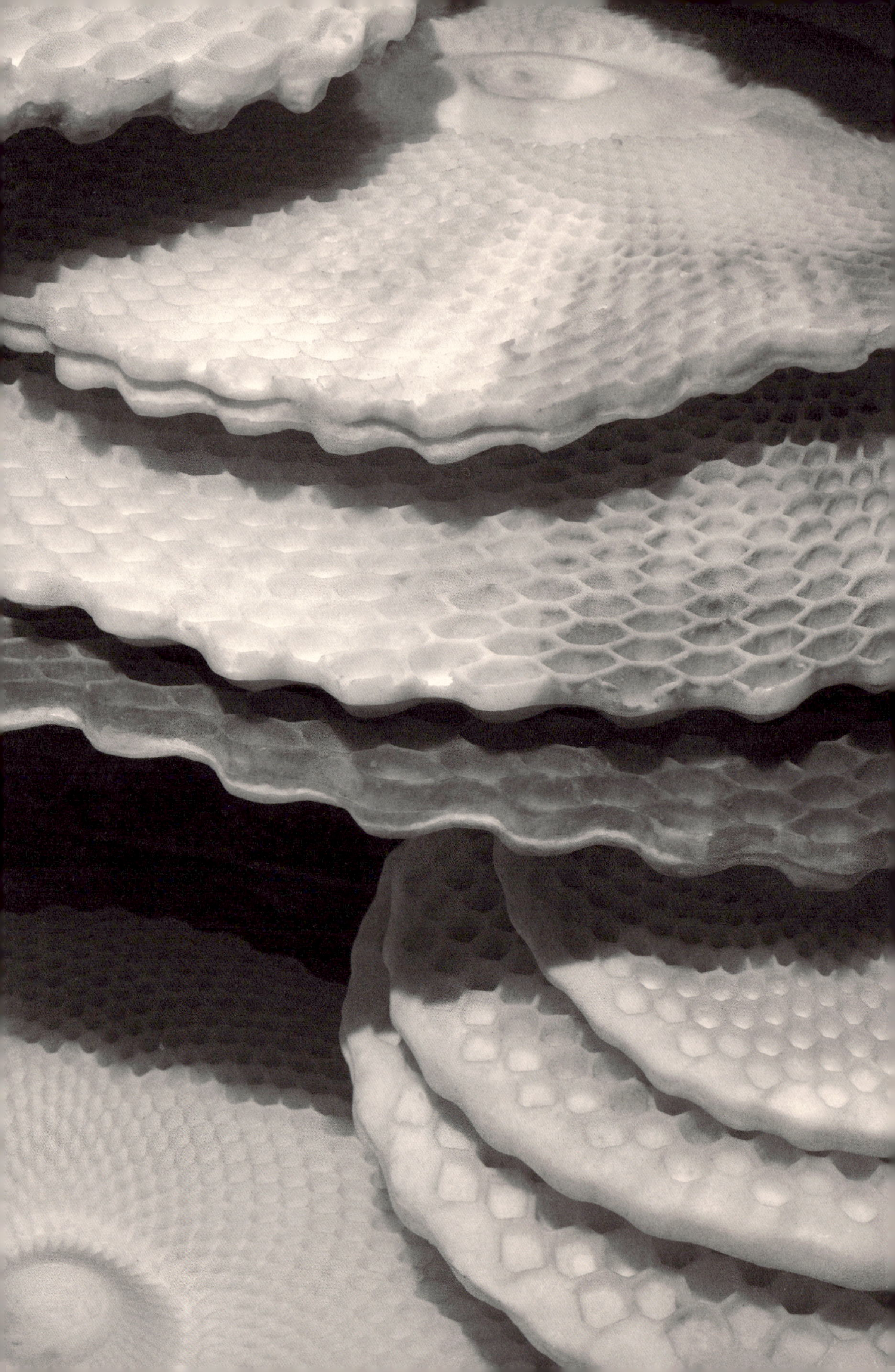

Through the transformative effects of accumulation and aggregation, the artist recasts common consumer goods – often brightly coloured plastic items with involute forms – into complex forms that remind us of characteristic patterns of growth.

In her intricately fabricated *The Guardian of Ancient Yeast* (2023, pp. 139–40), Marguerite Humeau elaborates a hybrid sculptural vocabulary that draws on architectures of the insect world. Made with an eclectic mix of materials that include wax and wood partially eaten by worms and fungi, Humeau's sculptures are inspired in part by beehives and termite mounds – collectively forged structures whose surfaces often reveal the countless movements involved in their making (it is worth mentioning that Humeau's considerable research process led her to the writings of early twentieth-century naturalist Eugène Marais (1871–1936), who regarded termite habitats as living organisms). Other works in the series replicate the gills of mushrooms or reference vessels used for brewing yeast-fermented cultures – a nod to the long history of complex interconnections between human societies and microorganisms. A layering of sculptural 'voices' – breathy and percussive soundscapes created by experimental saxophonist Bendik Giske – adds a sonic dimension to the lively aura of activity that animates these materially varied sculptures, evoking the sense of ongoing conversations taking place within this diverse network of forms.

Collaborating with Materials

It is plainly observable how matter imposes its own form upon form. — HENRI FOCILLON[17]

If a naturalist can consider a termite mound a living system – one whose inhabitants, like the cells in a body, work together to grow and maintain it – can we also regard certain works of art from a similar perspective? Certainly, many of the artists in this survey regard their work as the outcome of a collaborative engagement with both their chosen materials and with gravity. With her poured sculptures like *Quartered Meteor* (1969, cast 1975, pp. 68–69), Benglis deliberately set up a production method that ensured the malleable nature of her materials and her process of making would be directly reflected in the appearance of the finished sculptural form. As if in accord with Focillon's observation that 'matter imposes its own form upon form', the resulting sculpture reflected a decentred notion of authorship, inasmuch as the outcome depended as much on the particular characteristics of the materials being used as it did on the actions of a human agent.

In similarly abandoning traditional claims to exclusive authorship and aesthetic authority, later artists such as Blazy and Humeau have moved away from the anthropocentric bias of most human cultural activity. Blazy, who has said that he regards his sculptures as 'living beings', describes his approach as if he were a kind of caretaker or curator of material processes: 'My gesture as a sculptor often consists of triggering a process that takes shape on its own; I try to create the right conditions for a material to perform.'[18] Humeau has spoken of her own thinking in similar terms: 'I don't make sculptures, I make beings that are alive … I conceive them as processes so they are alive. They have their bloodflows, or heartbeats that we can hear in the background.'[19]

Marguerite Humeau,
The Holder of Wasp Venom, 2023 (detail)

This way of thinking about art as a kind of living system chimes with current concerns about the need for human beings to give up our self-centred perspective, and to reimagine our place in the world in a manner that recognises our co-dependency with the natural environment. Yet curiously, as Franz West once noted, the idea of collaborating with materials also relates to a conception of art that in Western Europe, at least, dates back to the roots of classical civilisation. 'It is well-known that the Greek sculptors said they were like an extension of the tool that was working on the material', West related. 'I think it is a bit like that in my case too. One is, so to speak ... only a handmaid for the finished sculpture ... That sounds childish and stupid, but it is real.'[20]

In contrast with the art produced in Ancient Greece, however, West's 'finished sculptures' tend to have a distinctly provisional quality. As was the case with other artists such as Barlow, the approach of collaborating with one's materials often resulted in sculptures that appear to be perpetually improvised 'works in progress'. A similar sense of contingency infuses many of Paloma Bosquê's sculptures – a work like *Two Stones* (2017, pp. 78–79) suggests a precarious arrangement of materials still open to further possibilities of development. This intimation of potential change enhances the physical liveliness that characterises the work of these artists: distinguished by rough, irregular contours, misshapen lumps and unexpected indentations, their sculptures teeter on the edge of formal resolution but never quite convey the impression of having reached a final state of equilibrium.

In this respect, their work corresponds with Barlow's definition of sculpture as an 'extremely restless' medium. Because you observe different aspects of a sculpture whilst walking around it, Barlow maintained that 'you can never quite hold on to what it is. Sculpture unfolds and refolds and unfolds again.'[21] This is especially true of the irregular, organic or eccentric forms that make up the artworks under consideration here. Seen from different viewpoints, the unexpected swellings, wobbly outline or complex curves of a particular sculpture might suggest alternative associations: an element that resembles a bodily organ from one angle may look more like a gently rounded hilltop or a scoop of melting ice cream when seen from the other side. Through simple changes of perspective, our perception and experience of such work can move in a variety of alternative directions. As Tara Donovan has remarked: 'Because the surfaces of my work often shift and follow the perspective of the viewer, there is a perceptual movement that coincides with a person's physical movement within the gallery space.'[22]

The Strange Motility of Knots

Everything is a knot. — LYNDA BENGLIS[23]

That kind of enlivening encounter – in which our perception of a sculptural object radically shifts as we move around it – highlights the potentially dynamic character of form. It also underscores the ways in which forms are inextricably entangled with their surroundings, as it is not only the topological profile of the sculpture that changes as we circumnavigate it, but also the space within which it appears to us. Schooled in such experiences, attentive observers must look askance at the traditional notion that forms delineate fixed and circumscribed boundaries, as if marking the borders of autonomous entities. In order to explore the interweaving of forms with their environs, several artists presented here have created works that exhibit knot-like structures. Asawa was an early explorer of this artistic territory: in her hanging sculptures woven from metal wire, forms are made visible through and within other forms, as if coexisting in a kind of entangled spatial volume that defies our usual distinctions of internal and external – conjuring forms, as she noted, that were 'inside and outside at the same time.'[24]

Many of Martin Puryear's exactingly fabricated wooden sculptures – such as *Untitled* (2015, pp. 165–66) – subvert traditions of sculpture as solid mass by fashioning forms in which 'inside' and 'outside' are equally visible. More classically knot-like, Jean-Luc Moulène's tabletop sculptures of glass and metal conjure complex Möbius loops; the artist has described these works as 'surfaces, with no inside or outside, only holes'.[25] While we commonly think of knots as fixing things in place, Moulène's sculptures instead suggest circuits of perpetual motion, eliding our attempts to mentally unwind their paradoxical configurations.

Lynda Benglis, who has spent much of her career experimenting with knot-like sculptural forms, links this motif to patterns of growth. 'Everything is a knot', she has observed. 'A growing plant is a knot, a body is a knot, every embryo is a knot.'[26] Her polished, highly reflective bronze sculpture *Power Tower* (2019, pp. 65–66) comprises a twisting, melting configuration of curving surfaces and perforations; viewers who walk around the work in order to explore its volatile, hyperbolic geometries may find themselves – and mirrored images of their bodies – enmeshed in an entangled and rubbery space in which everything feels loosely linked, as if joined by invisible knots (which, rather than fixed points, function in this kind of topological space as infinitely flexible joints).

Holly Hendry, in discussing her serpentine installations made with industrial ducting, has described a relationship between her work and its architectural site in which 'outside and inside are totally interrelated ... I imagined the building being eaten, chewed up, spat out by [the work's] monstrous form.'[27] In confounding our customary spatial division of inside and outside, such sculptures ultimately illuminate the interconnectedness of forms. They remind us that the incessant visual dialogue between forms carries on across all boundaries and conventional lines of demarcation. These works also implicitly speak to our experience of being *of* the world, rather than standing apart from it – a notion that was influentially elaborated (among other places) in the writings of early twentieth-century philosopher Georges Bataille (1897–1962). Bataille envisioned the human body as a site of ceaseless exchange between inside and outside – a viewpoint in sharp contrast to a humanist tradition that defines the individual as an independent, self-contained subject, a sealed system with solid borders separating it from other people and the world at large.

As if rearticulating that Bataillean perspective, Nairy Baghramian's *Chin Up (First Fitting)* (2016, pp. 51–55) presents paired, open aluminium structures that resemble greatly enlarged versions of orthodontic braces. Displayed high on a gallery wall, they appear as receptacles waiting to receive some missing content (an enormous tooth, perhaps?). At the same time, the work prompts viewers to wonder whether it positions us as though we were inside a giant mouth, gazing outwards, or vice versa. Collapsing oppositions of inside and outside, content and form, growth and restraint, Baghramian's sculpture intimates the possibilities of a social space in which our 'normal' sense of personal and institutional boundaries no longer holds sway. 'I am interested in the thin membrane separating the inside from the outside in physical and social spaces', Baghramian has noted. 'It is about inclusion or exclusion.'[28]

A Flow of Associations

*Form is surrounded by a certain aura: although it is our most
strict definition of space, it also suggests to us the existence
of other forms.* — HENRY FOCILLON[29]

One of the key ways in which the artworks discussed here evince an energetic liveliness is by triggering myriad and diverse associations. If they refuse to lie down and be accountable, as it were, it is in large part because they are constantly starting up conversations with a wide range of other forms. When viewed from different angles, irregular and complex (as opposed to geometric) forms can appear radically different, and this, in turn, multiplies the manner in which such forms inevitably bring to mind other, vaguely similar things: forms that may be present in the same space or even within the same work, but also forms from elsewhere, from the world at large, from history and the inventories of our visual memory. Inasmuch as they continually prompt this restless dialogue of comparison and contrast, irregular forms are never immobile. Our encounters with them invariably unleash a fluid stream of related associations.

Ambiguity is a crucial characteristic that enables this kind of open-ended interpretative play. Consider the sculptures of Hans Arp, one of the pioneers of biomorphic art: the semi-organic forms in his work seemingly allude to parts of living organisms, yet avoid any explicit or directly representational reference. This undefined or in-between status – seeming at once familiar yet impossible to fix in place – allows them to slip and slide in relation to an ever-evolving range of possible associations, and so to continually suggest new avenues of potential meaning. Form, when freed from its conventional obligation of demarcating recognisable boundaries and identities, turns out to be the sliding signifier par excellence.

Form's endlessly mobile, fluidly associative character is abundantly evident in Matthew Ronay's exquisitely shaped, textured and painted wooden sculptures which, like Arp's work, traffic in a lexicon that relates to both the biological and the botanical. Though modestly scaled, Ronay's sculptures – which are composed of distinctively shaped and differently coloured parts – bring into play a vast repertoire of reference. They exhibit resemblances and correspondences with the structures of fungi, insects, plants, sexual organs, coral, ganglia, miscellaneous orifices and microscopic diatoms of algae – to name but a few. As Ronay has put it: 'I started to realise that all these things that you think you invented, nature thought of them first. Beautiful textures, and colours and divine geometries – just real brilliance of pattern, humor, theatre, and a way in which nature embodies thoughts.'[30] By displaying his sculptures in grouped clusters, the artist draws attention to the complex

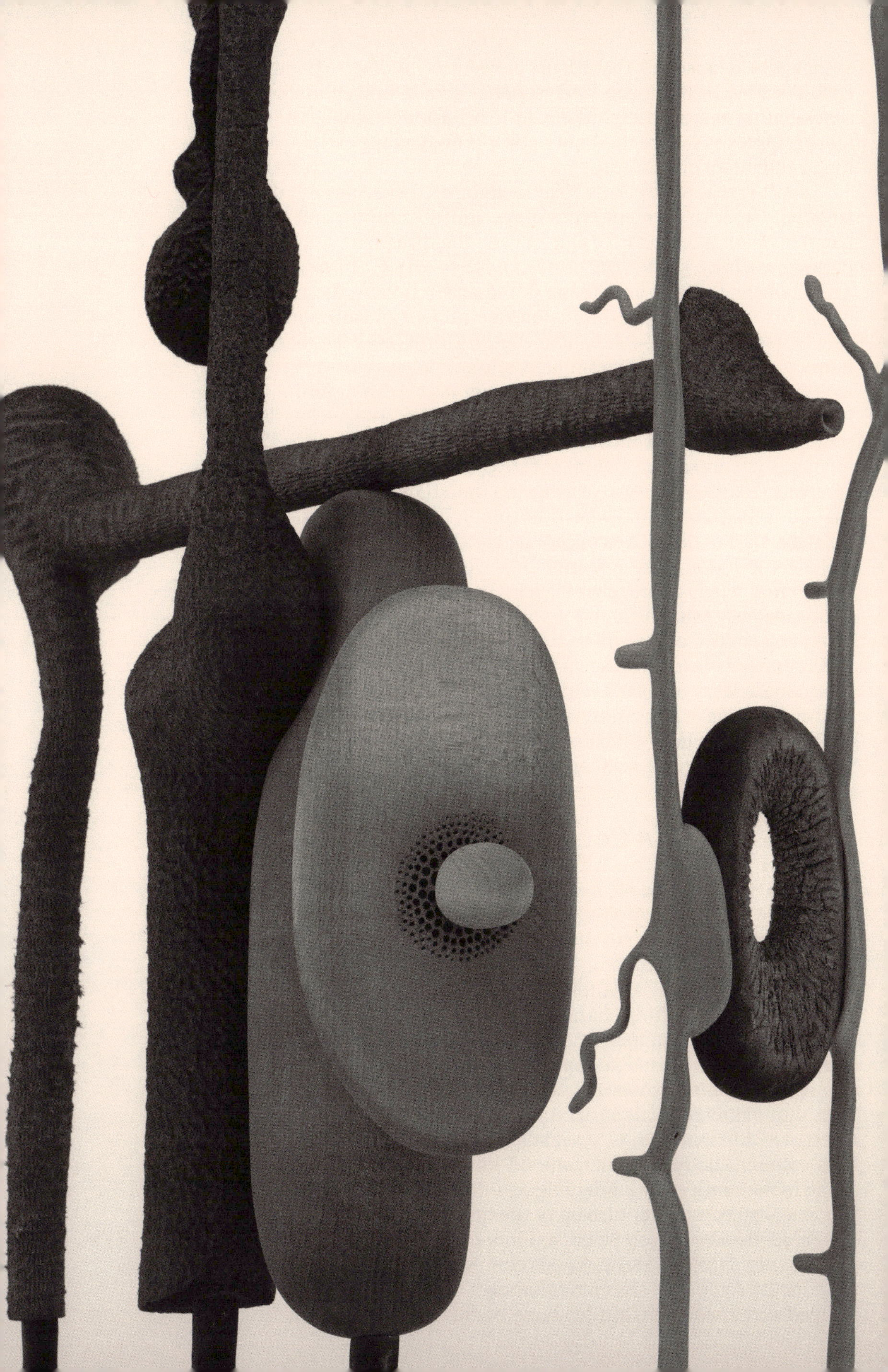

exchange and cross-talk that occurs between such diverse points of reference. Like tiny aesthetic ecosystems, Ronay's sculptural ensembles sustain a blossoming interconnectedness of form, whilst highlighting the ways that more complex structures harbour networks of dynamic exchange between their constituent parts.

Another type of associative play is engineered by sculptures that allude simultaneously to different types of recognisable forms, and so leave us hanging on an interpretative cliff's edge. The three-part configuration of Barlow's *untitled: girl ii; 2019* (2019–20, pp. 59–61), for instance, seems to ambiguously combine architectural and anthropomorphic references; it brings to mind both a megalithic stone monument and an enormous, truncated torso resting on swollen haunches. Its forms seem at once teasingly familiar and elusively indeterminate, and this allows the work to not only to disarm our habitual patterns of response (as we can never fully resolve its 'identity') but also to haunt us – not in any kind of spooky way, but in the sense of a lingering encounter. It stays with us for longer.

In a not dissimilar manner, Teresa Solar Abboud's *Tunnel Boring Machines* (2021–23, pp. 179–85) instigate a traffic jam of competing allusions that can cause our mental wheels to spin in place while we search vainly for some kind of definitive conceptual traction. Most of the works in this series combine joint-like clay structures with aerodynamic forms reminiscent of fins, wings or propeller blades, spray painted in saturated colours. Simultaneously naturalistic and cartoonish, appealing and off-putting, these sculptures arouse our desire to touch them while evincing an enigmatic otherness that makes them seem impossibly, coolly distant. The peculiarly mixed materiality of Solar's work, along with its references to both industrial and organic processes, allows it to escape our usual categories. Indeed, the almost unnervingly animated presence of these works is fuelled, in large part, by a sense of their oscillating hybrid identities.

A Comedy of Forms

There is a playful and delicately absurd aspect to the animated interplay of forms in Ronay's sculpture. Writing about his work, one critic observed that the sculptures seem to 'enact tense little comedic dramas and interactions in the ways they lean, droop or are stacked'.[31] Vividly realised in strong colours, Ronay's sculptures seem like quasi-abstract cousins to the antic, shape-shifting characters of mid-twentieth century cartoons. Notes of physical humour also percolate in sculptures by Franz West and Olaf Brzeski. West's *Kain naht Abel (Kain approaching Abel)* (2009, pp. 190–91) confronts viewers with a pair of precariously balanced 'figures' – ungainly collections of bumpy parts and protuberances, casually painted in different colours – that fail to add up to any conventional image of a coherent body. Energetically off-kilter, like slapstick actors struggling to maintain their vulnerable equilibrium, these sculptures exude a comical abjection reminiscent of the unstable, eccentric characters in a Samuel Beckett novel. Striking a more languid note, Brzeski's series *Little Orphans* (2009–14, pp. 84–87) comes across like a slacker's take on minimalist sculpture: slumping blocks of corten steel are languorously draped across chairs as if they were bodies collapsing from fatigue or boredom. Along with West's errant figures, these sculptures playfully burlesque classical sculpture's self-regarding gravitas, along with modernist ideals of verticality and rectitude.

Physical comedy springs not only from our failure to successfully resist the force of gravity (as in the slips and pratfalls of slapstick), but also in the surprise of unexpected deviations from conventional form. When Senga Nengudi's installations stretch unusual media, like nylons and ropes, into strange contortions as if enacting a sequence of gags and routines, the artist is subverting the visual values associated with traditional sculpture, as well as its aspirations to permanence and transcendent posturing. A comical incongruity also informs Phyllida Barlow's unwieldy and out-of-sync assemblages of disparate materials. Barlow once described her art as comprising an 'adventure of objects', and in some works that sense of adventure is largely fuelled by formal collisions between the multifarious media she employed, and by their apparent resistance to 'aesthetic' manipulation. As she once observed: 'I just want materials to do a job for me, and I like the way those materials might begin like that but they rebel against it and that's where the humour is, this anarchic thing about materials, they won't do what you want them to do.'[32] Even in the world of forms, failure and mishaps lie at the heart of comedy.

The Duties of Form

Summing up conventional thinking on the subject, art historian Rosalind Krauss wrote that 'the duties of form' consist of 'creating binaries ... separating the world into neat pairs of opposition'.[33] Yet clearly this is not the 'duty' taken up by the myriad artworks discussed here. Instead, these sculptures illuminate the restless activity of form; they underscore its mobile and permeable character, which takes shape through continual and ever-evolving negotiations with the world around it. They perpetually remind us of Focillon's insistence that form is dynamic – rather than being defined by a fixed border, form is more like a set of fluid relationships.

In their adventurous engagement with the life of forms, the artists in this exhibition have contributed to an incredibly rich and significant chapter of recent art history. Strangely, it is a chapter that remains largely neglected. Yet, in an era when our encounters are increasingly digitised and disembodied, the work of these artists seems increasingly urgent in returning us to an active exploration of physical experience, and an overdue rethinking of how we make sense of the forms around us. Ingeniously, and often joyously, their restless sculptures remind us that everything in the world – inorganic as well as organic matter – is moving, seething, changing, transforming.

Our understanding of form, as the artists featured here make abundantly evident, is not merely an academic concern. Our future may depend in part on evolving the way we comprehend this subject and, consequently, the way we move through the world. As Marguerite Humeau has pointed out: 'As humans we're starting to understand that we have to merge with the greater goal of life, we have to flow together with other life forms, or we're not going to make it on Earth.'[34] Can we learn, alongside these artists, to think anew through the interlinking, relational character of form? It is a way of seeing, one suspects, that informed Leonardo's contention that everything in the world is connected to everything else – a perspective we continue to ignore at great peril not only to ourselves but to all forms of life.

1   Ellie Brown, 'Unlocking the senses: Getting a feel for the somatic and tactile sculpture of Eva Fàbregas's, *Present Space* (12 January 2023), https://www.presentspace.com/story/the-work-of-eva-fabregas-seems-to-teeter-between-binaries1 (accessed 24 November 2023)

2   Holly Hendry speaking in a 2020 video produced by Jared Schiller/Stephen Friedman Gallery, https://vimeo.com/461845719/c72ea78d47 (accessed 23 November 2023)

3   Henri Focillon, *The Life of Forms in Art*, trans. by George Kubler (New York: Zone Books, 1992)

4   Quoted in Andrew Bonacina/Bibiana Obler/Nora Lawrence, *Lynda Benglis* (London: Phaidon Press, 2002), p.18

5   Sherman Sam, 'Interviews: Phyllida Barlow', *Artforum* (3 October 2011), https://www.artforum.com/columns/phyllida-barlow-talks-about-her-exhibition-at-hauser-wirth-198474/ (accessed 23 November 2023)

6   Focillon 1992, p. 17

7   Natalie Hegert, 'Repondez s'il vous plait: An Interview with Senga Nengudi', *Mutual Art* (28 September 2016), https://www.mutualart.com/Article/Repondez-sil-vous-plait--An-Interview-wi/71B964571BB7D4AF (accessed 24 November 2023)

8   Hilton Als, 'The Dance' in *Martin Puryear* (Wassenaar: Voorlinden Musuem, 2018), p. 10

9   '*Studio Drift SHYLIGHT*' (9 March 2015), https://vimeo.com/121664339 (accessed 24 November 2023)

10   Lonneke Gordijn, 'Finding the Rhythm', *DRIFT: Choreographing the Future* (London: Phaidon, 2022), p. 16

11   Quoted in Alexandra Foradas/Makayla Bailey, 'EJ Hill: Brake Run Helix' (North Adams, MA: MASS MoCA, 2022), p. 3, https://massmoca.org/wp-content/uploads/2022/11/EJHill_GalleryGuide_MECH.pdf (accessed 16 November 2023)

12   Brown 2023

13   Ruth Asawa (2000), https://www.brooklynmuseum.org/opencollection/exhibitions/1202 (accessed 19 December 2023)

14   'Ruth Asawa: Sculpture', https://ruthasawa.com/art/sculpture (accessed 24 November 2023)

15   Tara Donovan, 'Interview', in Jutta Mattern/Mette Marcus/Jean Rank Schelded (eds.), Tara Donovan (Copenhagen: Louisiana Museum of Modern Art, 2013), p. 16

16   Tara Donovan, interview (2004), https://hammer.ucla.edu/exhibitions/2004/hammer-projects-tara-donovan (accessed 2 December 2023)

17   Focillon 1989, p. 19

18   'Michel Blazy: Encourage the Matter', https://www.pca-stream.com/en/articles/michel-blazy-encouraging-the-matter-102 (accessed 24 November 2023)

19   'Conversations: Marguerite Humeau and Charlotte Burns', White Cube, https://www.youtube.com/watch?v=vrBmZOyKI8E (accessed 24 November 2023)

20   Andreas Reiter Raabe, 'Interview: Franz West', *Spike*, No. 16 (Summer 2008), https://spikeartmagazine.com/articles/interview-franz-west (accessed 24 November 2023)

21 Quoted in Alastair Sooke, 'Phyllida Barlow: Nothing Fixed', Tim Marlow (ed.), *Phyllida Barlow: Cul de Sac*, Royal Academy of Arts, London, 2009, p. 10

22 Tara Donovan 2013, p. 30

23 Judith Tannenbaum, 'Oral history interview with Lynda Benglis, 2009 November 20' (2009), https://www.aaa.si.edu/collections/interviews/oral-history-interview-lynda-benglis-15741 (accessed 24 November 2023)

24 Aiko Cuneo, 'Interview with Ruth Asawa' (20 October 2003), unpaginated. Ruth Asawa Papers, Department of Special Collections, Stanford University Libraries, Stanford, CA

25 Jo-ey Tang, '500 Words: Jean-Luc Moulène', *Artforum.com*, 4 November 2016, https://www.artforum.com/columns/jean-luc-moulene-discusses-his-exhibition-at-the-pompidou-231389 (accessed 24 November 2023)

26 Tannenbaum 2009

27 Holly Hendry, video interview '*Indifferent Deep* and *Invertebrate*: De La Warr Pavillon', www.dlwp.com/exhibition/holly-hendry-invertebrate (accessed 24 November 2023)

28 Kostas Prapoglou, 'Nairy Baghramian in conversation with Dr Kostas Prapoglou', *XIBT* (2021), https://www.xibtmagazine.com/2021/08/nairy-baghramian-in-conversation-with-dr-kostas-prapoglou (accessed 24 November 2023)

29 Focillon 1982, p. 34

30 'Modernist Abstraction and Ritualistic Objects: Matthew Ronay', Lecture, Nasher Sculpture Center, Dallas, TX (8 December 2013), https://www.youtube.com/watch?v=5wiXYGgaO3c&ab_channel=NasherSculptureCenter (accessed 24 November 2023)

31 Roberta Smith, 'What to See in Art Galleries Right Now, *New York Times* (6 June 2019)

32 Quoted in Marlow 2009, p. 43

33 Rosalind E. Krauss, *The Optical Unconscious* (Cambridge, MA: MIT Press, 1993), p. 166

34 Mark Hudson, 'Meet the artist who's resurrected sphinxes, mammoths and Cleopatra', *Telegraph* (1 April 2023)

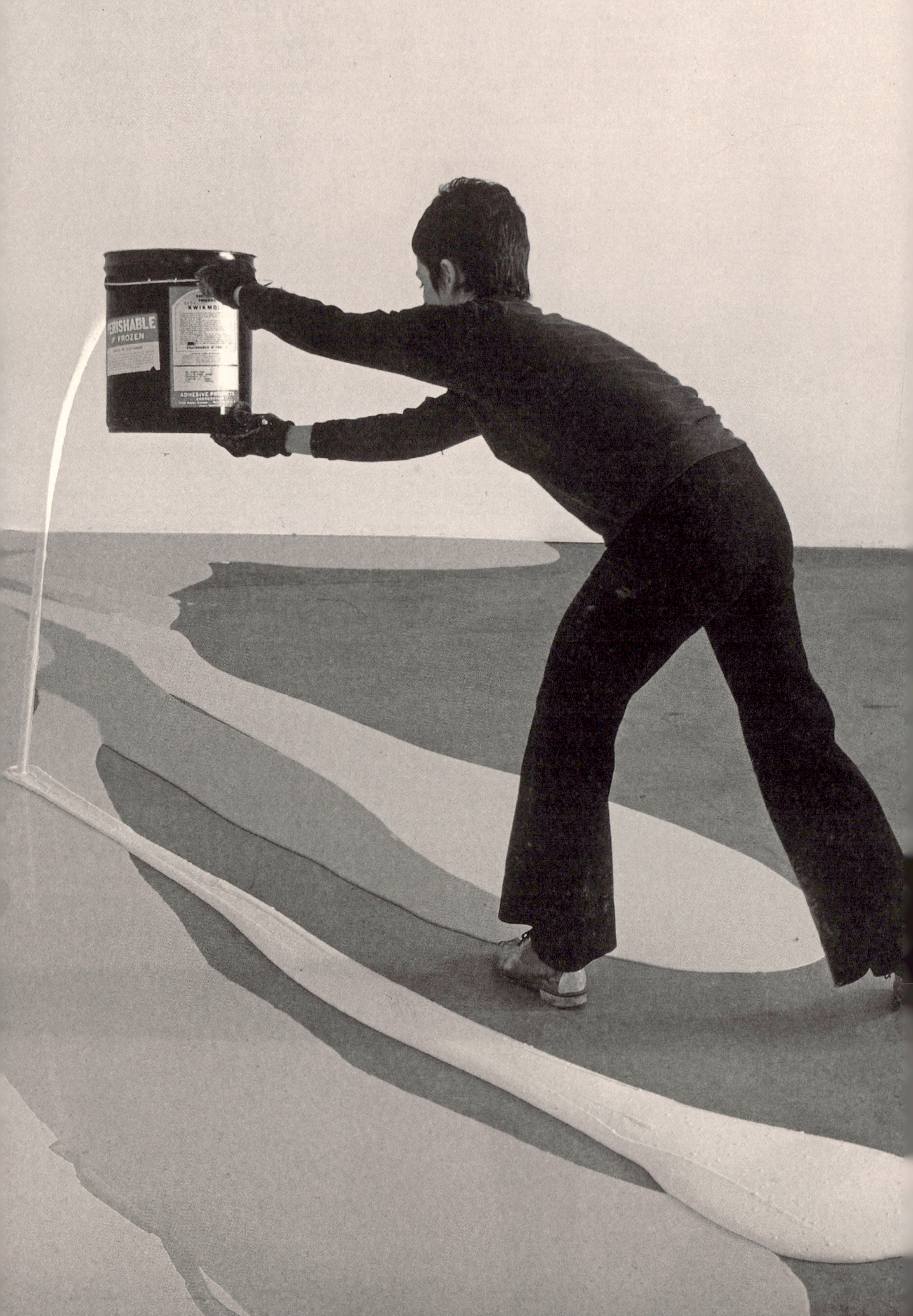

PERISHABLE
IF FROZEN
KWIKMOL
PERISHABLE IF FROZEN
ADHESIVE PRODUCTS
CORPORATION

Lynda Benglis, *Life Magazine*,
27 February 1970

Going with the Flow: Ways of Bringing Sculpture to Life

At first glance, one could be forgiven for thinking that all of the works in this exhibition were made yesterday. Animated, energised and engaging, these forms appear full of life. On closer inspection, it becomes evident that the widespread desire to activate sculpture has a long history. In and among the generous selection of recent work by younger generations of artists, one discovers relatively early examples of work by Ruth Asawa (1926–2013) and Lynda Benglis (b. 1941). There are also significant pieces by Phyllida Barlow (1944–2023), Senga Nengudi (b. 1943), Martin Puryear (b. 1941) and Franz West (1947–2012), all of whom were born during the 1940s. The inclusion of these works acknowledges the achievements of a long lineage of artists dedicated to the pursuit of bringing sculpture to life. Despite considerable differences in location and intention, each artist has embarked on a process of creative adventure. Going with the flow of materials and processes, all have created sensuous and elusive forms which elude easy categorisation. There is, however, a shared interest in fluidity and freedom, evidenced in a clear desire to unsettle preconceived hierarchies of genre and method, nature and culture. The sources of inspiration informing this work are equally diverse. If the lessons of postminimalism are embodied in these forms, then so too are many local and global influences gleaned through individual investigation. Following an examination of the legacies of postminimalism, this essay will assess the contributions made by these artists. The significance of material choices and making processes will be discussed, and consideration will also be given to the various strategic decisions taken to address matters of display, interaction and encounter. In taking a broad view, points of connection and areas of divergence begin to emerge. Furthermore, this process of looking back in time illuminates the intergenerational flow of ideas and innovations that have shaped the trajectories of contemporary art practice.

Embracing Change

The late 1960s provides an appropriate starting point for this account, as it was during these years that many of the artists under discussion were beginning to navigate the art world. Definitions of sculpture were pliant at this time, having been pushed and pulled in multiple directions by many artists, curators and critics across the decade.[1] Pop sculpture, with its predilection for recognisable forms inspired by consumer goods and everyday contexts, had achieved significant visibility in New York's gallery spaces during the early 1960s. For example, around 1962, Claes Oldenburg (1929–2022) received attention for his soft and spongy hand-stitched versions of fast foods and household fixtures, which he presented in slumped and sagging configurations. But by 1963–64, the repeated, geometric units of minimalism were on the ascendancy. Although the artists associated with minimalism eschewed human gesture and association – the preconceived, primary forms they employed were often produced by specialist fabricators[2] – the close attention artists such as Donald Judd and Robert Morris paid to the placement of their work revealed a clear acknowledgement of audience and context.

By mid-decade, a new wave of 'post-pop' and 'postminimal' attitudes was beginning to emerge. Absorbing the playful lessons of pop's everyday objecthood and acknowledging the importance of repetition and site to minimalism, many artists began to engage with a wider range of malleable and vulnerable materials, using their hands, bodies and gestures to activate and enliven their work. These actions often led to the creation of multipart installations which thrived on a spirit of impermanence. Frequently termed 'anti-form' or 'process' art, these new tendencies were informed by concurrent developments in performance art and contemporary choreography which foregrounded durational actions and involved a personal engagement with a given space.[3] The growing influence of conceptual art, with its rejection of commercial objects in favour of ideas and situations, also eroded the notion that sculpture must find a single, static, marketable form. By 1965 it was clear that the autonomy of the sculptural object was under attack from many directions.

One of the first exhibitions to account for this new tendency was *Eccentric Abstraction*, a group show curated by the critic and writer Lucy R. Lippard for New York's Fischbach Gallery in 1966. *Eccentric Abstraction* featured the work of eight artists, including Louise Bourgeois (1911–2010), Eva Hesse (1936–70) and Bruce Nauman (b. 1941), and was accompanied by an essay by Lippard bearing the same title.[4] Here, Lippard conceived of the new style as a heady fusion of the allusiveness of surrealism, the vulgar humour of pop art and the primary structures of minimalism, all topped off with a visceral sensuality. Although the work was essentially abstract, the body was evidenced through active making processes, unorthodox materials and in the suggestive curves and crevices of the resulting forms. Even the exhibition announcement card, printed on soft pink latex, appeared fleshy.

The exhibition was significant for its clear recognition of the important contribution made by women to this emerging tendency, with Lippard dedicating significant space and attention to the work of Louise Bourgeois and Eva Hesse in particular. In their hands, abstraction turned suggestive, messy, sexy, witty, slippery and dangerous. As Lippard declared: 'Eccentric abstraction offers an improbable combination of this death premise with a wholly sensuous life-giving element.'[5] Although Bourgeois's long career would flourish in a glow of late recognition, Hesse's intense creativity was cut short by her premature death from a brain tumour at the age of 34. During the years 1965–70, Hesse achieved rapid acclaim for an innovative body of work motivated by transformation and flux. Harnessing the potential of a wide range of materials, including fibreglass, latex and scavenged urban detritus, she created an embodied approach to abstraction, one which traversed boundaries of solid and liquid, organic and industrial, wall and floor. Hesse recognised a spirit of absurdity in these incongruous fusions of opposites. She also described her work as 'powerful yet precarious' – an unusual conflation which perfectly describes the unique energy of her sculpture.[6]

As an important centre of postminimal discourse, New York was an obvious draw for many artists in search of opportunities. Lynda Benglis left her home in Louisiana for New York in 1964, training initially as a painter at the Brooklyn Museum School of Art. By the end of the decade, she had achieved significant attention for her poured latex floor works in bold artificial colours. She became a leading exponent of the new process-driven art, engaging with contemporaries such as Eva Hesse, whom Benglis admired for her experimental work using liquid latex. In 1971 Senga Nengudi, too, set out for New York from her home in California, following the advice of one of her teachers: 'Well, you have to go to New York. New York is boot camp. Gotta do that if you want to be anything.'[7] Nengudi established herself in East Harlem, where she discovered a community of African American artists engaged in innovative performance-based work. Other artists chose to stay away from New York, their decisions often fuelled by a desire for independence or by a wider commitment to a local community, such as Ruth Asawa's dedication to teaching in San Francisco: 'I had a choice of pursuing a career in New York or somewhere like that, or go to the schools ... I chose to go to the schools. I think it's more important.'[8]

Of course, for many artists, particularly those based in Europe, relocating to New York was simply out of the question. Furthermore, international travel remained a luxury during these years, rendering difficult even short visits. For artists based away from major art centres, the importance of exhibitions, catalogues and international art journals cannot be overestimated, with *Artforum* providing a particularly rich source of information.[9] A tantalising glimpse of new possibilities emerged in the magazine's April 1968 edition, with the publication of Robert Morris's article 'Antiform'.[10] Morris was well known for his contribution to minimalism, but his pronouncements here revealed a discernible shift in attitude:

> *Recently, materials other than rigid ones have begun to show up. ... The focus on matter and gravity as means results in forms that were not projected in advance. Considerations of ordering are necessarily casual and imprecise and unemphasized. Random piling, loose stacking, hanging, give passing form to the material. Chance is accepted and indeterminacy is implied, as replacing will result in another configuration. Disengagement with preconceived enduring forms and orders for things is a positive assertion.*[11]

A similar emphasis on doing is discernible in the work and writings of the American artist Richard Serra (b. 1938), whose language-based drawing *Verb List* (1967–68), comprises an enticing inventory of performative actions for making and unmaking: 'to scatter, to arrange, to repair, to discard...' The work was published in *Avalanche* magazine in the winter of 1971.[12]

Such enticing offerings provided a huge source of inspiration to the London-based artist Phyllida Barlow. Scouring exhibition catalogues and art journals, and despite having to make do with poor-quality black and white illustrations, she discovered a wealth of possibilities:

> *The hearsay and rumours offered an entirely different experience … No more the need for permanency, weightiness, handicraft, the learnt, and to be taught restraints of what was and what was not sculpture. Instead, in with impermanency, temporariness, dematerialisation, the fugitive, the ephemeral, the here and now.*[13]

Barlow came to realise that these new tendencies in sculpture formed part of an increasingly globalised trend. Harald Szeemann's important survey exhibition *Live in Your Head: When Attitudes Become Form*, which toured from Kunsthalle Bern to the Institute of Contemporary Art in London in 1969, confirmed Barlow's suspicions.[14] The exhibition provided a firsthand opportunity to view not just recent examples of American sculpture by artists such as Hesse, Morris and Nauman, but also innovative work from across Europe: it featured a substantial selection of work by Italian artists associated with the Italian Arte Povera movement, who were also transforming cheap materials into radical, temporary forms which evaded commercialisation.[15] Writing in the catalogue, Szeemann acknowledged the increasingly international nature of a 'complex phenomenon' which lacked a 'satisfactory name'.[16] He noted how 'a lack of a real centre has persuaded increasing numbers of artists to remain in their home towns and to work against all the ideas and principles of the society in which they found themselves.'[17] These unnamed trends in sculpture were infectious and mobile: they could be absorbed and reinterpreted anywhere. This gradual shift away from New York as a central crucible of art world activity and towards a situation of multiple global sites of dialogue and creative exchange anticipates the globalised art world we know today.

It would be some years before this global phenomenon secured a consistent name. The American art critic Robert Pincus-Witten (1935–2018) first coined the term 'Post-Minimalism' in a 1971 article on Eva Hesse for *Artforum*,[18] and the publication in 1977 of his book *Postminimalism* helped cement it.[19] In the introduction to this anthology of art journalism, Pincus-Witten highlighted how the formalist abstraction of the late 1960s had been 'challenged by a new set of formal and moral values, imperatives tempered by despair over the conduct of American politics (Viet Nam, Watergate etc.).'[20] Although the Civil Rights Movement could be added to this list of important developments motivating artists at this time, Pincus-Witten's recognition of the women's movement is refreshing:

> *The new style's relationship to the women's movement cannot be overly stressed; many of its formal attitudes and properties, not to mention its exemplars, derive from methods and substances that hitherto had been sexistically tagged as female or feminine, whether or not the work had been made by women.*[21]

Although his book focuses predominantly on the work of male artists, Pincus-Witten's astute observations reveal how women's contributions were not only beginning to be valued but were also leading the debate.[22] Furthermore, the fact that the term 'postminimalism' first emerged in a posthumous article about Eva Hesse confirms the pre-eminence of her work within this context. Hesse's work was publicised and distributed during the years following her death, securing her legacy and influence.[23] Her example demonstrated to women that it was possible to succeed through a combination of talent, hard work and determination. As Hesse insisted: 'Excellence has no sex.'[24]

In the Flow

To emerge as an artist at a time of burgeoning postminimalism was to exist on a threshold of seemingly limitless possibility. Sculpture was no longer an impenetrable and static realm divorced from life and politics: boundaries could be crossed, and an ever-expanding range of methods and materials employed. These freedoms provided significant opportunities. Given the sheer diversity of approaches already at play, however, finding original ways to contribute was a challenge. All the artists featured in this essay found a way forward through sustained physical engagement, working with the inherent properties of materials and processes while channelling personal experiences and positions into the flow.

Often, these material adventures involved a clear determination to extend the field of vision beyond the established art world centres of the US and Western Europe. Many of the artists discussed here embarked on global travels and active research, in search of alternative ways of making; others took inspiration from their immediate environment, finding rich sculptural possibilities in the everyday interactions and textures of home. It is also important to acknowledge that many of these material adventures spanned decades, with artists sustaining their practices through long phases of limited critical attention. Although Lynda Benglis enjoyed early success, most of the older artists represented in this exhibition achieved recognition only much later in life. These practices, therefore, evidence an admirable spirit of endurance and perseverance.

A consideration of Lynda Benglis's work *Quartered Meteor* (1969, cast 1975, p. 69), reveals how an embodied engagement with materials can trigger a multitude of ideas and associations. Benglis has compared the physicality of her process to the moment of 'wrestling with your sheets as you come out of a dream state, being overwhelmed by the unmanageability of a material.'[25] It is through this whole-body interaction with materials that forms emerge: 'I like to work in a way that the image flows out of some information about the material itself. There is a tension in the forms as the materials are pushed to their limits.'[26] Having brought her earlier floor-hugging latex pieces to a natural conclusion, Benglis began to experiment in the late 1960s with polyurethane foam, enjoying its voluminosity. With heft and determination, Benglis poured this toxic industrial sludge onto the floor and into corners, creating amorphous lava-like heaps. Due to the impermanence of the material, only casting could preserve these forms in the long term. Casting in lead transforms *Quartered Meteor* into a dead weight, one which appears to have found its final resting place only through violent impact. Keen to elevate and enlarge her work, Benglis subsequently poured the polyurethane foam on wall-based armatures, creating gigantic wing-like gestures which spread across the gallery space. Benglis's foam works could be described as hybrids, playing in the space between liquidity and solidity, between painting, sculpture and performance.[27]

Through the transformation of fluid materials procured in the city, she evoked the natural features of the landscapes of her Louisiana childhood and her extensive subsequent global travels:

> *I see those landscapes [of childhood] in most of my work, the rivers and the swamps, and even the crawfish mounds in what used to be the open rice fields but all my experiences of the natural world somehow find their way into my work.*[28]

Equally compelling is the way in which Benglis engaged in a complex power play between the gendered associations of powerful 'macho' gestures and the 'feminine' qualities of softness, sensuality and natural flow. According to Benglis, these contradictions 'mock the idea of having to take sexual sides – to be either a male artist or a female.'[29]

Benglis was not alone in her personal and material responses to gender. Although many women working in sculpture were engaged with and supportive of the women's liberation movement, when it came to the work, aspects of gender percolated in more nuanced ways. As Phyllida Barlow succinctly expressed it: 'The more personal the process of discovering a gender for the work, or issues about gender, the more interested I am. The way decisions can be ignited beyond manifestos, doctrines and theories is what inspires me.'[30]

Like Benglis, Barlow was deeply committed to physical material adventure. Intent on manipulating vast quantities of commonplace materials such as polythene, plaster and chicken wire, Barlow created a multitude of forms – some tiny, some gigantic, yet all intent on an intimate dance between the natural, the urban and the sensate. Barlow enjoyed the tussle of making, explaining that 'my ambition to make work is quite aggressive.'[31] Working in a studio next door to the home she shared with her husband, the painter Fabian Peake, and, by 1981, their five young children, Barlow 'brought into that space a kind of masculine way of working – even if that's an incredibly simplistic way of describing it. It's to do with cutting and breaking, pulling and shoving.'[32] Nevertheless, Barlow's approach cannot be described as purely 'aggressive', for she has also acknowledged the importance of tender gestures and actions gleaned from parenting her young children.[33] Going with the flow of her art and life, Barlow engaged in a precarious kind of juggling act, finding creative ways to balance making and mothering, conflict and care, and embracing the casual 'make do' gestures associated with being stretched as a parent.

Senga Nengudi has never considered herself to be pushing a specific political agenda: 'I'm doing it from a personal level', she has explained.[34] Her work emerges from her individual perspective on 'what it feels like to be an artist who is black, who is American, who is a mother, who is a daughter.'[35] Nengudi trained in art and dance, and a spirit of interdisciplinarity, coupled with a bodily engagement with materials, informs much of her work. Through a proactive process of research and travel, she discovered a global range of possibilities, including West Coast assemblage art, African ritualistic practices, Japanese Noh theatre, and the experimental art of the Gutai Art Association.[36] Following a research trip to Japan in 1966–67, Nengudi returned to New York and embarked on a series of heat-sealed plastic sculptures filled with water. These forms could at once be said to reflect postminimal sculptural developments, and to evoke the ephemeral and playful nature of Gutai art. Nengudi enjoyed the associative

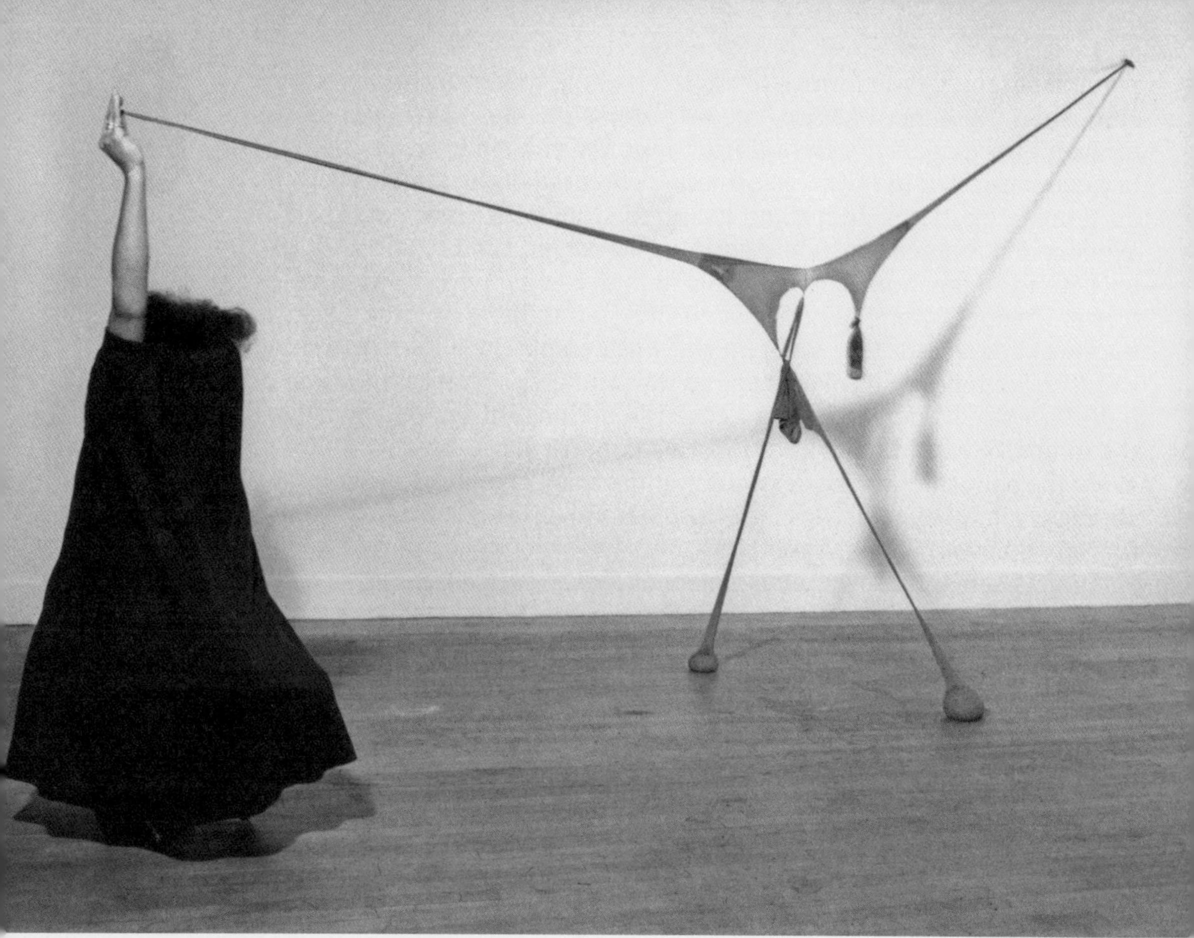

31

potential of these fluid forms: 'If you felt them, it was really quite sensual, and it had this sense of body, because it was pliable.'[37] However, it was through the experience of giving birth to her first child in 1974 that the artist became interested in the transformative potential of the female body, its usefulness, its stretchability, and its interactions with gravity. As she has explained: 'From tender, tight beginnings to sagging end … The body can only stand so much push and pull until it gives way, never to resume its original shape.'[38] Nengudi discovered in nylon tights – or pantyhose, as they are known in the US – a material of considerable elasticity which could be filled, stretched and splayed across wall and floor, bearing the strain of hard work and labour, operating as used skin. Nengudi has acknowledged the influence on these works of Eva Hesse, particularly Hesse's ability to evoke the body through the dextrous manipulation of found materials. The sheer portability of pantyhose was also helpful, given the limited market for Nengudi's work at this time:

> *There was always an issue about money, my concept was I could take a whole show and put it in my purse. I could take it out of my purse and there would be no costs for installing or shipping. I liked this idea that a woman's life is in her purse.*[39]

The life of these works did not cease at the point of installation. Collectively titled *R.S.V.P.* ('respond, if you please'), these works invited interaction. Collaborating with fellow artist and dancer Maren Hassinger (b.1947), Nengudi staged a series of performances with the works, which were then photographed. These iconic images reveal the two artists at work to create new shapes and gestures, bodies and materials entwined. As Nengudi recalls: 'We were explorers, ever investigating and finding new ways to use commonplace materials that we could use in ways that would charge our works with energy and layered meaning.'[40]

The process of energising sculpture need not involve a wide range of materials and processes. Ruth Asawa's fascination with industrial wire first emerged during her childhood, when she would unravel the wire tags on the vegetable crates at her parents' farm in California, retwining them to make jewellery and figures. In 1947, during her time as a student at Black Mountain College, Asawa made a trip to Toluca, Mexico, where she learned a looping technique from a community of wire basket weavers. Asawa now had everything she needed: a material, a method and an absolute belief in the value of hard work. From these limited components, Asawa created a prolific body of looped wire suspended forms of increasing formal complexity. Asawa's exquisite and intricate forms are decidedly organic, inspired by her daily observations of nature, but also blossoming out of her drawing practice:

> *My curiosity was aroused through the idea of giving structural form to the images in my drawings. These forms come from observing plants, the spiral shell of a snail, seeing light through insect wings, watching spiders repair their webs in the early morning, and seeing the sun through the droplets of water suspended from the tips of pine needles while watering my garden.*[41]

Asawa became aware that her work, which danced on the boundaries between drawing and sculpture, art and craft, did not fit within established art categories. Rather than dwell on such matters, however, she remained focused on 'finding solutions to problems', paying close attention to the flow of the wire as it meandered in and out of individual works, and across groups and series.[42] There are no performative gestures here, no instant flashes of inspiration, but rather a multitude of small repeated actions which birth beguiling shapes, some of which nestle lovingly inside one another. As Asawa explained: 'I'm not so interested in the expression of something. But, I'm more interested in what the material can do. And so that's why I keep exploring.'[43] Asawa's adventures with wire continued unabated for the rest of her life, enriching her concurrent commitments as a teacher, a passionate advocate for arts education, and mother to her six children.

Martin Puryear's work also evolves from the devoted manipulation of a choice selection of materials, particularly wood. Between 1964 and 1966, Puryear was posted as a Peace Corps volunteer in Sierra Leone, where he observed the formidable talents of local carpenters and craftspeople. Subsequent studies in Sweden introduced Puryear to Nordic design and furniture, which he admired for its fusion of beauty and functionality. Puryear's sculptural forms take on an organic life of their own. *Untitled* (2015, pp. 165–66), for example, comprises an elegant wave of Alaskan yellow cedar which sweeps around and down the wall with sinuous determination. In his hands, the hard, volumetric properties of wood soften and billow, like fabric or poured water. As the art critic Jonathan Crary noted: 'Puryear usually concentrates on reducing his forms to surfaces and lines. His thinking never addresses itself to problems of volumes. ... Puryear focuses on the surface, on its flows and seductiveness, on a mobile, indeterminate contour.'[44] Puryear's works are resolutely crafted. Additive processes, such as laminating, joining and layering are used to assemble each elusive form. As he has explained, 'I enjoy and need to work with my hands, with tools ... they give you a measure of the mind and body ... they keep ideas of the work connected to the man making them.'[45] If Puryear's haptic techniques evoke postminimalism, then his refined abstract creations could be said to recall minimalist sculpture. Some of his works also reference aspects of his African American heritage. Overall, Puryear intends for his sculptures to reach beyond the specific and towards universal concerns and poetic associations.

Let Loose

This discussion has so far focused on expanded material choices and liberated processes of making. Of equal importance to these artists is the subsequent life of a form once it is released into the world. This could be described as a partnership of sorts: between artist and audience, material and environment. How an artwork functions in a particular space and time has been the source of prolonged debate. We have seen how the artists associated with minimalism reflected deeply on matters of positioning and placement – efforts roundly criticised by the modernist critic Michael Fried (b. 1939) in an impassioned *Artforum* article in 1967. According to Fried, an artwork should be autonomous in form and universal in presence and meaning, and he considered these artists' attempts to situate an artwork within a wider context as 'corrupted or perverted by theatre.'[46] Despite Fried's vociferous criticism, issues of place, context and public engagement have continued to play a crucial role in the display and reception of much of the sculpture and installation produced during the past 50 years, with notions of theatricality and interactivity perceived as sources of significant strength and possibility rather than potential weaknesses.

Indeed, it is hard to ignore the heightened theatricality evident in many of the works on display here. An enlarged scale, clashing colours and exaggerated, bulbous contours fuel the drama. Take, for example, Franz West's two-part work, *Kain naht Abel (Kain approaching Abel)* (2009, pp. 190–91), which draws the viewer into the heart of this murderous religious story. The two looming figures engage in direct combat, limbs outstretched like sore thumbs or swollen appendages, equally threatening and preposterous. West's decision to balance his writhing combatants on spindly footings adds to the sense of risk and unpredictability. Similar strategies of ungainly bulk, emphatic upscaling and implied structural precarity are evident in the work of Phyllida Barlow.[47] The colossal phallic body of *untitled: girl ii; 2019* (2019–20, pp. 59–61) teeters upon three rotund legs which dwindle to mere tiptoes. Stretching over four metres in length, this cumbersome creature appears to be in limbo, at once dominating the space and yet constrained by her own expansive proportions. There are many echoes of the past here, not least of Louise Bourgeois's outsized penises and precarious pointed leg forms, but also Eva Hesse's love of the absurd and her fusion of power and precarity. At the heart of Barlow's sculptural endeavours, however, lies a desire to engage with an audience in the here and now.

Heightened theatricality in a gallery setting is not the only display strategy available for the release of sculptural energies. Ruth Asawa sought a more harmonious relationship between her work and its context. Her suspended forms interact with gravity, air and light, unleashing gentle movements and soft shadows. Equally compelling is the way in which Asawa embraced domestic space as a setting for her work (a decision motivated to some degree by limited exhibition opportunities during her lifetime). She made and presented a generous selection of her work within the family home, enabling her art to become part of the intimate flow of family life and to provide a daily reminder to her children of the value of graft. A lack of institutional support also prompted Phyllida Barlow to display her work in her family home, and in the homes of her friends, during the 1990s. In a humorous series titled *Objects for...* (1994–99), Barlow created bizarre appendages for ironing boards, armchairs and television sets. Following these unorthodox collisions of art and life, Barlow pushed the idea a stage further, taking to the streets to create anonymous objects for lamp posts and street furniture and leaving them in situ until the point of disintegration or forcible removal. In her most extreme act of experimentation with the flow of external forces, Barlow made a series of undocumented works which she threw into the Thames. This liberating method enabled Barlow to present her work in 'a place that's restless, a non-place'.[48] Such actions resonate with Barlow's reflections on the creative potential of being ignored: 'To be non-visible, to be invisible and not showing, it leaves this enormous space to sort of wander wherever you like.'[49] Given Barlow's embrace of a process of creative wandering, it stands to reason that she would propel her works along a similarly fluid path. Via different means, then, Asawa and Barlow engaged in a process of delegation, inviting the forces of nature and circumstance to channel their work along new trajectories.

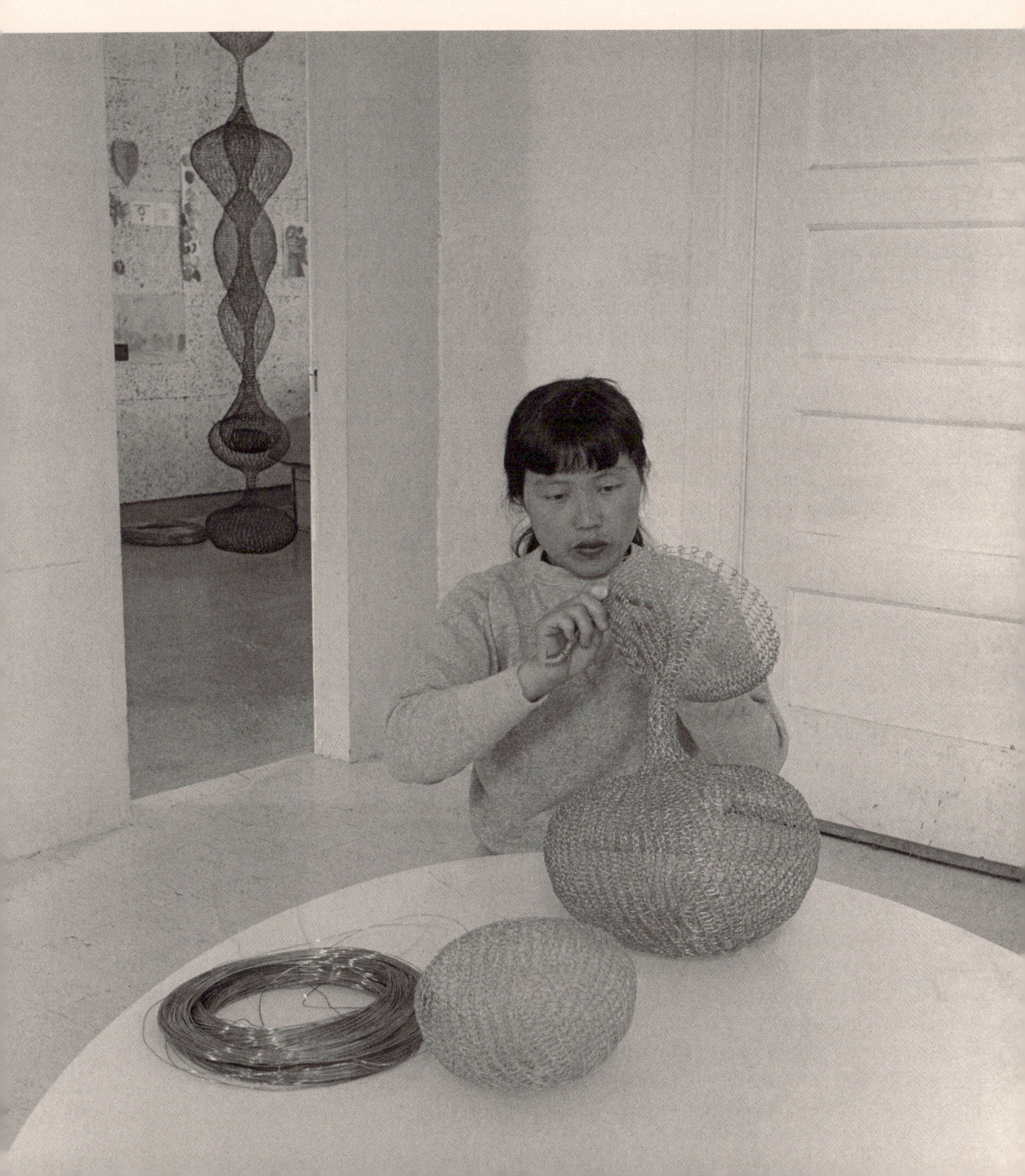

Ruth Asawa
at work, 1956

Another powerful way of unlocking the potential of sculpture involves a loosening of the reins of authorship to provide space for the active involvement of other people. The role of participation in art has a long history. From the late 1950s, the artists associated with the Brazilian art movement of neo-concretism pioneered an approach to art that was sensual and experiential. Artists including Lygia Clark (1920–88), Hélio Oiticica (1937–80) and Lygia Pape (1927–2004) invited public interaction by creating playful opportunities to enact, inhabit or manipulate their works. Describing her practice in 1960, Clark explained how these processes of participation enabled a detachment from 'everything that is fixed and dead'.[50]

As has already been discussed, Senga Nengudi extended the life of her pantyhose works through her collaboration with Maren Hassinger. Nengudi has also engaged with many other artists, performers and dancers across her career, working within and beyond the gallery space. Franz West's desire for discourse with other people prompted him to collaborate with many artists throughout his lifetime, while his work invites audiences to interact in a variety of direct and playful ways. Born and raised in post-war Vienna, West was a self-taught artist who refused to fit into the mainstream yet insisted on a positive outlook: 'I preferred to look into the future, which I saw as being optimistic. The forerunners of Pop art became known here in Vienna at that time, and art with a connection to daily life and to colour was important.' His early works of the 1970s, titled *Passstücke* (Adaptives), comprised quirky papier-mâché forms designed to be worn and activated by members of the public. In later works, West often employed the humble chair as an engagement device, inviting gallery visitors to sit, interact, observe and think. West's notion of art as an inhabitable, interactive and time-based activity resonated with Nicolas Bourriaud's analysis of an emerging relational art. In his influential 1998 book *Relational Aesthetics*, Bourriaud delineates art as 'a period of time to be lived through, like an opening to an unlimited discussion'.[51] The chair in West's *Epiphanie an Stuhlen (Epiphany on Chairs)* (2011, p. 187) is not a passive piece of gallery furniture but a fundamental part of the work, one which invites an individual to contemplate the preposterous pink sputnik dangling from the ceiling. In doing so, the viewer-protagonist can engage with West's wry reflections on the ability of art to unlock groundbreaking personal revelations. That said, one must not overlook the simple pleasure and joy to be found in contemplating this bulbous, deliberately cack-handed confection, which refuses to conform to conventions of taste.

Sensuous pleasure emerges in much of the work of this older generation, unfurling in carnivalesque bursts of delicious colour, in the seductive glisten of a polished surface, in the gratifying tug of every sinew, twist and meander. These forms are generous, open to interpretation, interaction and enjoyment. This spirit of congeniality extends to the long-standing commitment many of these artists have made to teaching and mentoring.[52] This eagerness for intergenerational dialogue has forged a direct and lived connection between recent art history and the contemporary moment. Overall, this older generation has extended the possibilities of postminimalism, adding new layers of meaning gleaned from sustained interaction with materials and engagement with the world at large. At times, success has been hard-won, achieved through acts of resilience and perseverance, often in the face of art world inattention. Occupying this precarious territory has yielded surprising outcomes, including the discovery of unorthodox materials, processes and display methods. In accepting uncertainty and change, these artists have developed a keen awareness of when to hold on and when to let go, when to get involved and when to make space for other energies. This is fertile territory for sculpture, a place of continuing rewards. And going with the flow remains a highly generative strategy, for it is alive with possibilities.

1   For a succinct assessment of the various successive waves and trends in 1960s sculpture, see Richard Armstrong, 'Introduction', in Richard Armstrong/Richard Marshall (eds.), *The New Sculpture 1965–1975: Between Geometry and Gesture* (New York: Whitney Museum of American Art, 1990), p. 8

2   For further information about the relationship between sculptors and sculpture fabricators at this time, see Jonathan D. Lippincott, *Large Scale: Fabricating Sculpture in the 1960s and 1970s* (Princeton: Princeton Architectural Press, 2010)

3   For insights into the close relationship between minimalism, postminimalism and choreography, see Stephanie Rosenthal, 'Choreographing You: Choreographies in the Visual Arts', in Stephanie Rosenthal (ed.), *Move: Choreographing You: Art and Dance Since the 1960s* (London: Hayward Publishing, 2010), pp. 11–14

4   The exhibition took place from 20 September to 8 October 1966, and featured the work of Alice Adams, Louise Bourgeois, Eva Hesse, Gary Kuehn, Bruce Nauman, Don Potts, Keith Sonnier and Frank Lincoln Viner. Lippard's accompanying essay originally featured in *Art International*, Vol. 10, No. 9 (November 1966), and was reproduced in Lucy R. Lippard, *Changing: Essays in Art Criticism* (New York: E.P. Dutton & Co., Inc., 1971), p. 100

5   Ibid

6   Hesse's conflation of precarity and power emerged in her written analysis of her 1969 work *Expanded Expansion*, now in the collection of the Guggenheim Museum. Extending over 25 feet across a given space, this curtain construction, made from latex-dipped cheesecloth, is propped provisionally against the wall, therefore operating as both painting and sculpture. Hesse described the work as 'large looming, powerful yet precarious. Its positioning as a unit or sectional units could take many stands. The flexible and also inflexible quality is there and in contrast.' Cited in Lucy R. Lippard, *Eva Hesse* (New York: New York University Press, 1976), p. 152

7   Elissa Auther/Senga Nengudi, 'Senga Nengudi in conversation with Elissa Auther', in Stephanie Weber/Matthias Mühling (eds.), *Senga Nengudi: Topologies* (Munich: Hirmer, 2019), p. 289

8   Emma Ridgway/Vibece Salthe, *Ruth Asawa: Citizen of the Universe* (London: Thames & Hudson, 2022), p. 36

9   In 1979, the writer and critic Rosalind Krauss reflected on how *Artforum* 'for a time became the centre and the medium of art world discourse'. See Rosalind E. Krauss, 'Eva Hesse', in Rosalind E. Krauss/Nicholas Serota, *Eva Hesse 1936–1970: Sculpture* (London: Whitechapel Art Gallery, 1979), p. 5

10 Robert Morris, 'Antiform', *Artforum*, Vol. 6, No. 8 (April 1968), p. 33–35

11 Ibid, p. 35

12 Richard Serra, '*Verb List*, 1967–68', *Avalanche*, No. 2 (Winter 1971), pp. 20–21. *Verb List* is now in the collection of the Museum of Modern Art, New York: www.moma.org/collection/works/152793 (accessed 6 November 2023)

13 Julia Peyton-Jones/Hans Ulrich Obrist, 'Interview with Phyllida Barlow,' in Kathryn Rattee/Melissa Larner (eds.), *Nairy Baghramian and Phyllida Barlow* (London: Serpentine Gallery, 2010), p. 50

14 Charles Harrison/Harald Szeemann, *Live in Your Head: When Attitudes Become Form – Works, Concepts, Processes, Situations, Information* (London: Institute of Contemporary Arts, 1969)

15 For an assessment of the reception of this exhibition in London, see Lisa Tickner, *London's New Scene: Art and Culture in the 1960s* (London: Paul Mellon Centre for Studies in British Art, 2020), pp. 278–85. The exhibition featured work by artists based in Belgium, Germany, France, Holland, Italy, Switzerland, the UK and the US

16 Harrison/Szeemann 1969. Szeemann provides a generous selection of 'names so far suggested': 'Anti-Form, Micro-Emotive Art, Possible Art, Impossible Art, Concept Art, Arte Povera, Earth Art.'

17 Ibid, n.p.

18 Neil Genzlinger, 'Robert Pincus-Witten, art critic and historian, is dead at 82', *New York Times* (31 January 2018), https://www.nytimes.com/2018/01/31/obituaries/robert-pincus-witten-art-critic-and-historian-is-dead-at-82.html (accessed 6 November 2023)

19 Robert Pincus-Witten, *Postminimalism* (New York: Out of London Press, 1977)

20 Ibid, p. 14

21 Ibid, p. 16

22 The book features 17 previously published texts, four of which focus on the work of women: one article a piece on Eva Hesse and Jackie Ferrara and two on Lynda Benglis, including Robert Pincus-Witten, 'Lynda Benglis: The Frozen Gesture,' in *Artforum*, Vol. 13, No. 3 (November 1974), pp. 54–59

23 A memorial retrospective exhibition was held at The Solomon R. Guggenheim Museum in New York in 1972. See Robert Pincus-Witten/Linda Shearer, *Eva Hesse: A Memorial Exhibition* (New York: Guggenheim Museum, 1972). Lucy Lippard's monograph *Eva Hesse* provided an important companion for many women working in sculpture (see Lippard 1976). A major European touring exhibition of Eva Hesse's work was staged in 1979; opening at the Whitechapel Art Gallery, London (4 May – 17 June 1979), *Eva Hesse 1936–1970: Sculpture* toured to Rijksmuseum Kröller-Müller, Otterlo (30 June – 5 August 1979) and Kestner-Gesellschaft, Hannover (17 August – 23 September 1979). See Krauss/Serota 1979

24 Cindy Nemser, *Art Talk: Conversations with 12 Women Artists* (New York: Charles Scribner's Sons, 1975), p. 9

25 Ibid, p. 27

26 Susan Krane, 'Lynda Benglis: Theatres of Nature', in Susan Krane, *Lynda Benglis: Dual Nature* (Atlanta: High Museum of Art, 1991), p. 21

27 For illuminating insights into the hybridised 'neither nor' working methods evident in women's abstract sculpture see Anne M. Wagner, 'What Women Do, or The Poetics of Sculpture', in Paul Schimmel/Jenni Sorkin (eds.), *Revolution in the Making: Abstract Sculpture by Women 1947–2016* (Skira, 2016) p. 90

28 Lynda Benglis/Andrew Bonacina, 'Interview: Andrew Bonacina in conversation with Lynda Benglis', in Andrew Bonacina/Nora Lawrence/Bibiana Obler, *Lynda Benglis* (London: Phaidon, 2022) p. 15. This interview provides illuminating insights into the range of non-art sources that have informed Benglis's art across her career, including classical architecture, her Greek heritage, scuba diving, oil slicks, Mardi Gras parades and Halloween festivals

29 Laura Hoptman, 'For the Amusement of a Goddess', in Franck Gautherot/Caroline Hancock/Seung-Duk Kim (eds.), *Lynda Benglis* (Dijon: Les Presses du Réel, 2009), p. 233

30 Peyton-Jones/Obrist 2010, p. 53

NATALIE RUDD

31   Ronnie Simpson/Phyllida Barlow, 'Between a Stroke and a Smack: Phyllida Barlow in conversation with Ronnie Simpson', in Ronnie Simpson (ed.), *Phyllida Barlow: STINT* (Coventry: Mead Gallery, University of Warwick, 2008), p. 33

32   Ibid

33   Phyllida Barlow/Anna Maria Maiolino, 'In Conversation: Art, Politics, Motherhood', *New York Times Style Magazine* (28 November 2018), p. 3

34   Auther/Nengudi 2019, p. 296

35   Ibid, p. 297

36   After graduating from California State University, and having read about Japanese art and culture in books, Nengudi spent a year at Waseda University, Japan in 1966–67, keen to learn more about Japanese culture. She was also fascinated by the work of the Gutai Art Association. Formed in 1954, the group used a wide range of materials and processes, including performance and theatre, to engage in a holistic expression of the body and the spirit, art and life.

37   Auther/Nengudi 2019, pp. 289–90

38   Senga Nengudi, 'Artist's Statement, Late 1970s', in Begum Yasar (ed.), *Senga Nengudi* (New York & London: Dominique Lévy Gallery, 2015), p. 81

39   Jori Finkel, 'Q&A: Maren Hassinger and Senga Nengudi', *Los Angeles Times* (27 November 2011), https://www.latimes.com/entertainment/la-xpm-2011-nov-27-la-ca-pst-kellie-jones-interview-20111127-story.html (accessed 6 November 2023)

40   Auther/Nengudi 2019, p. 294

41   Handwritten artist's statement, June 5, 1995. Courtesy Ruth Asawa Lanier, Inc.

42   Tamara H. Schenkenberg, 'Life's Work', in Tamara H. Schenkenberg (ed.), *Ruth Asawa: Life's Work* (St Louis: Pulitzer Arts Foundation in Association with Yale University Press, 2019), p. 16

43   Ibid

44   Jonathan Crary, 'Martin Puryear's Sculpture', *Artforum,* Vol. 18, No. 2 (October 1979), p. 29

45   Margo A. Crutchfield, *Martin Puryear* (Washington: University of Washington Press, 2002), pp. 4–5

46   Michael Fried, 'Art and Objecthood', *Artforum* (Summer 1967), p. 23

47   Again, an interest in conflict drives the decisions, as Barlow has explained: 'My interest in size and dimension and in making works that are bigger than myself is connected to arguing with space … Perhaps this combative response to space is in essence female, being protective and defensive at the same time.' See Peyton-Jones/Obrist 2010, p. 53

48   Peyton-Jones/Obrist 2010, p. 59. The date of these actions is unknown, but they are likely to have taken place during the early 1990s, at the time of Barlow's *Objects for…* works. In this interview, Barlow also commented: 'I don't want to add to pollution, but I'd love to do something where the work gets lost in the sea when the tide comes in – to take a ramp down to the coast, for instance.'

49   Phyllida Barlow, 'For No Reason: Townsend Memorial Lecture, Slade School of Art, 5 November 2014', in Sara Harrison (ed.), *Phyllida Barlow: Collected Lectures, Writings and Interviews* (London: Hauser & Wirth, 2021), p. 28

50   Anna Dezeuze, *Almost Nothing: Observations on Precarious Practices in Contemporary Art* (Manchester: Manchester University Press, 2016), p. 101

51   Nicolas Bourriaud, *Relational Aesthetics* (Dijon: Les Presses du réel, 1998), p. 15. For an illuminating discussion of West's chair works, see Darsie Alexander, 'Franz West: What to Do?', in Darsie Alexander (ed.), *Franz West: To Build a House You Start with the Roof* (Cambridge, MA: MIT Press, 2008), pp. 80–84

52   The teaching careers of Ruth Asawa, Phyllida Barlow and Senga Nengudi are well established. Franz West nurtured many fruitful friendships and collaborations with younger artists, including Sarah Lucas and Urs Fischer, and also supported many emerging artists through employment in his collegiate studio space

Ruth Asawa 194
Nairy Baghramian 196
Phyllida Barlow 198
Lynda Benglis 200
Michel Blazy 202
Paloma Bosquê 204
Olaf Brzeski 206
Choi Jeong Hwa 208
Tara Donovan 210
DRIFT 212
Eva Fàbregas 214
Holly Hendry 216
EJ Hill 218
Marguerite Humeau 220
Jean-Luc Moulène 222
Senga Nengudi 224
Ernesto Neto 226
Martin Puryear 228
Matthew Ronay 230
Teresa Solar Abboud 232
Franz West 234

Ruth

Asawa

Installation view, *Ruth Asawa*, David Zwirner Gallery, New York, 2017   p. 46–47 and detail

Untitled (S.154, Hanging Nine-Lobed, Single-Layered Continuous Form), c. 1958   p. 45

Untitled (S.142, Hanging Five-Lobed, Multi-Layered Continuous Form within a Form), 1990   p. 44

Untitled (S.065, Hanging Seven-Lobed, Multi-Layered Continuous Form within a Form with Spheres in the Second, Third, Fourth, and Sixth Lobes), c. 1960–63   p. 43

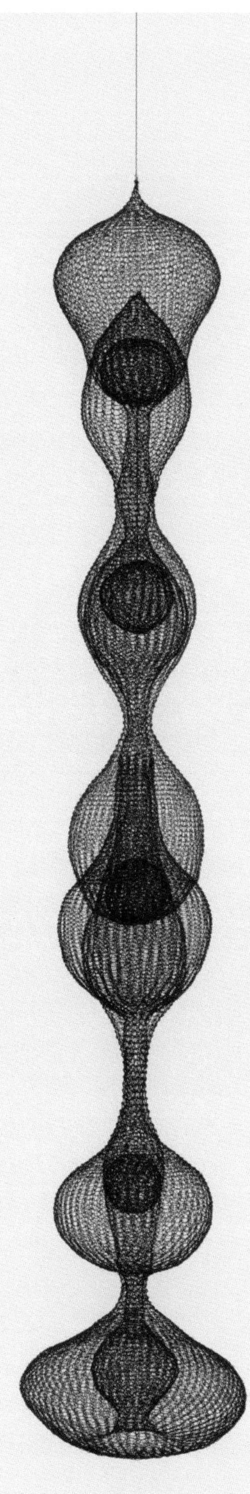

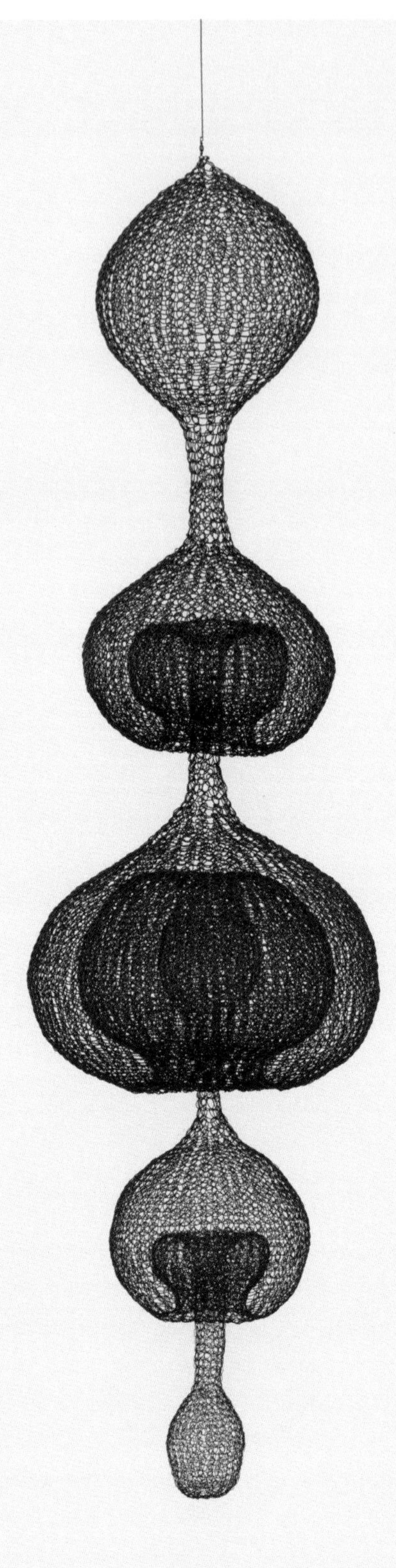

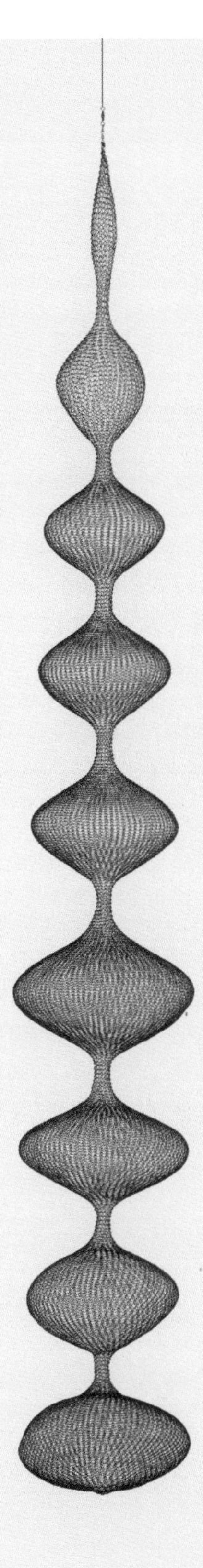

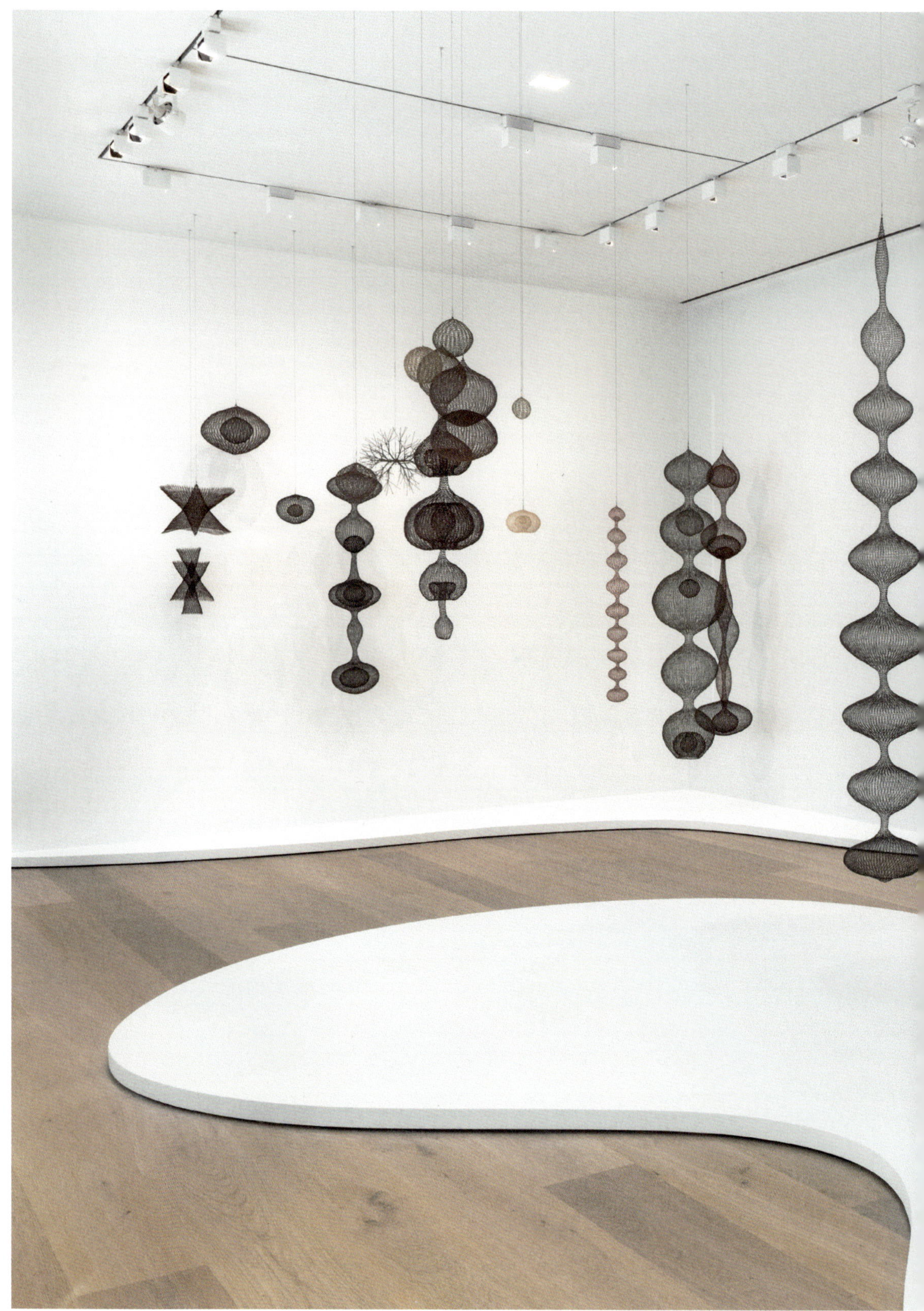

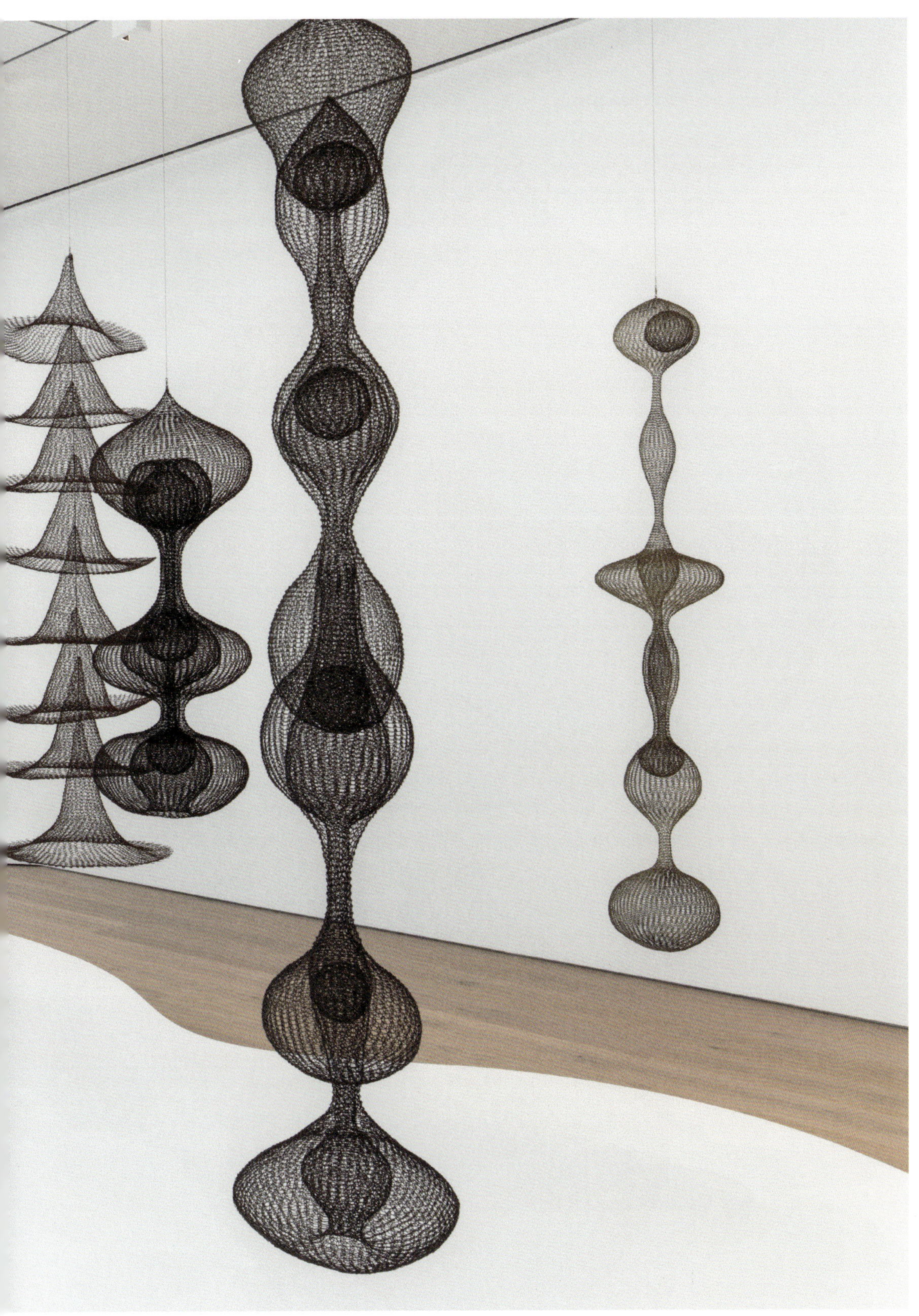

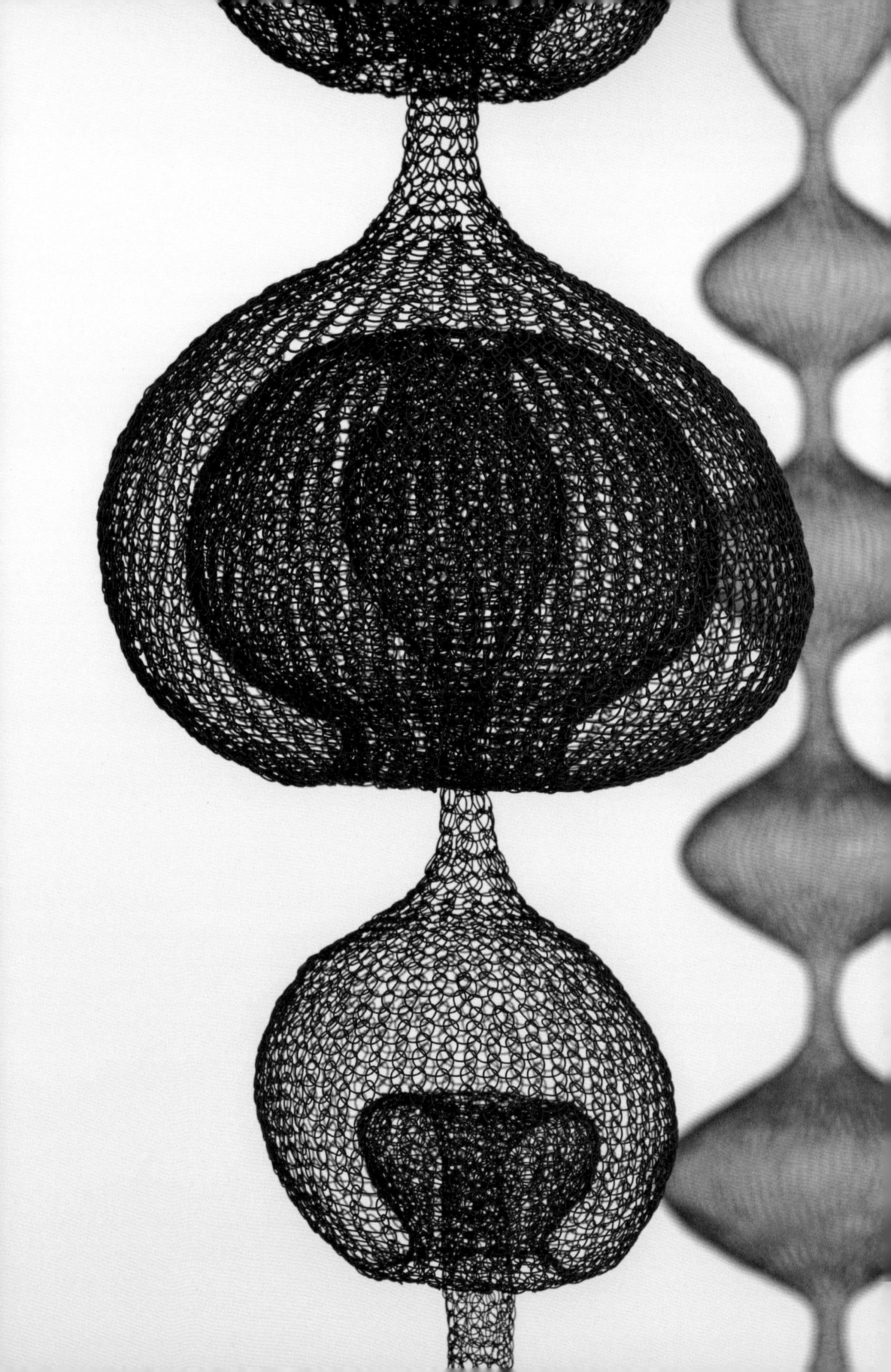

My curiosity was aroused by the idea of giving structural
form to the images in my drawings. These forms come from
observing plants, the spiral shell of a snail, seeing light
through insect wings, watching spiders repair their webs
in the early morning, and seeing the sun through the droplets
of water suspended from the tips of pine needles while
watering my garden.   RUTH ASAWA

Nairy

Baghramian

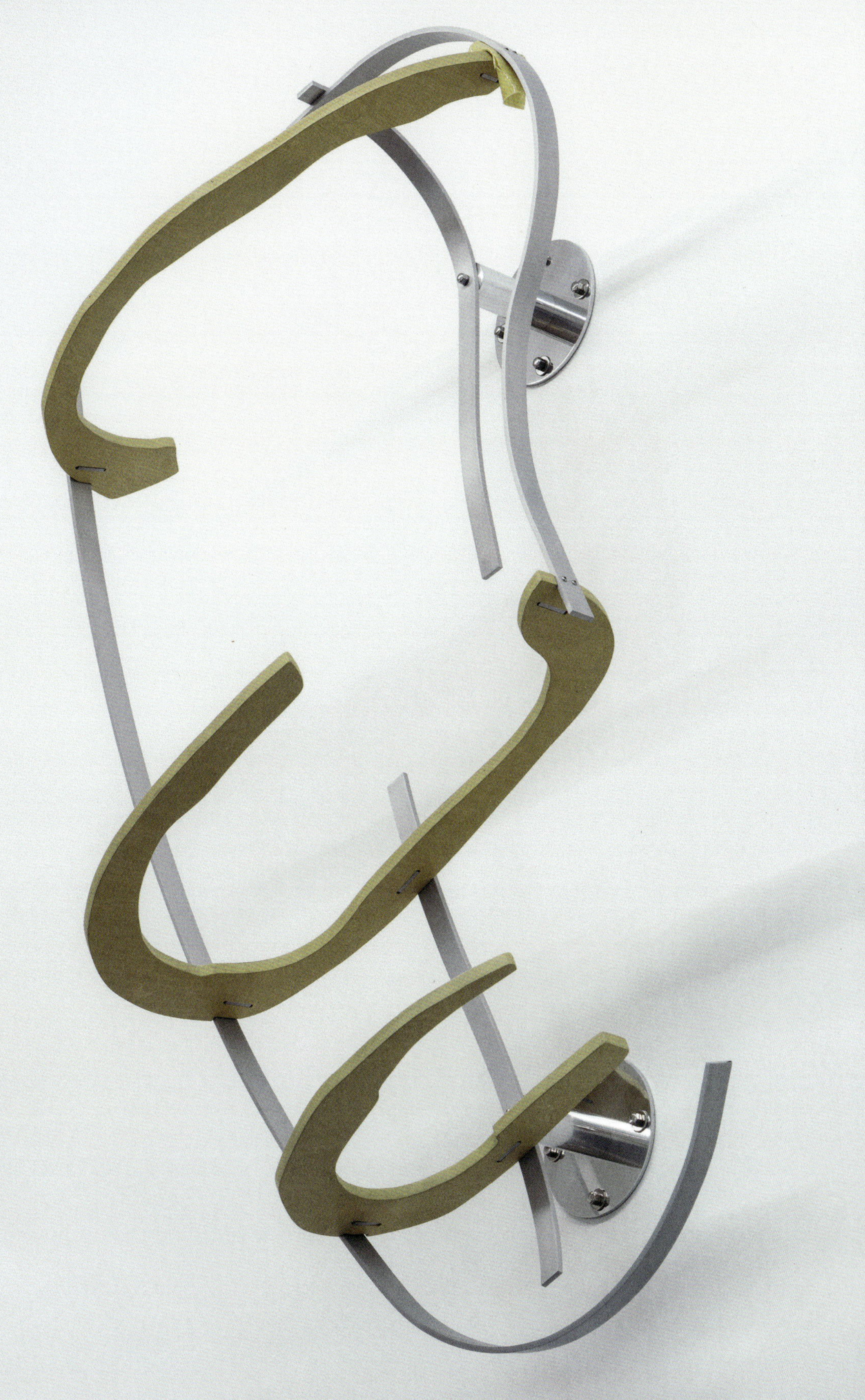

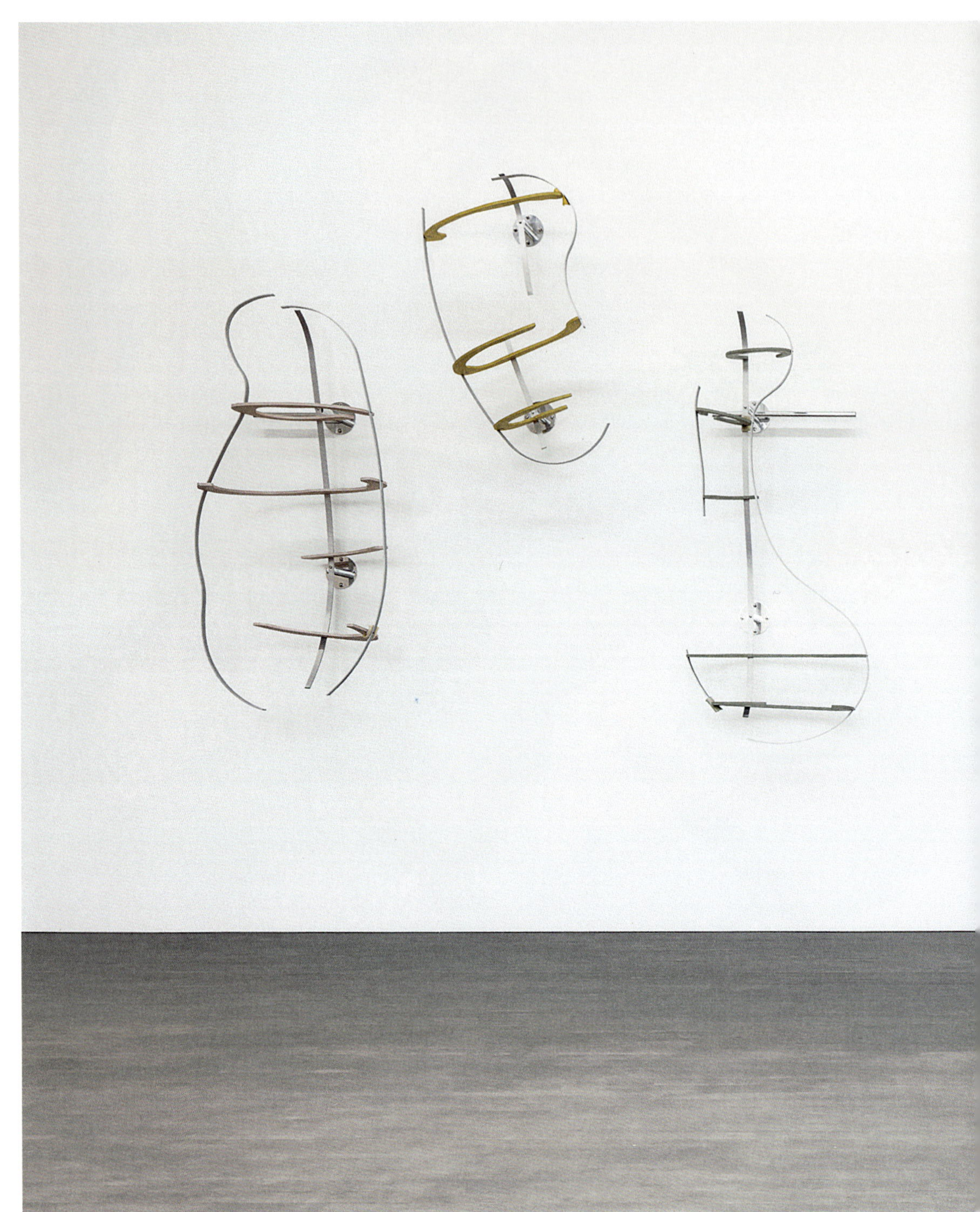

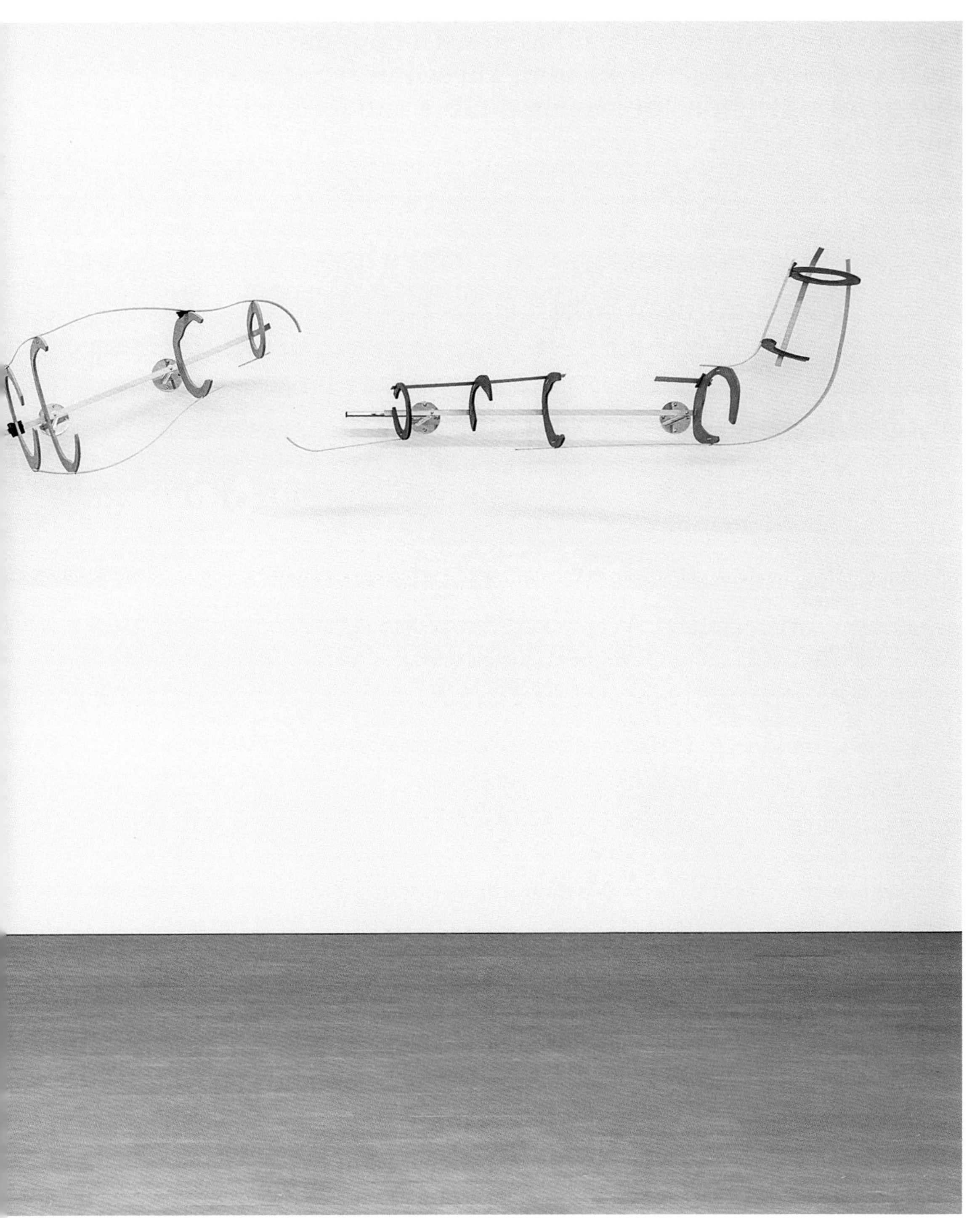

I like to intervene in spaces that mark a boundary
so I can cross and rethink them. These interspaces are
places for reflection, for raising doubts and for posing
questions. NAIRY BAGHRAMIAN

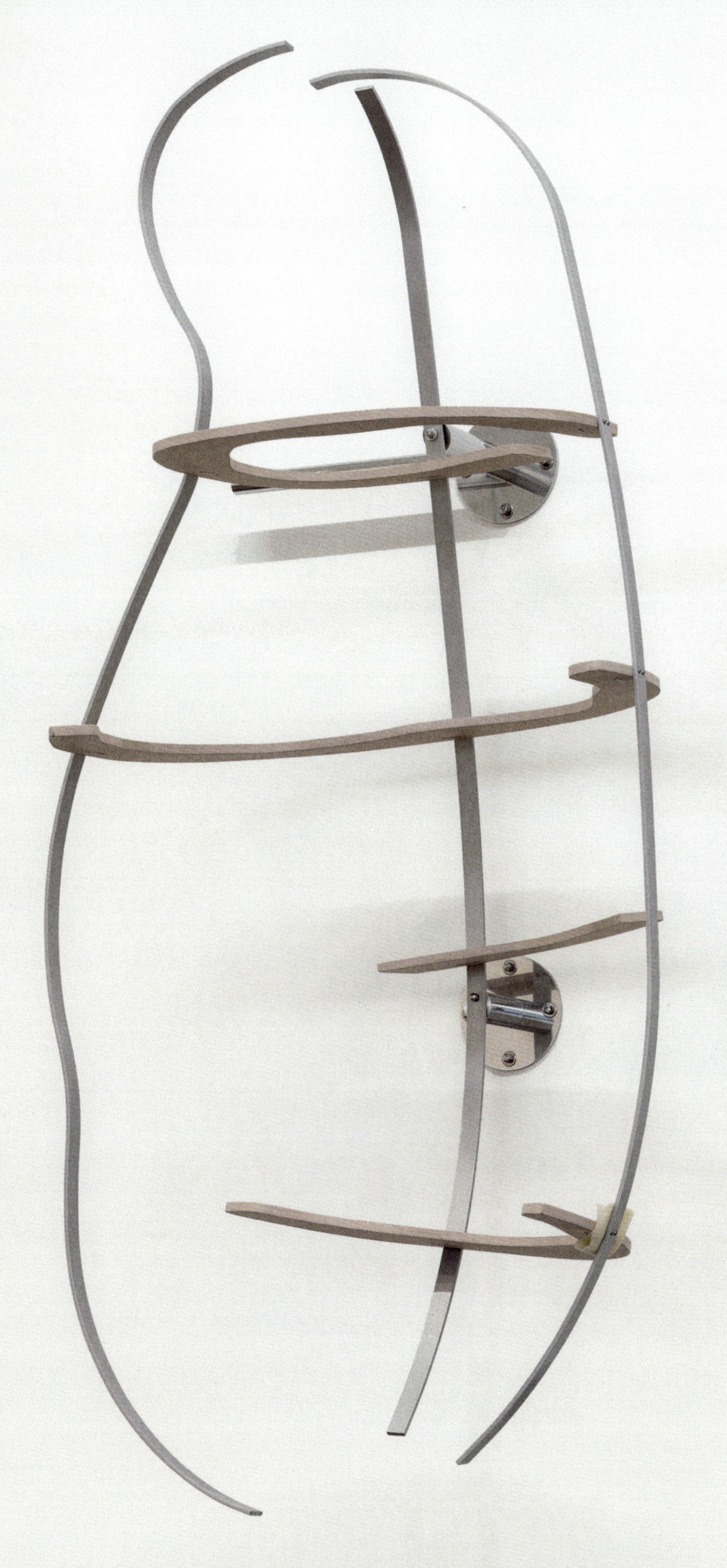

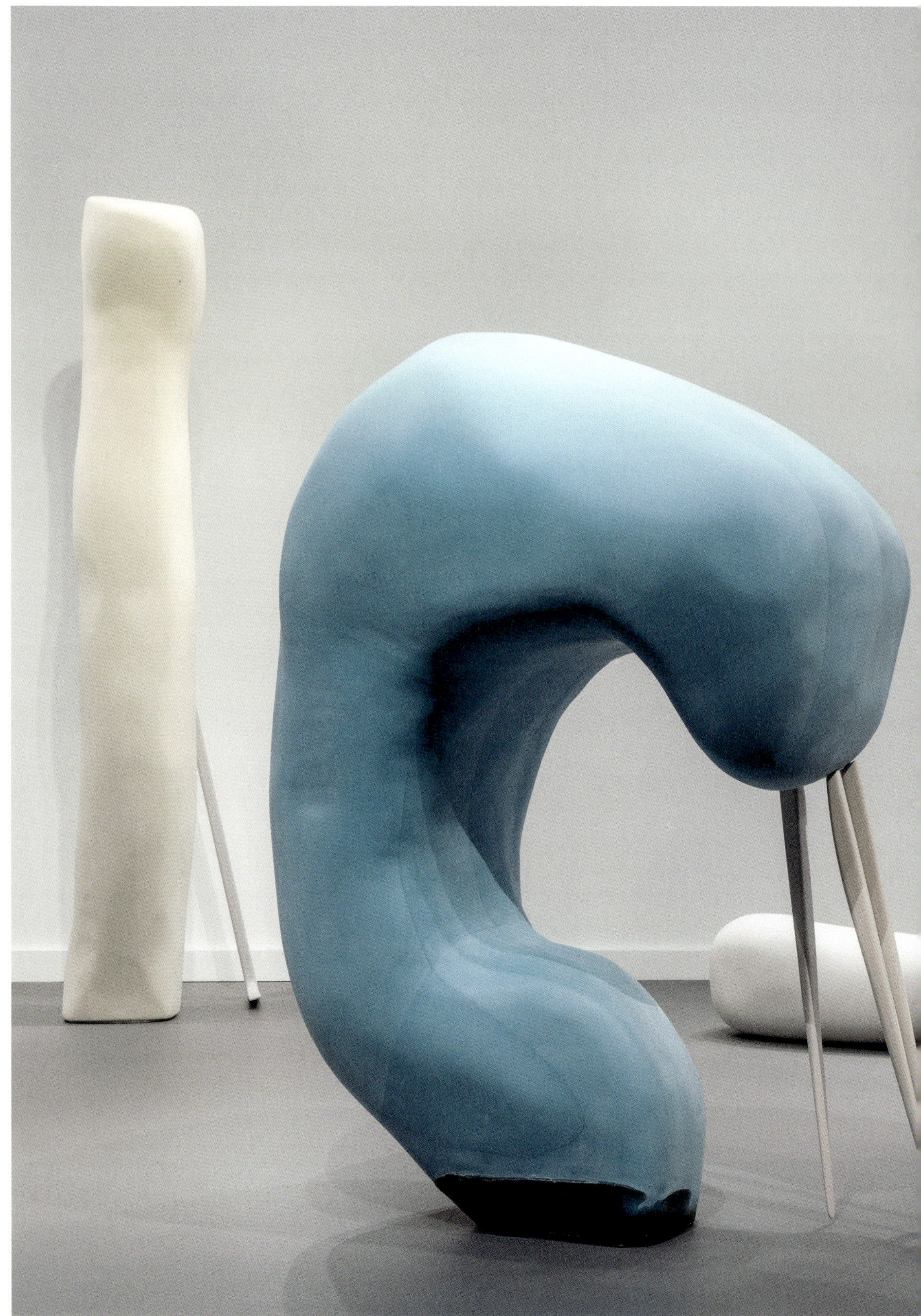

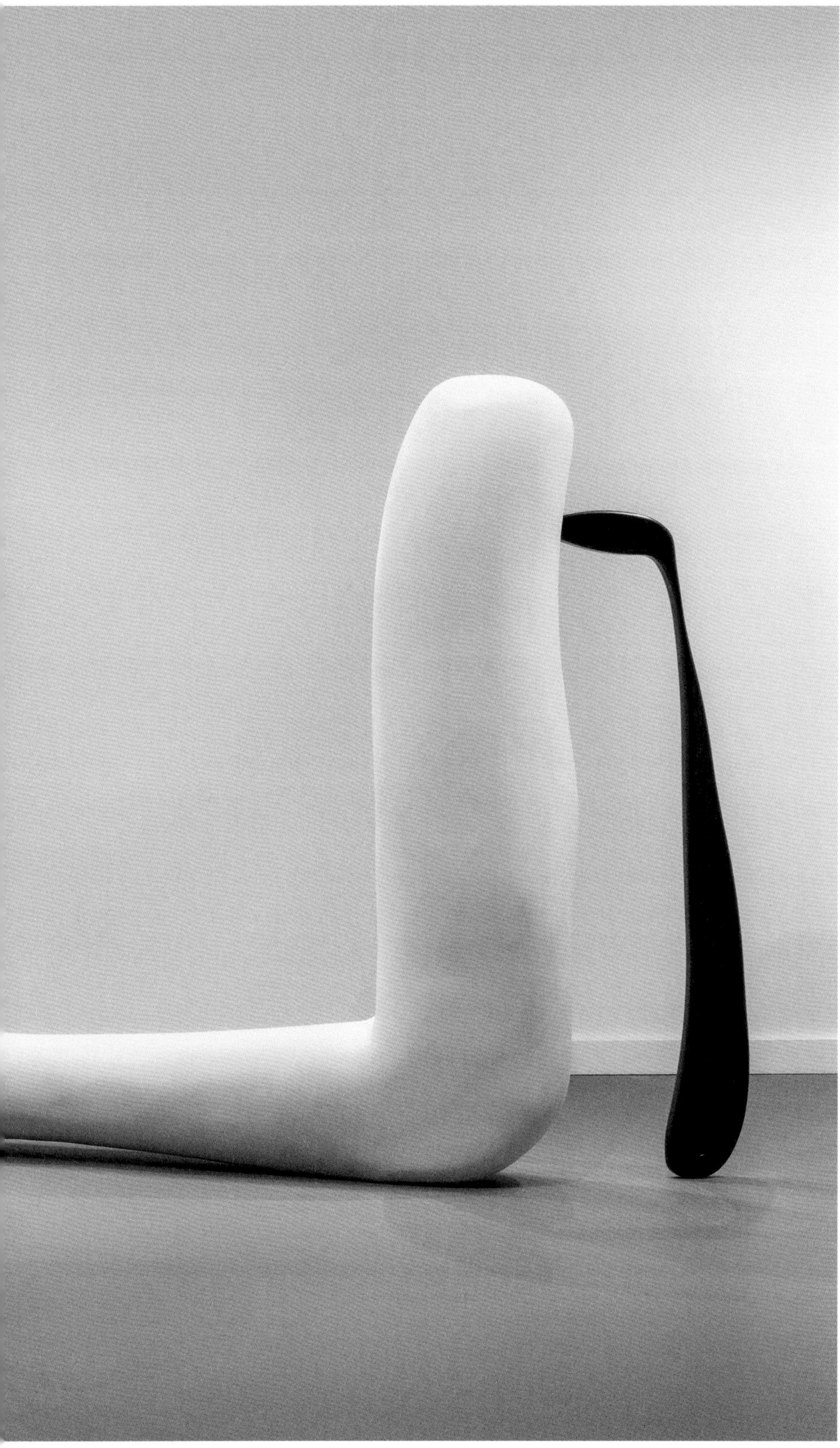

Stay Downers,
2017

Phyllida

Barlow

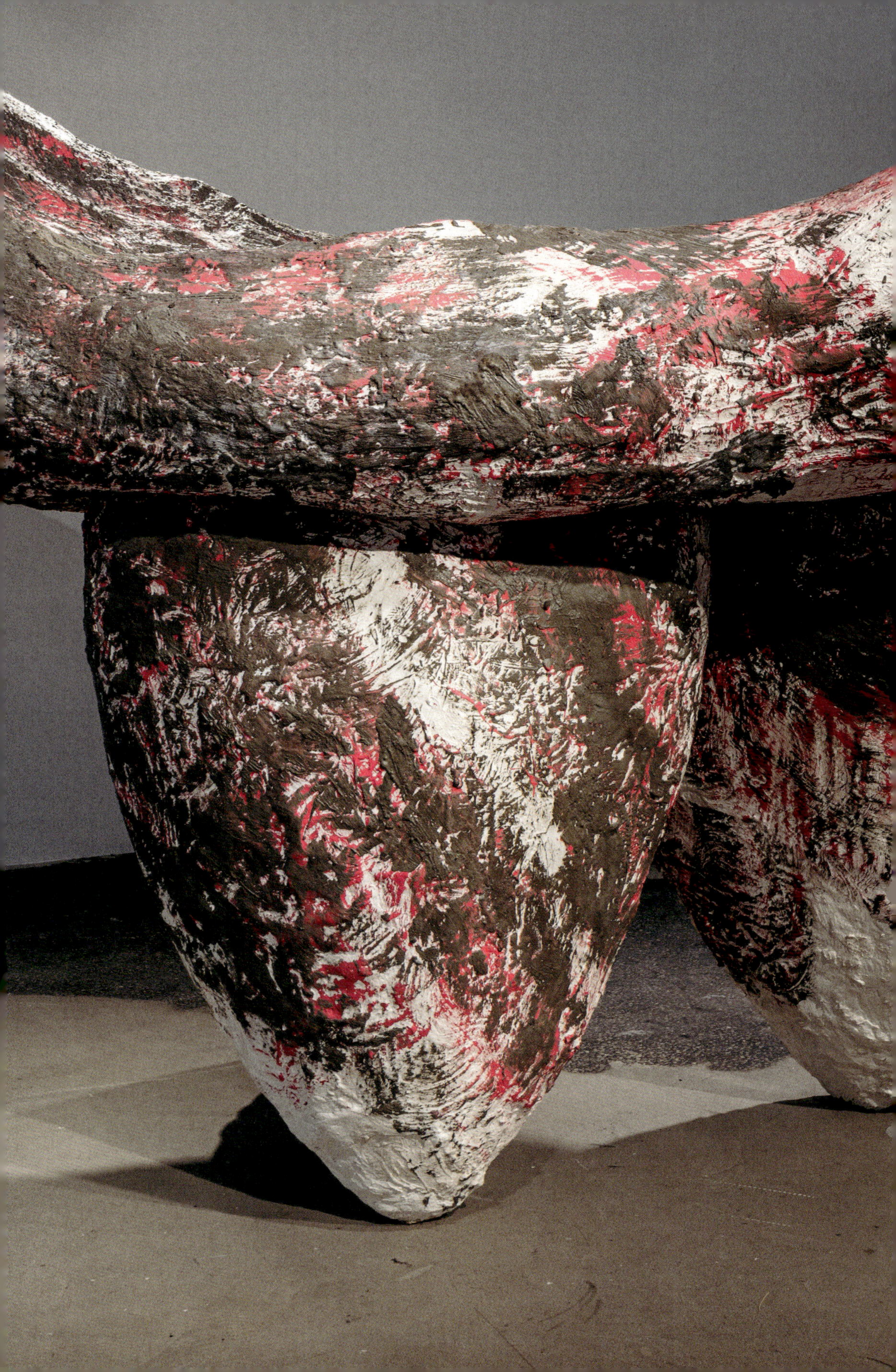

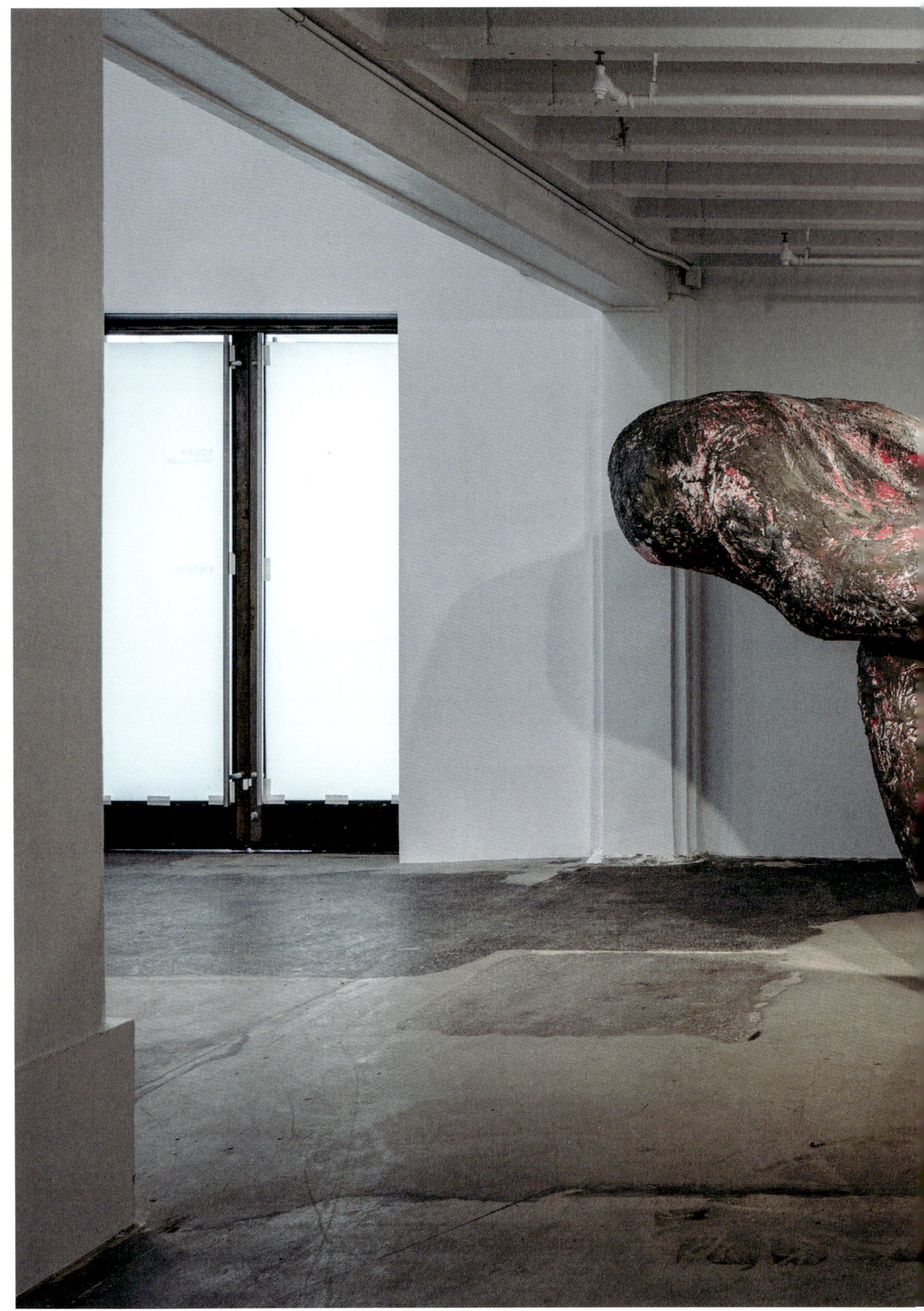

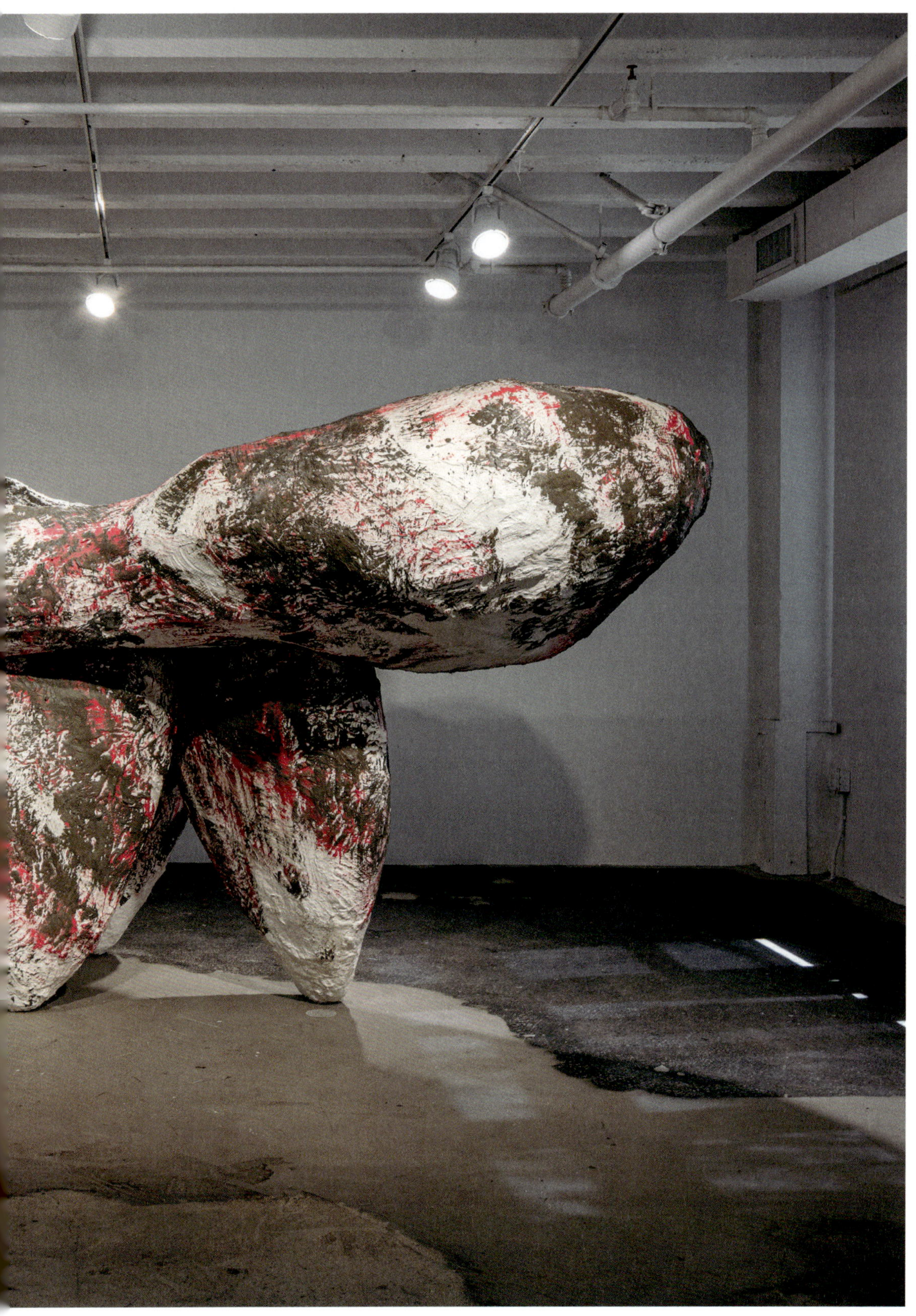

61

The experience of walking around it, the fact that you can never quite hold on to what it is. Sculpture unfolds and refolds and unfolds again. It's extremely restless.   PHYLLIDA BARLOW

untitled: modernsculpture; 2022, 2022

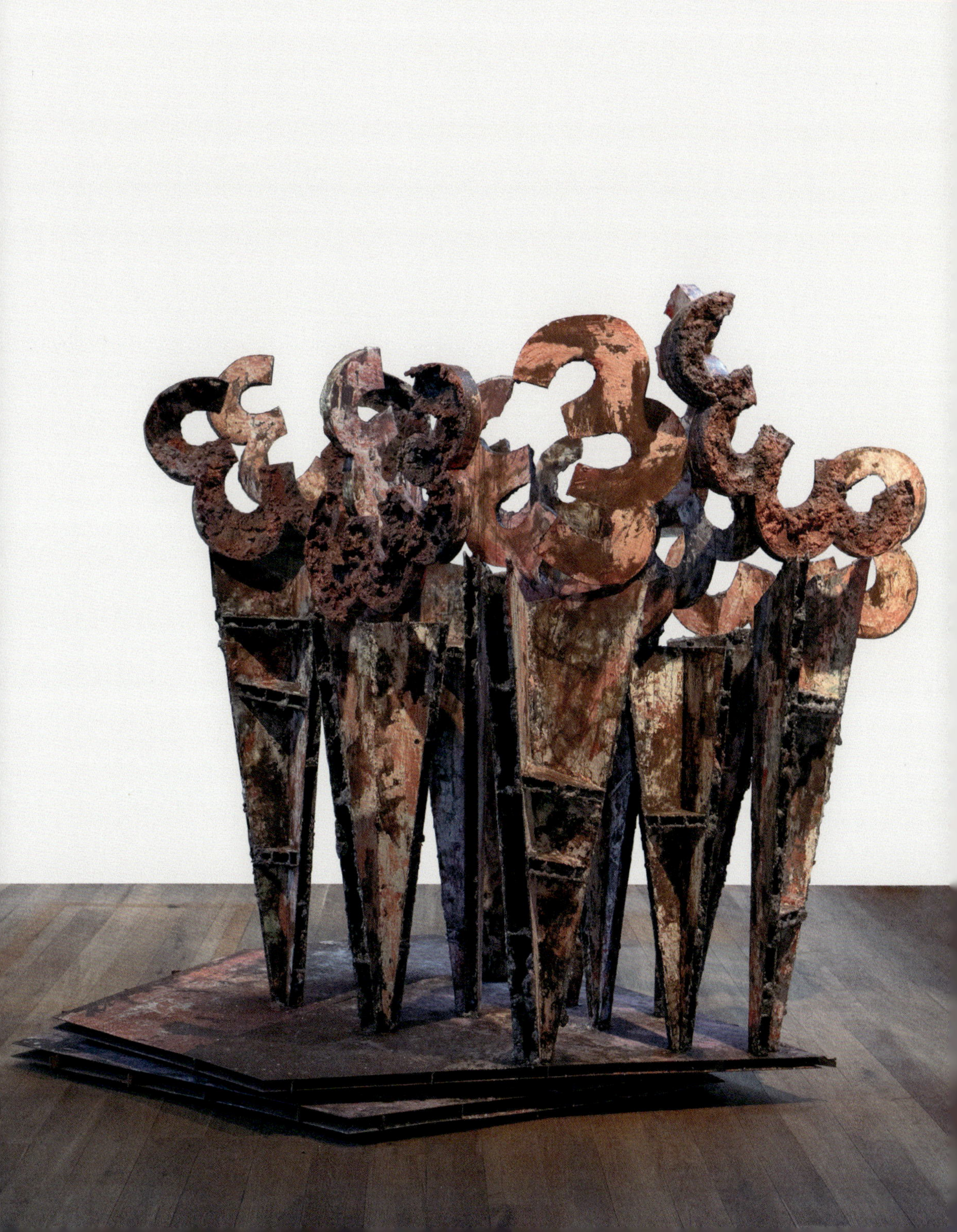

Lynda

Benglis

Power Tower, 2019
(detail and p.66)

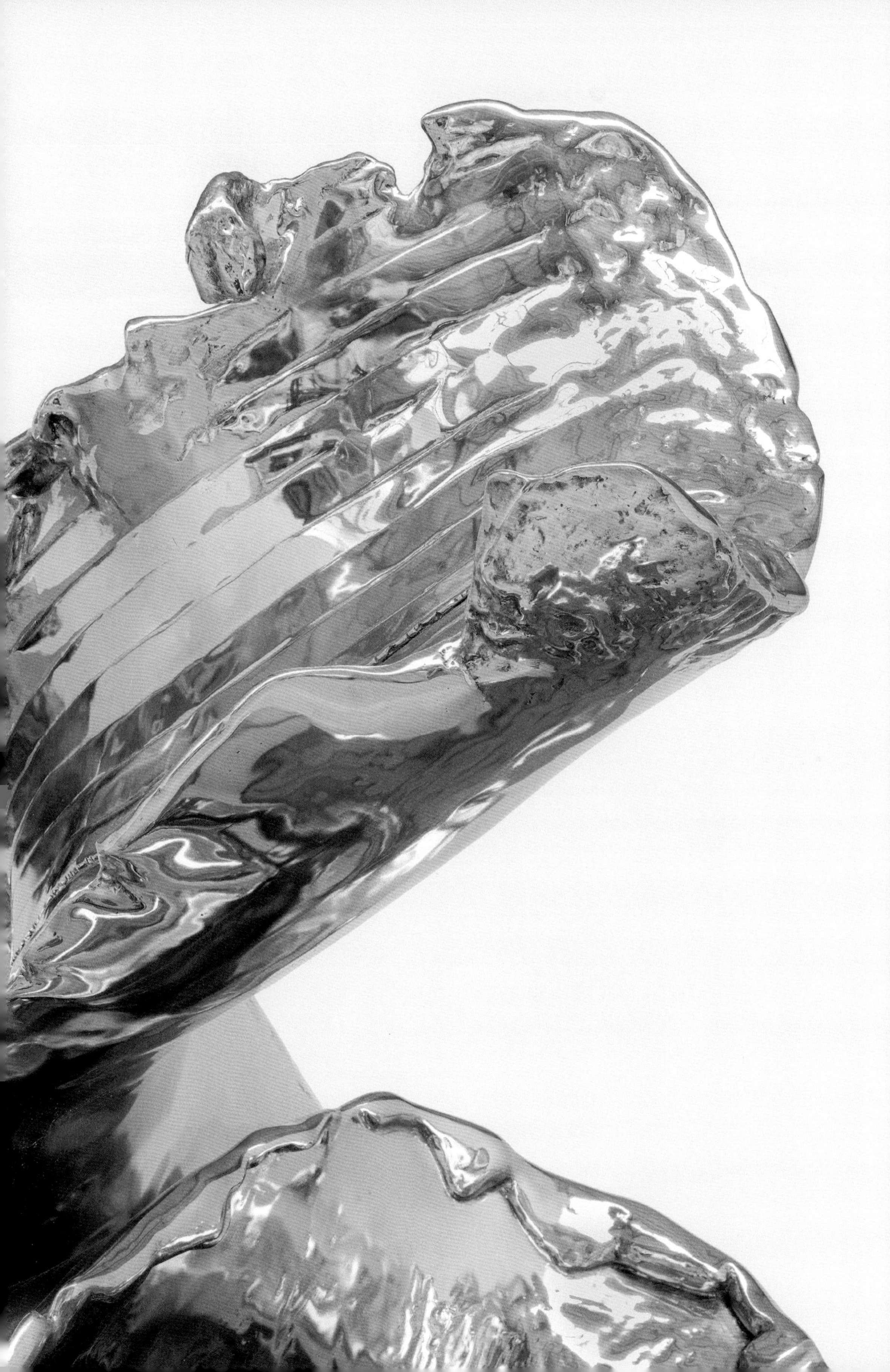

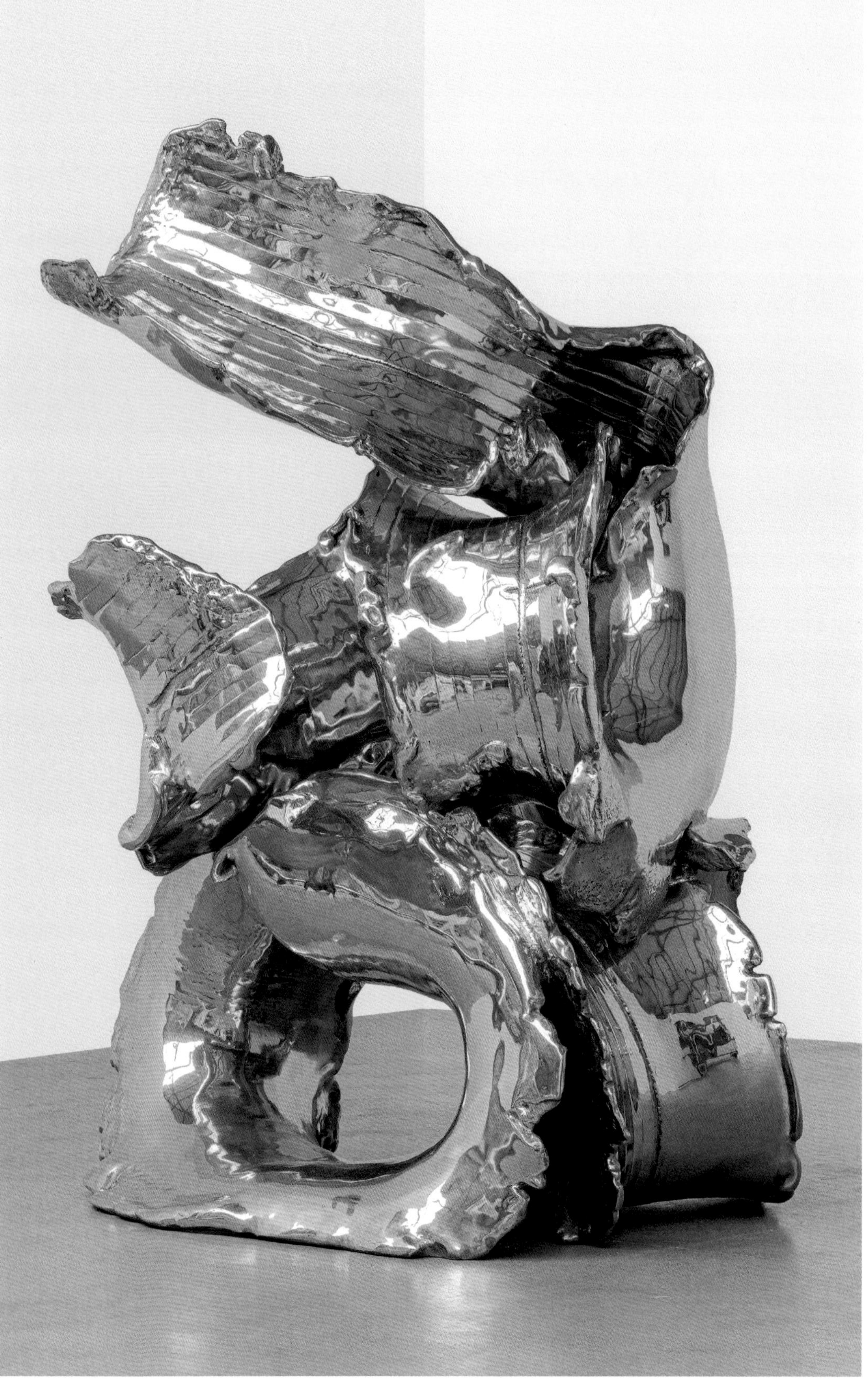

In my work, I am involved with bodily response so that the viewer has the feeling of being one with the material and with that action, both visually and muscularly. It is a matter of completing the artistic illusion, allusion, not in the literal sense – as done by a still life or landscape painter – but creating the illusion through feeling, both tactile and visual, through muscular response.   LYNDA BENGLIS

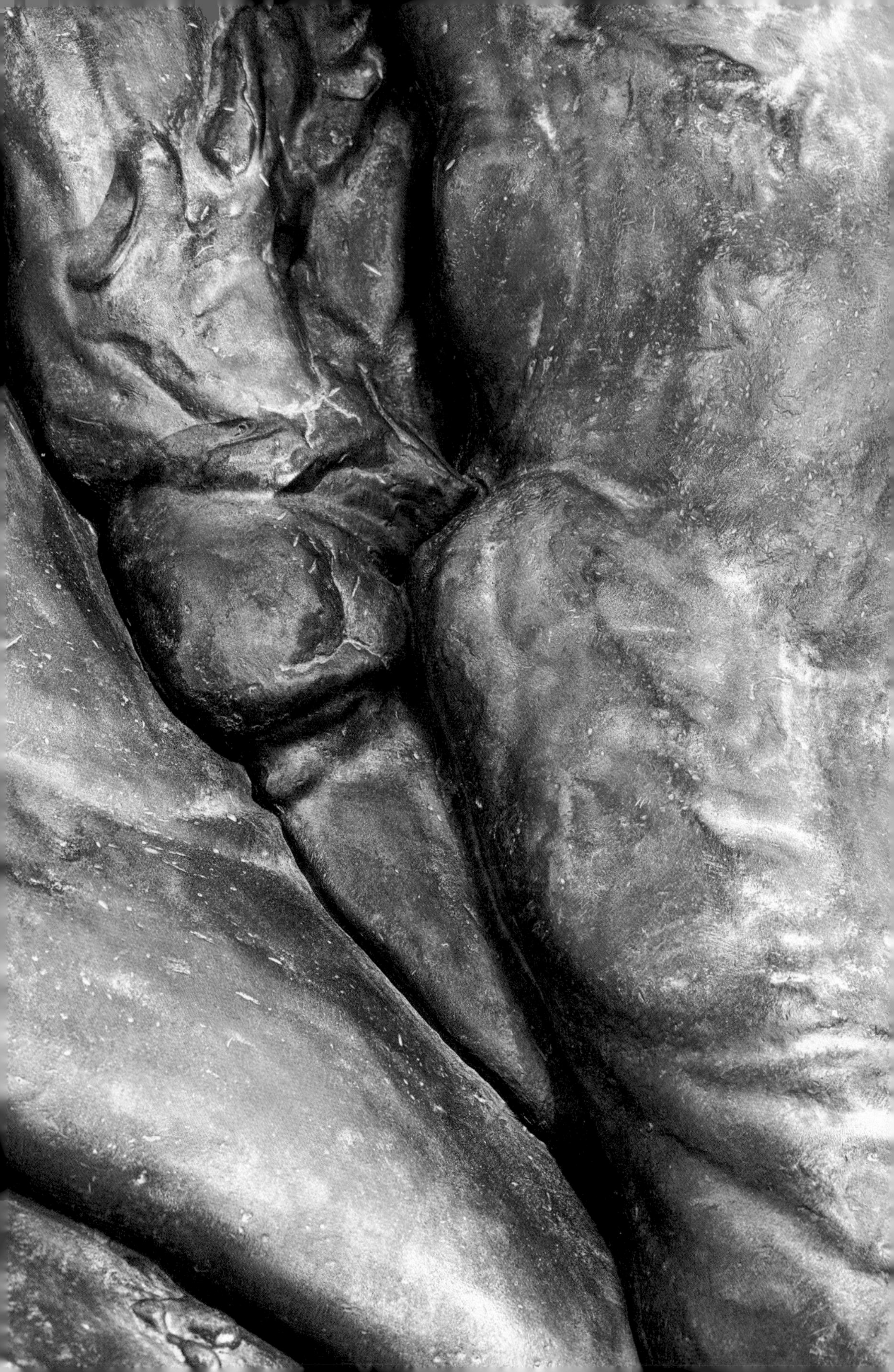

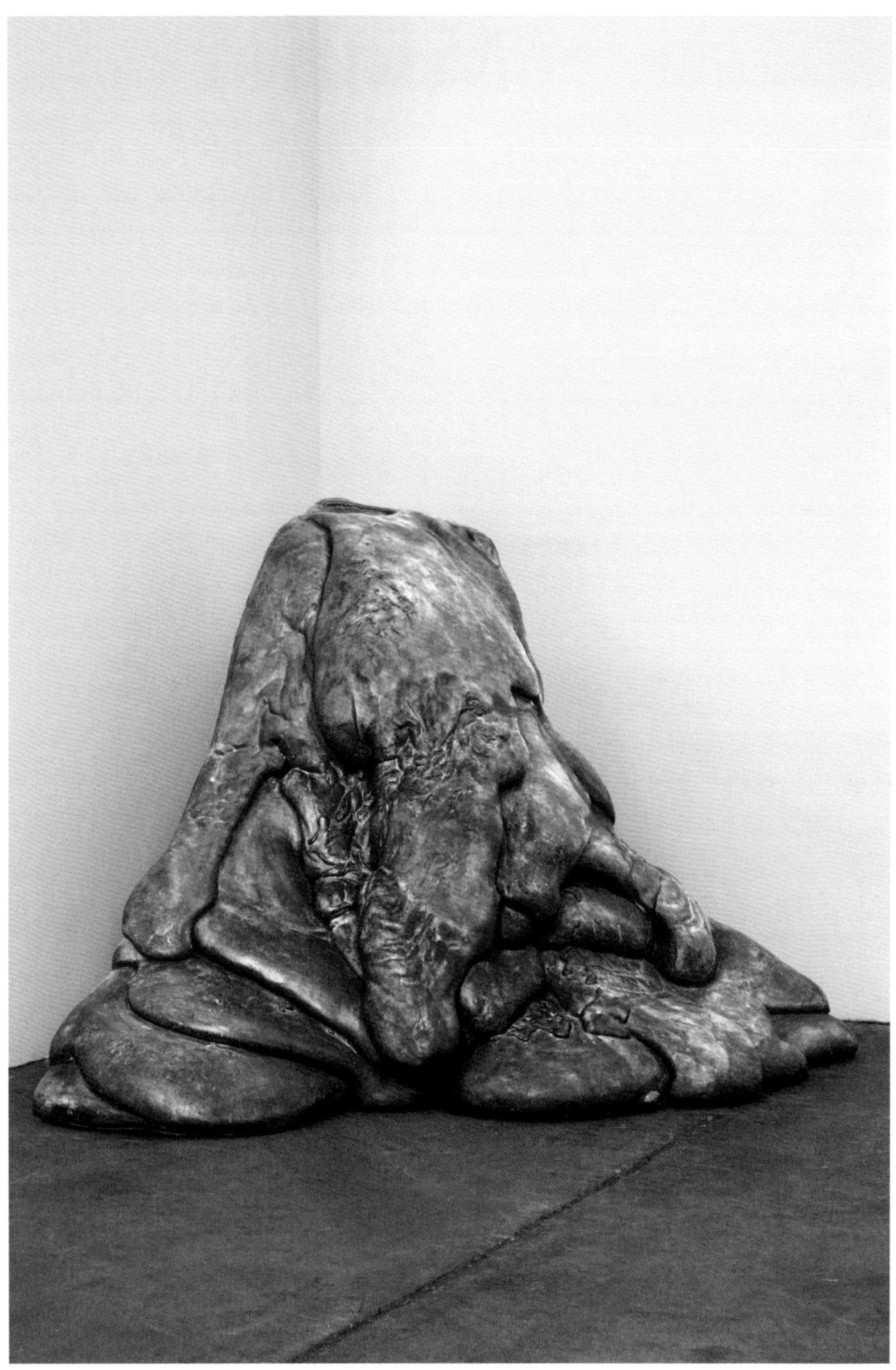

Quartered Meteor, 1969,
cast 1975 (and detail)

69

Michel

Blazy

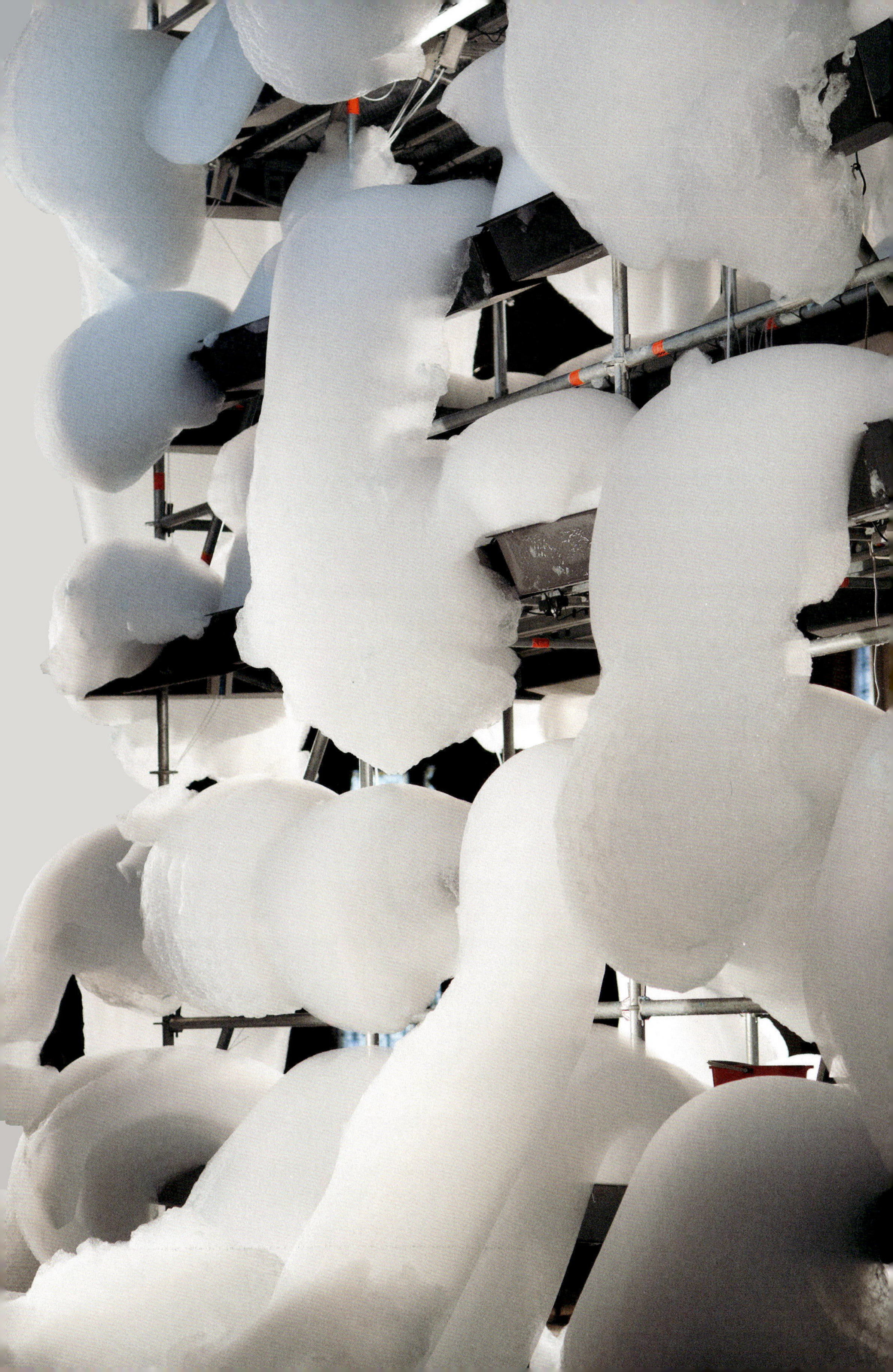

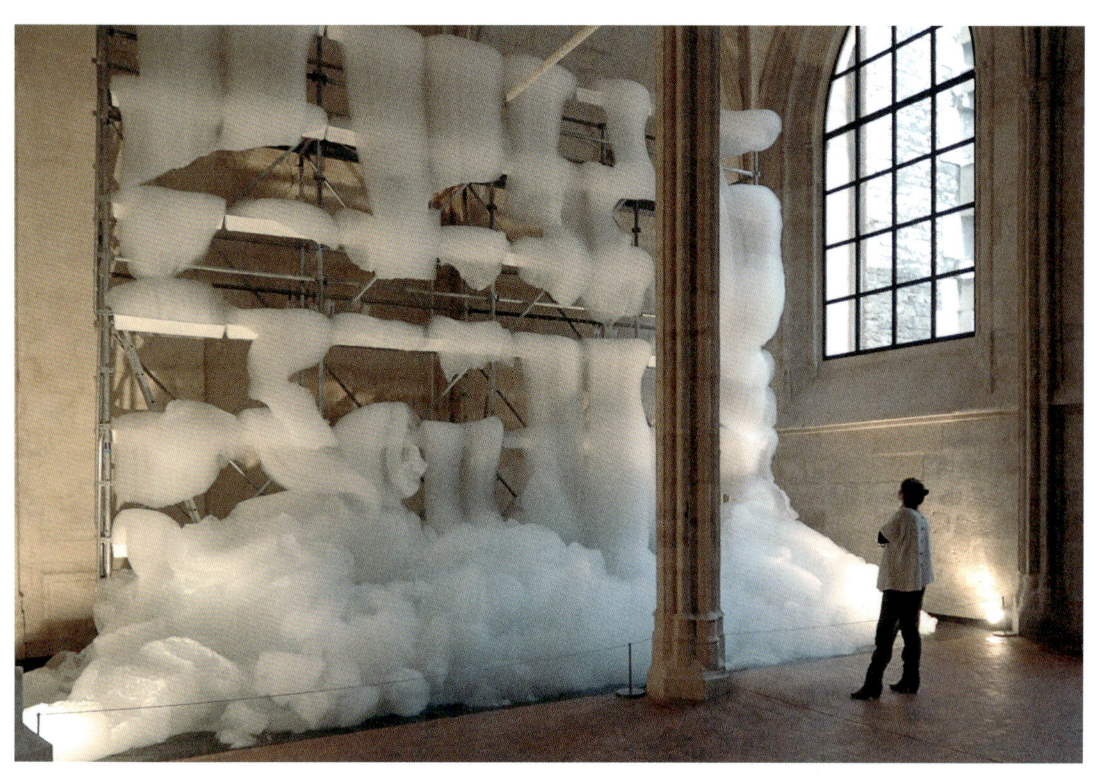

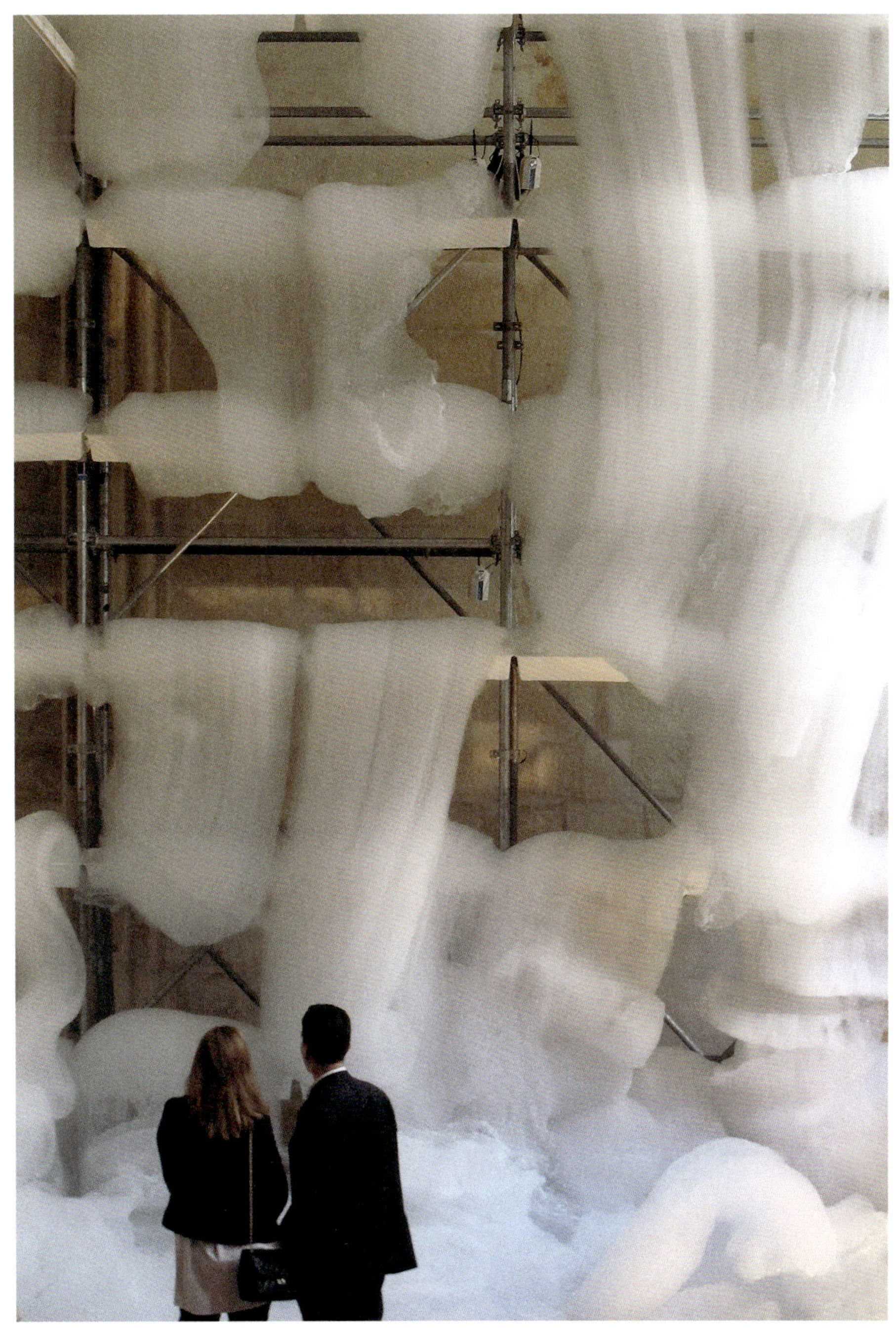

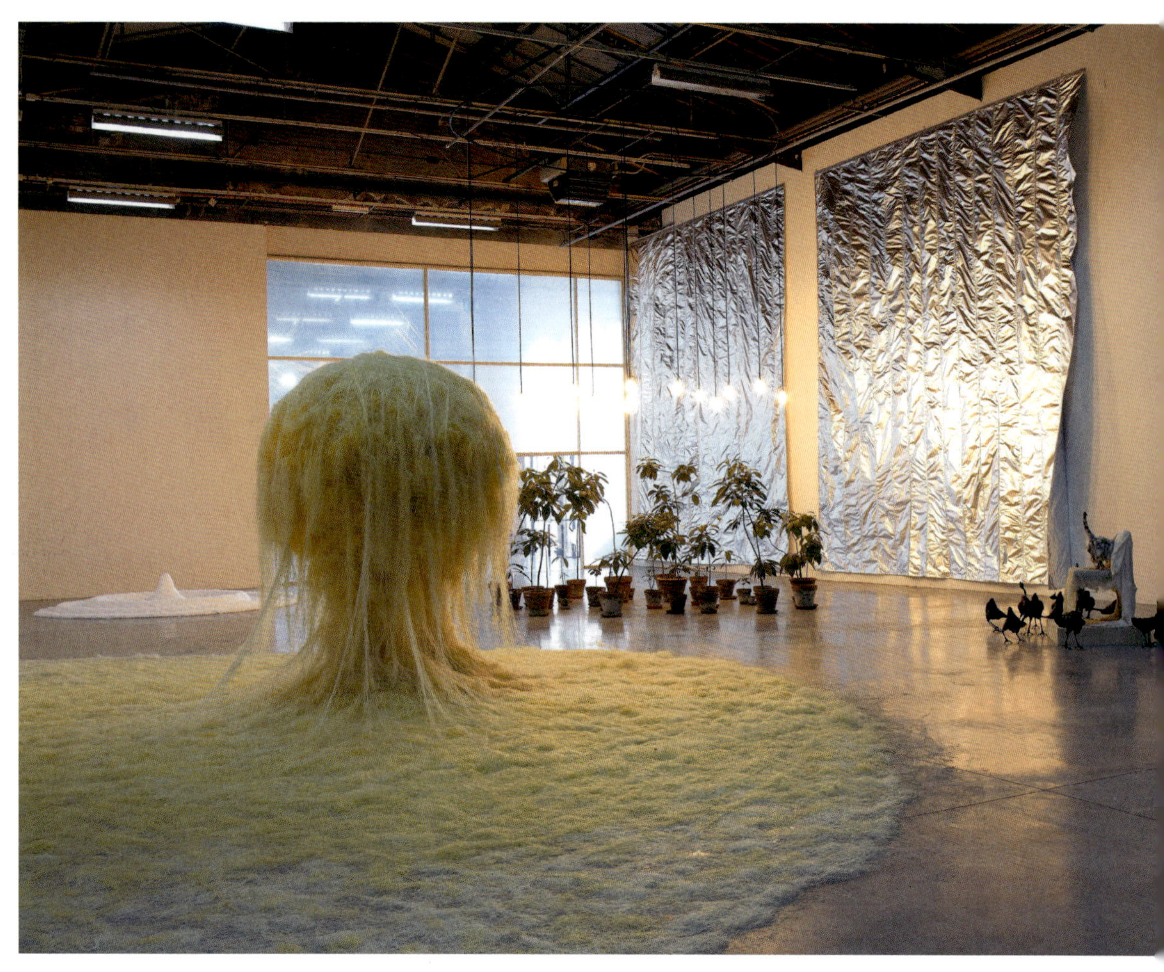

Patman 2,
2006

My philosophy is more about nurturing matter, just like
a gardener who would take the necessary measures to ensure
that things actually happen, even if they arise from forces
far beyond their understanding... I am not trying to prevail over
things, nor to bend them to my will, but rather to observe
them, to understand how they function and what their needs
are to ensure that they flourish. MICHEL BLAZY

Paloma

Bosquê

Two Stones, 2017
(detail and pp. 78–79)

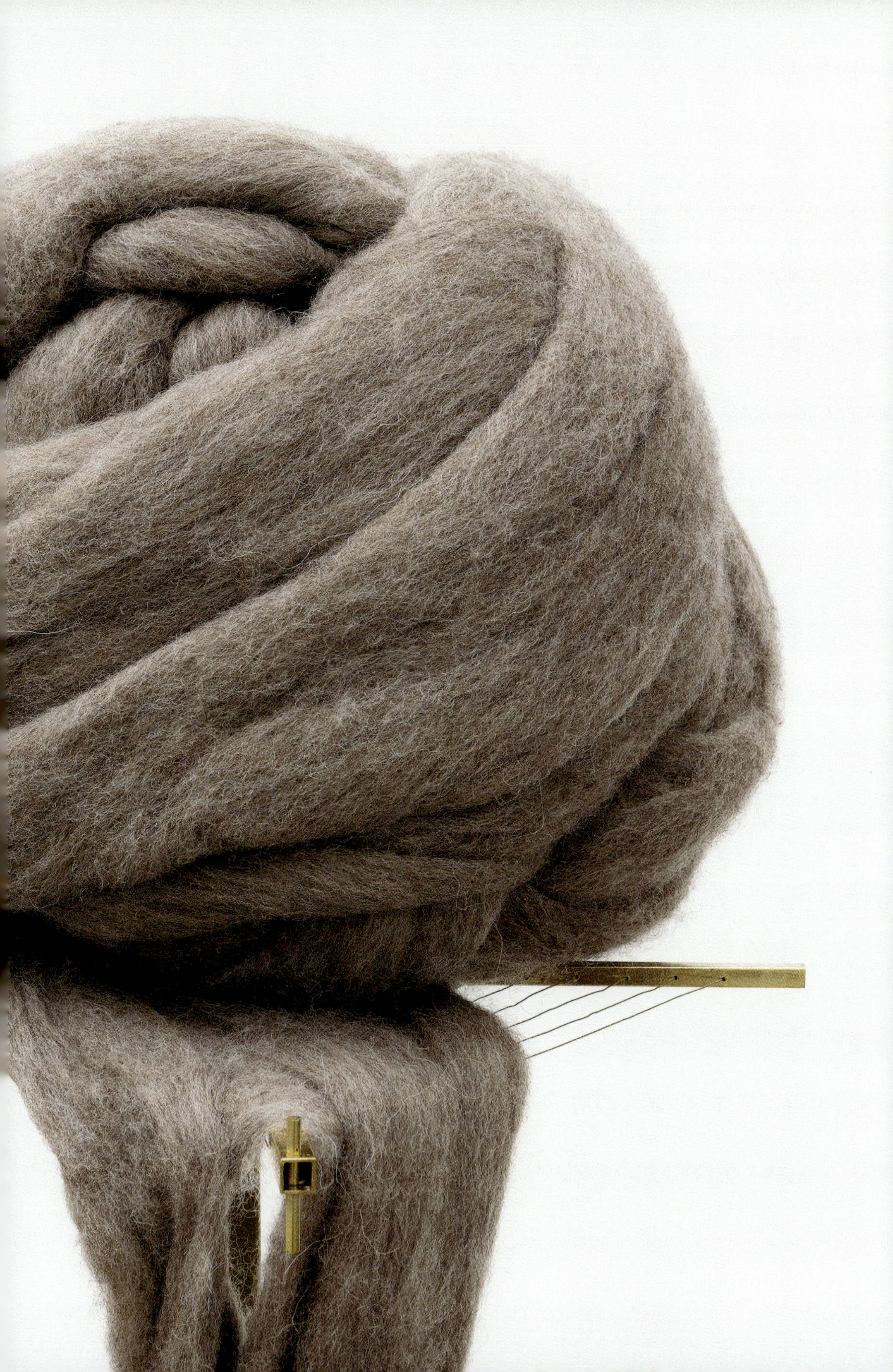

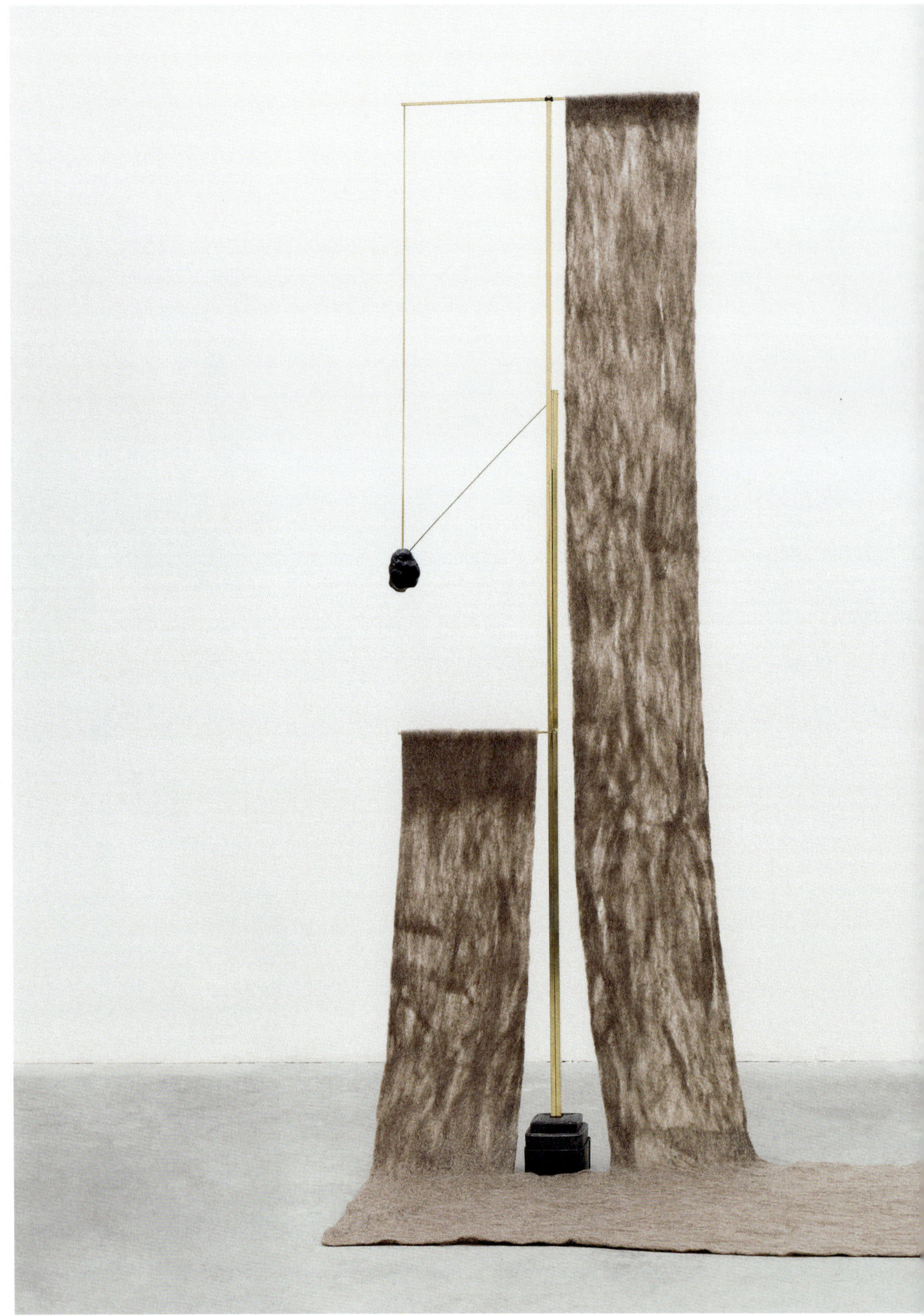

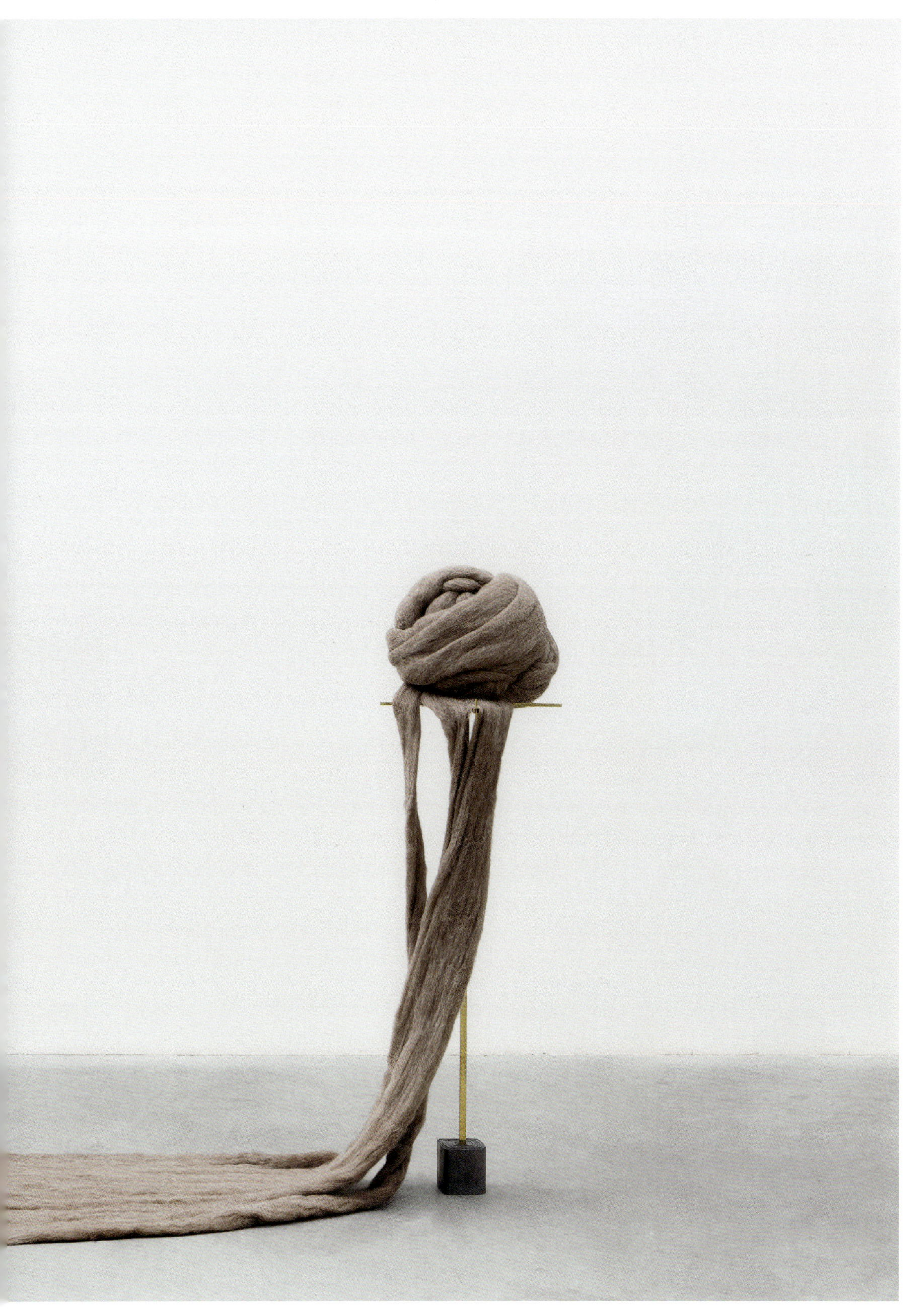

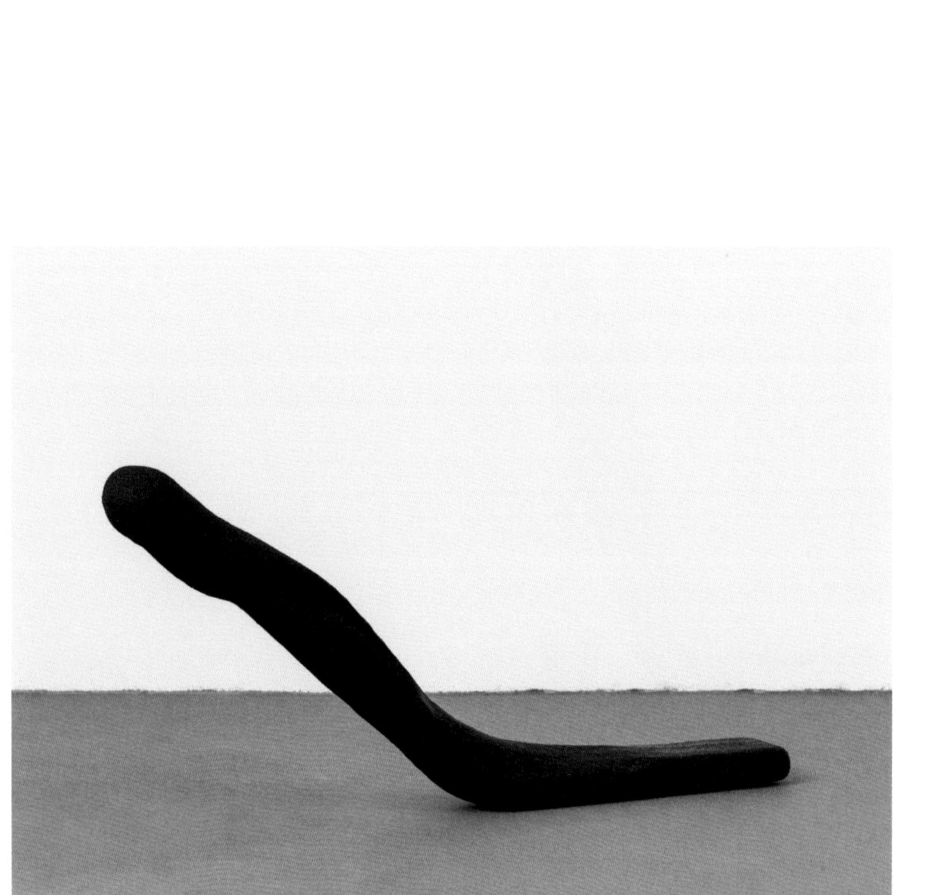

Snake,
2020

80

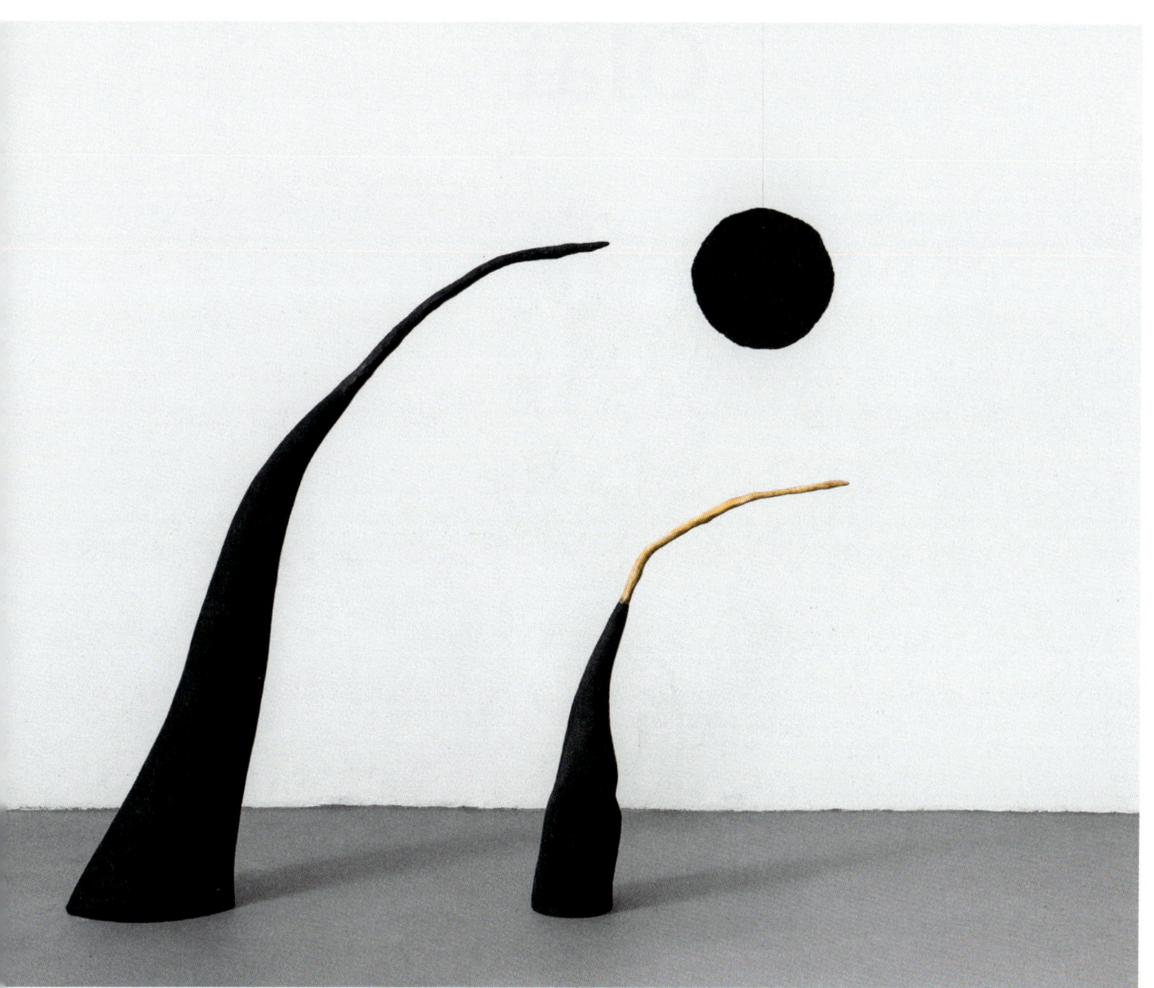

In the mechanics of tropical nature – my first experience
of nature – things are in a constant state of transformation,
everything decays very quickly and is born very quickly too.
In this state, everything needs to be constantly remade,
nothing remains unchanged. I am particularly interested in
the state of things at the borderline of this transformation.
A kind of 'in-between' moment.   PALOMA BOSQUÊ

81

Olaf

Brzeski

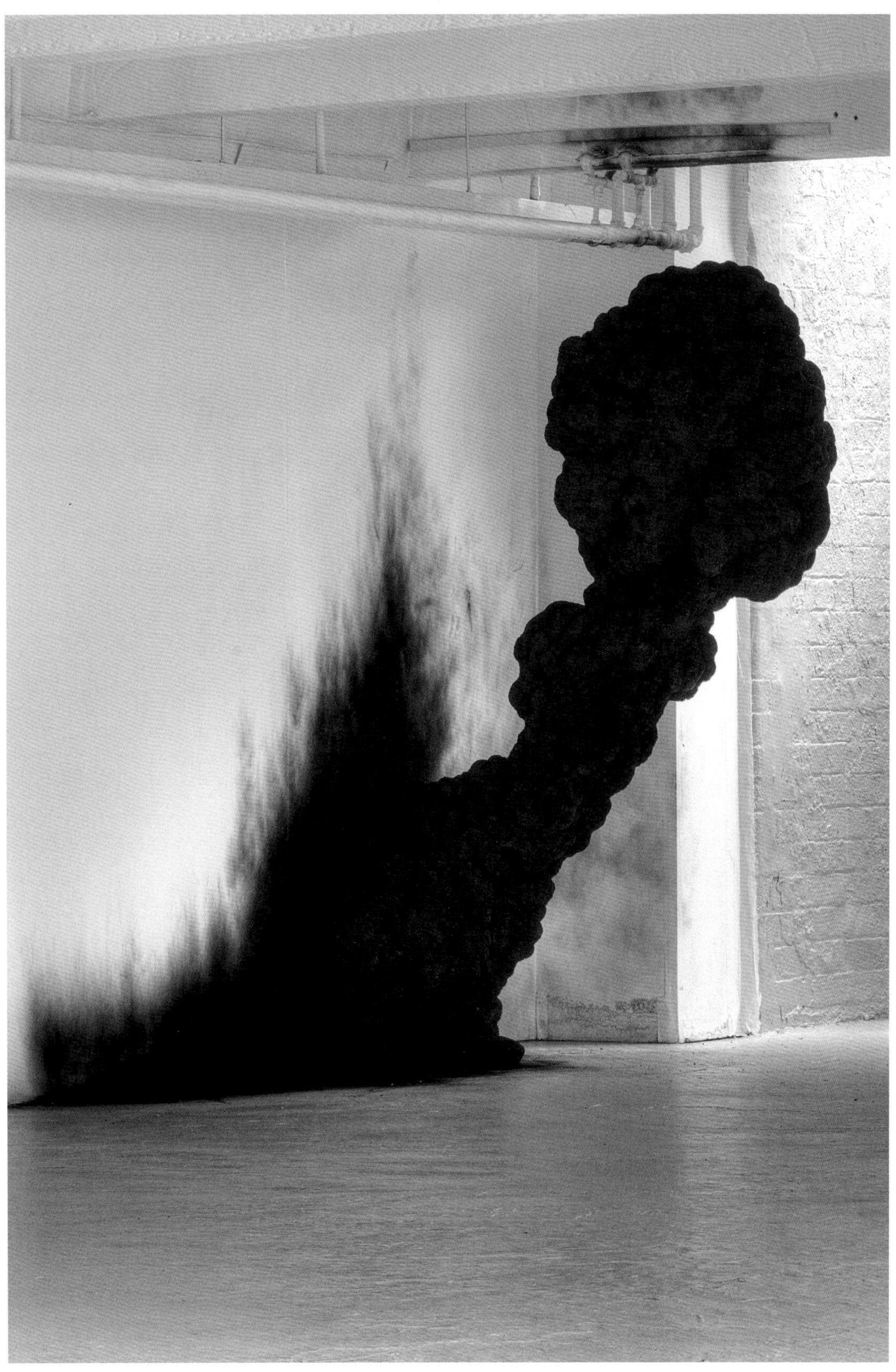

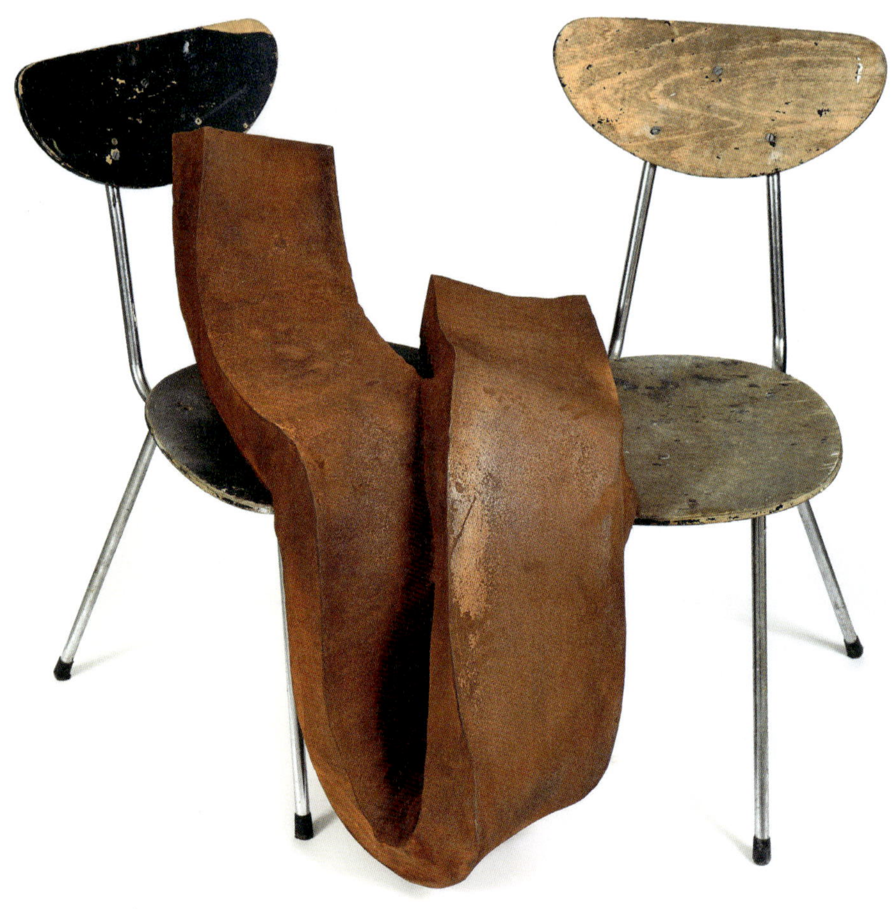

Untitled (from the Little
Orphans series), 2009

84

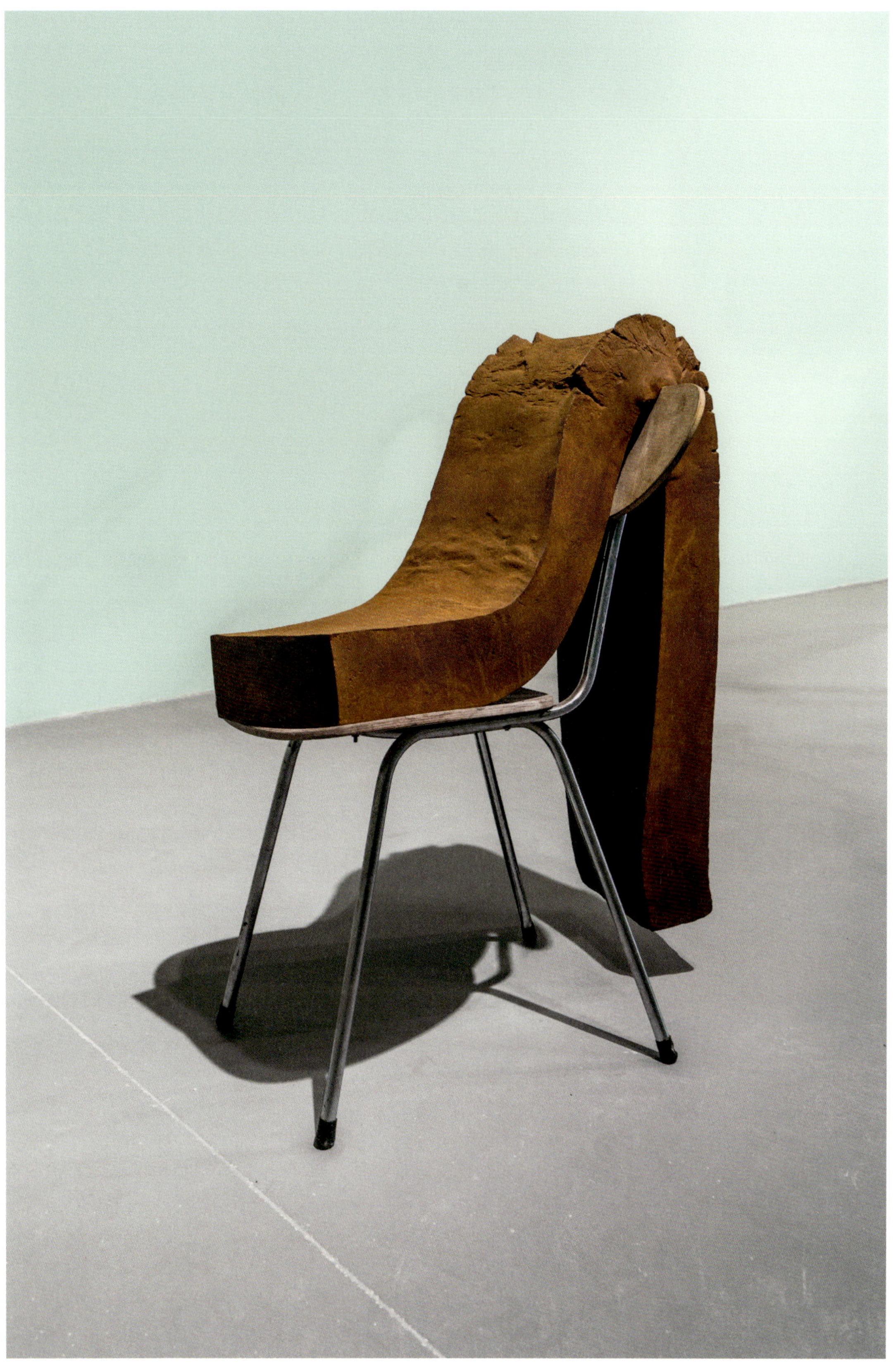

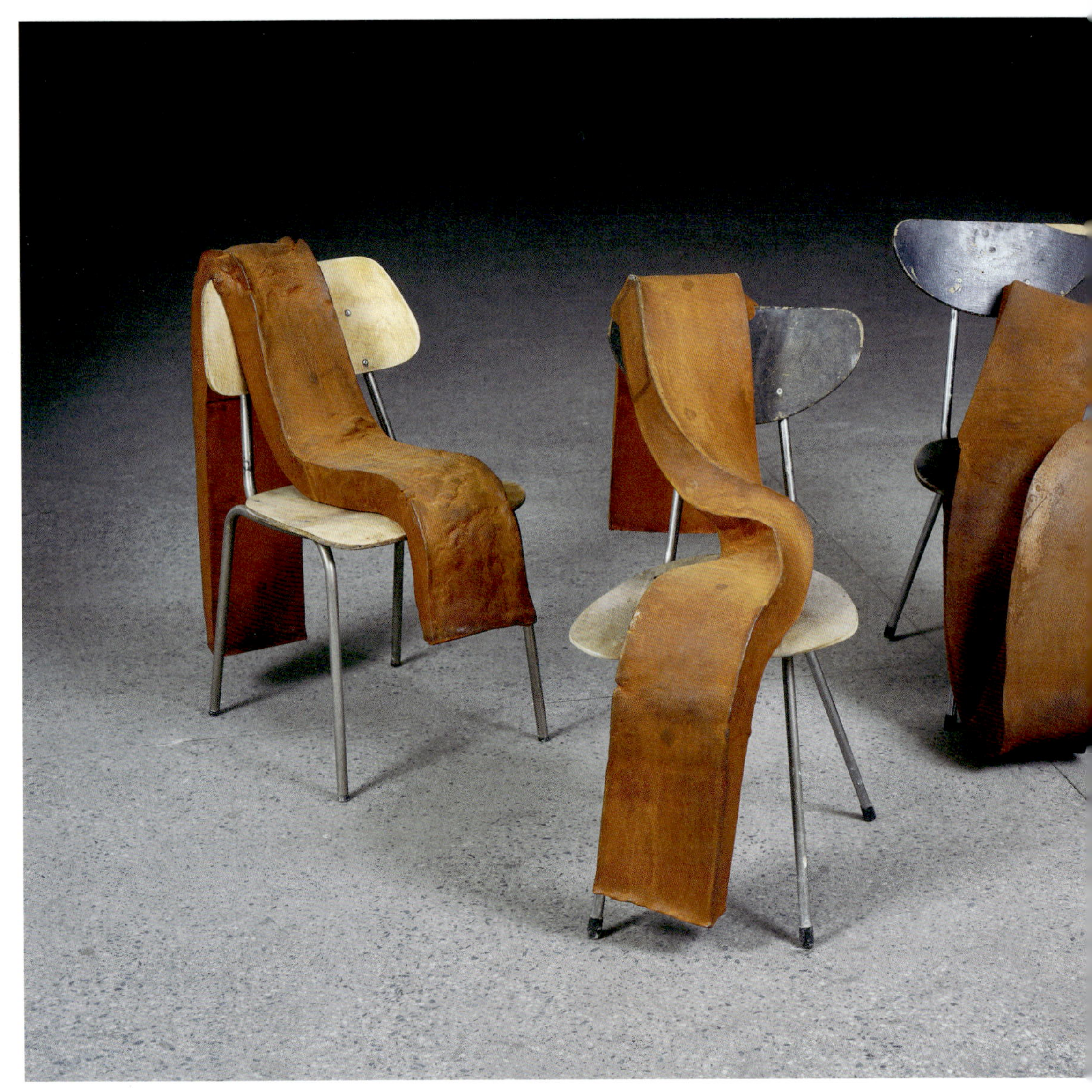

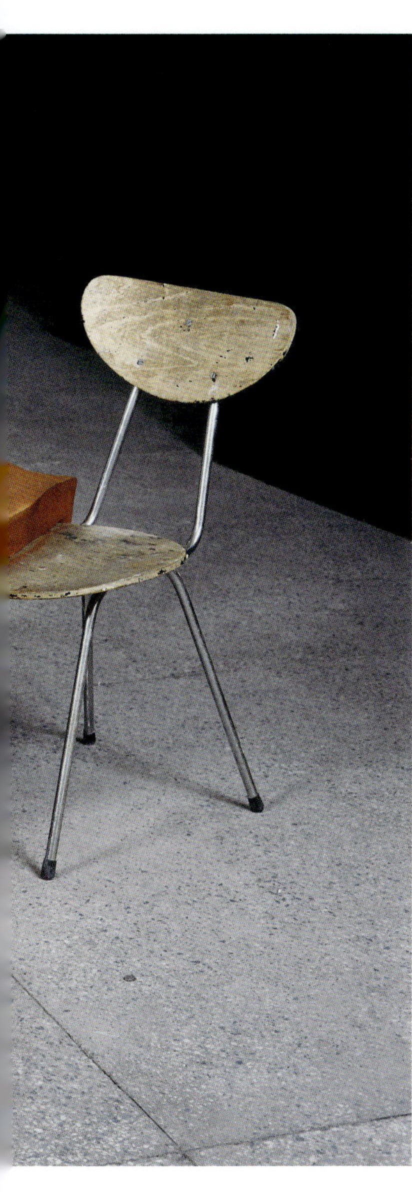

They creep slowly down. They are so tired of sitting
on their socles that they're totally slacking. OLAF BRZESKI

Choi

Jeong

Hwa

All works from the *Blooming matrix series*, 2018

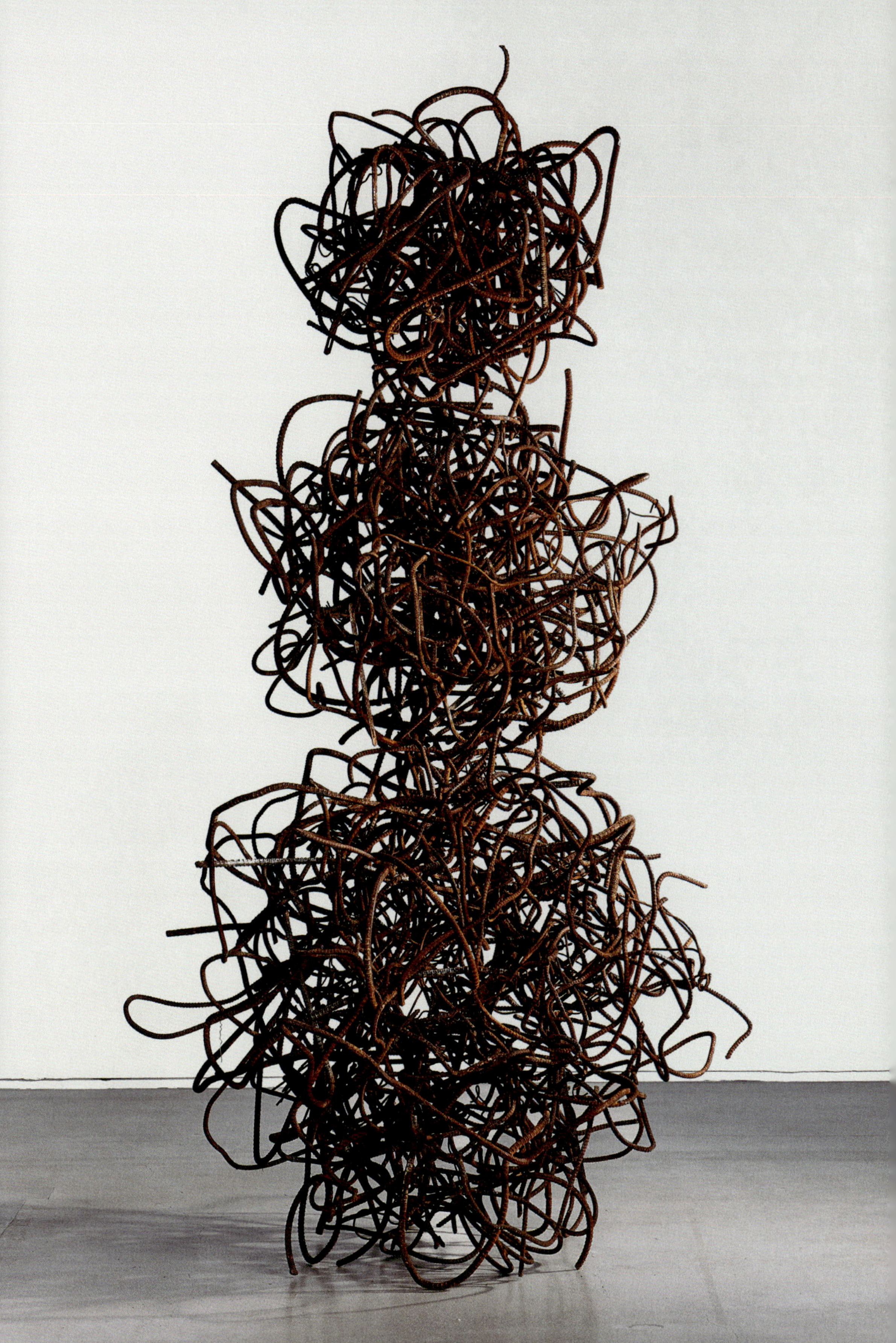

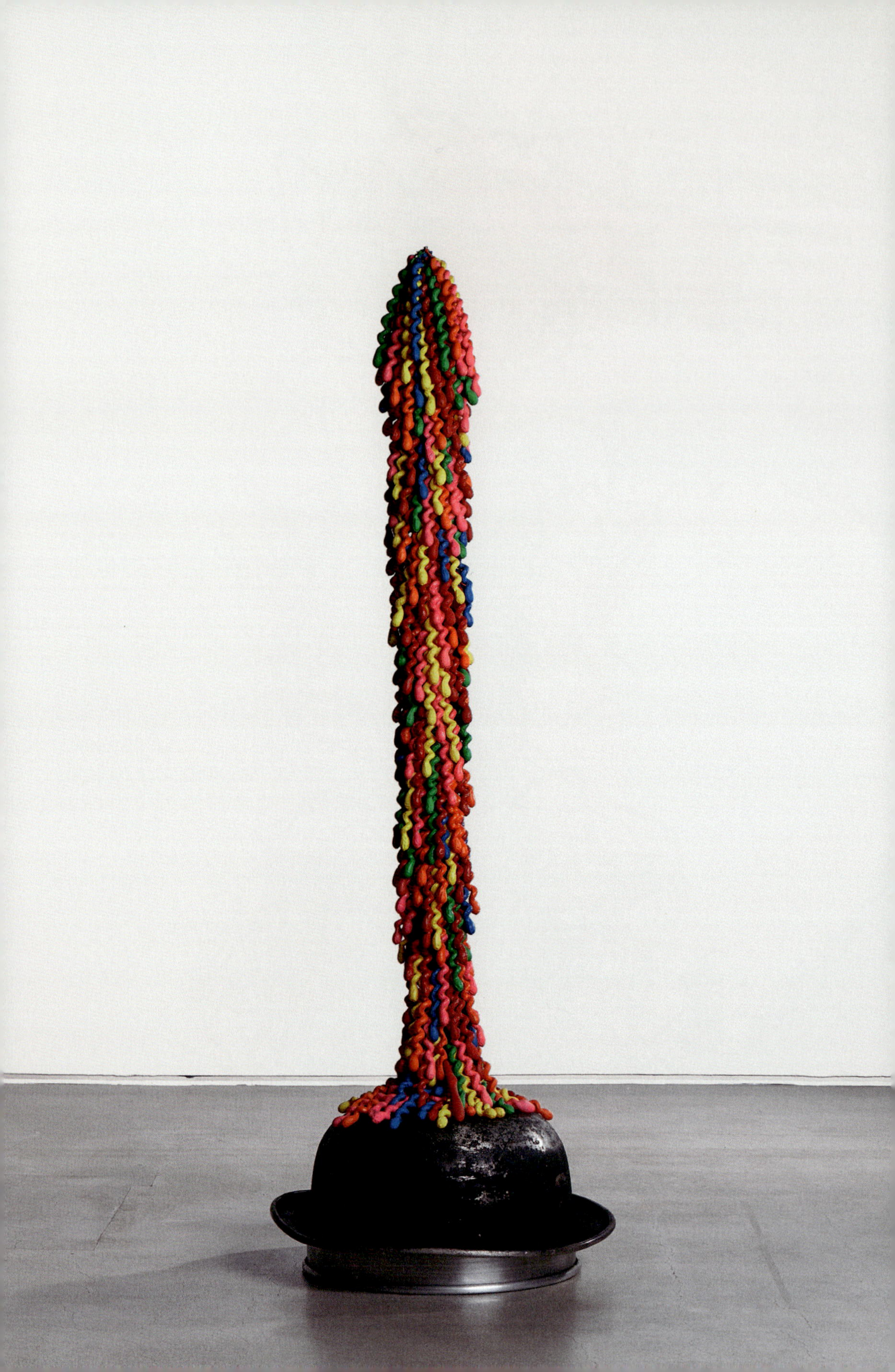

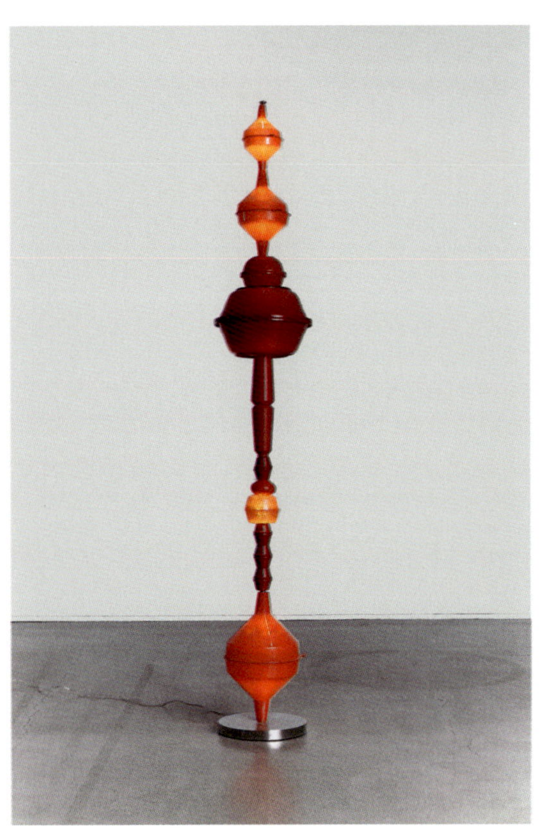
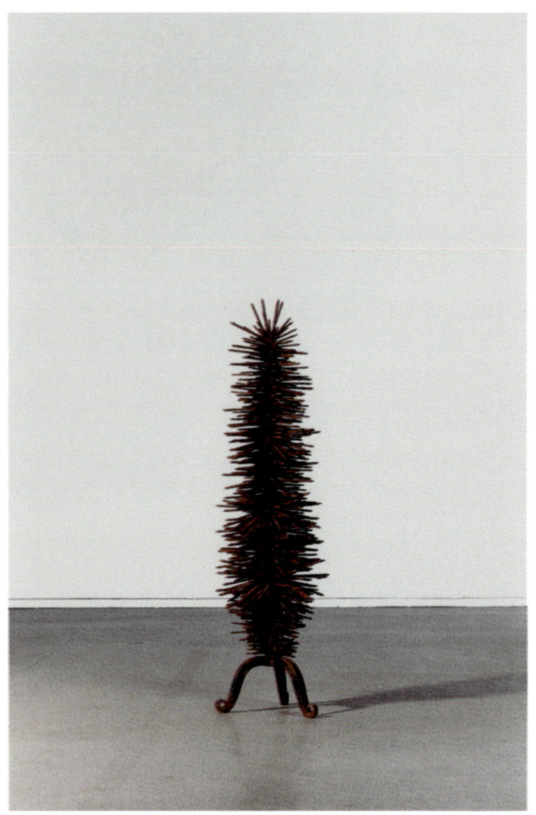
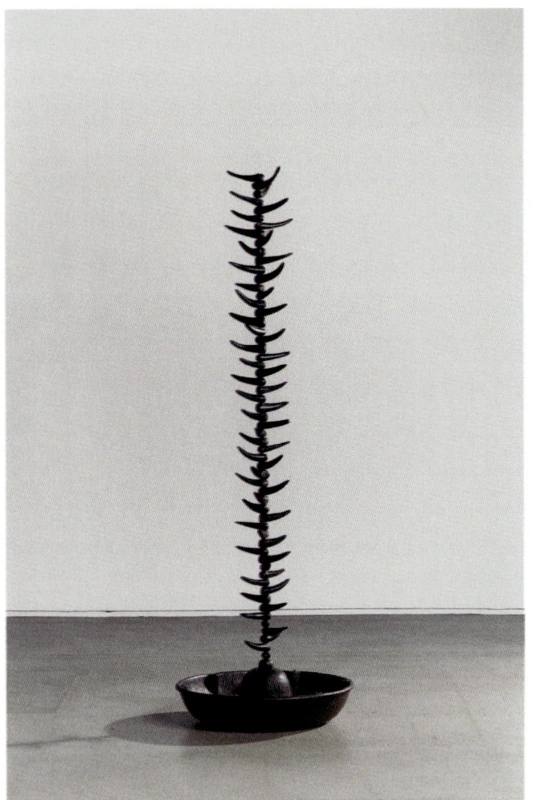
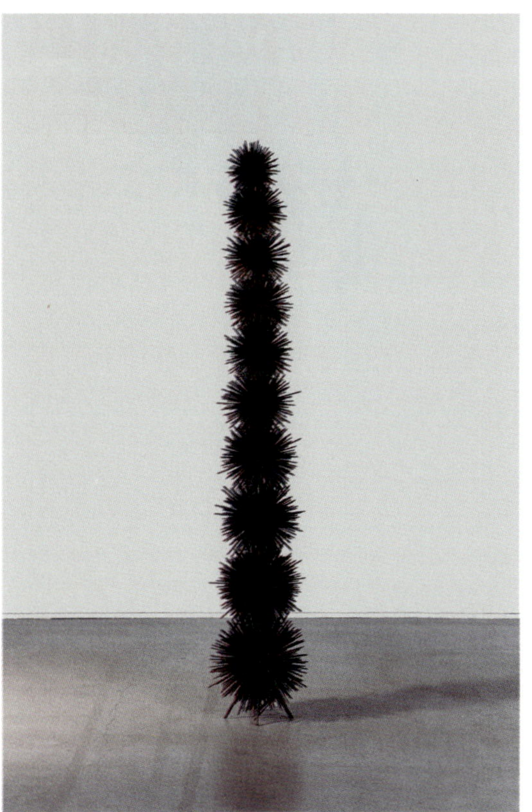

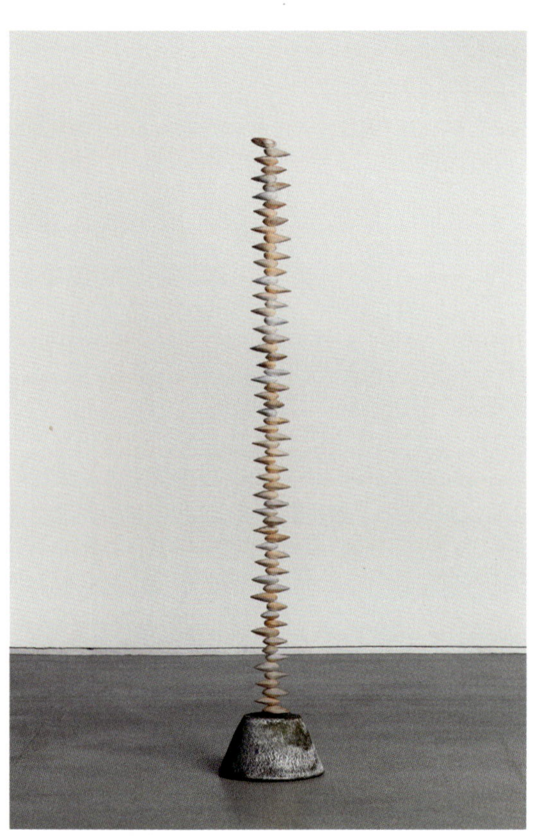
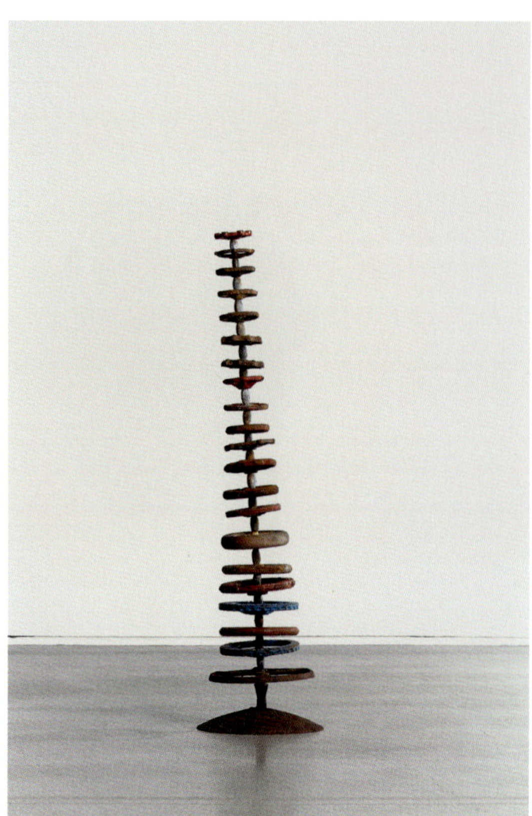
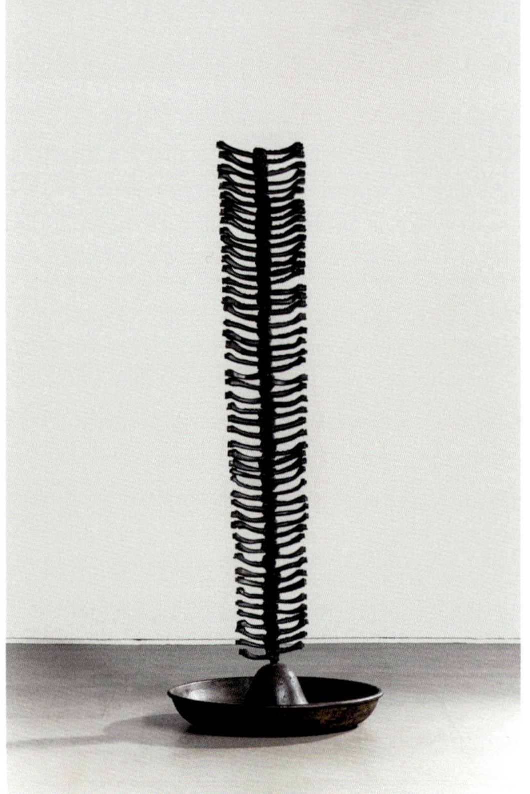
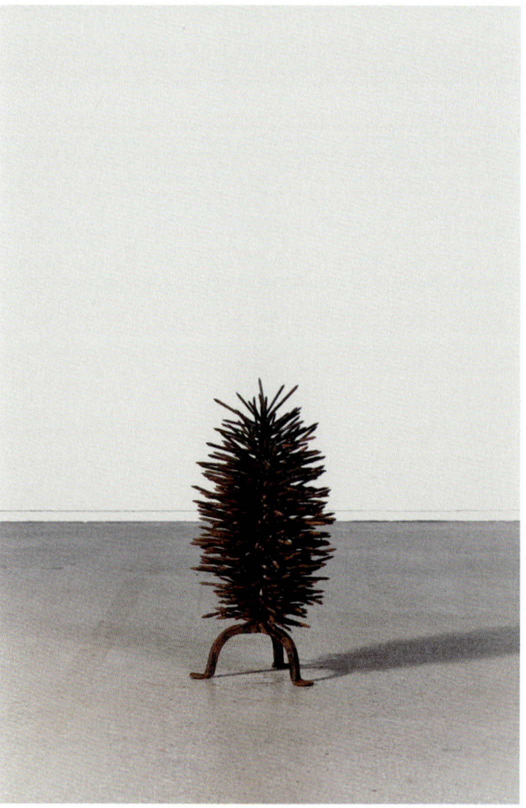

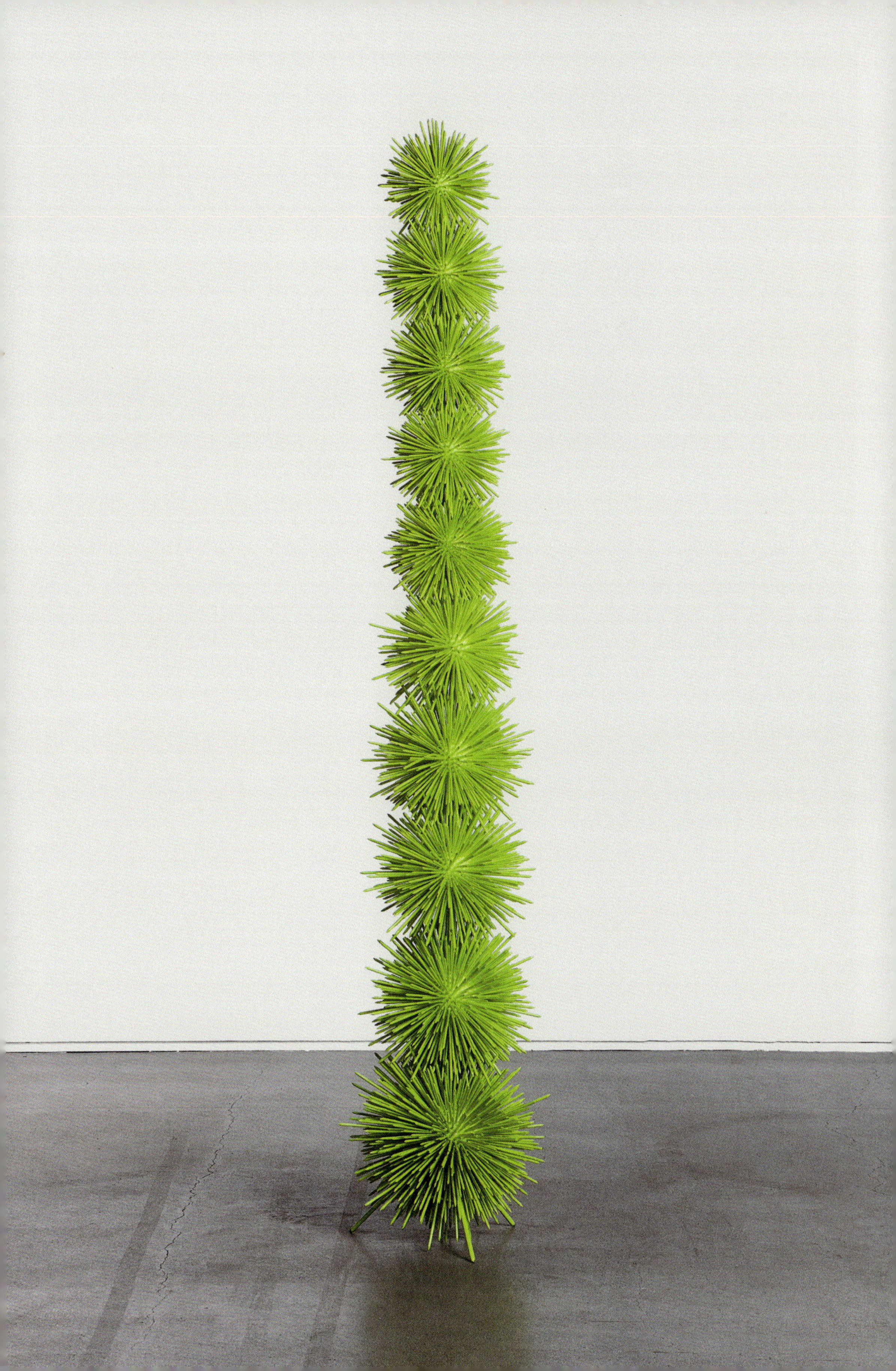

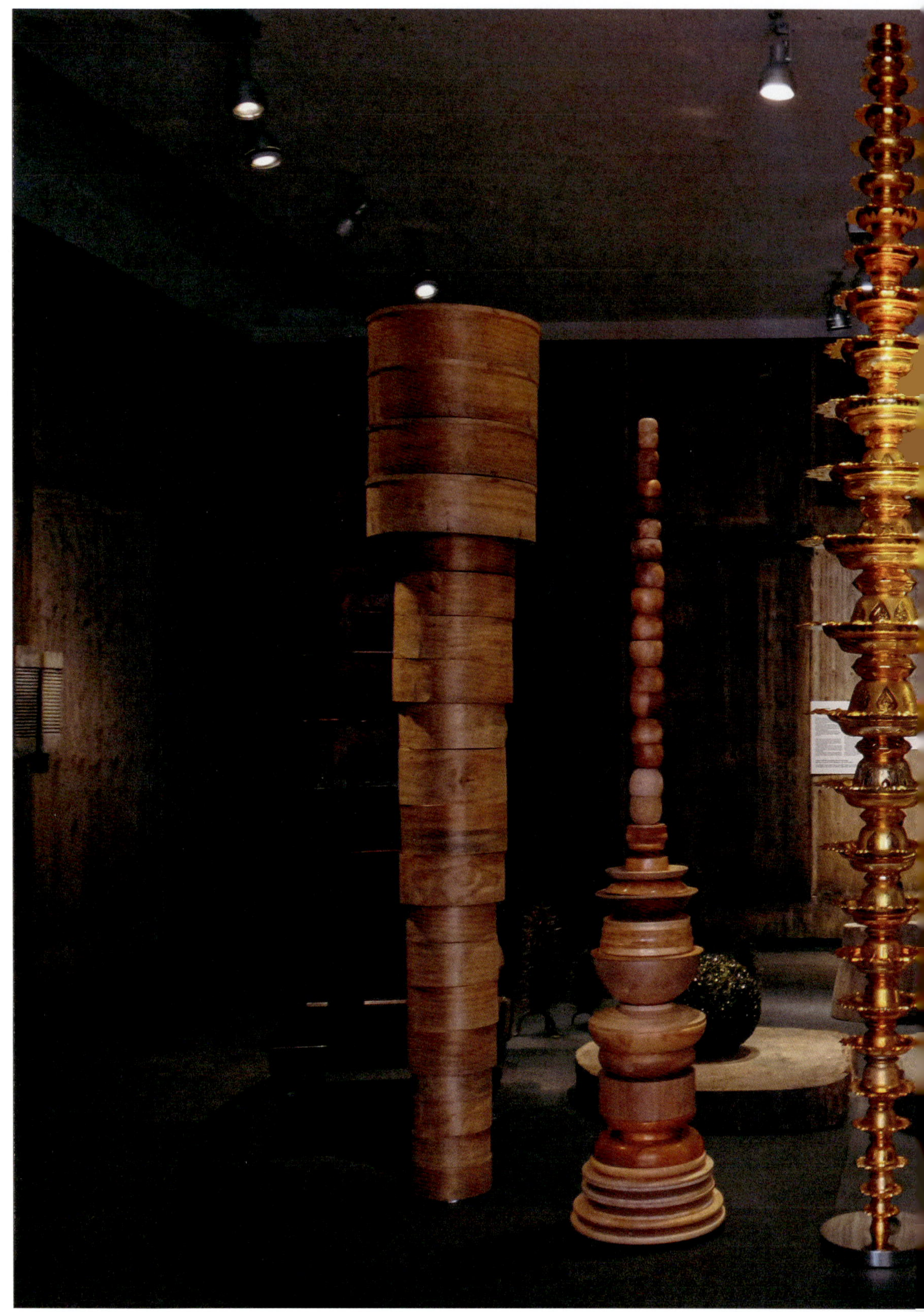

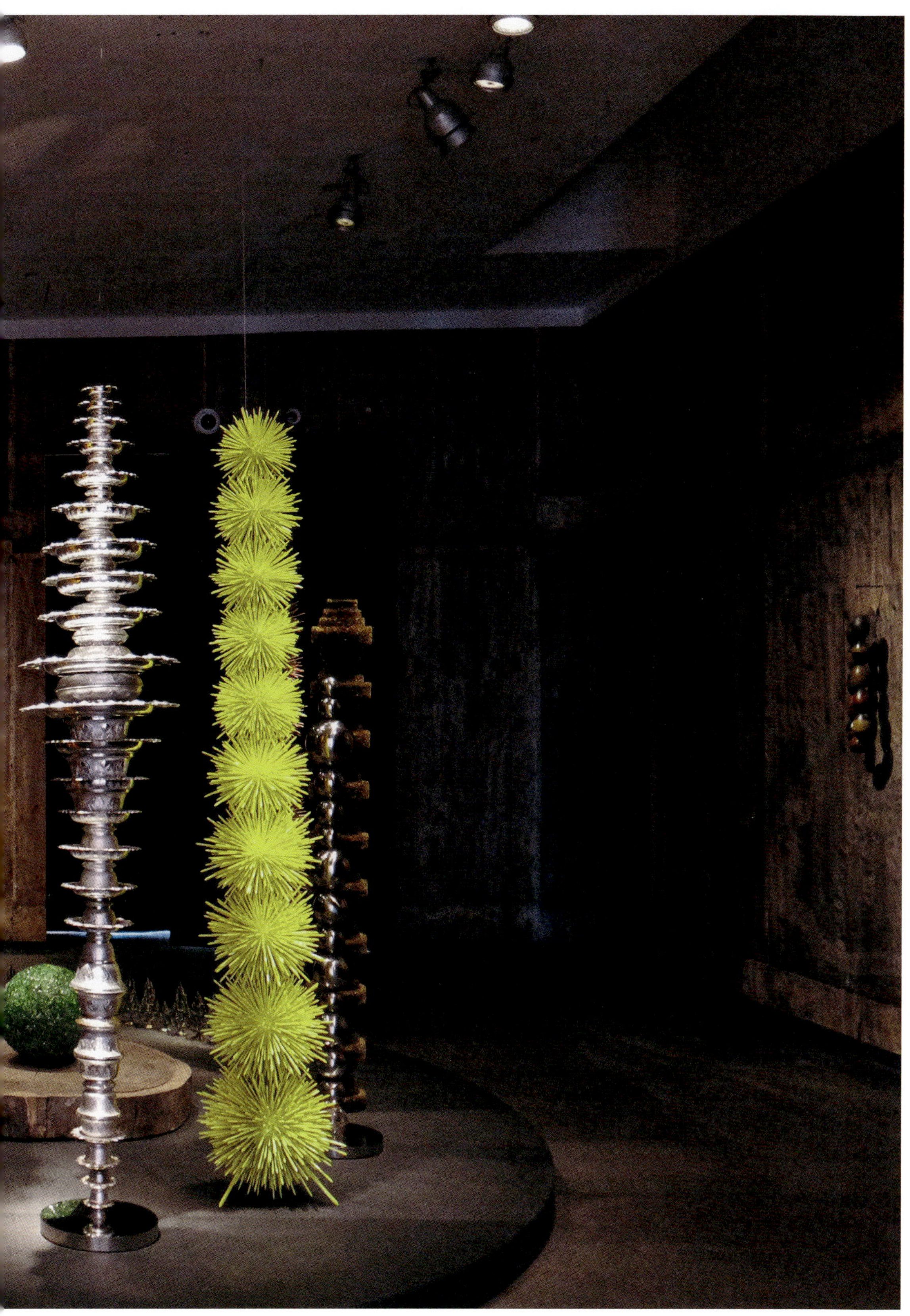

Tara

Donovan

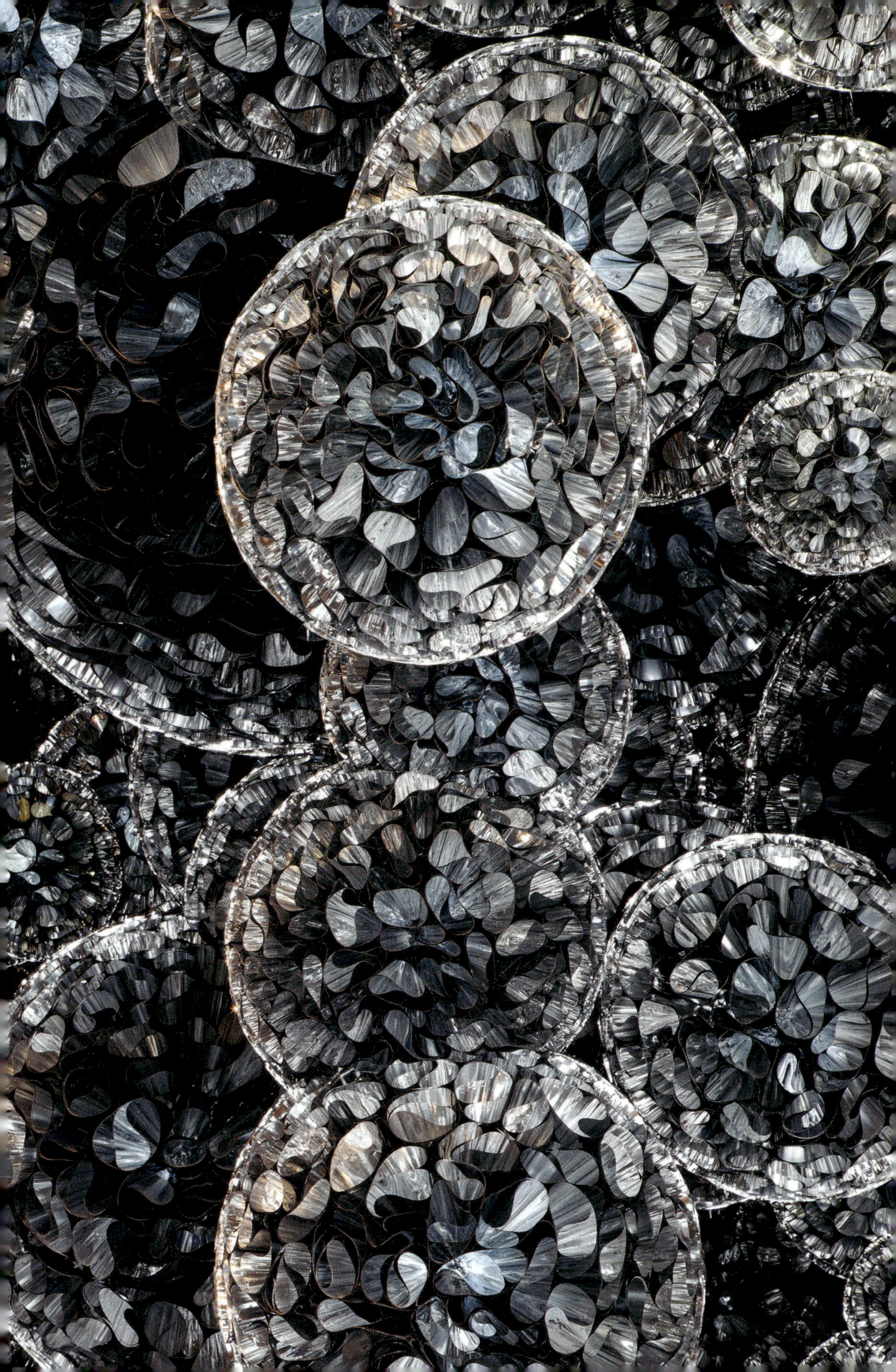

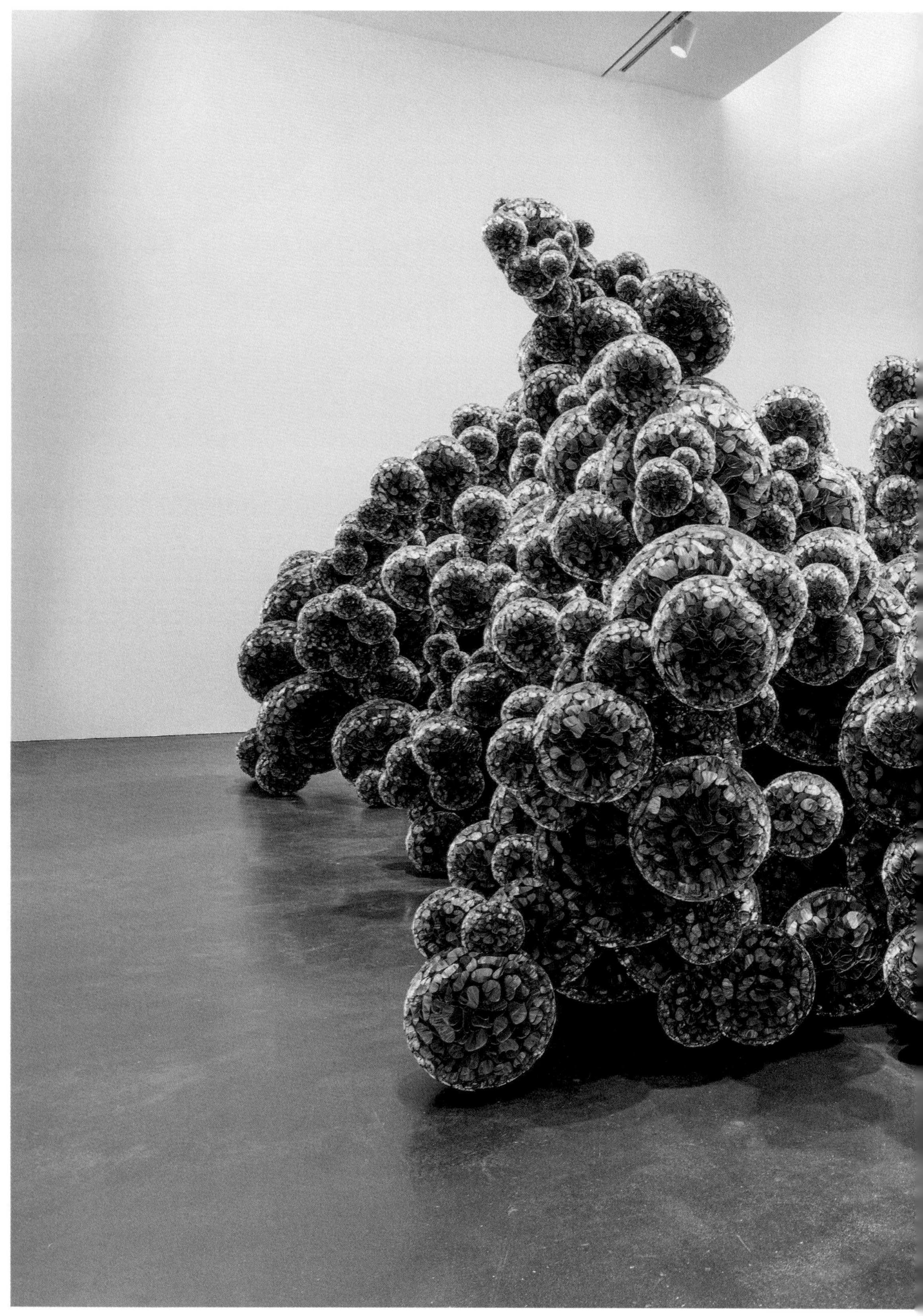

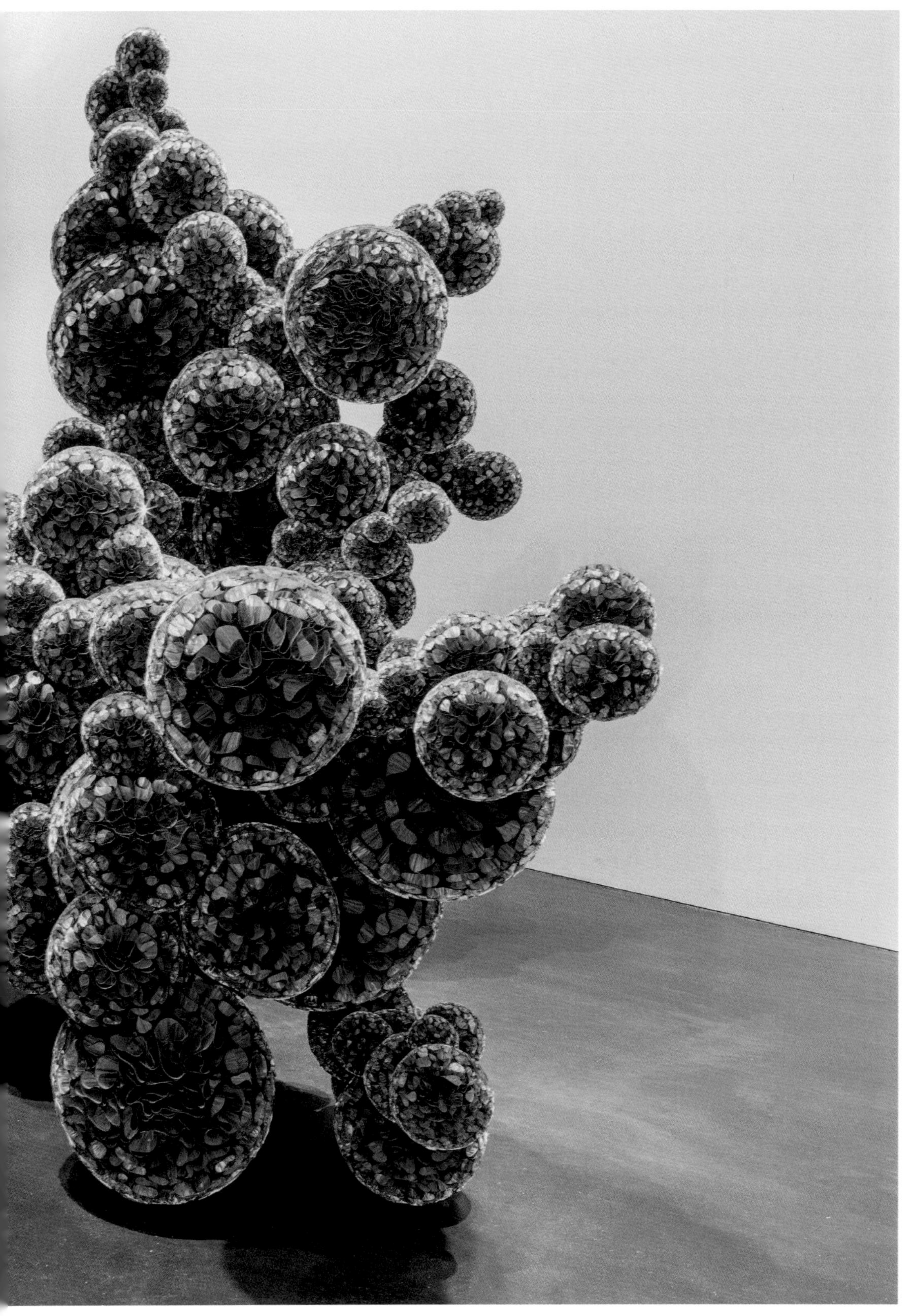

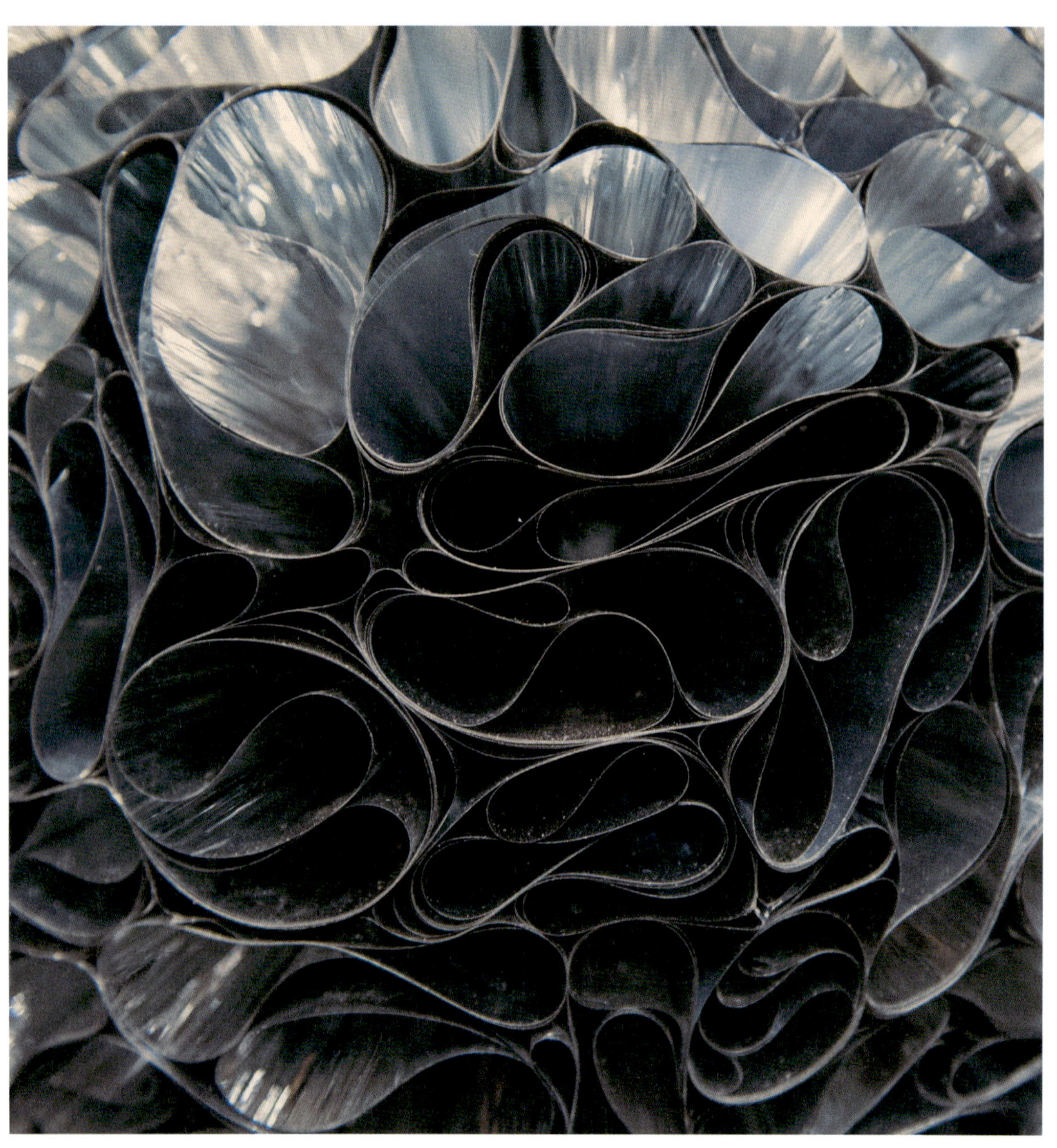

The idea of growth is central to my understanding
of how I work. ... In my work, growth happens through
a process of accumulation, which somehow manages
to combine patterns of both consumption and entropy
as a means to achieve structural aesthetic qualities
that are nearly universally described as biological, organic,
or terrain-like. TARA DONOVAN

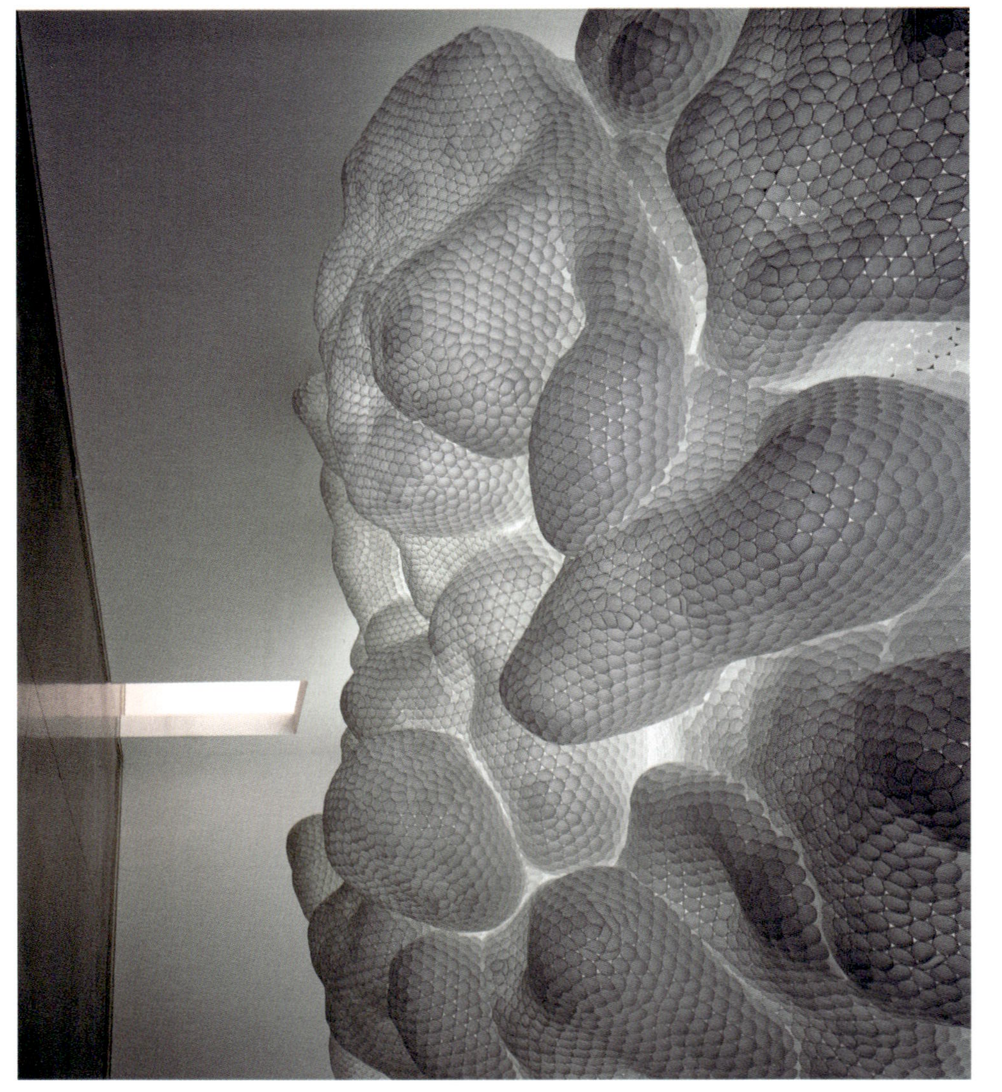

Untitled (Styrofoam cups),
2004/2008 (and detail)

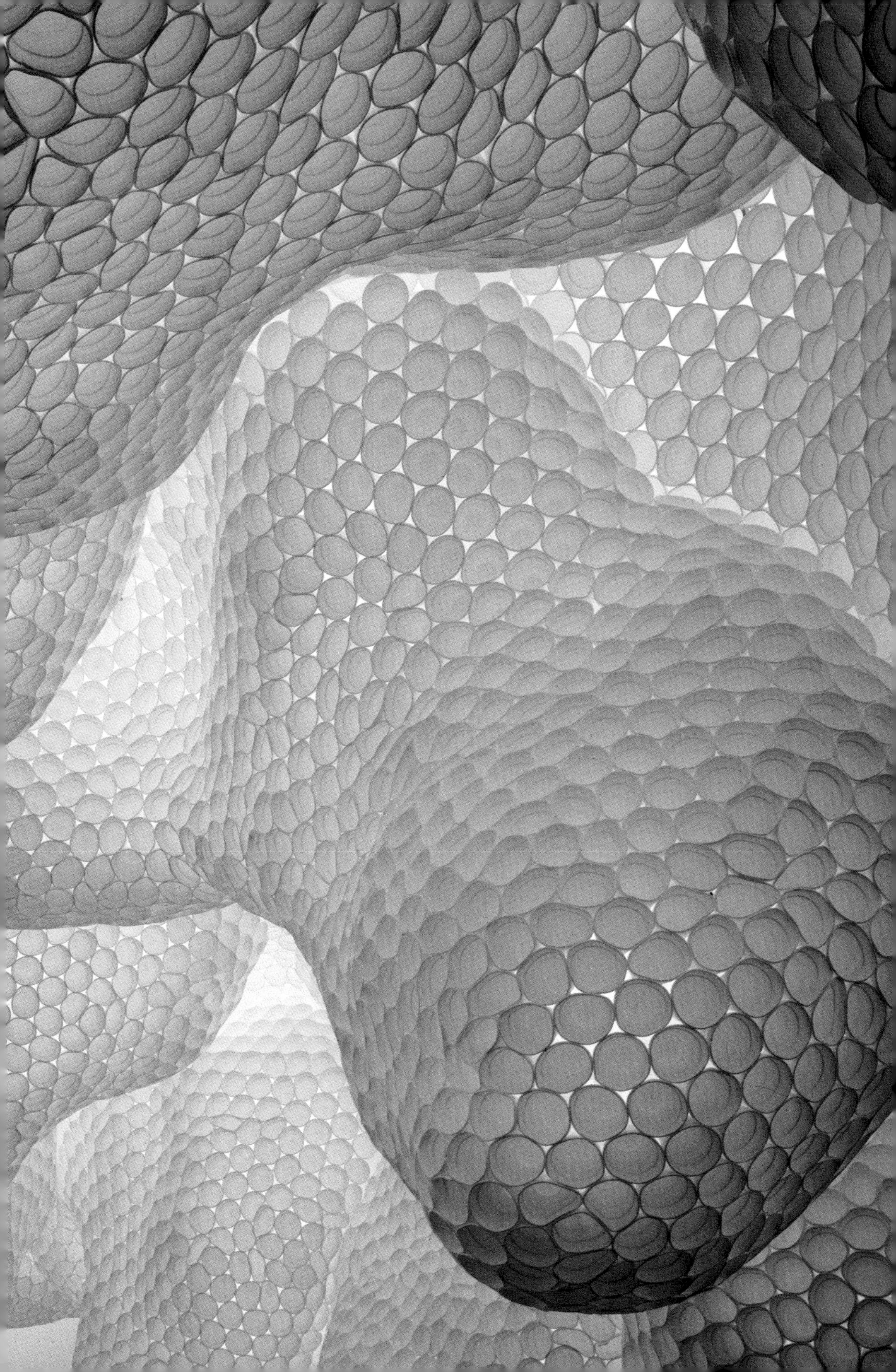

DRIFT

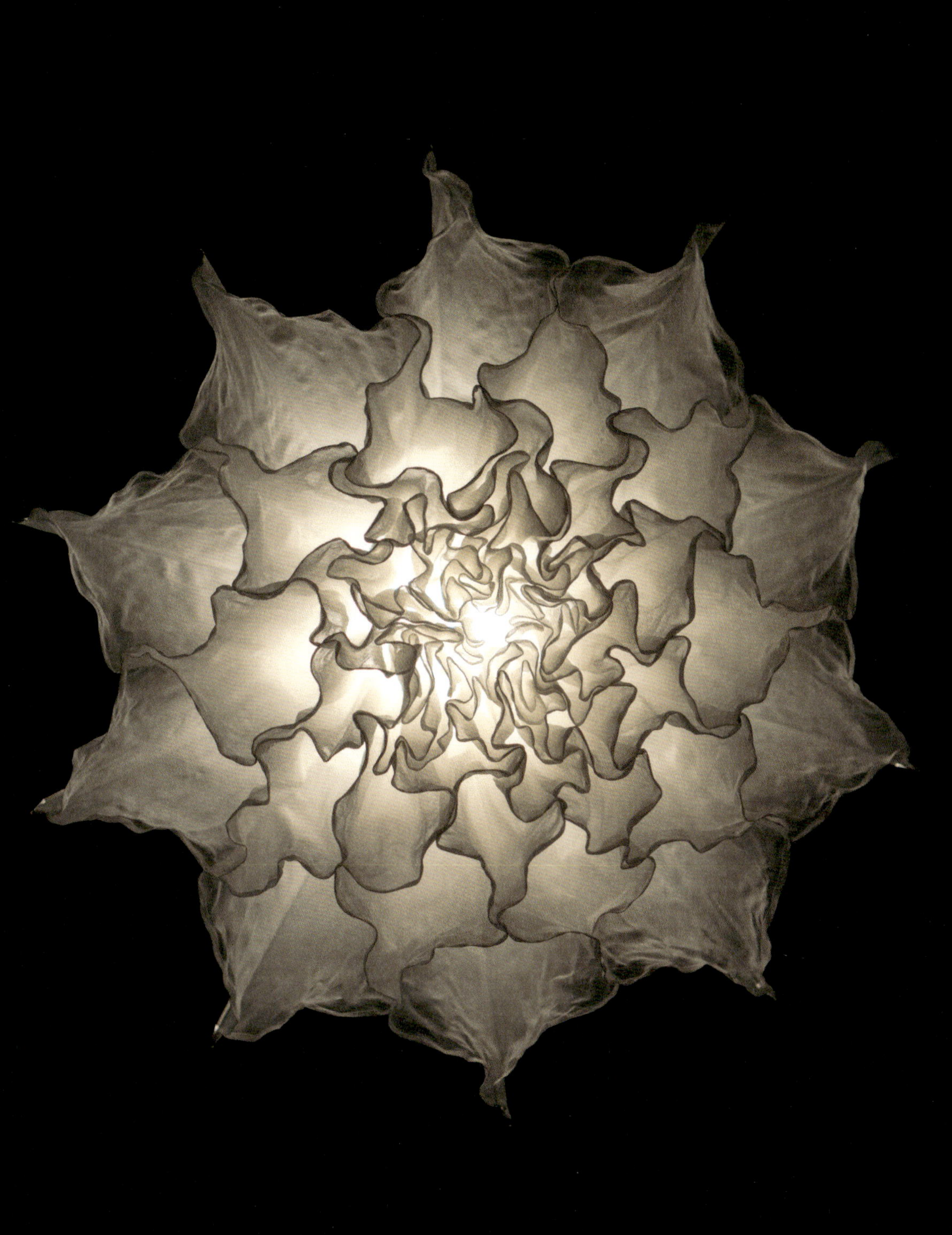

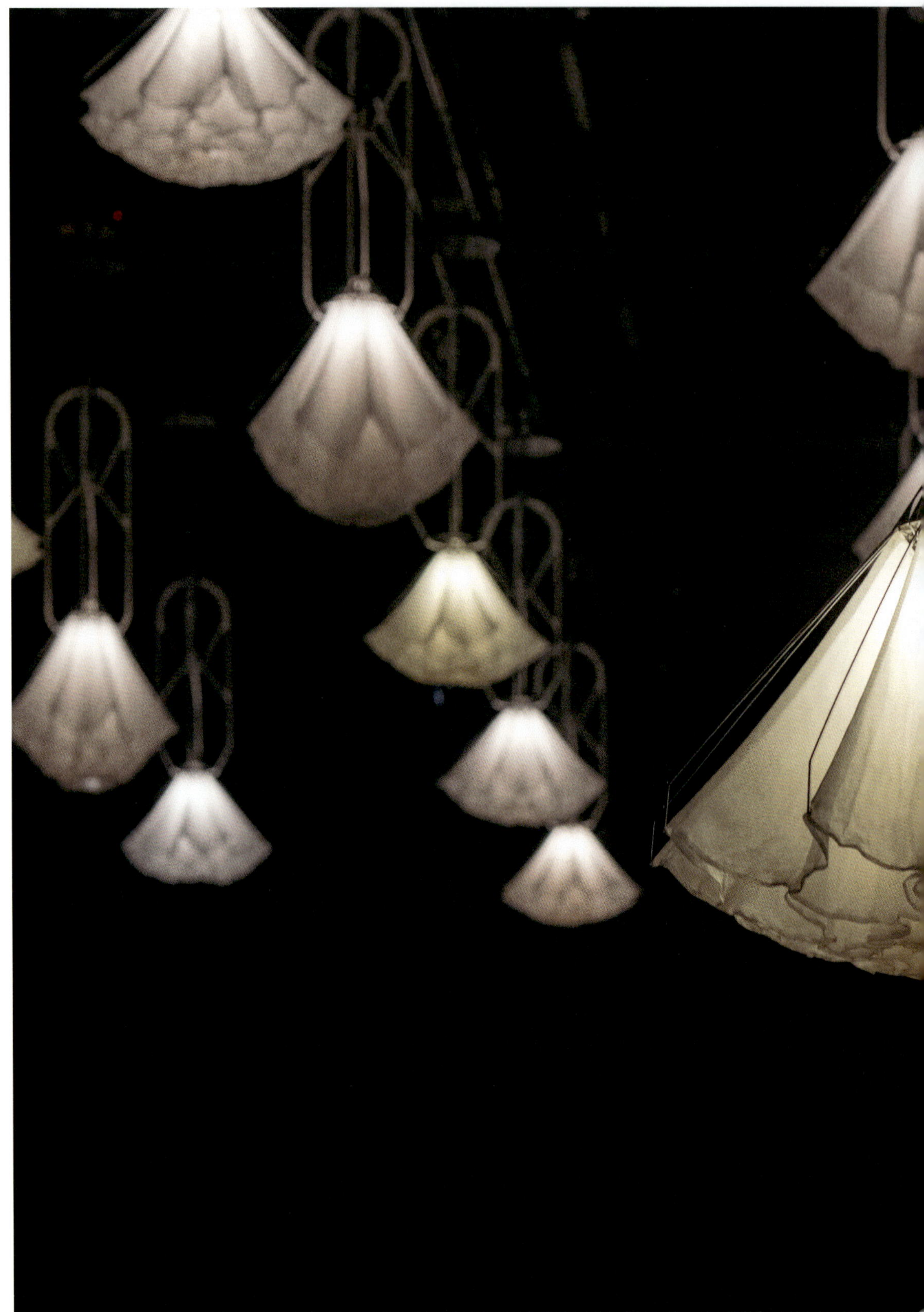

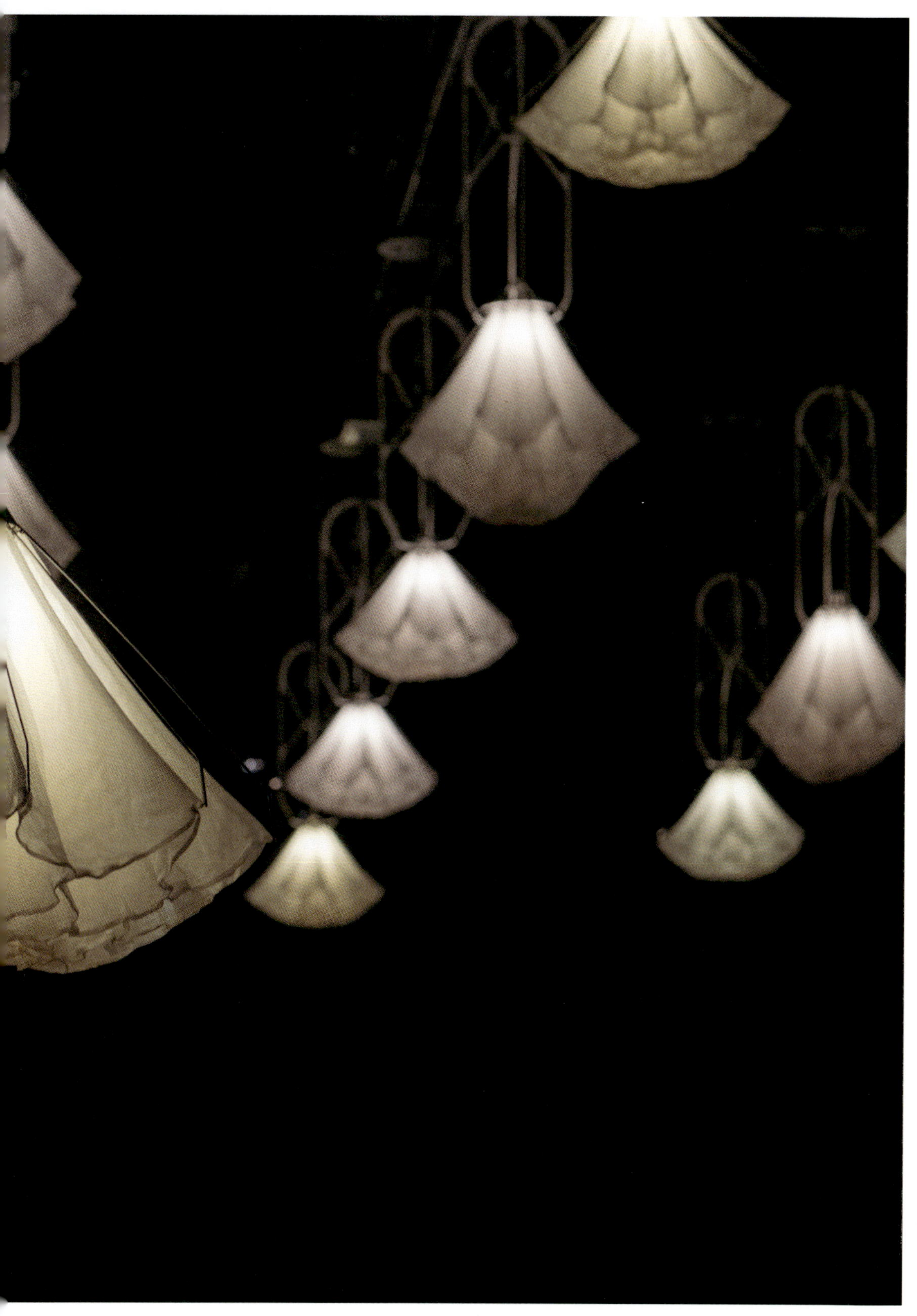

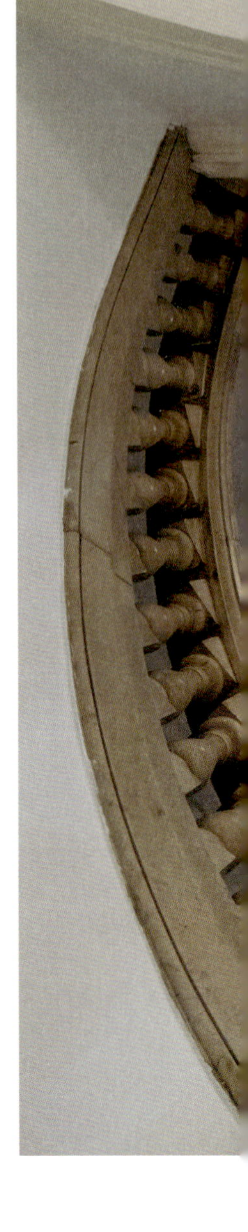

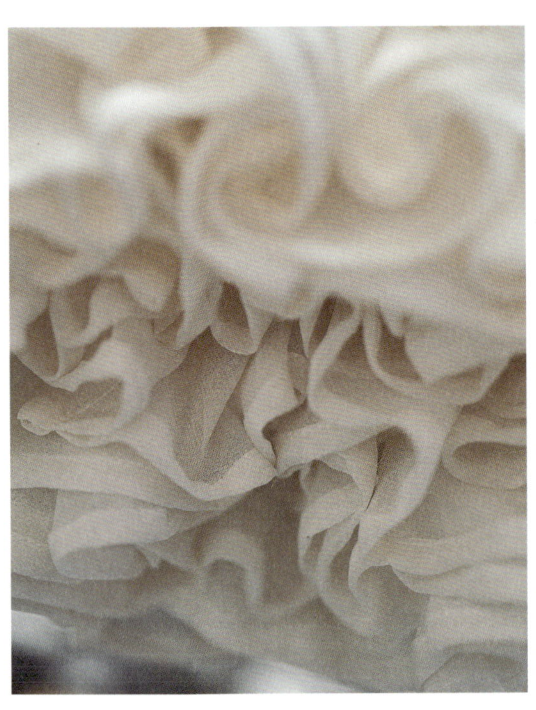

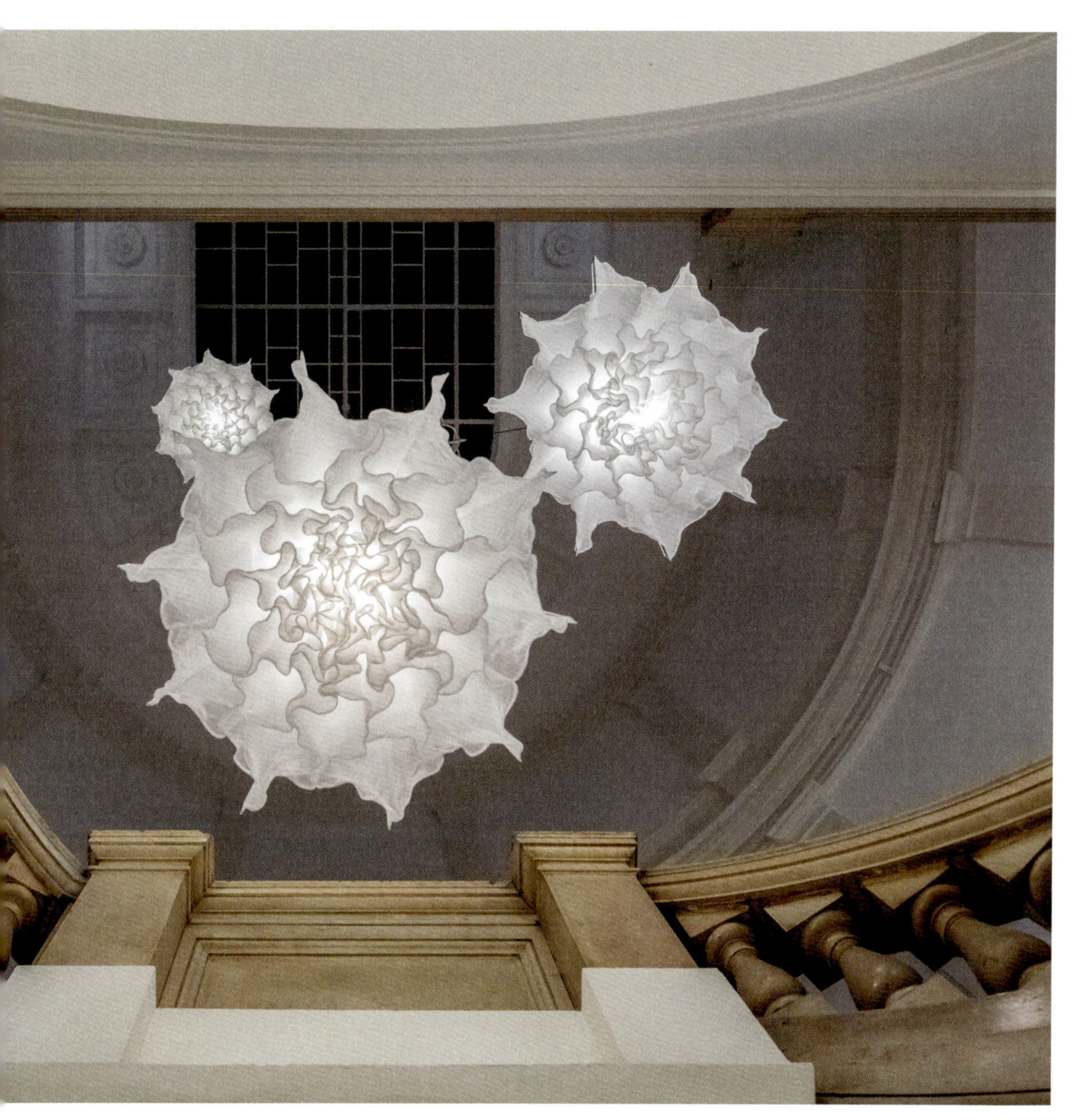

Shylight is a performative sculpture. When you enter the space, it becomes a kind of dance that is performed in front of you. DRIFT

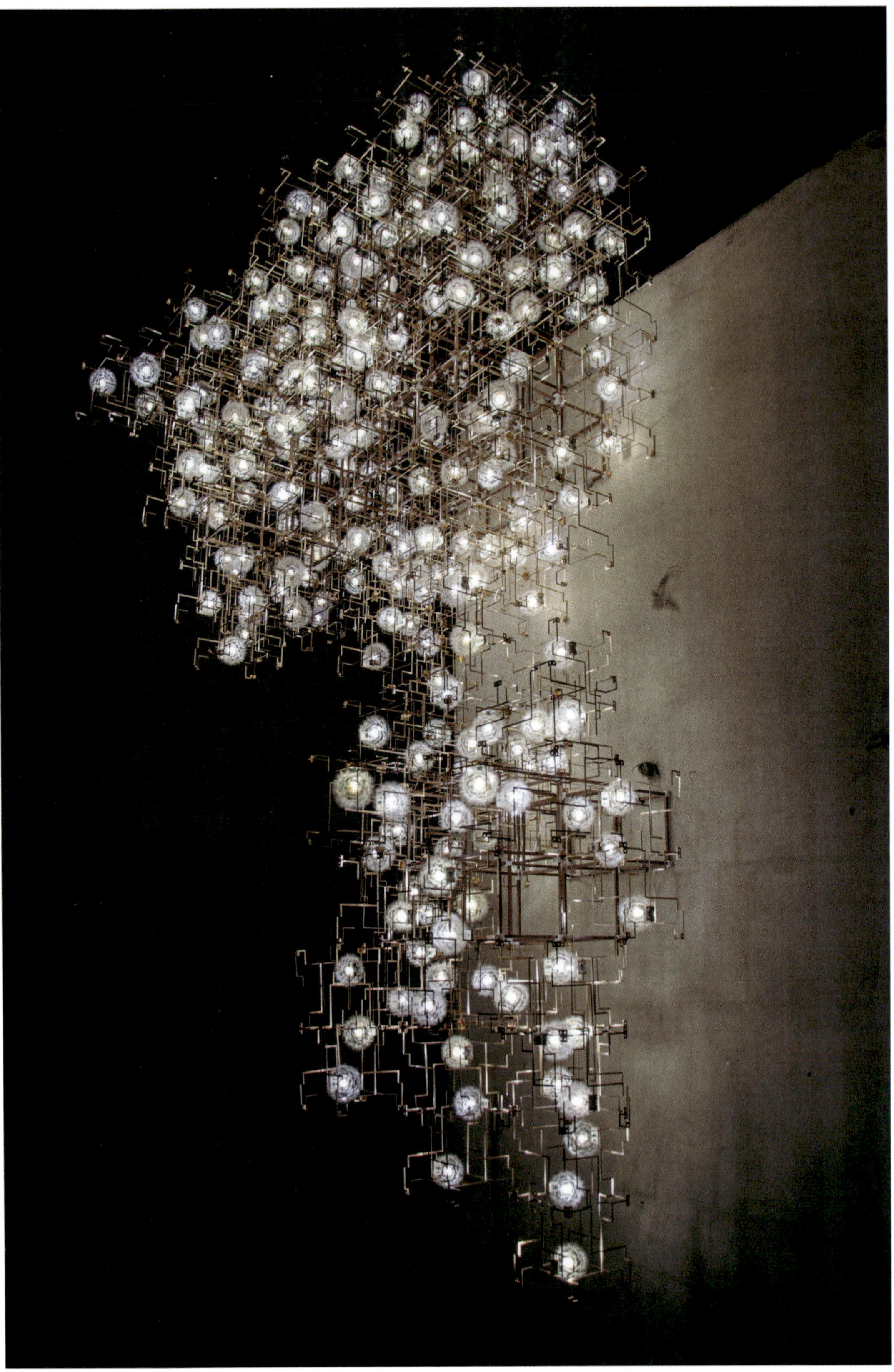

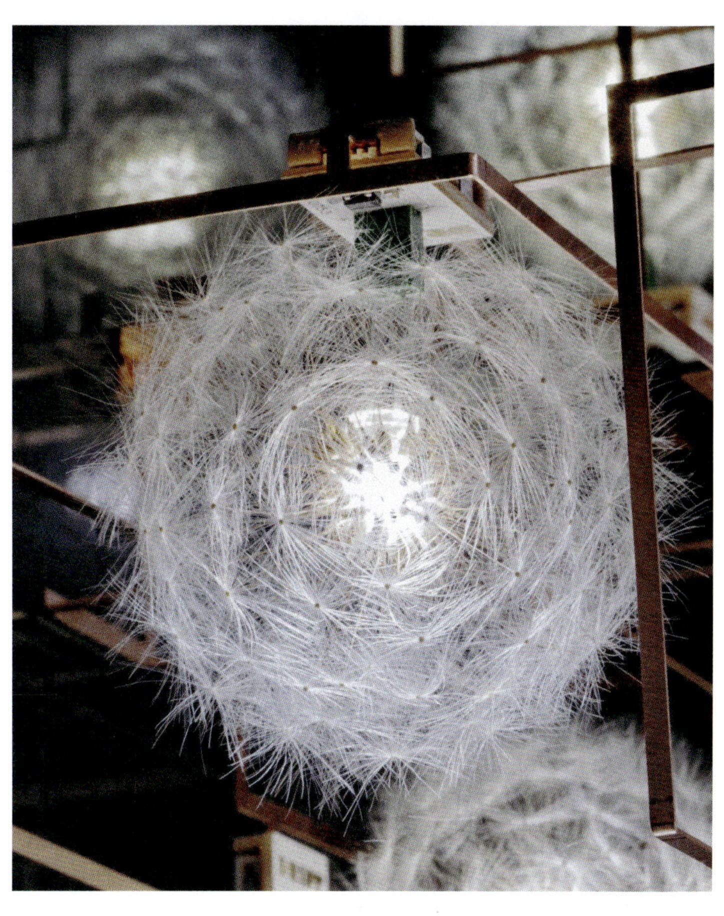

Fragile Future,
2000–ongoing

Eva

Fàbregas

Pumping, 2019
(pp. 113–117)

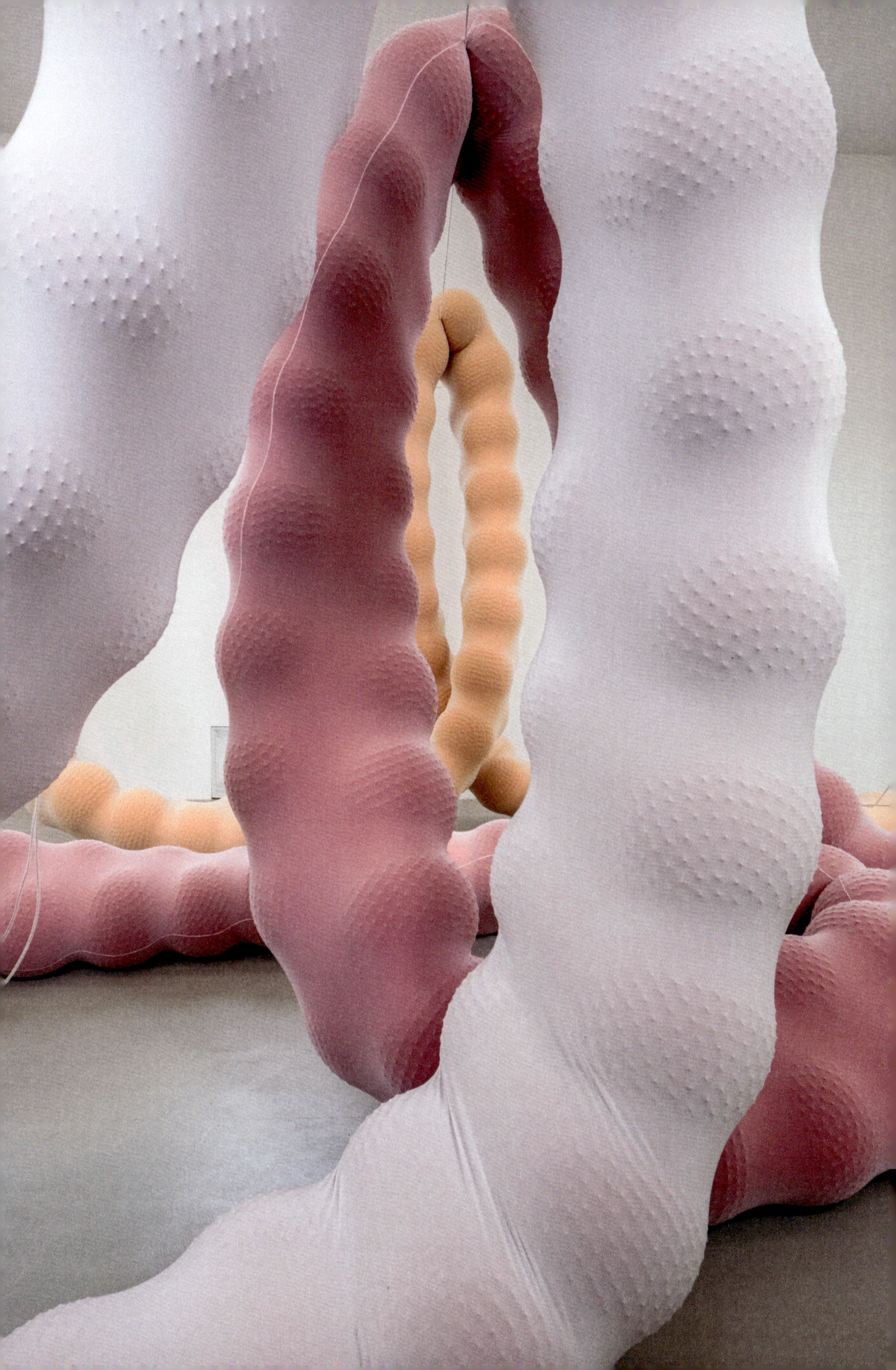

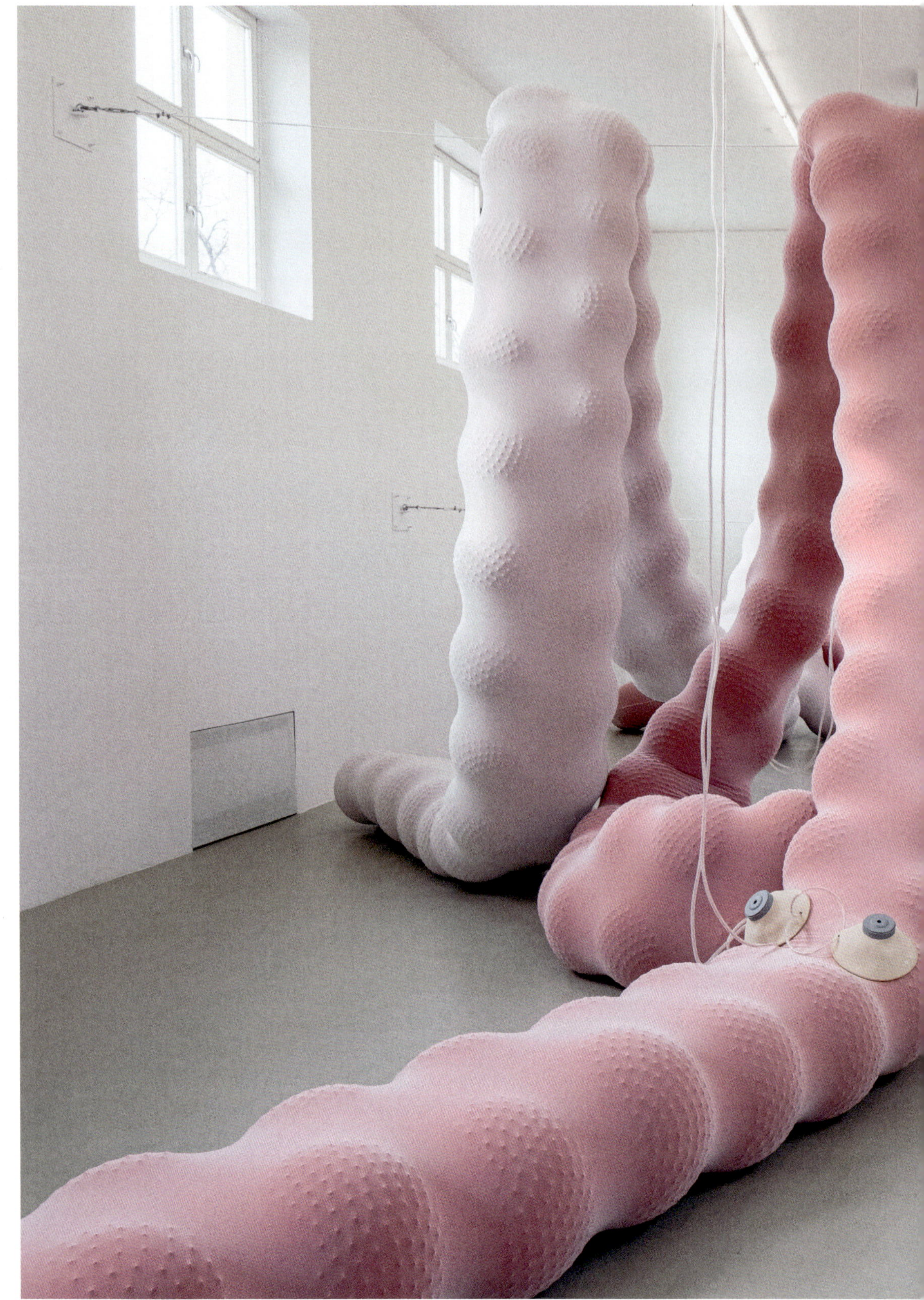

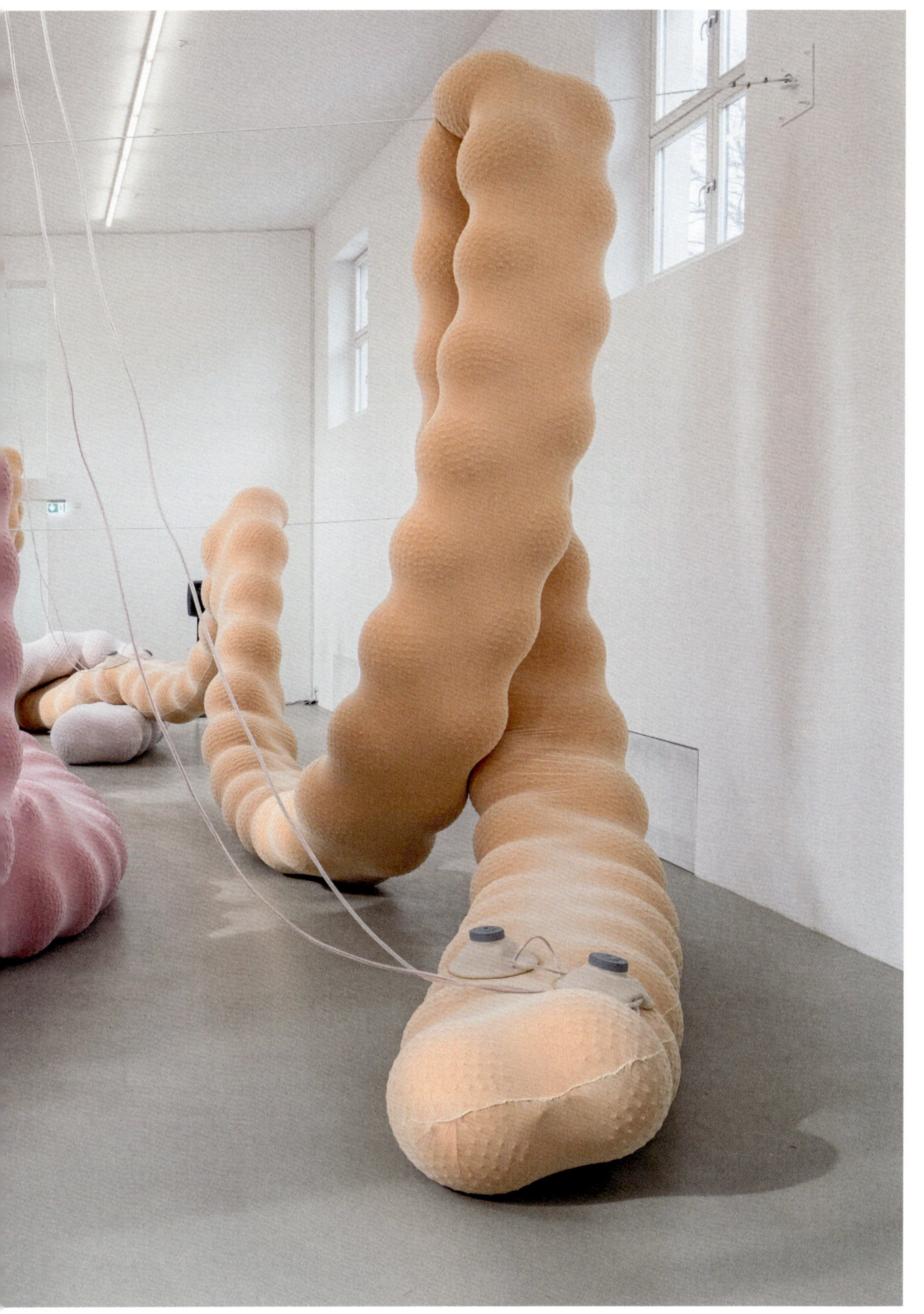

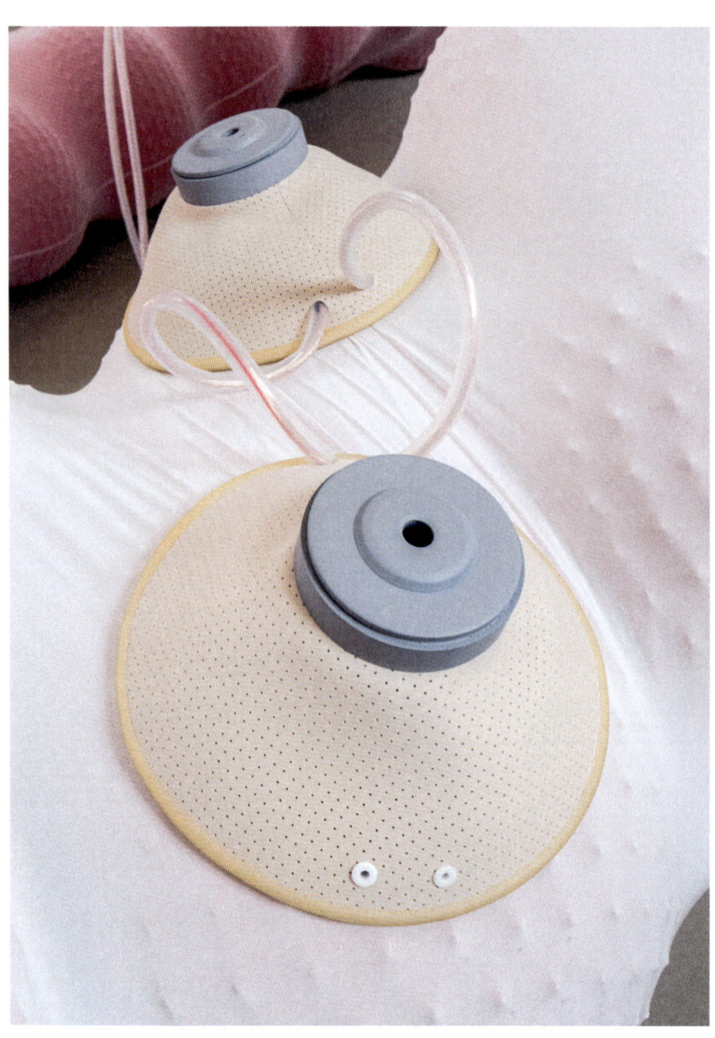

I see my work as creatures that can help us imagine other possible bodies, other ways of living, and new forms of desire and affect. EVA FÀBREGAS

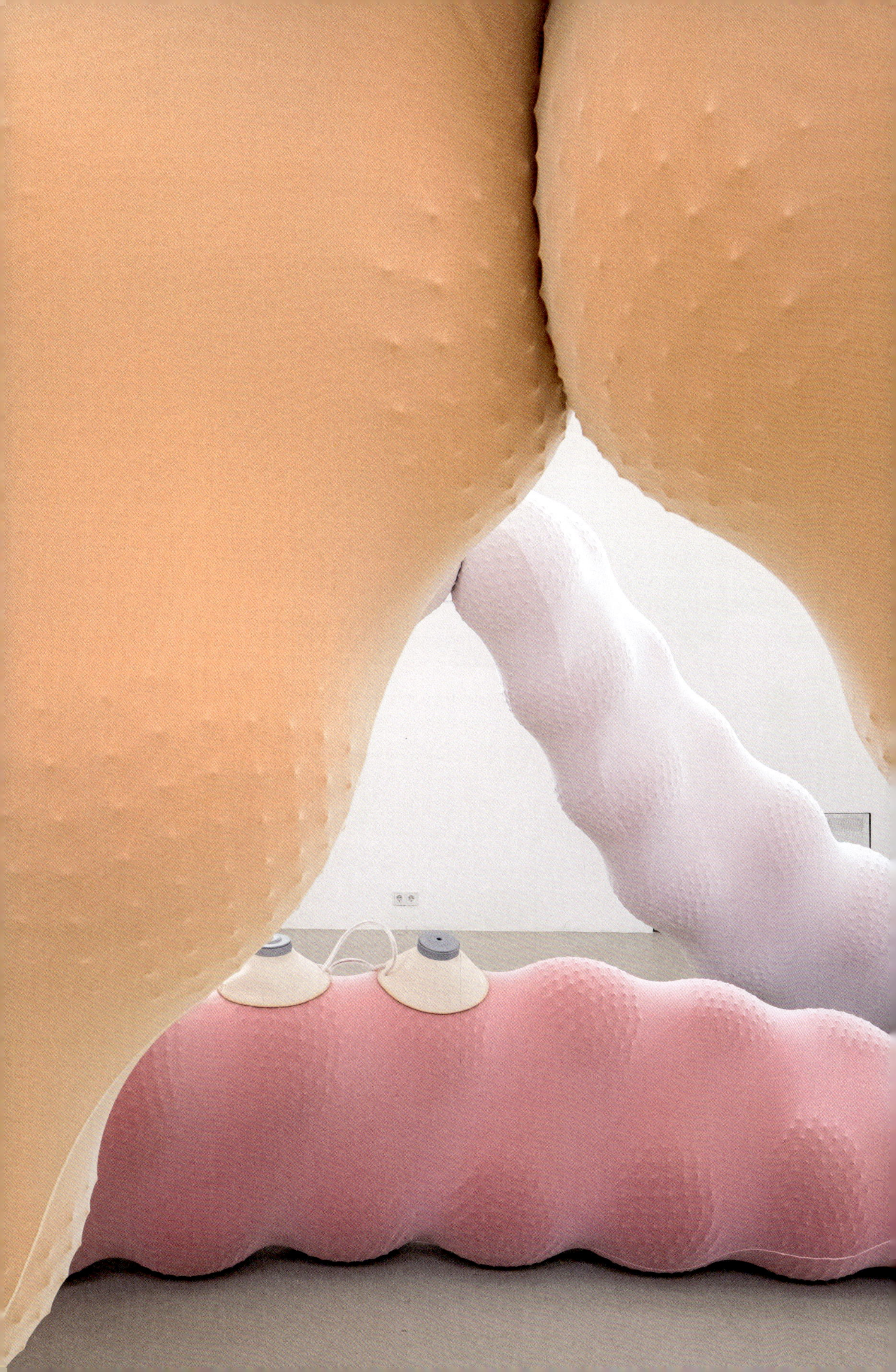

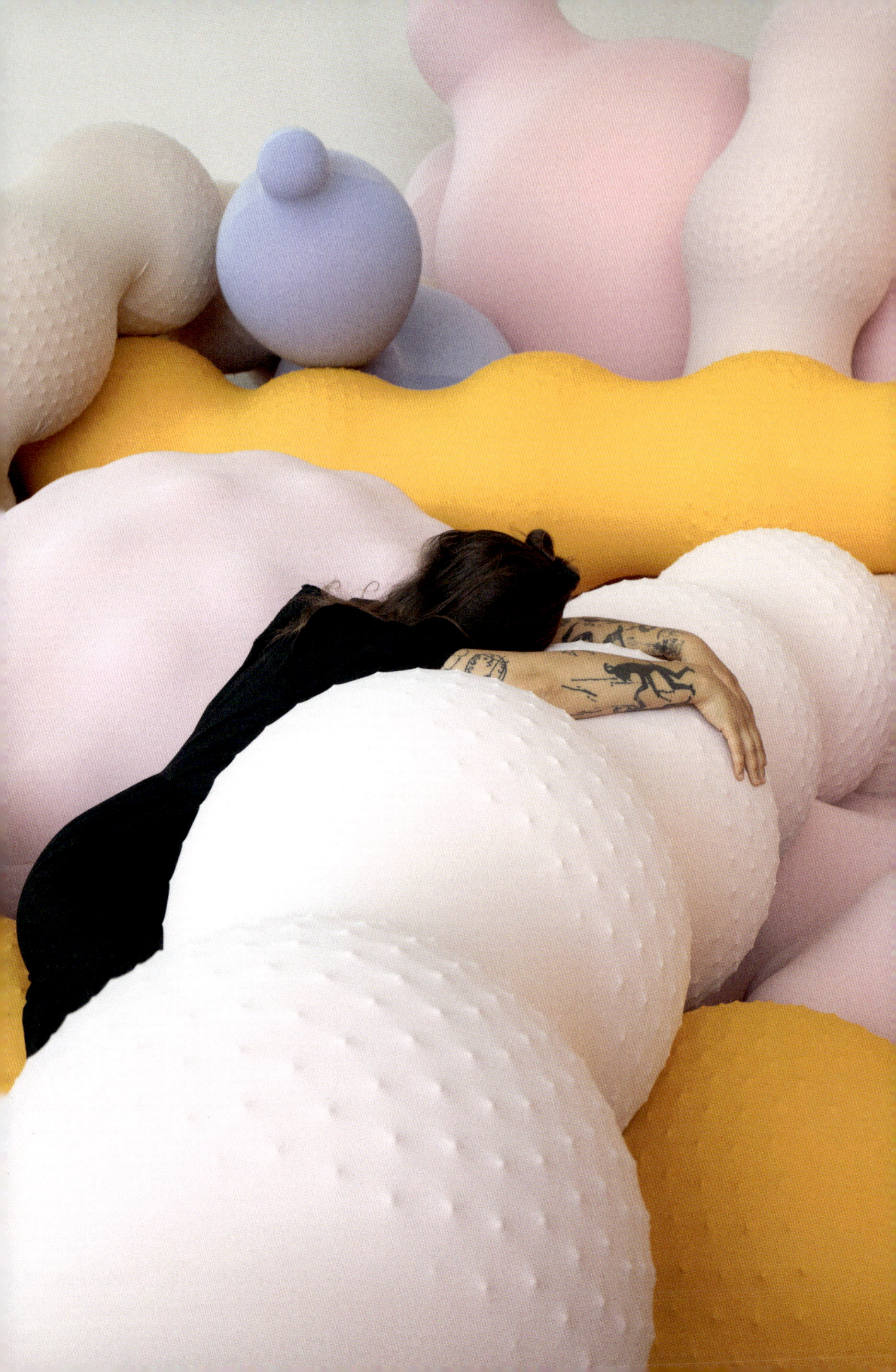

Oozing,
2023

Devouring Lovers,
2023

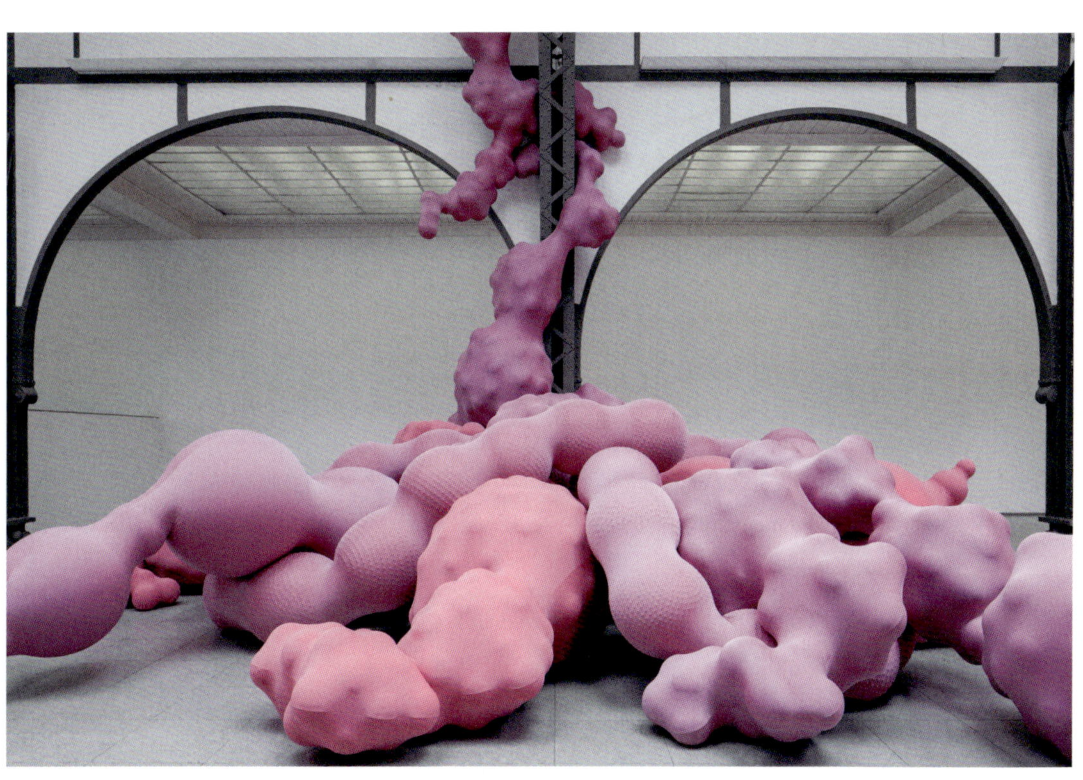

Holly

Hendry

Deep Soil Thrombosis, 2019
(detail and pp. 122–23)

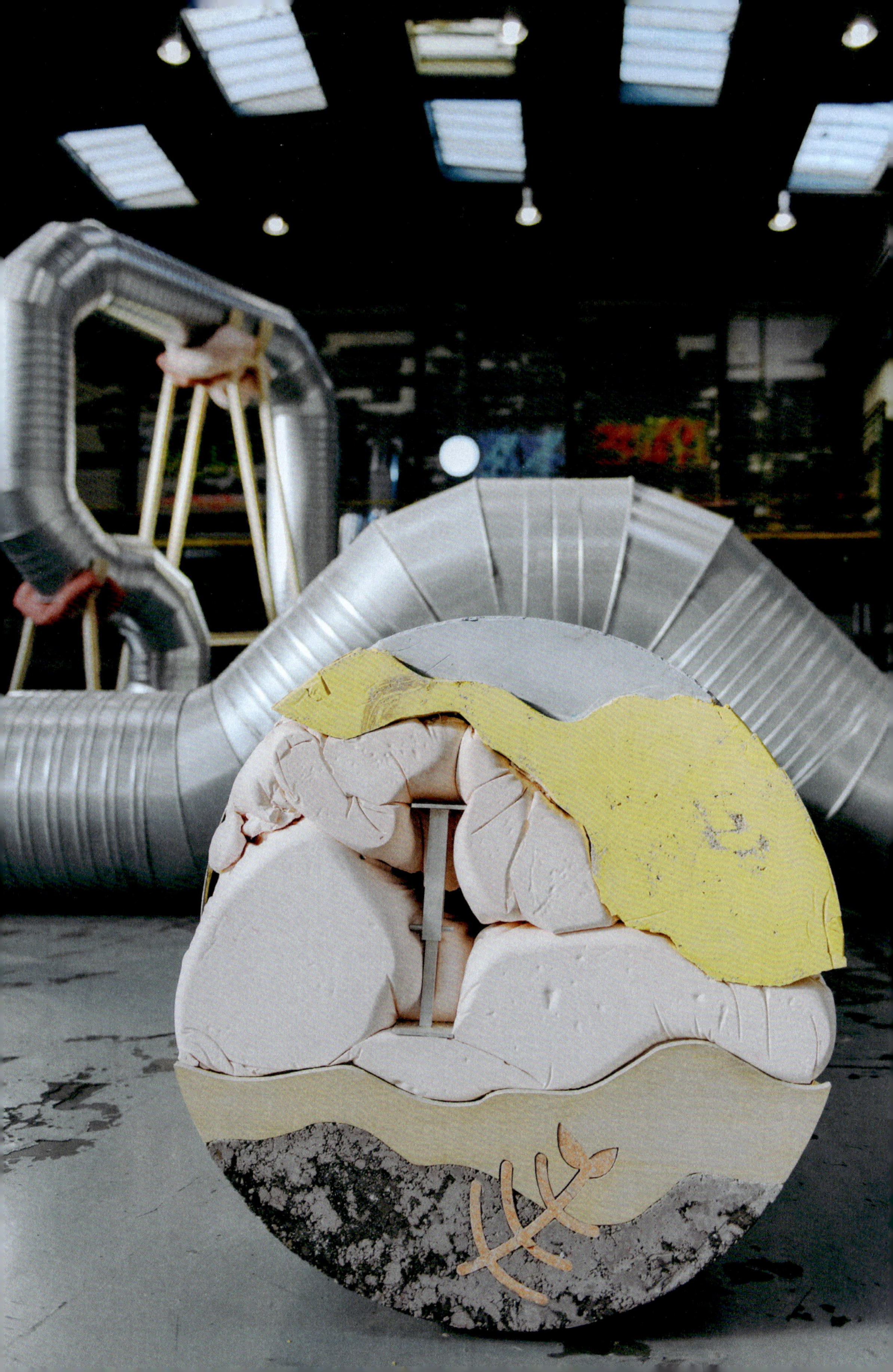

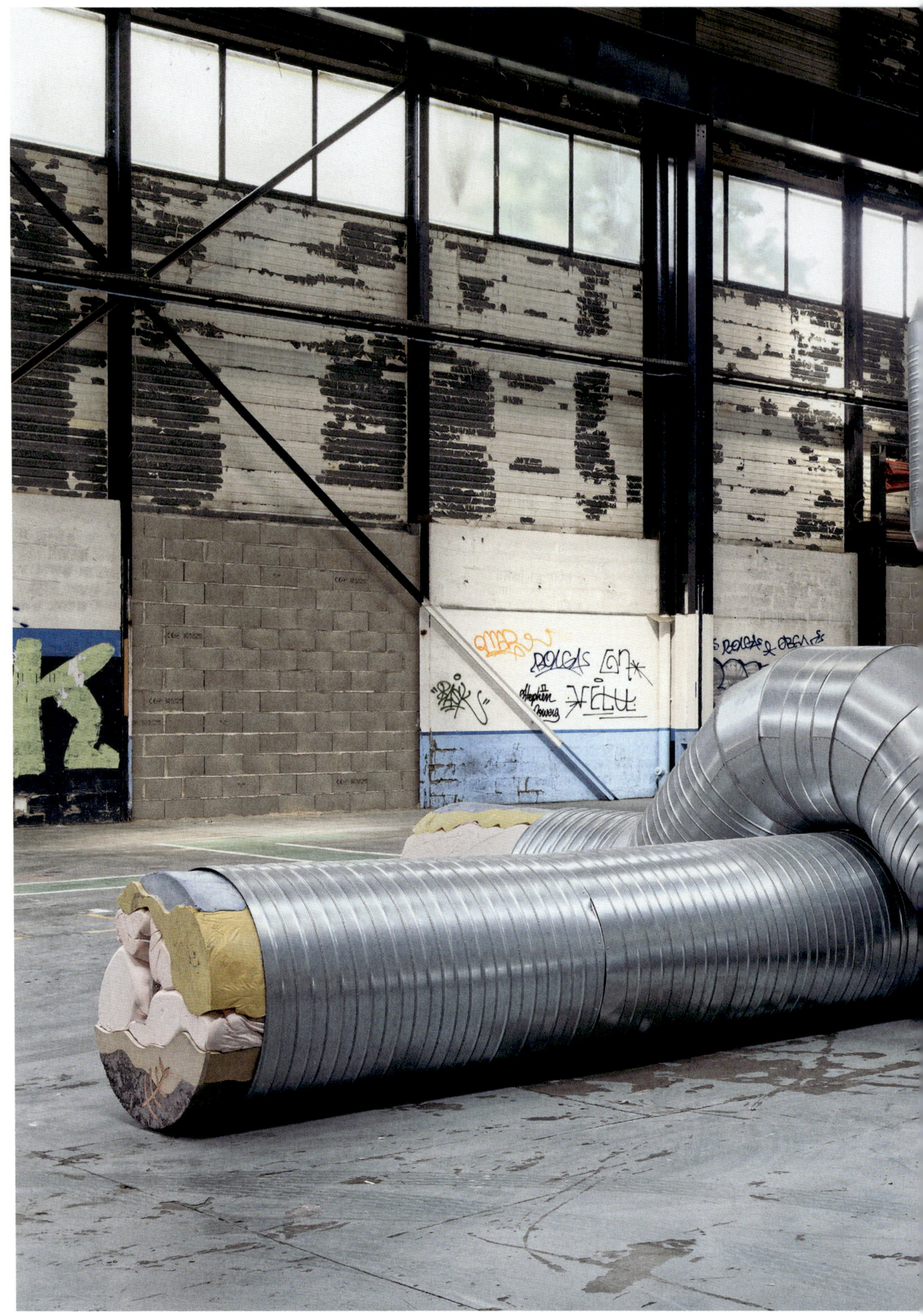

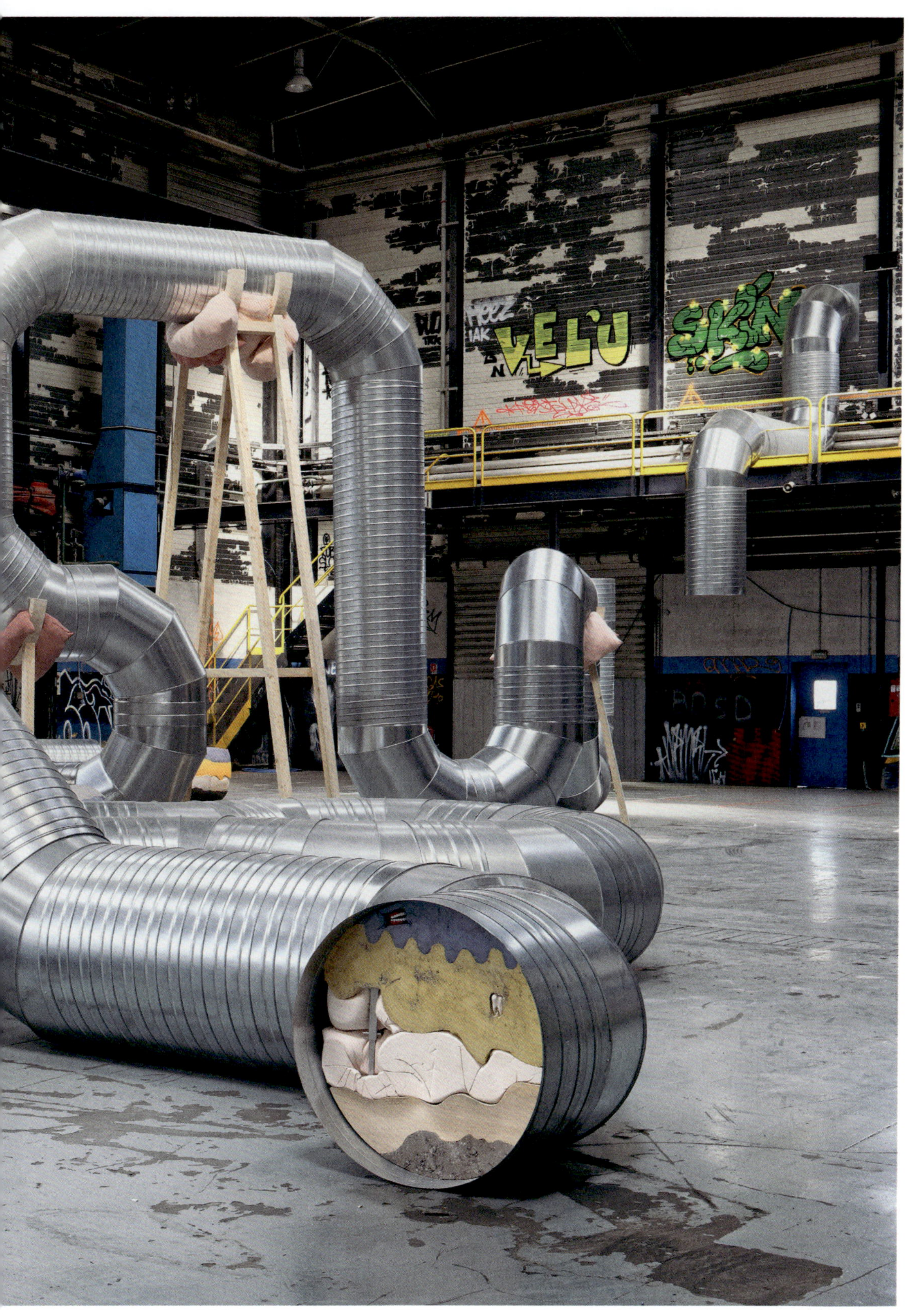

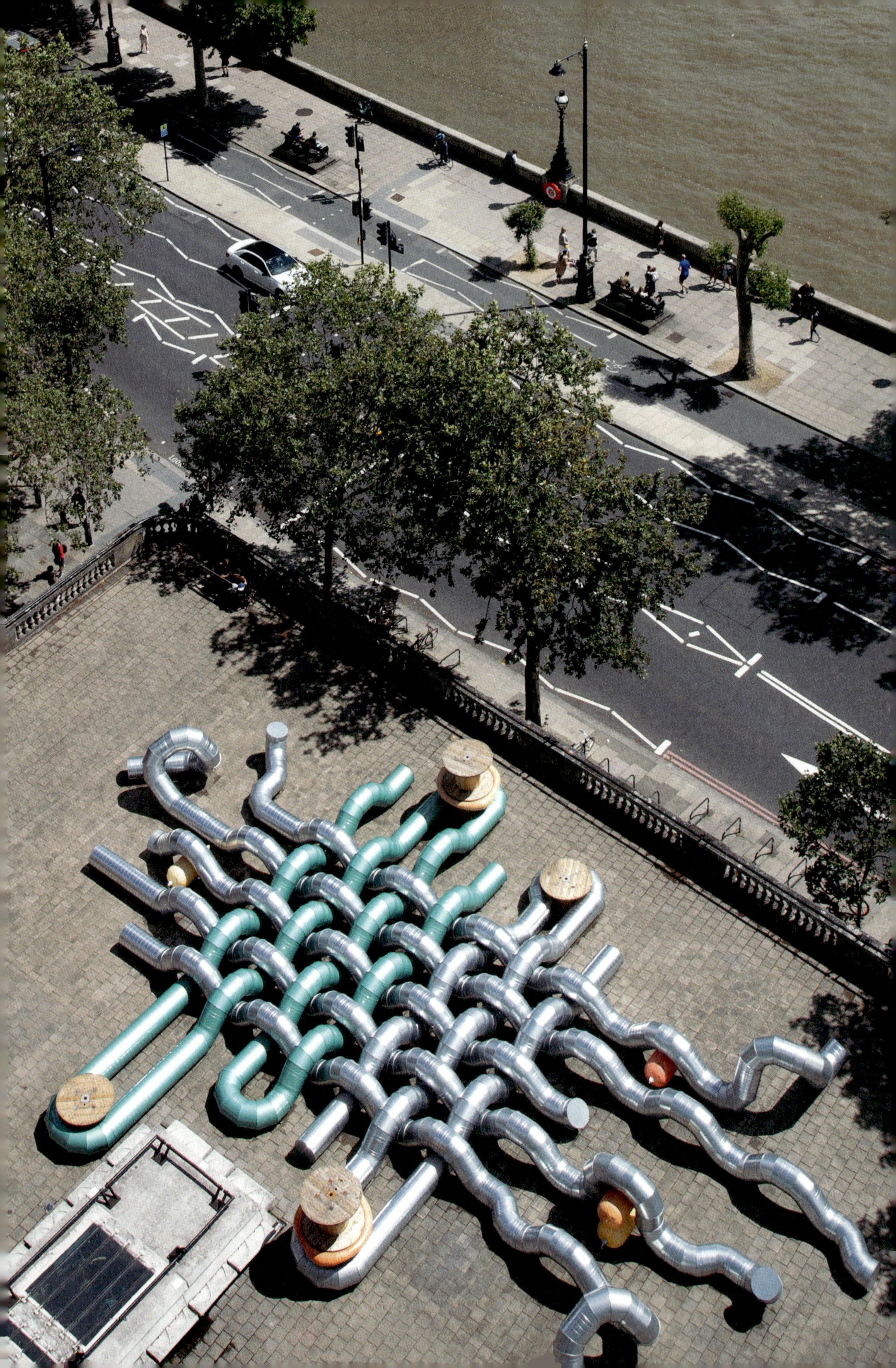

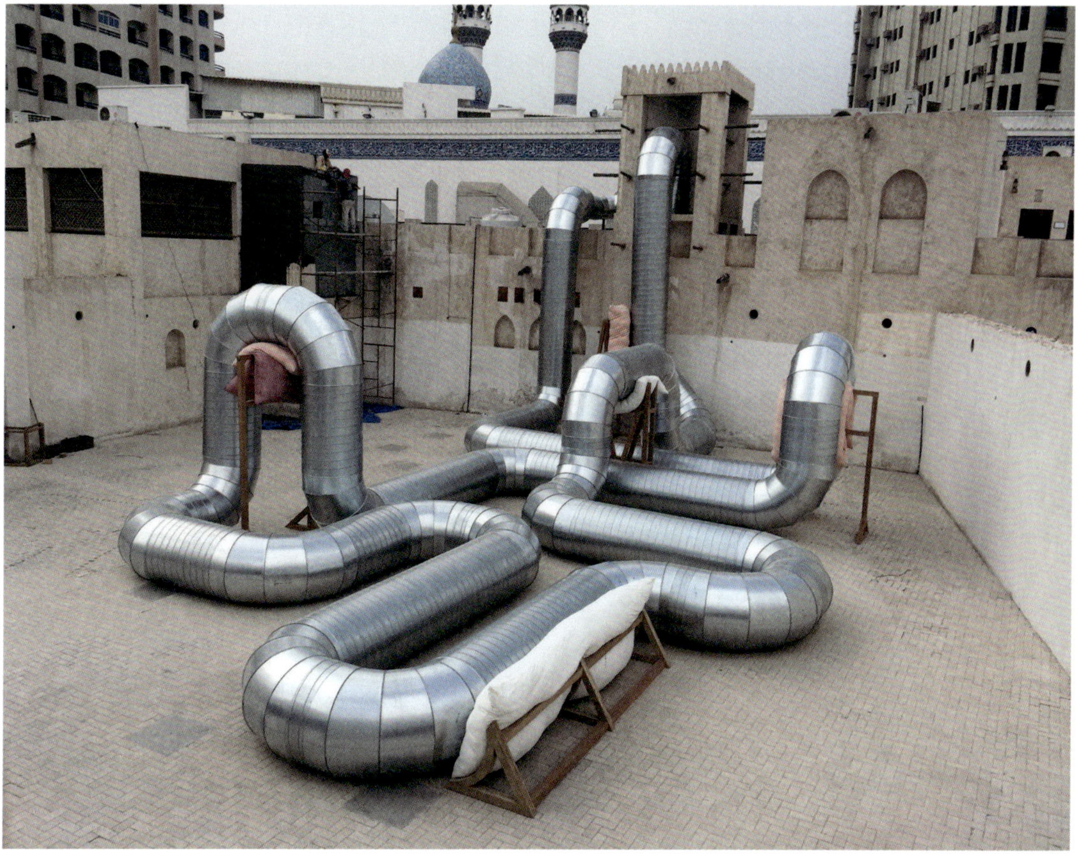

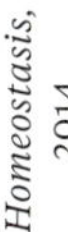

Homeostasis,
2014

Slackwater,
2023

Acts of digestion that happen within the building, sculpture and materials relate to edges and the breakdown of edges; this idea of incorporation where edges change and morph. Like when you chew something up, there is an intermingling of edges, where those outlines become part of you. Ideas of undoing, redoing and reconstituting were very important in my thinking. HOLLY HENDRY

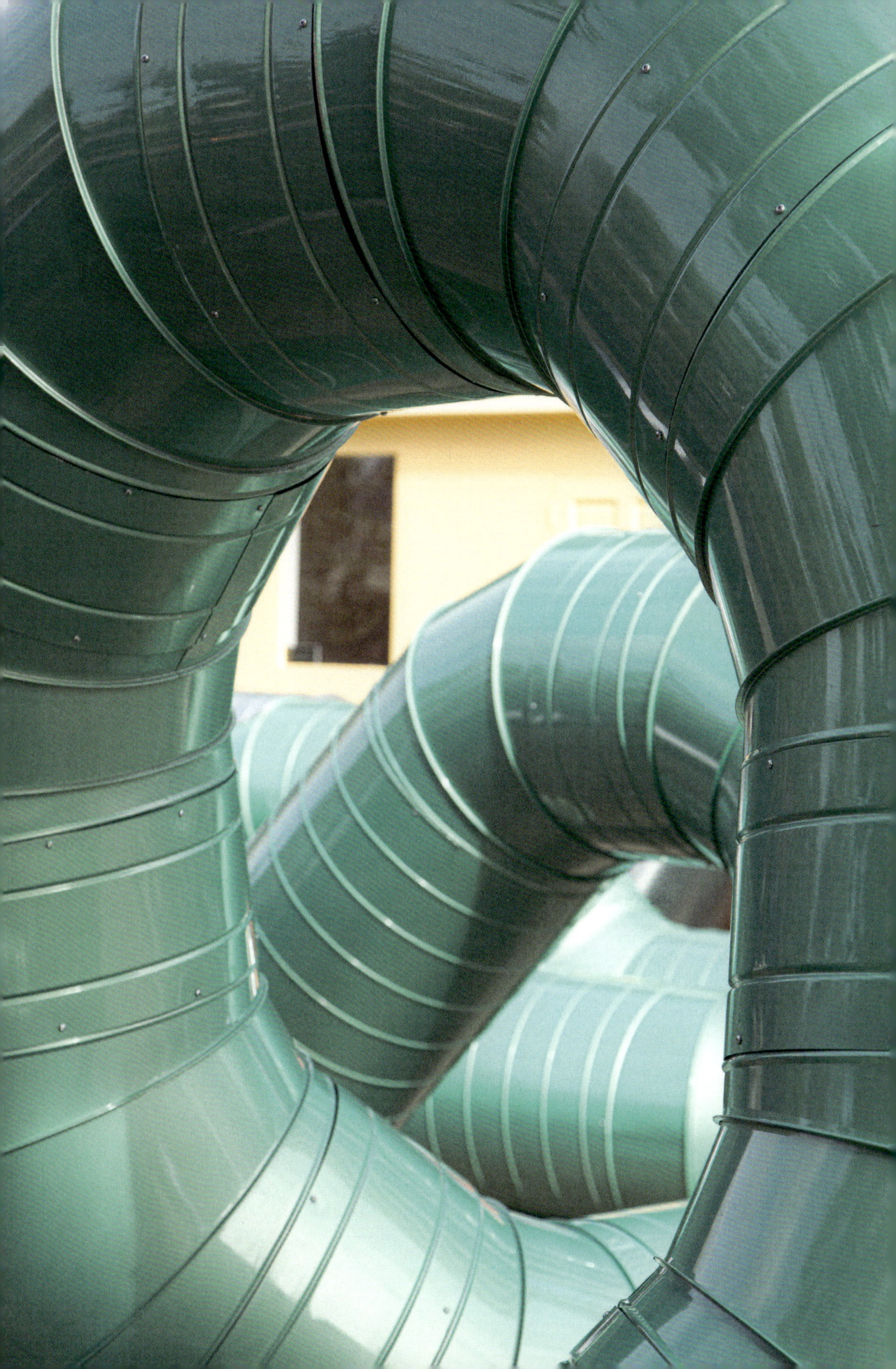

EJ

Hill

Pillar, 2017

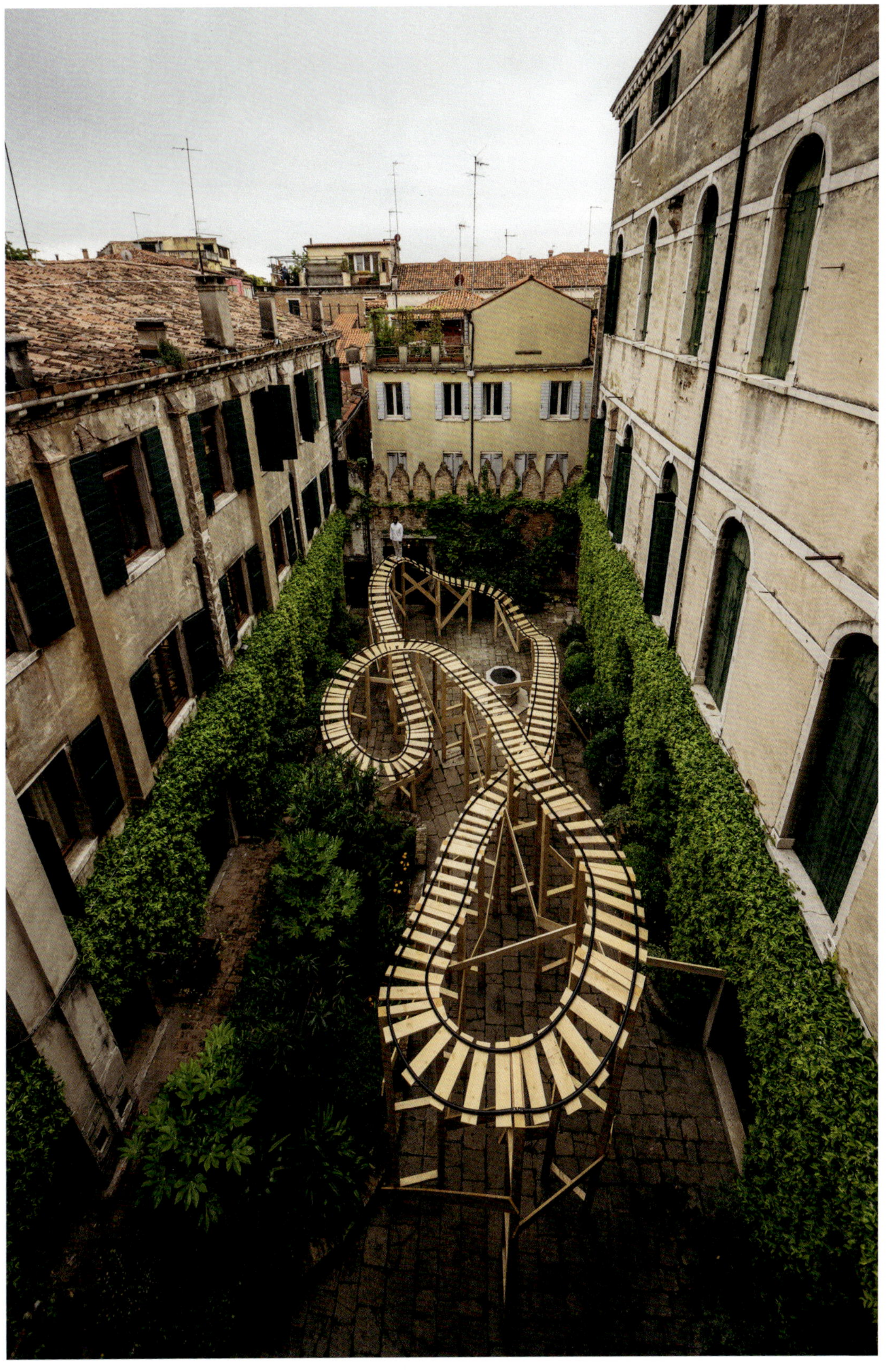

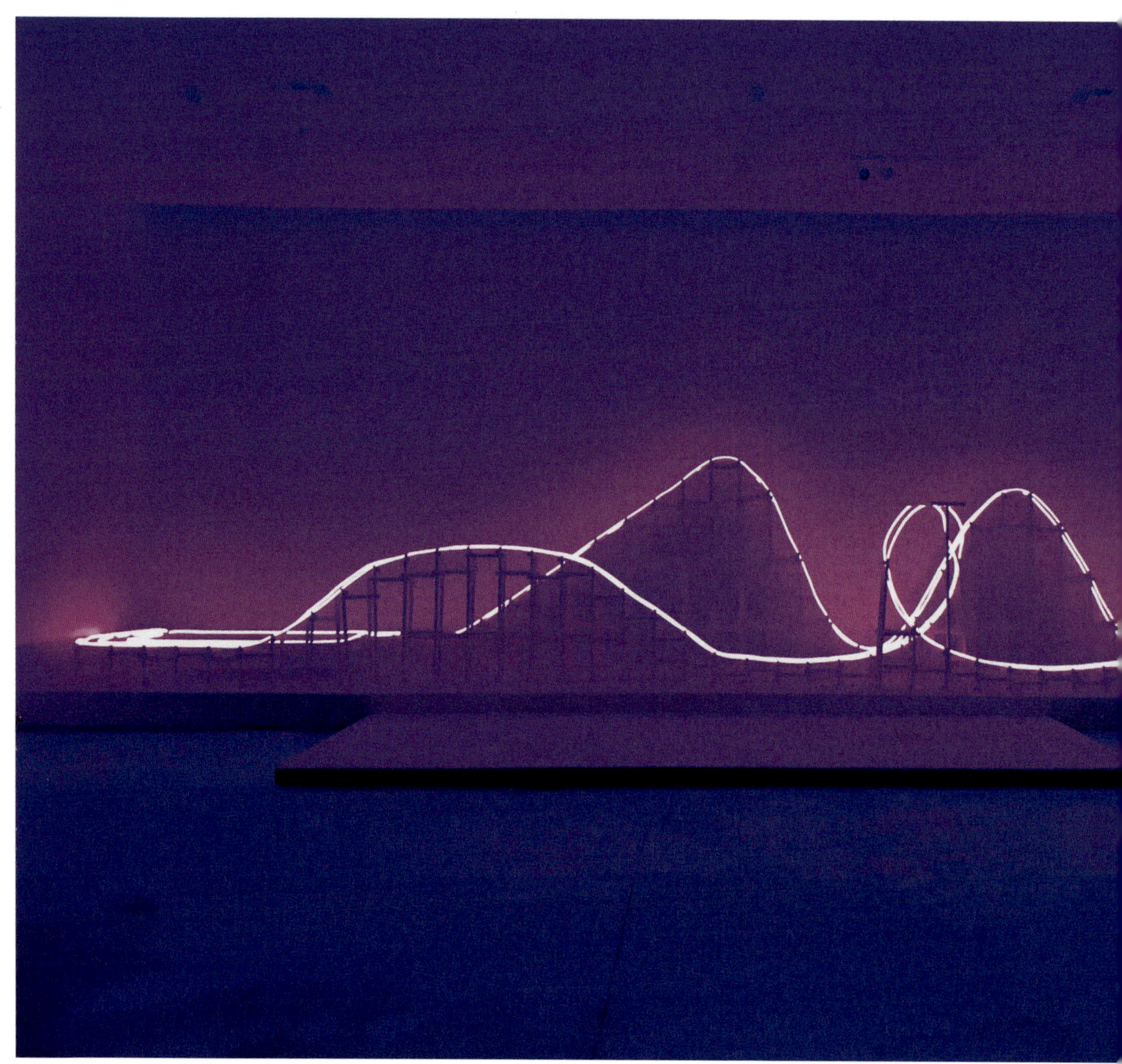

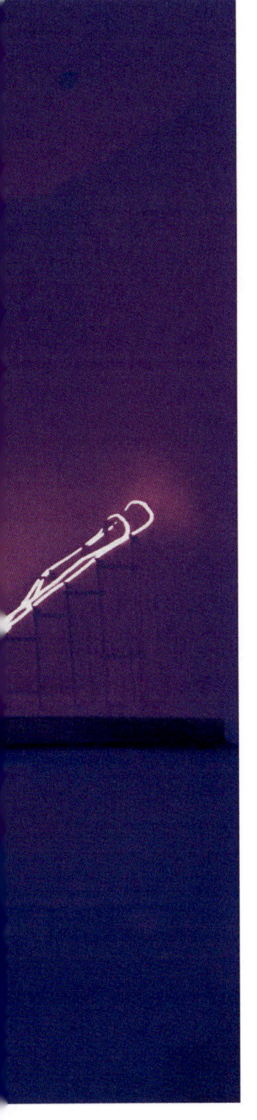

A Subsequent Offering,
2017

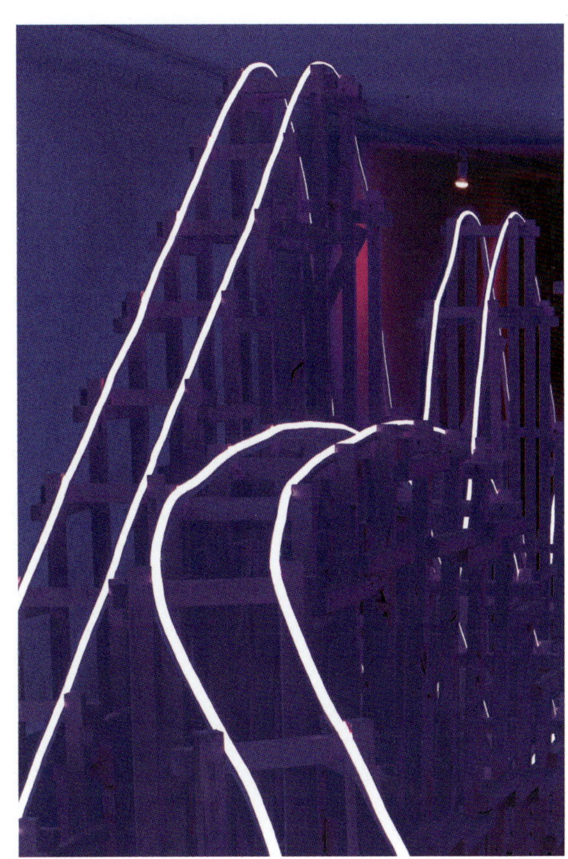

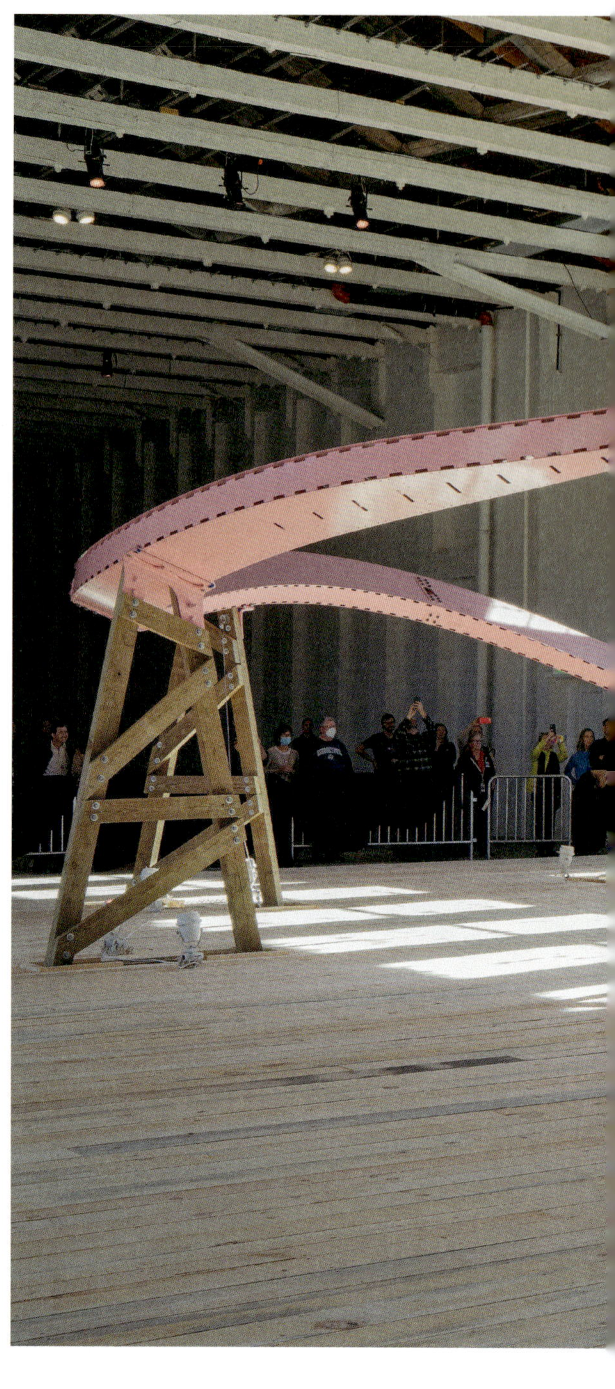

Thinking about rollercoasters, is one way for me
to communicate ideas that I have about struggle and
mortality and the impulse to go higher and faster
and test our physical and mental limits.   EJ HILL

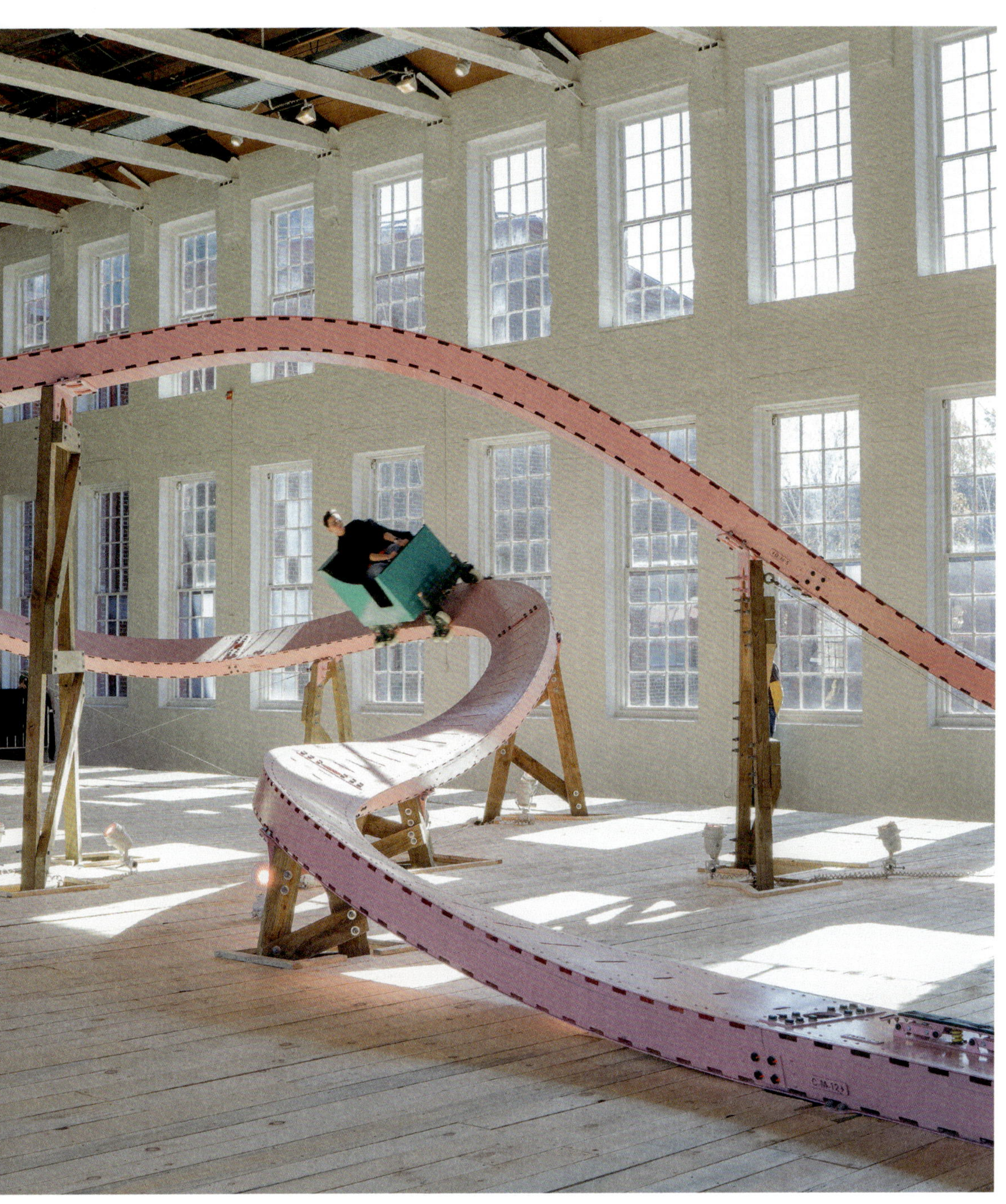

Brava, 2022

Marguerite

Humeau

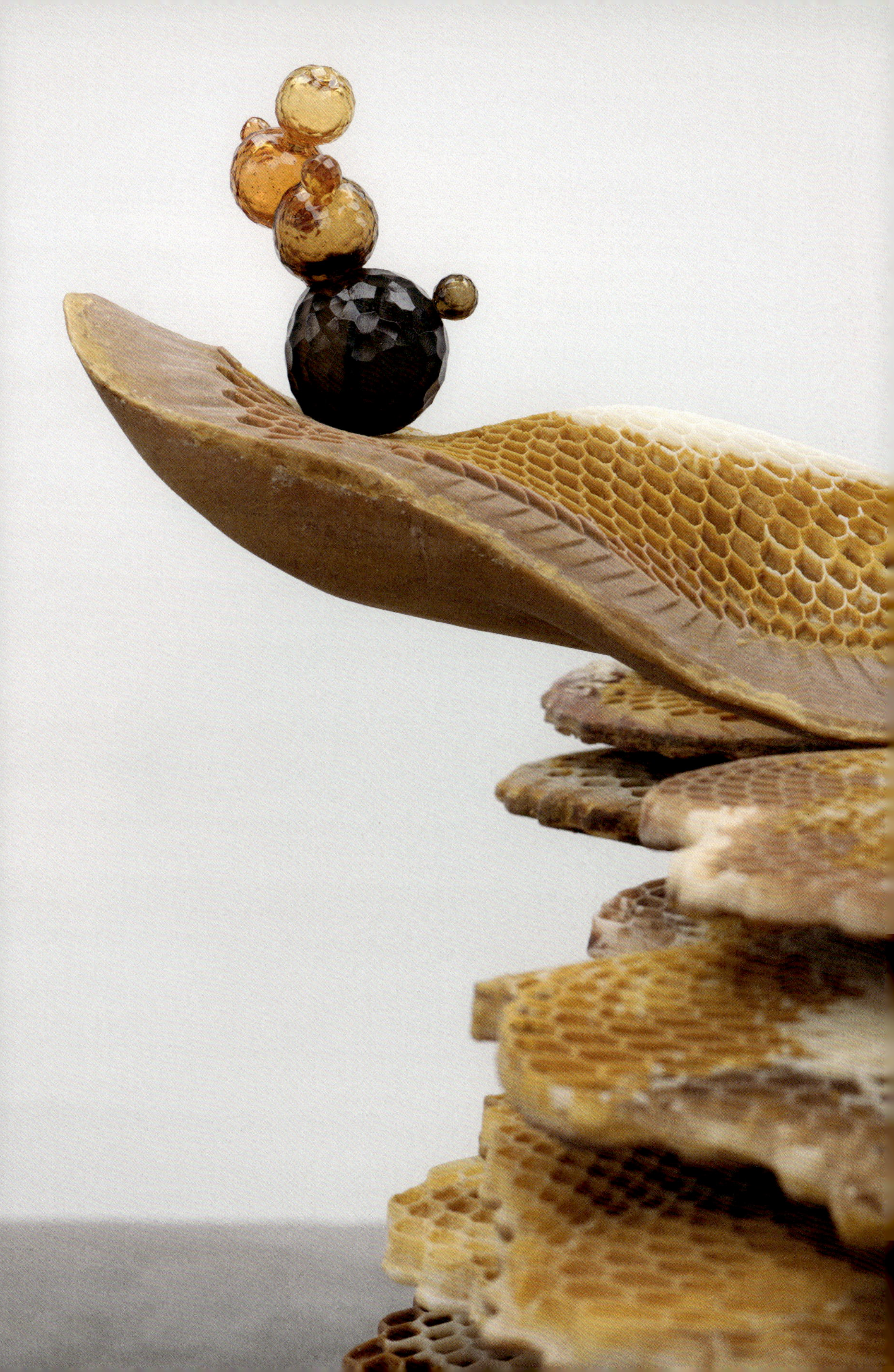

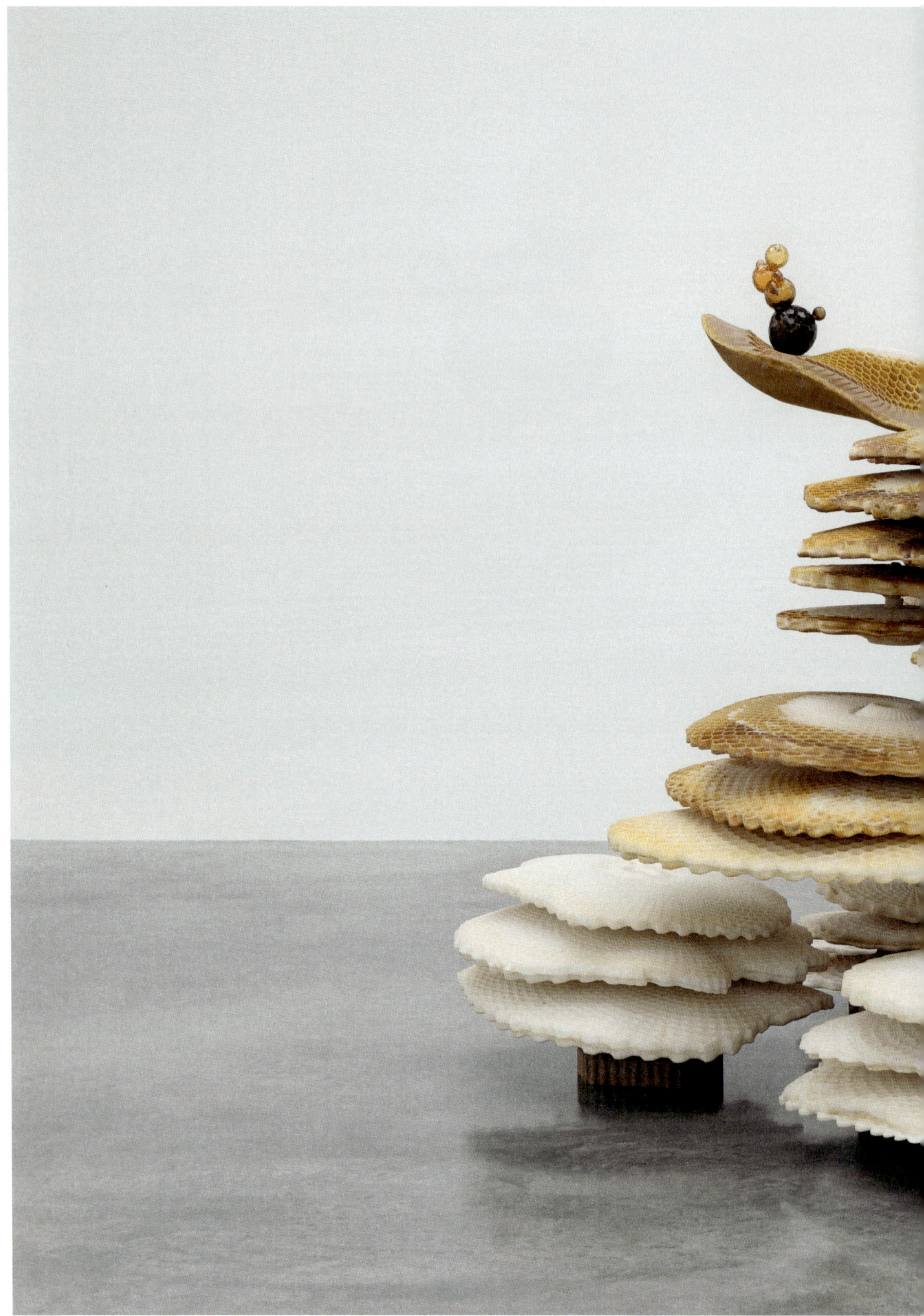

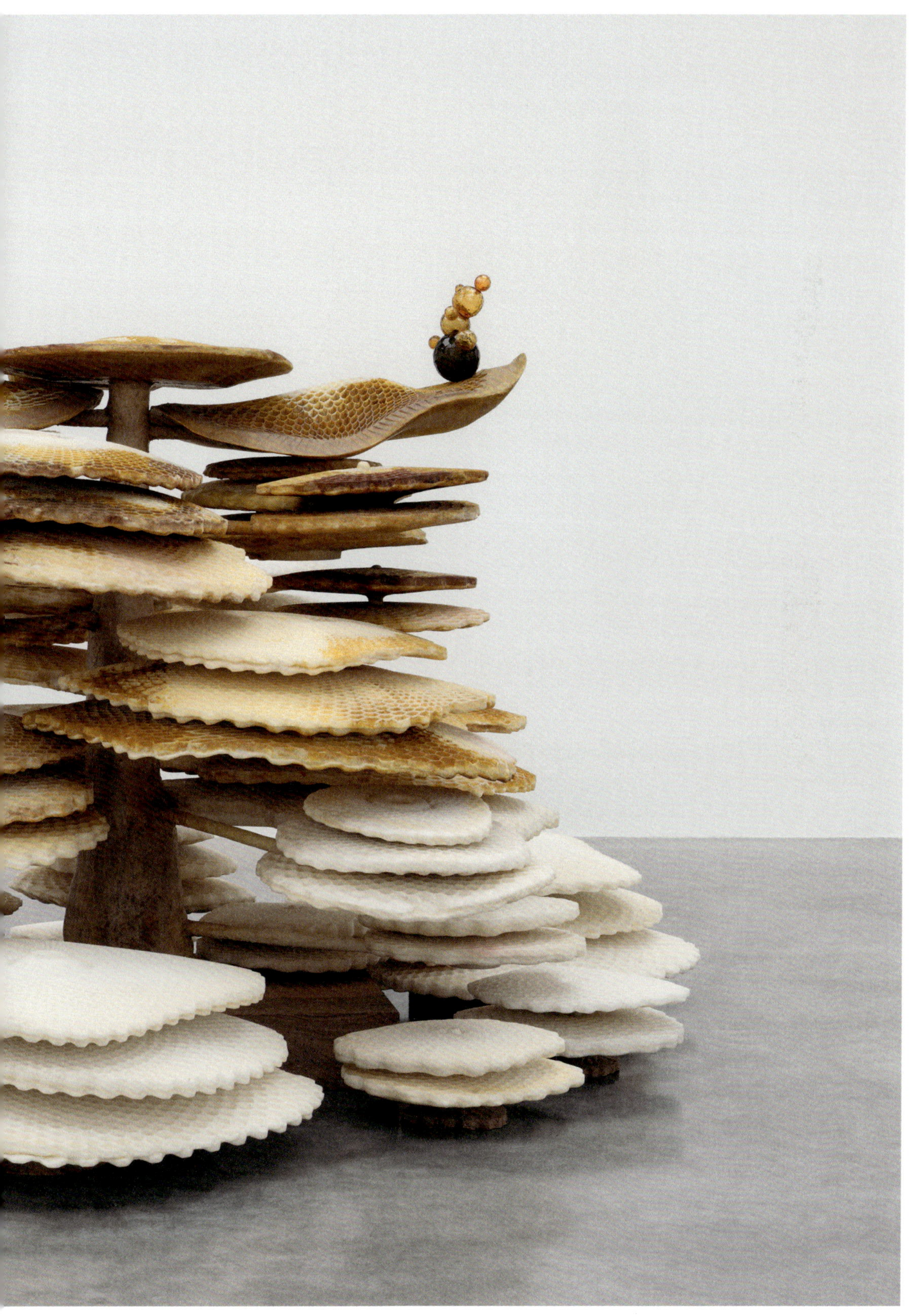

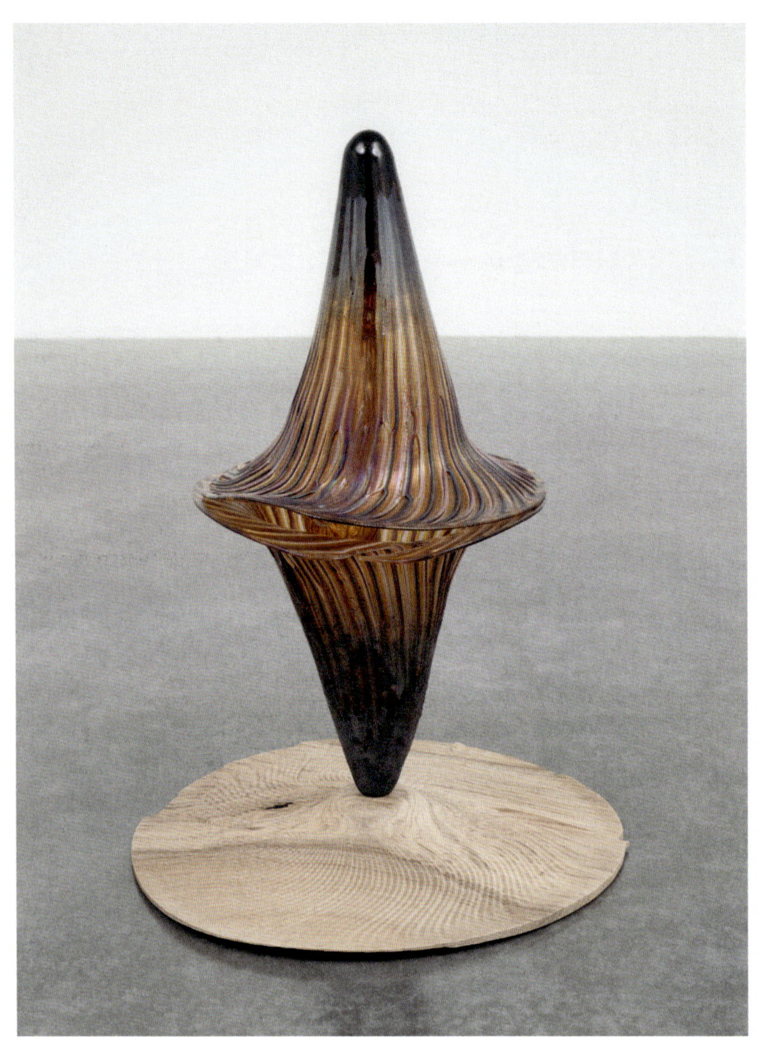

The Brewer,
2023

The Guardian of Ancient Yeast,
2023 (and detail)

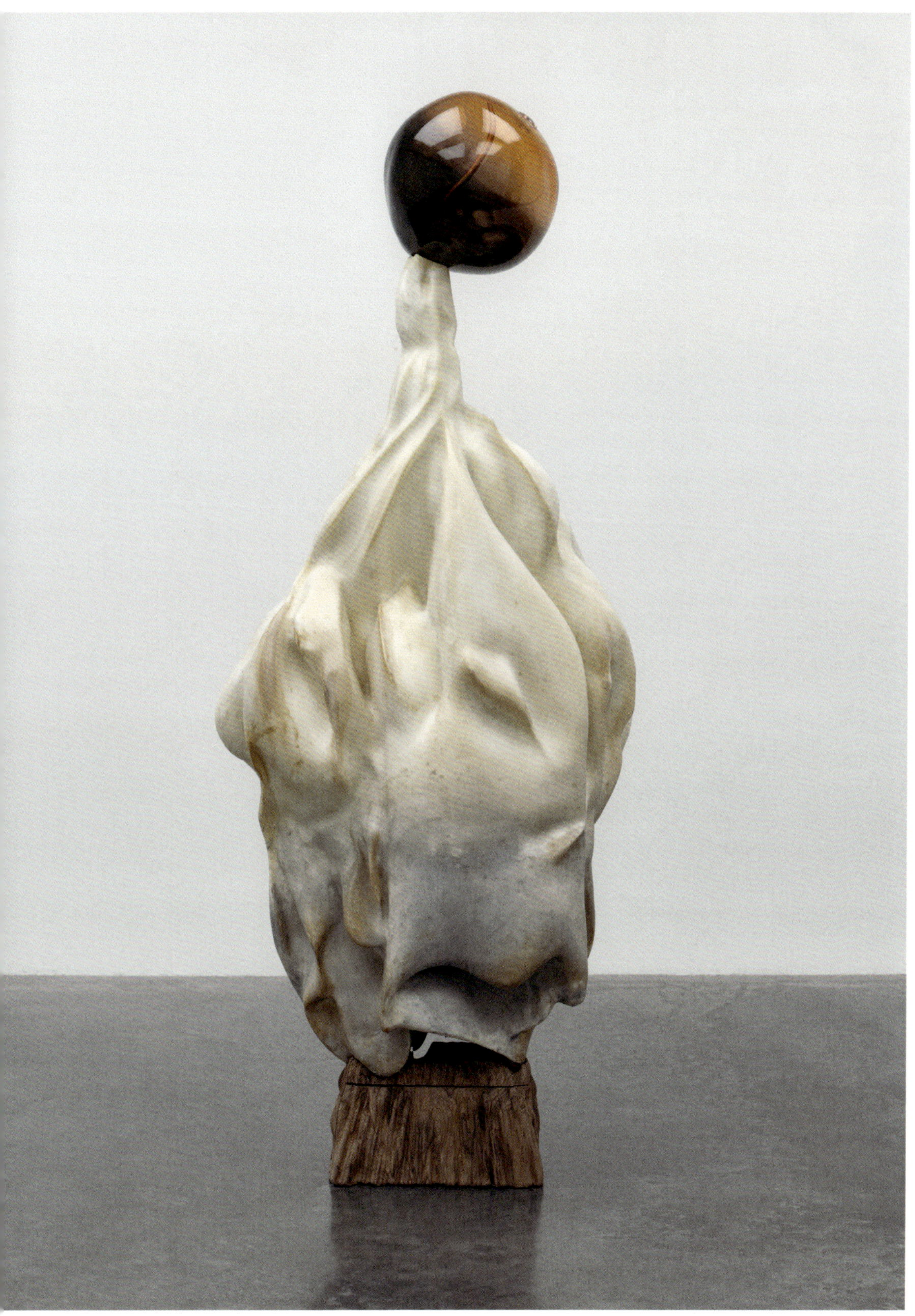

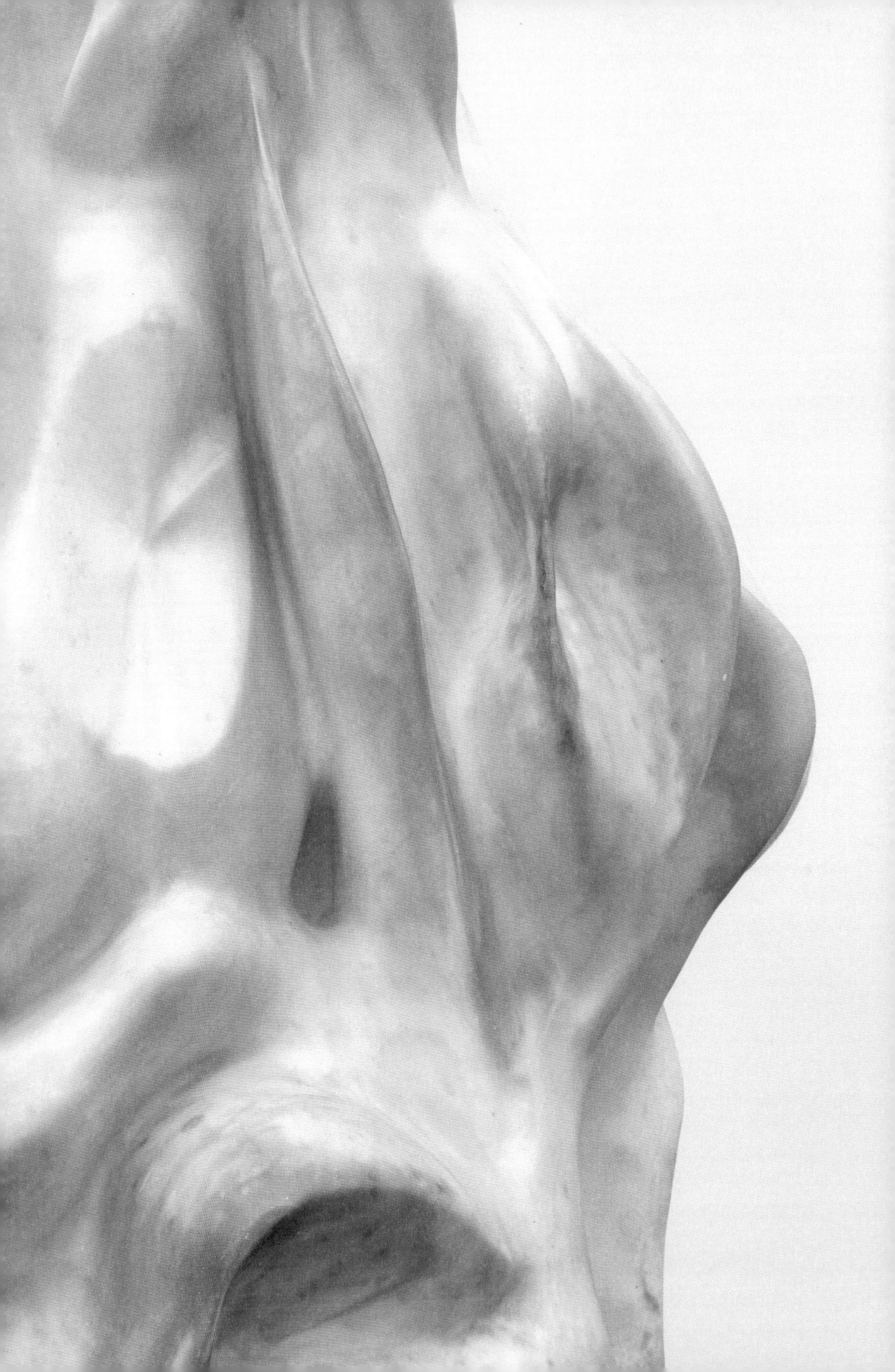

I don't make sculptures, I make beings that are alive.
They have their bloodflows, or heartbeats that
we can hear in the background. ... I didn't design them,
I designed processes. MARGUERITE HUMEAU

141

Jean-Luc

Moulène

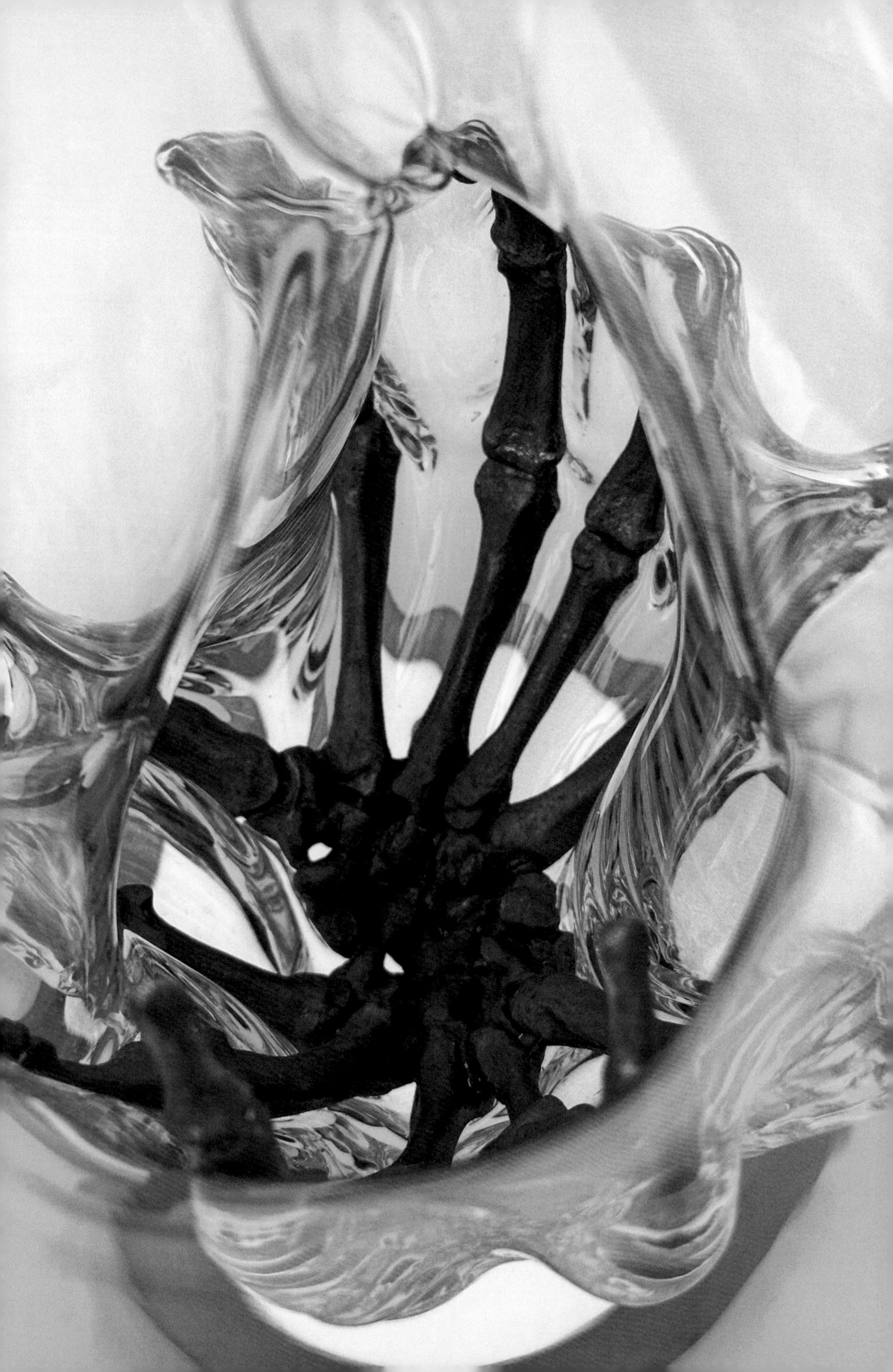

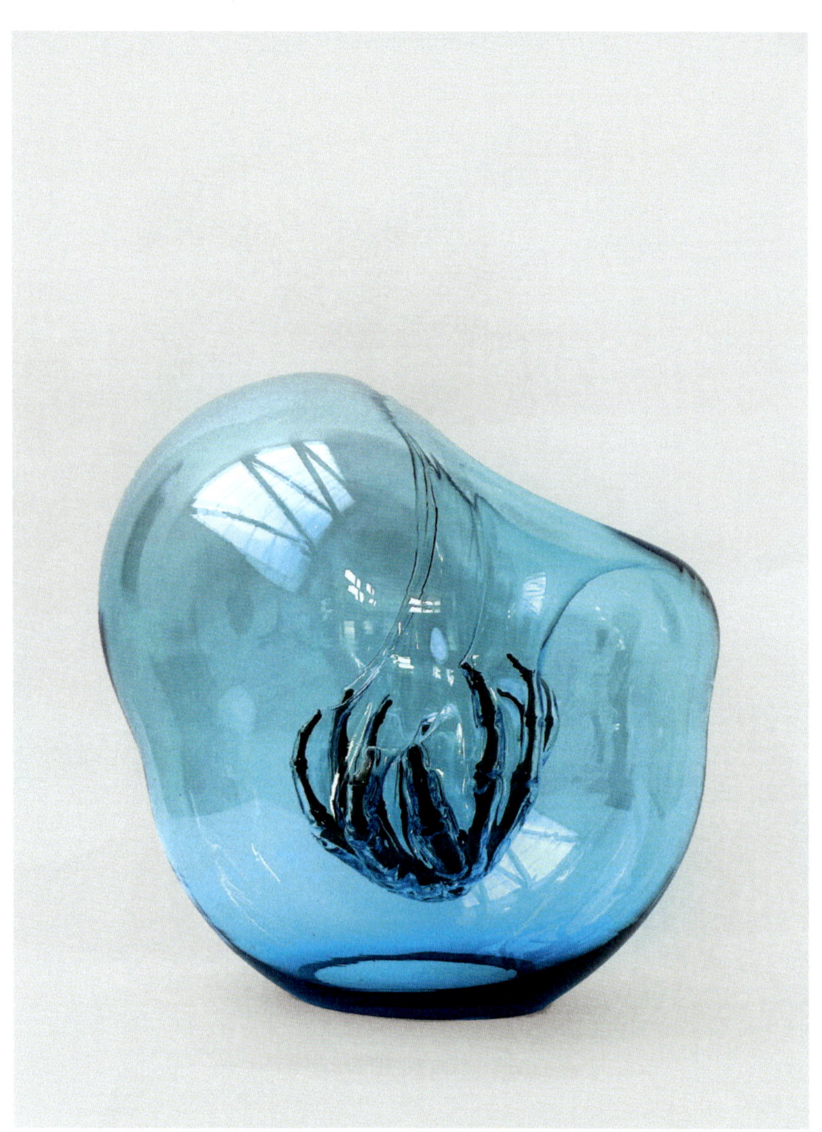

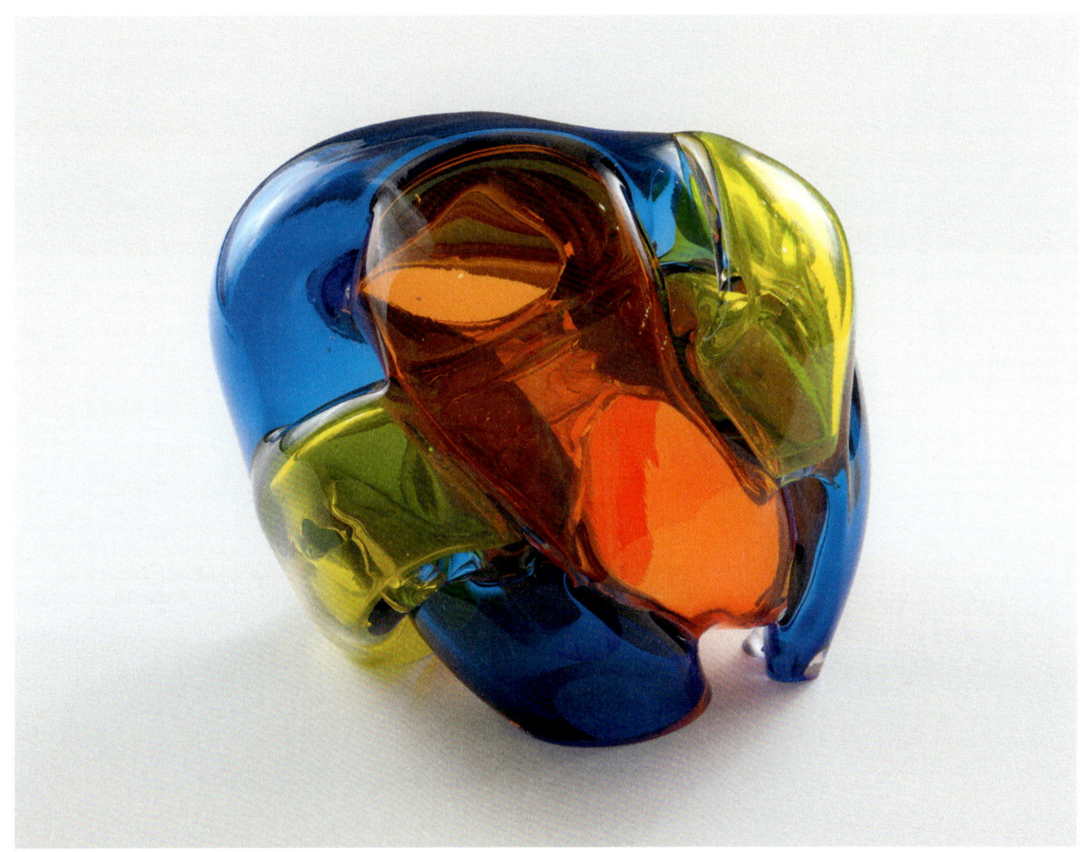

Blown Knot 6 $^3_2$ *(Borromean)*
Varia 06, Marseille 2012

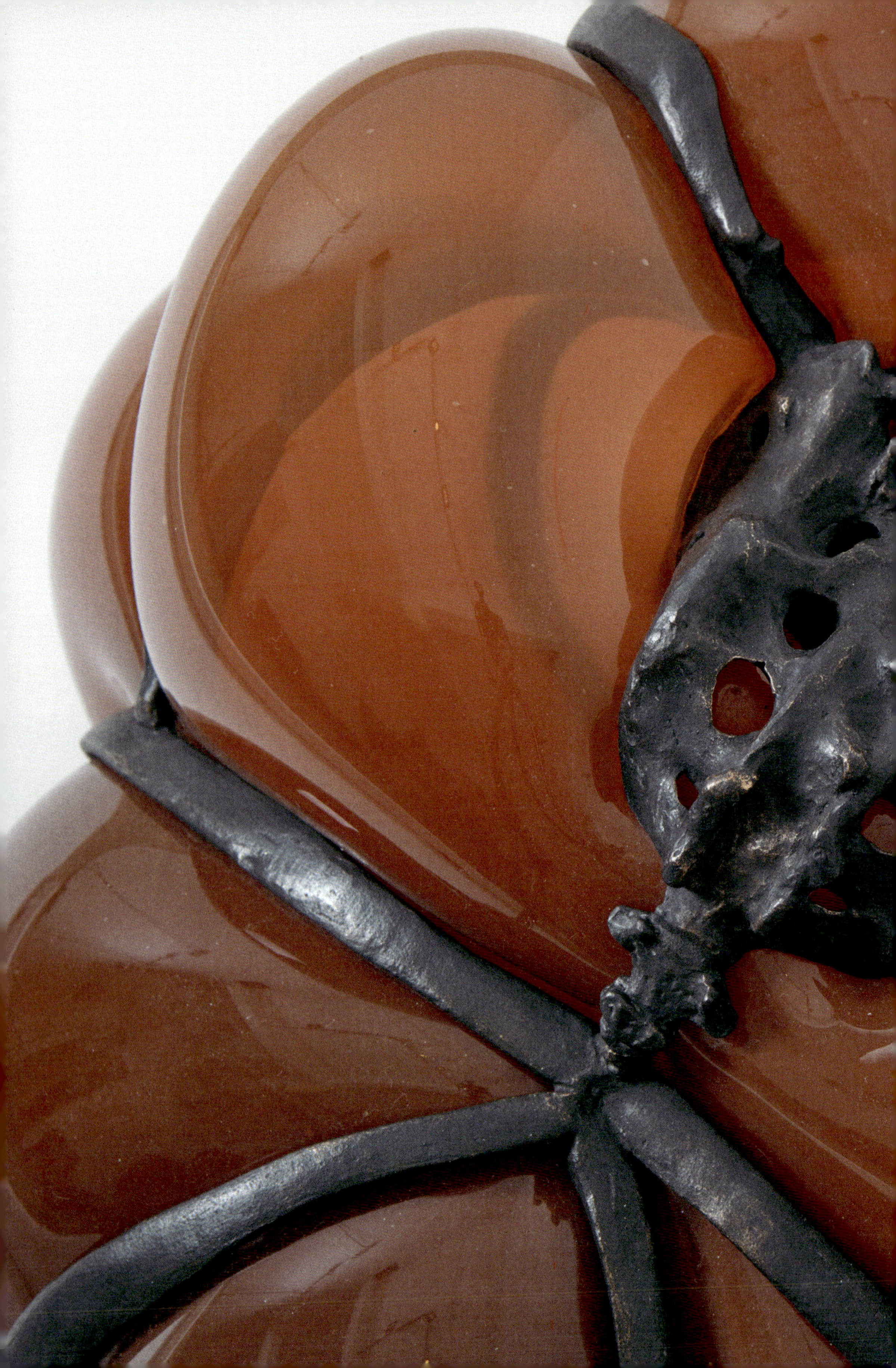

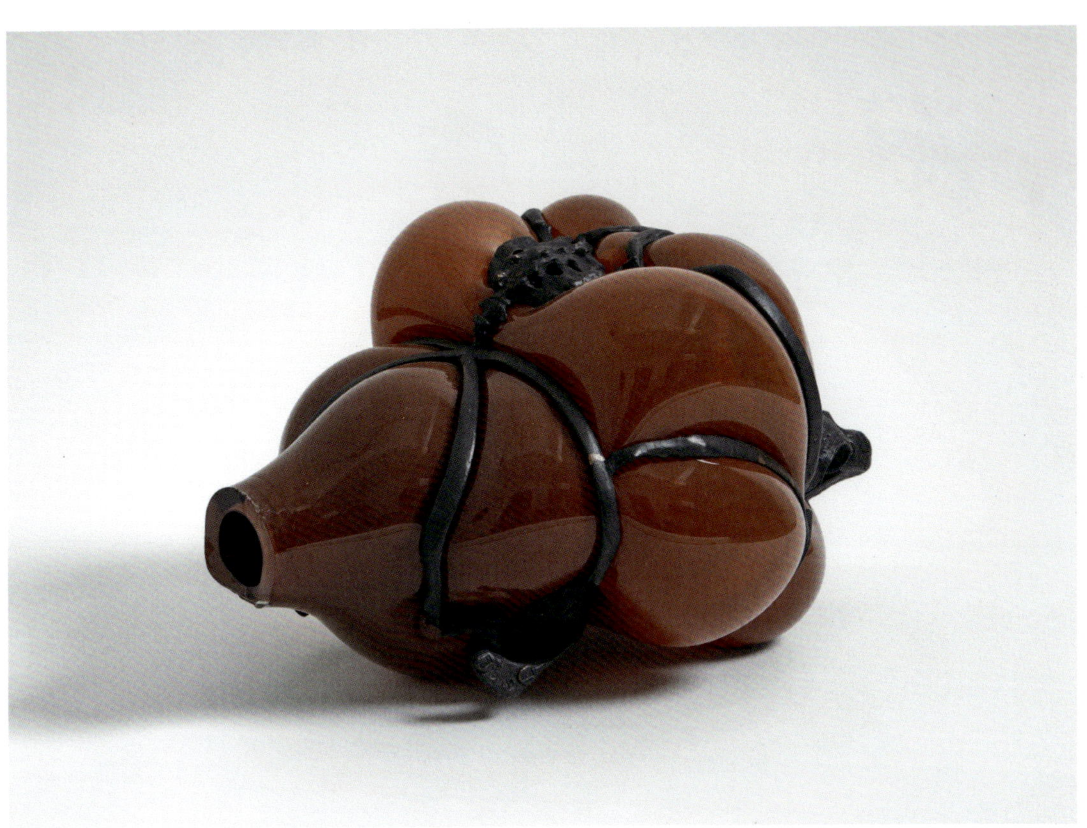

My objects are surfaces, with no inside or outside, only holes.
Through the holes there are other surfaces. JEAN-LUC MOULÈNE

147

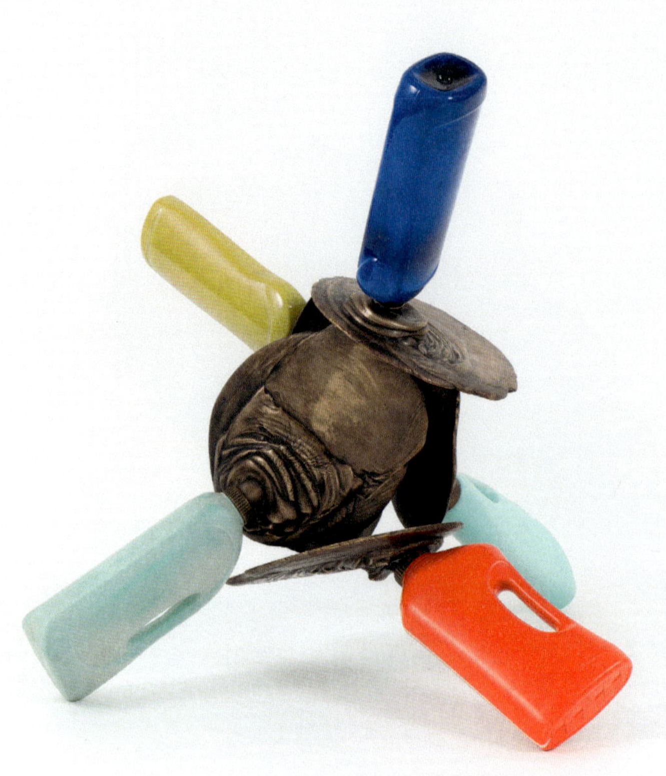

Ressort flou,
Le Buisson 2022 (top)

Méduse,
Paris 2018 (bottom)

148

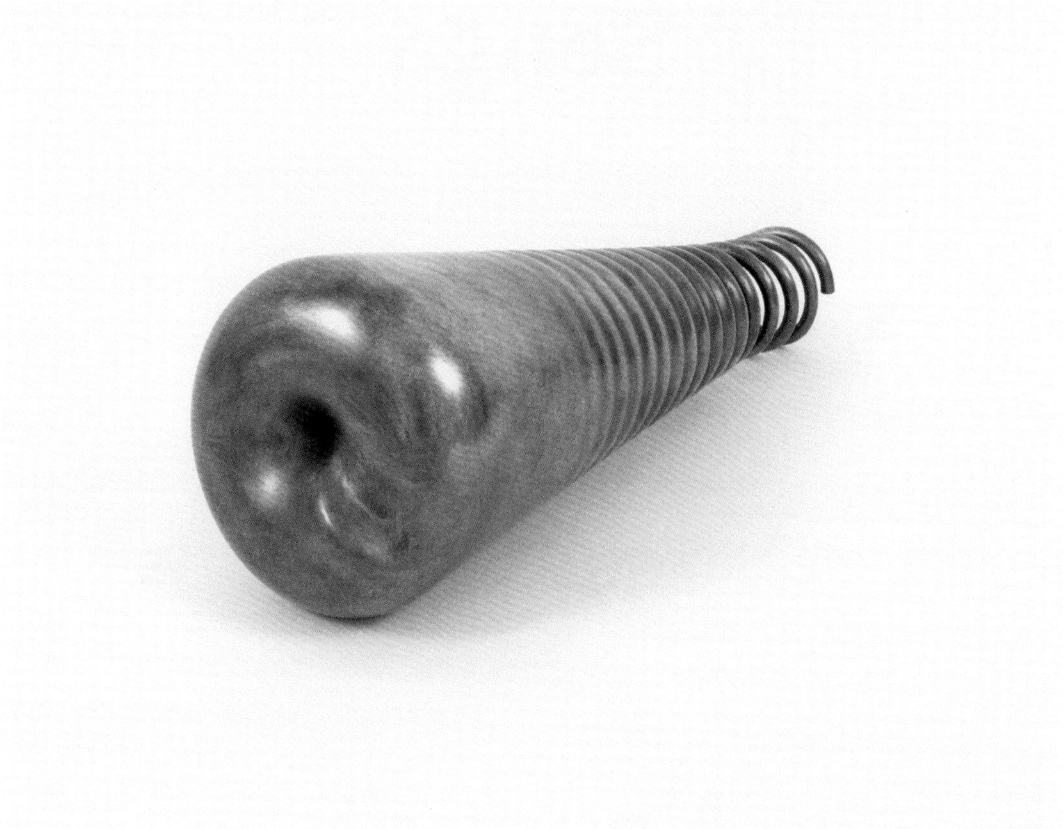

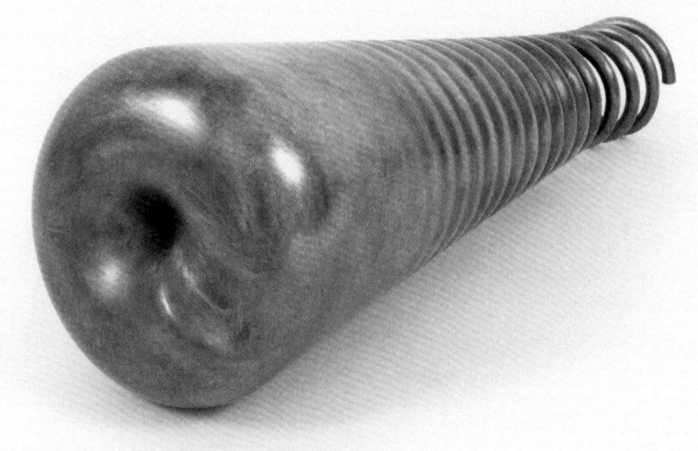

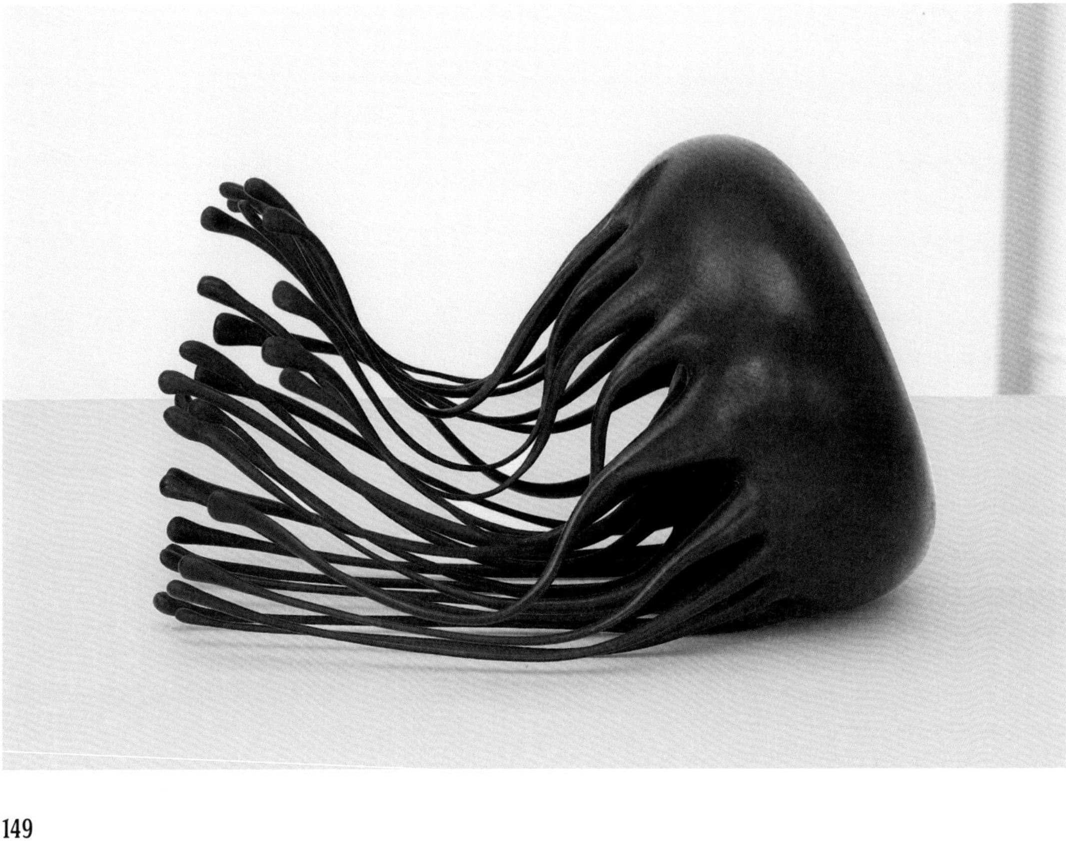

Senga

Nengudi

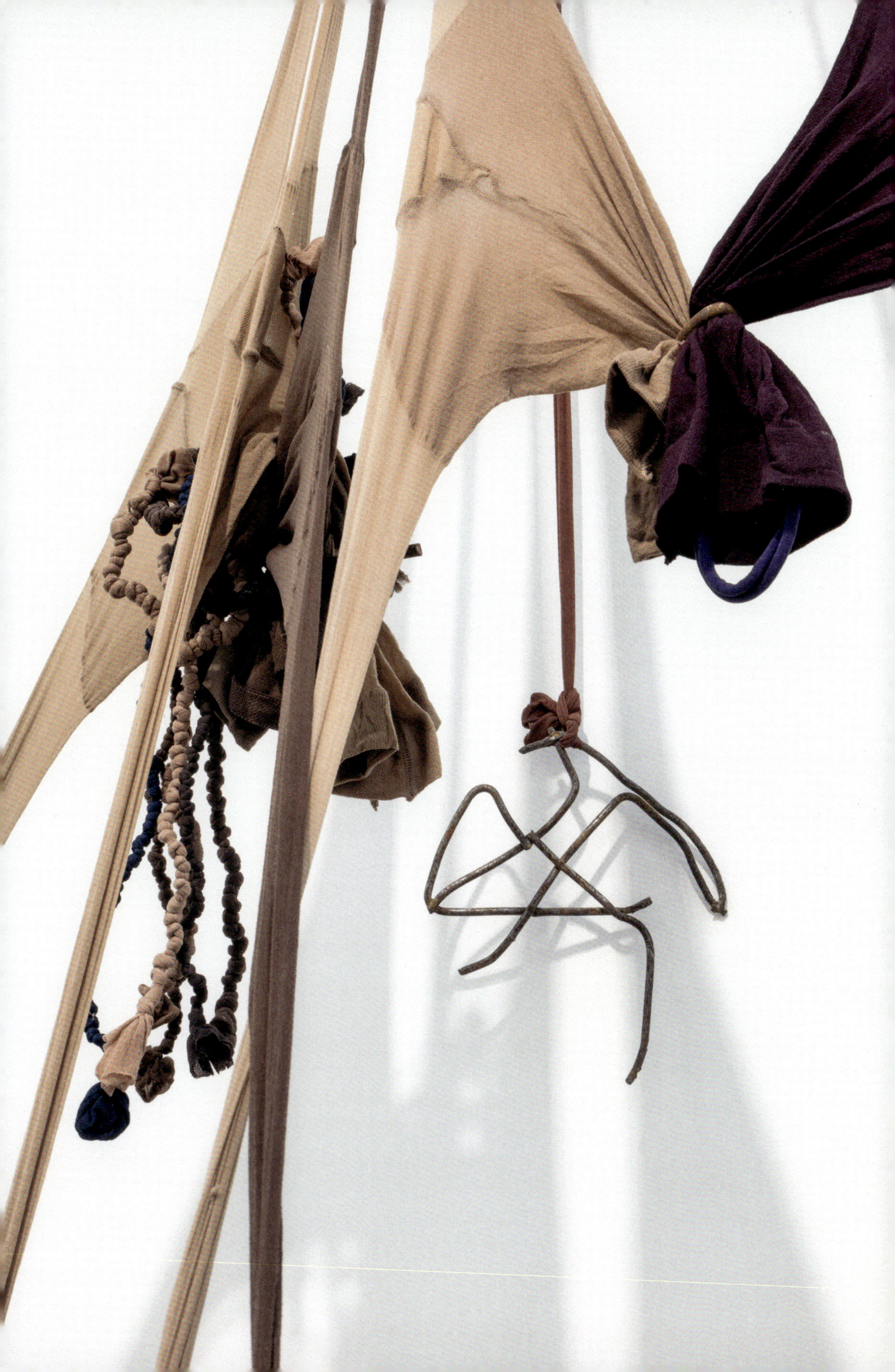

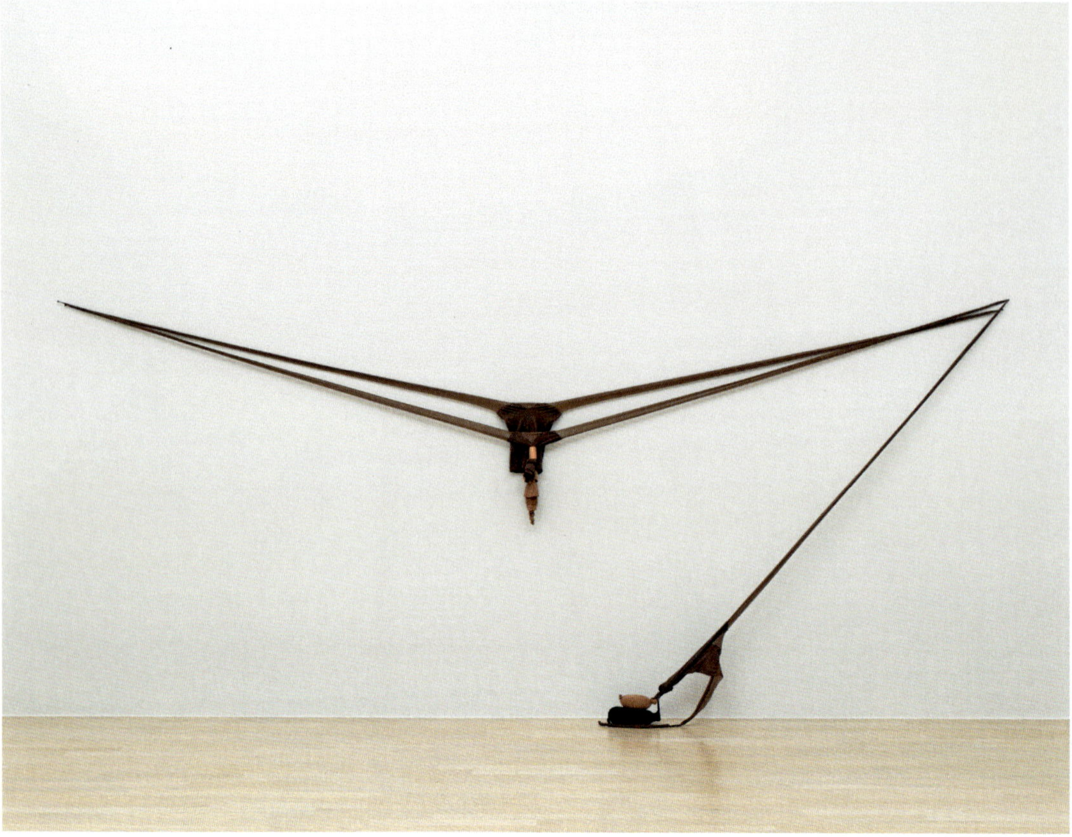

R.S.V.P. Reverie 'D',
2014

R.S.V.P. Reverie (Scribe),
1977

152

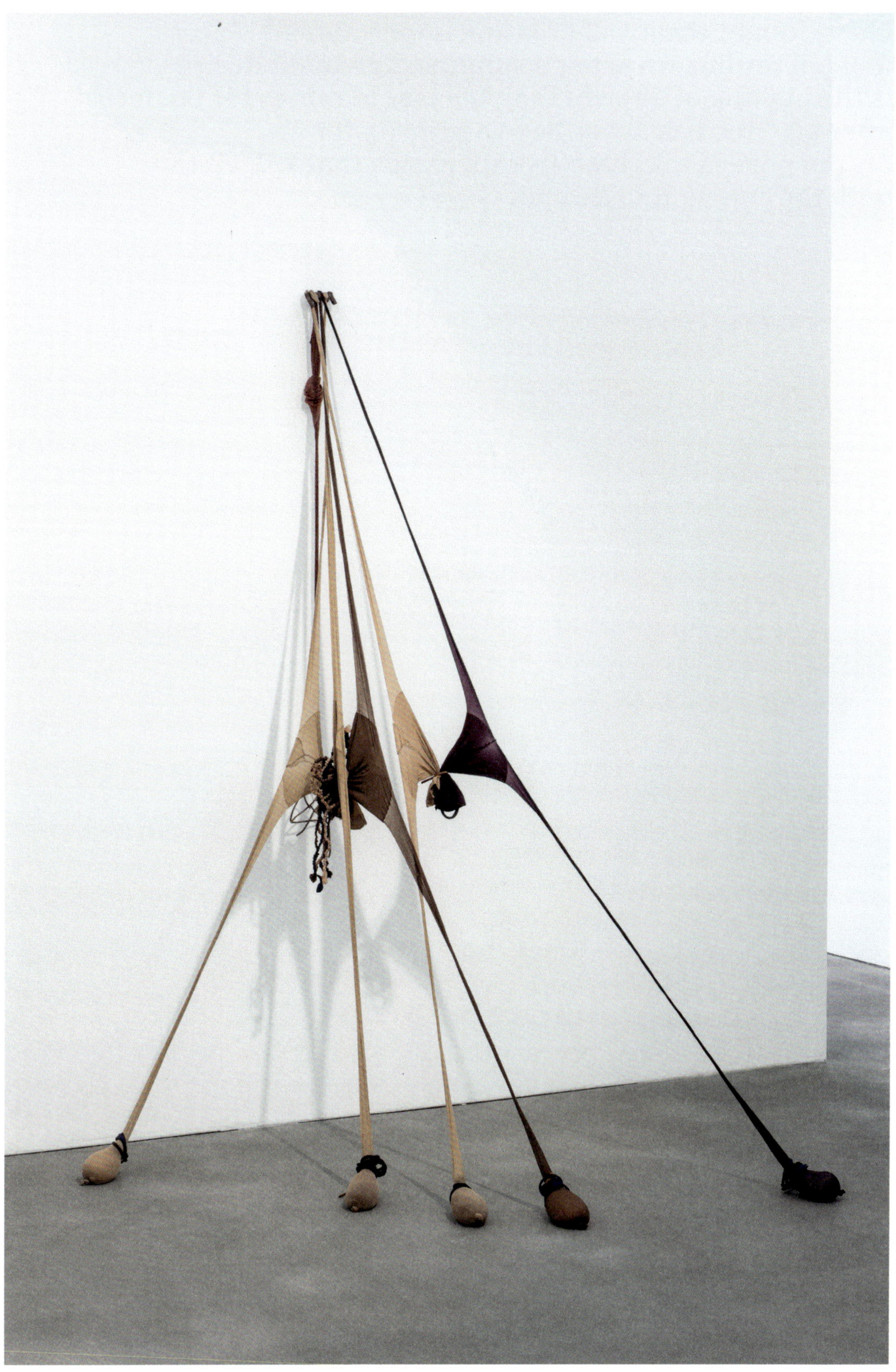

I have fought the joy of creating impermanent objects
most of my life. An artist's supposed greatest desire
is the making of objects that will last lifetimes for posterity
after all. This has never been a priority for me.
My purpose is to create an experience that will vibrate
with the connecting thread. SENGA NENGUDI

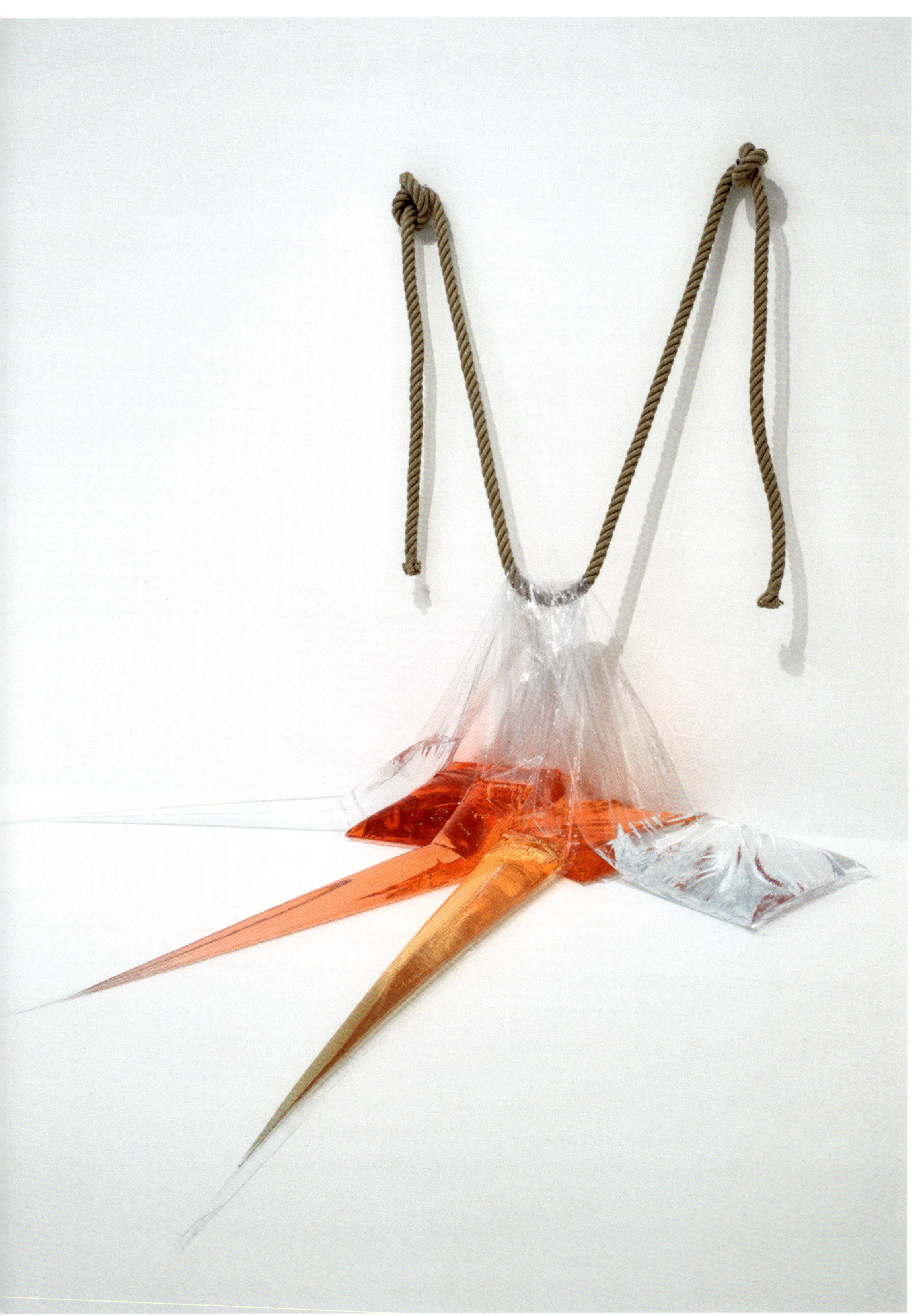

Ernesto

Neto

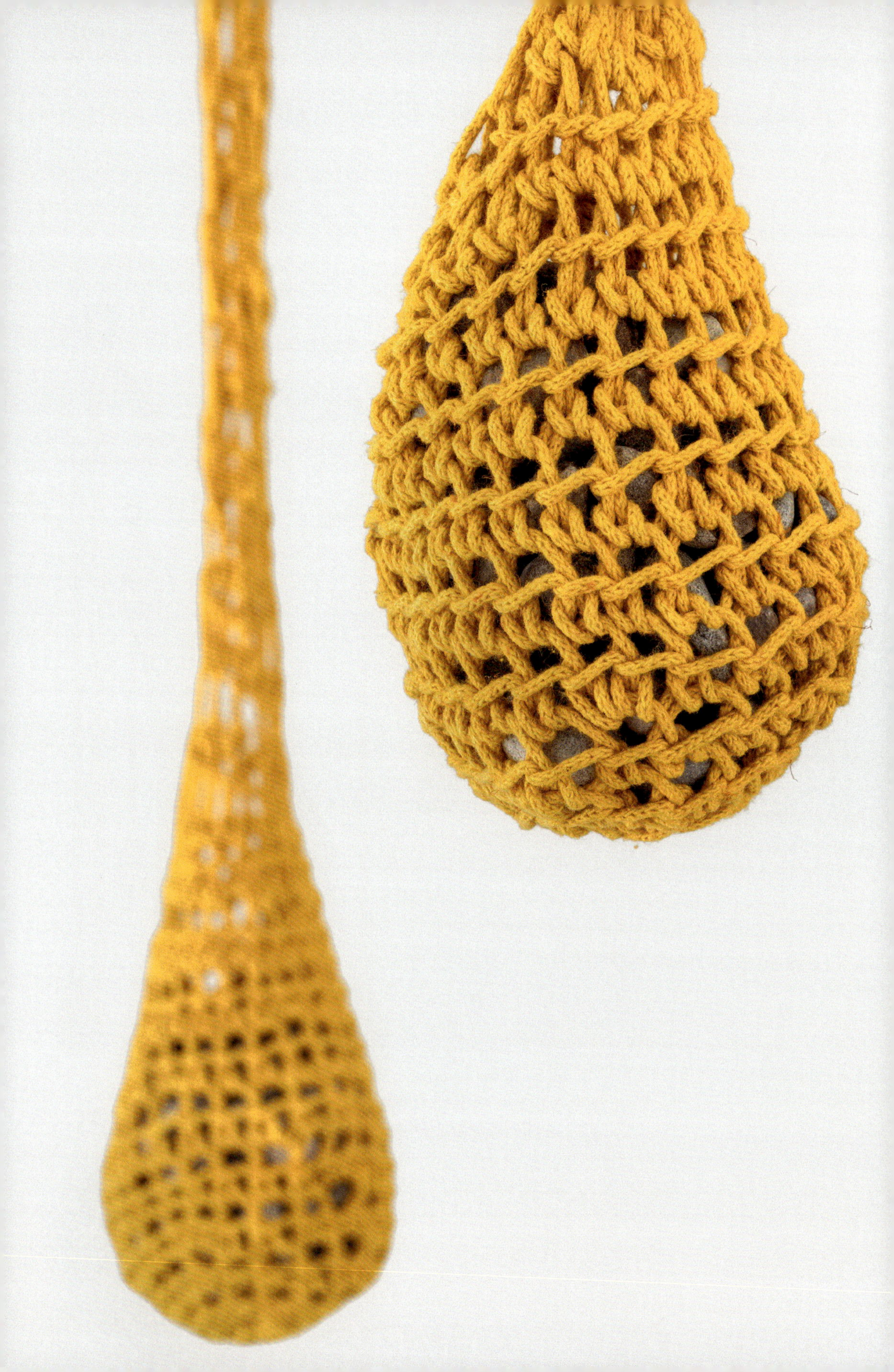

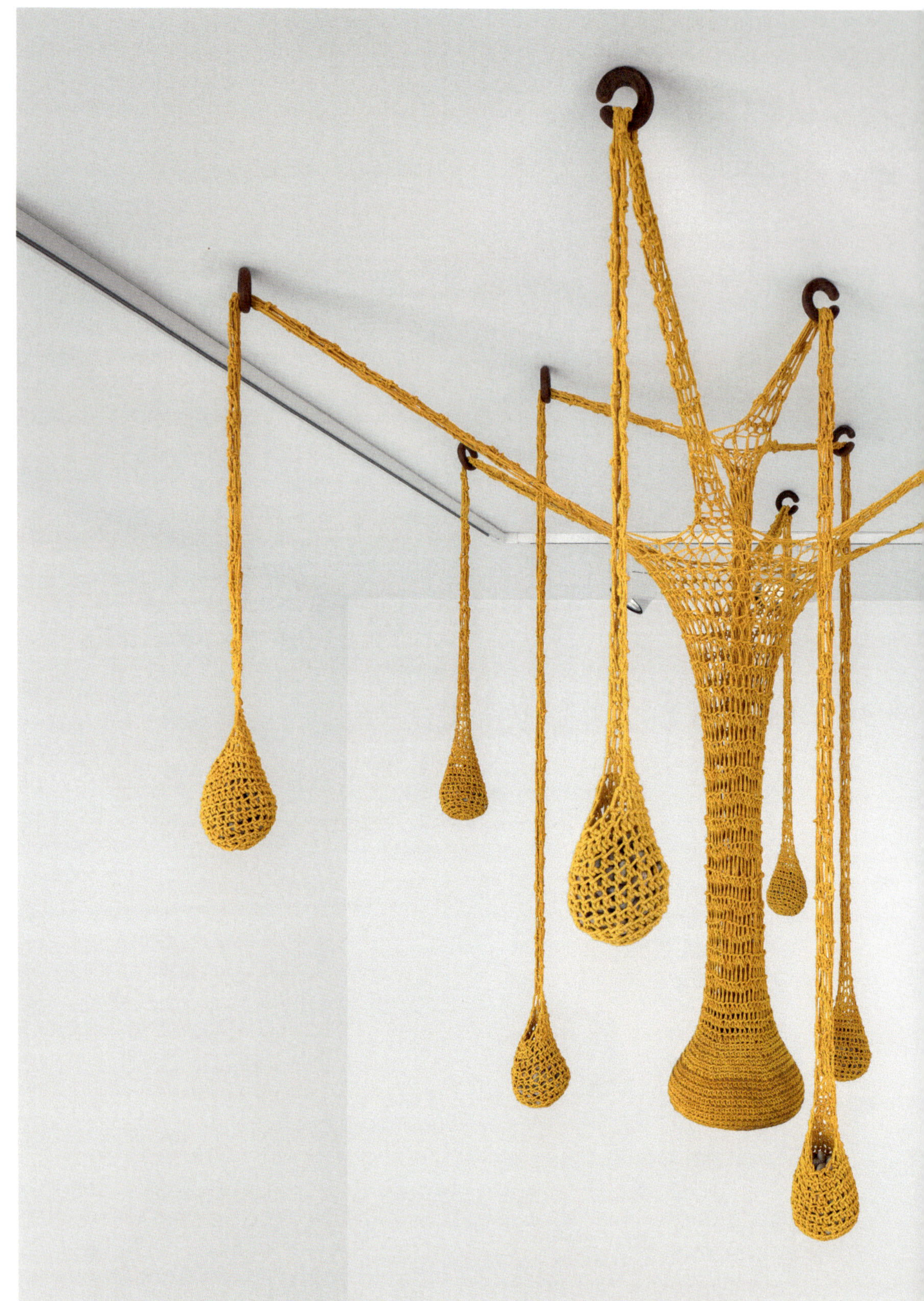

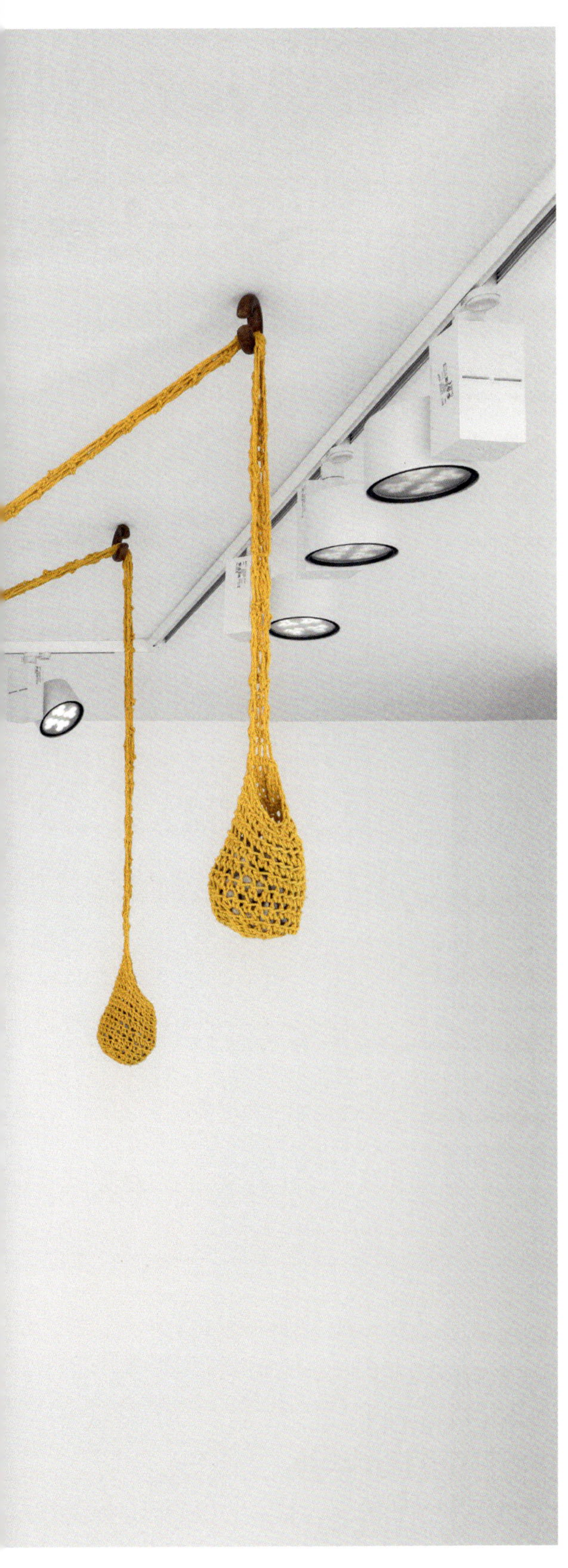

Art is a way of being in the world, it happens
all the time, everywhere, invisible and inexplicable,
an unnameable dream. Art spreads, pulsates,
guides, blows, sings and dances life.   ERNESTO NETO

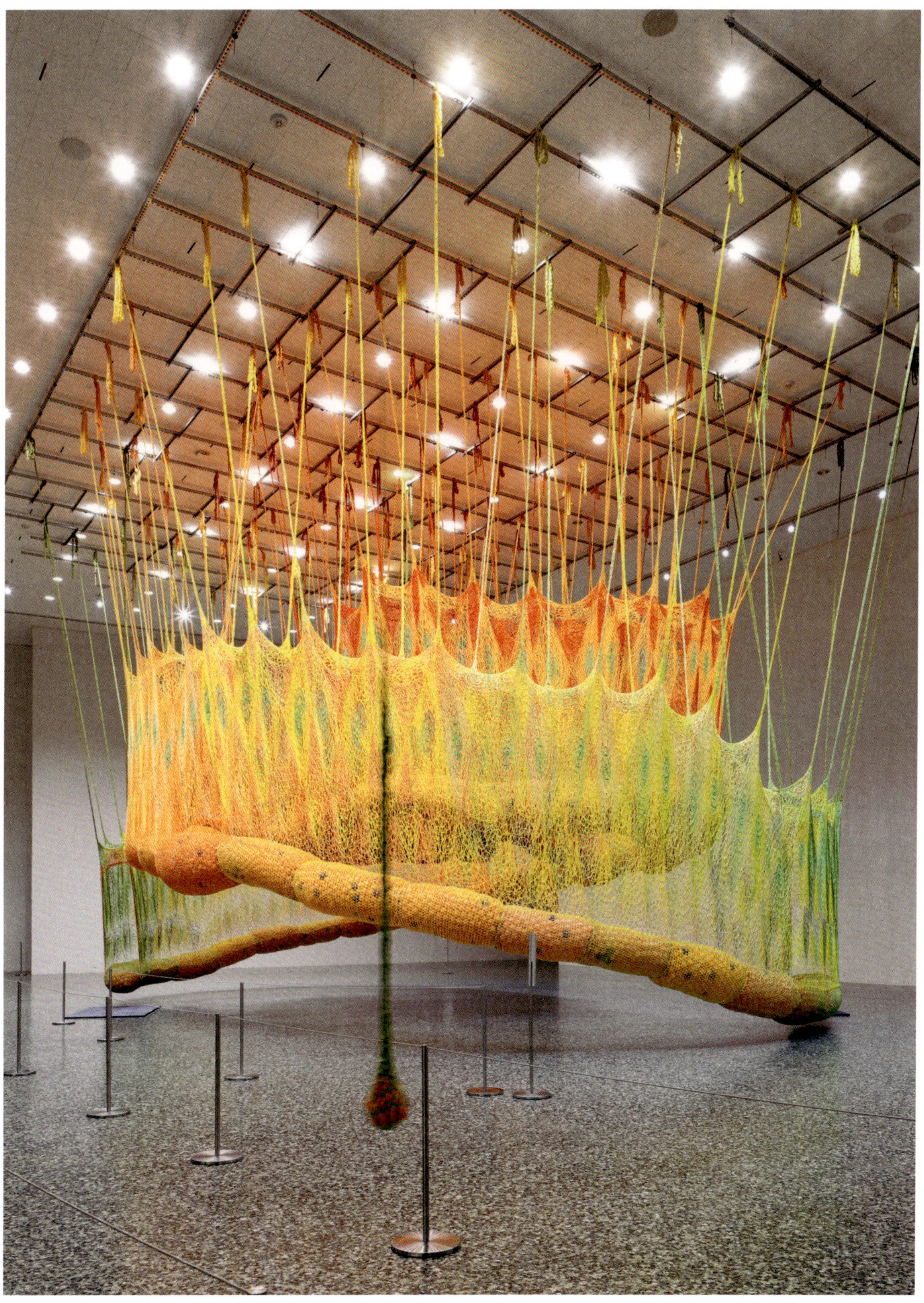

161

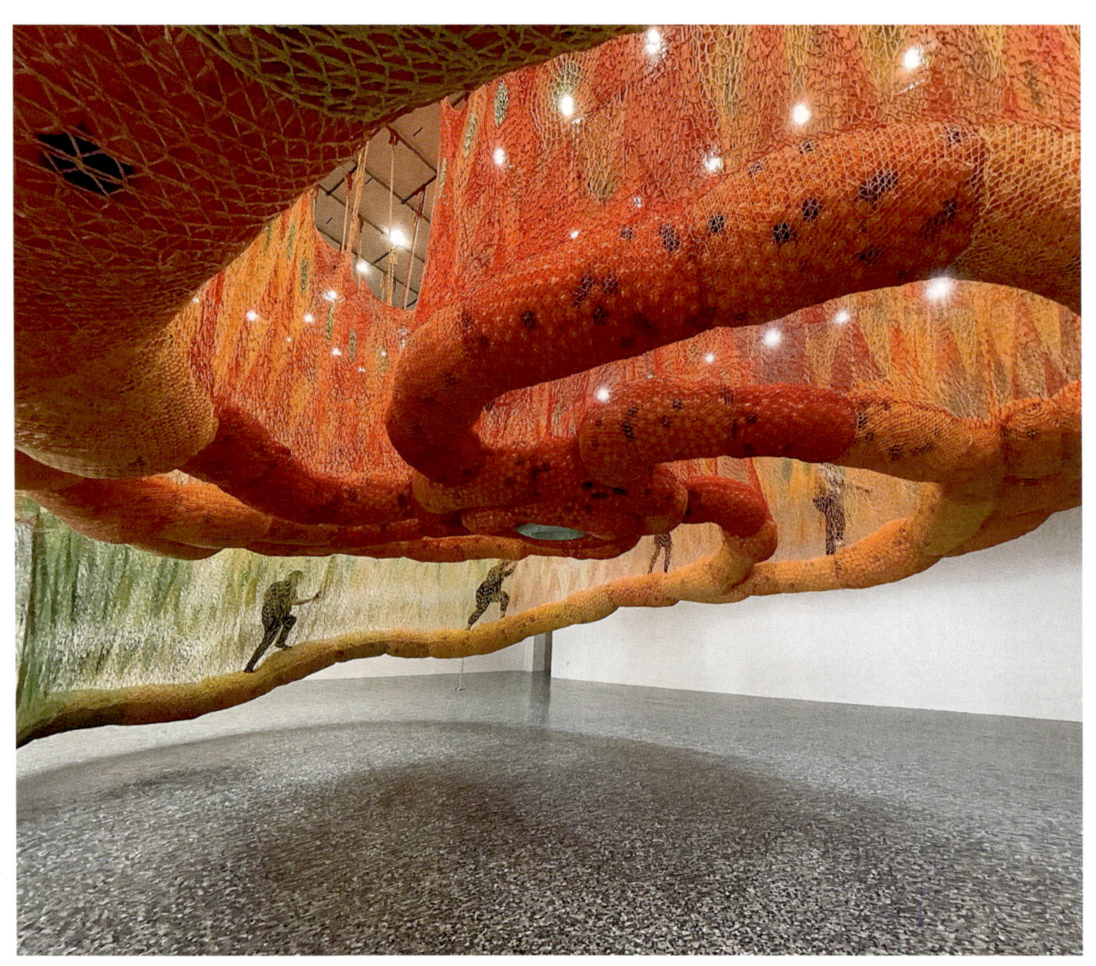

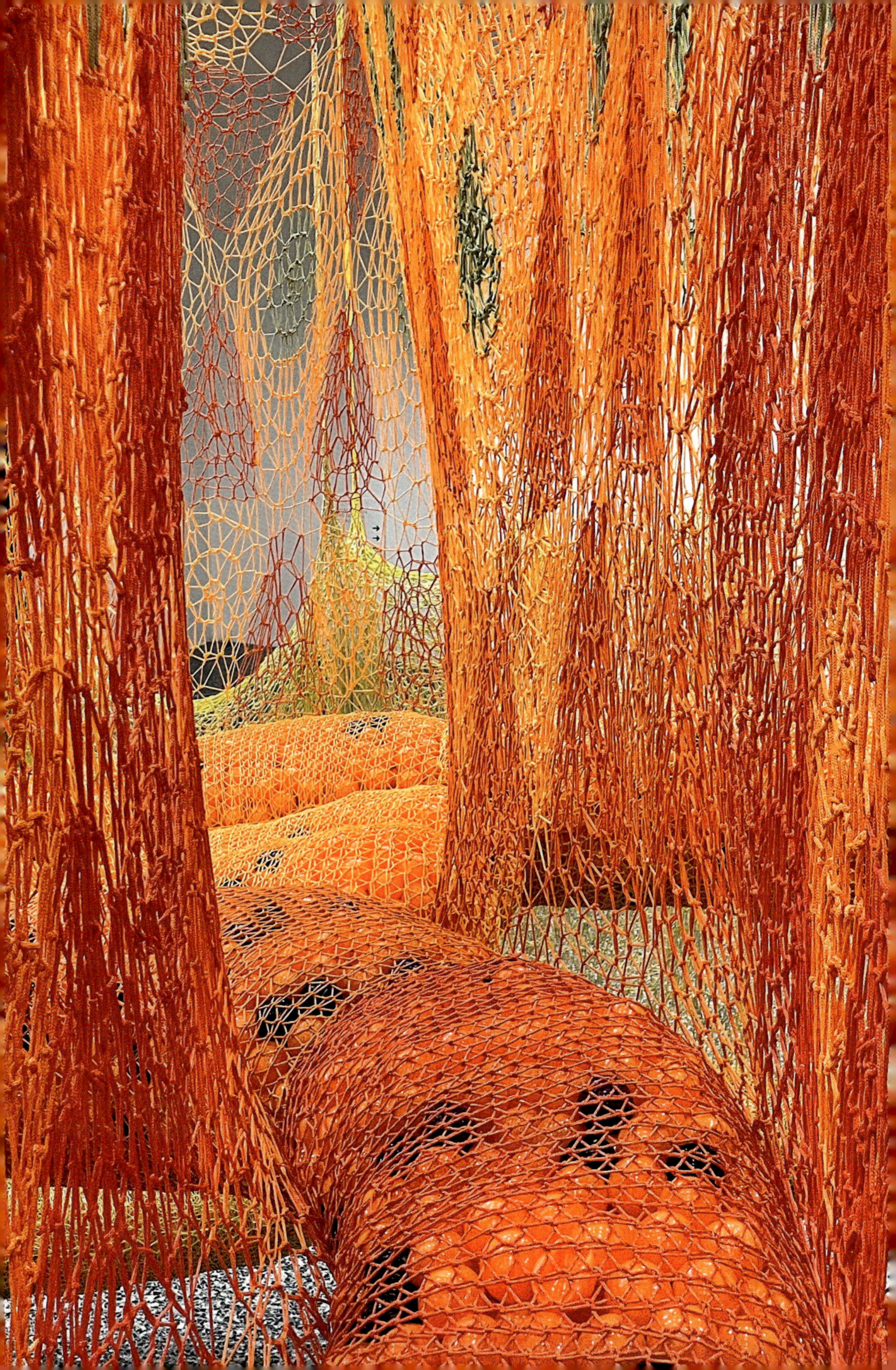

Martin

Puryear

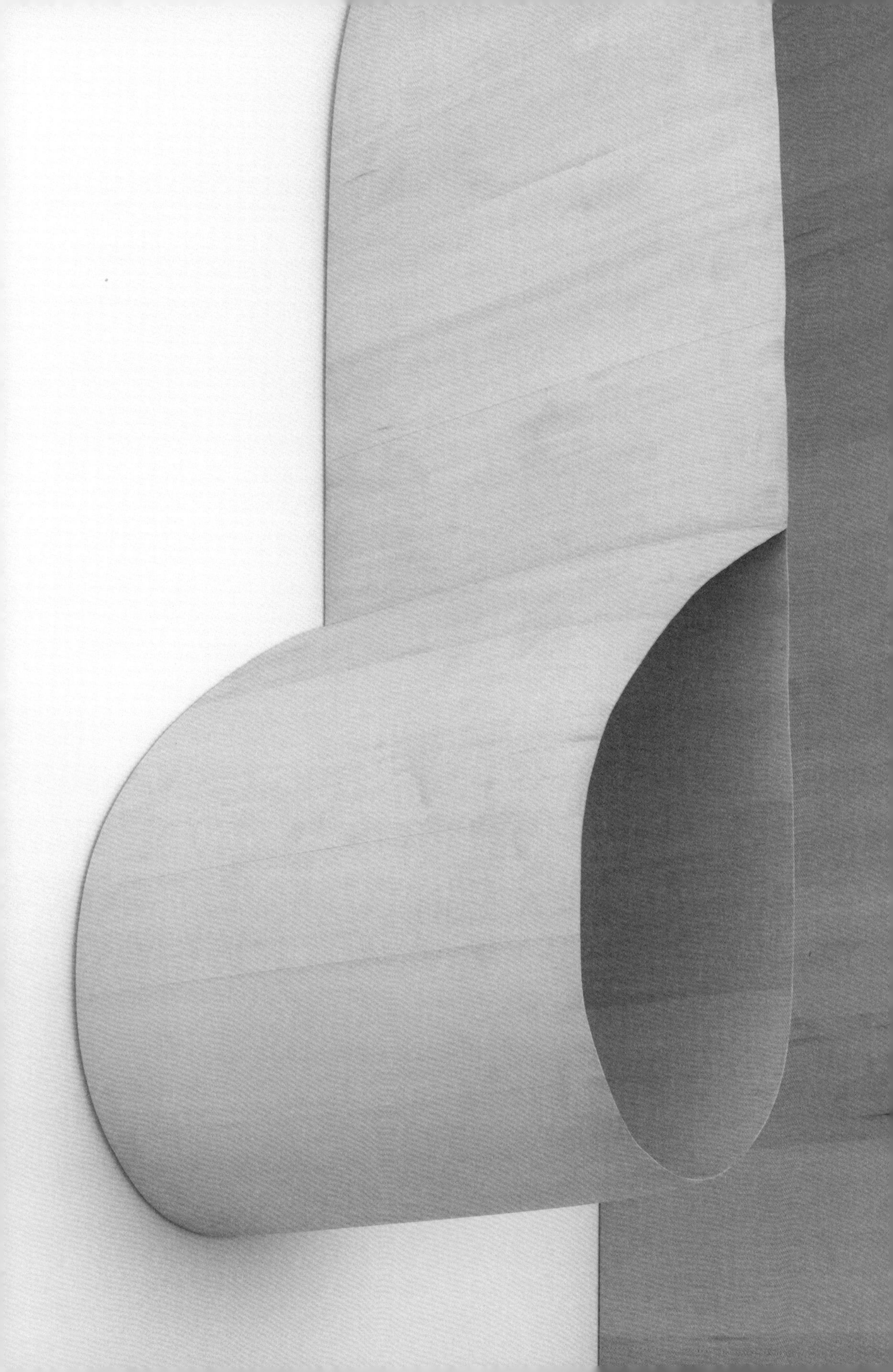

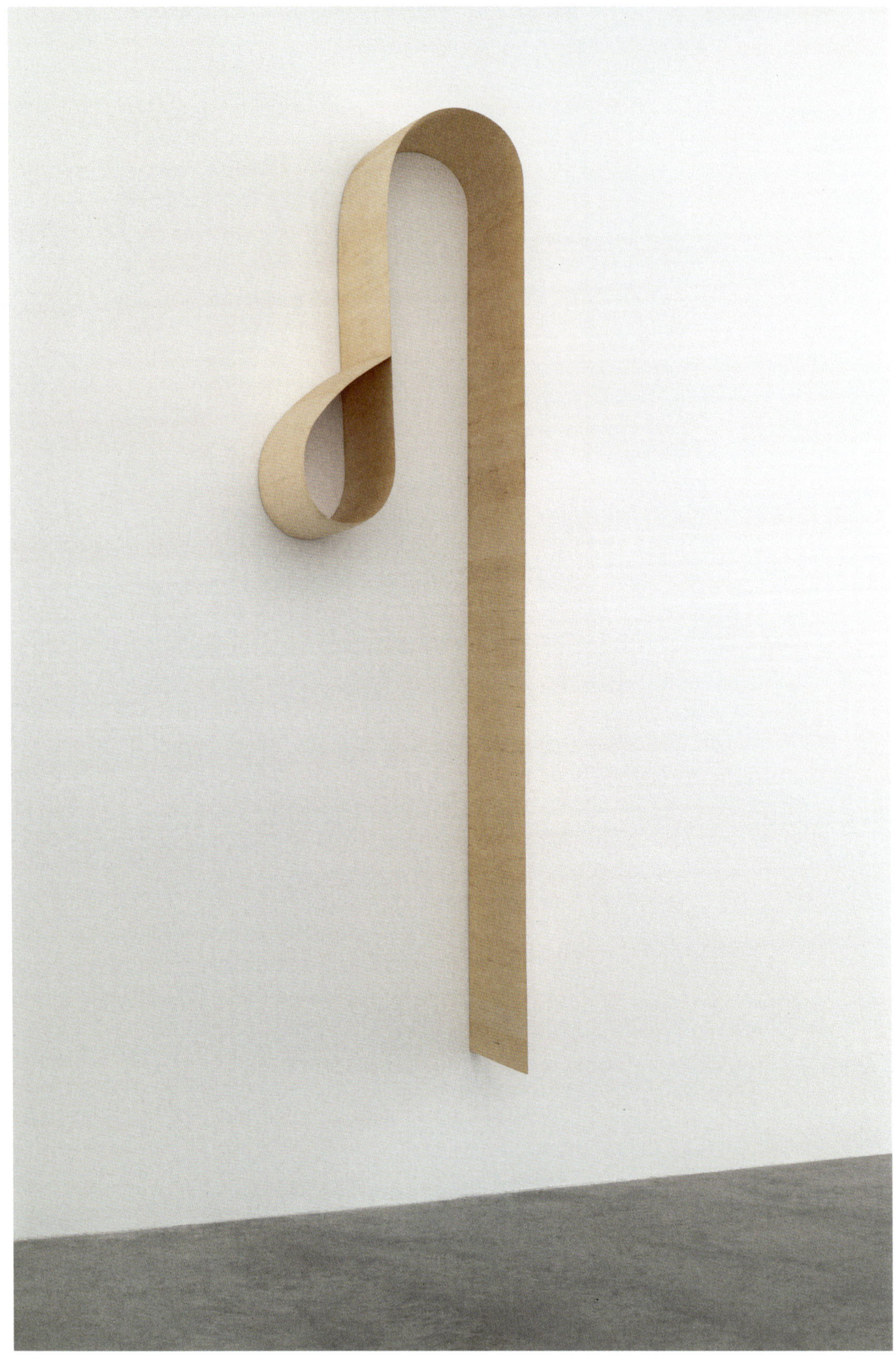

I value the referential quality of art, the fact that
a work can allude to things or states of being without
in any way representing them.   MARTIN PURYEAR

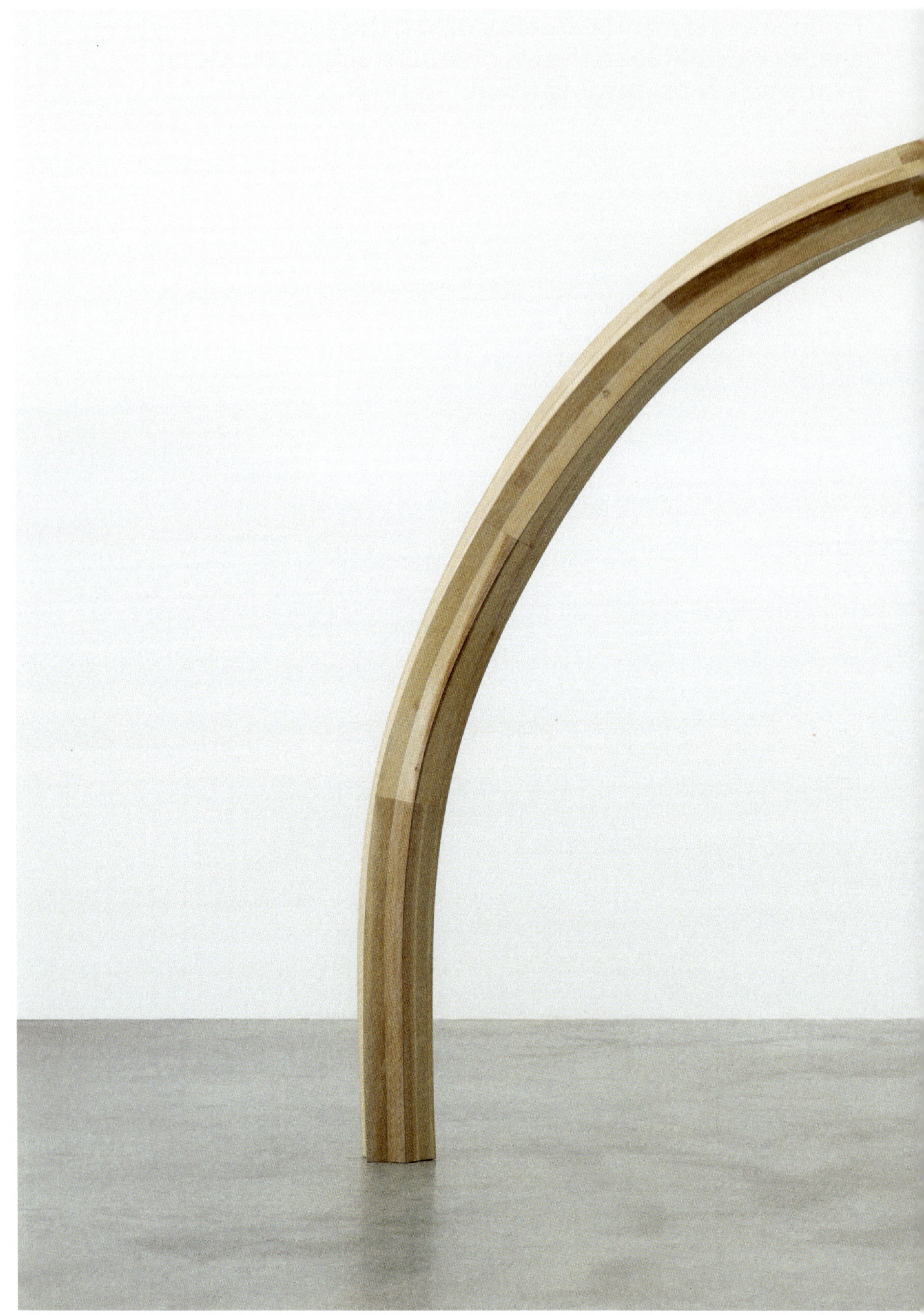

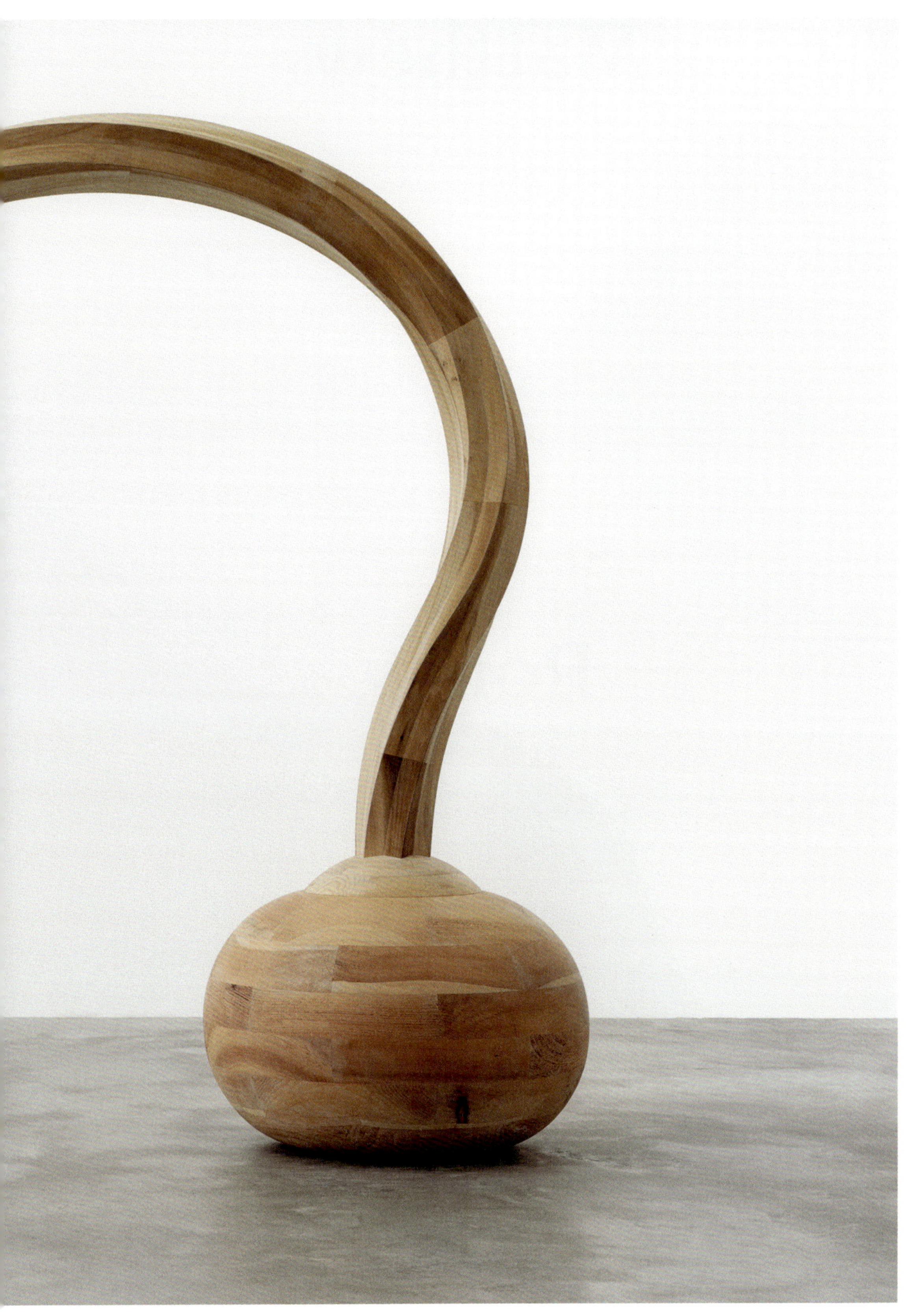

Matthew

Ronay

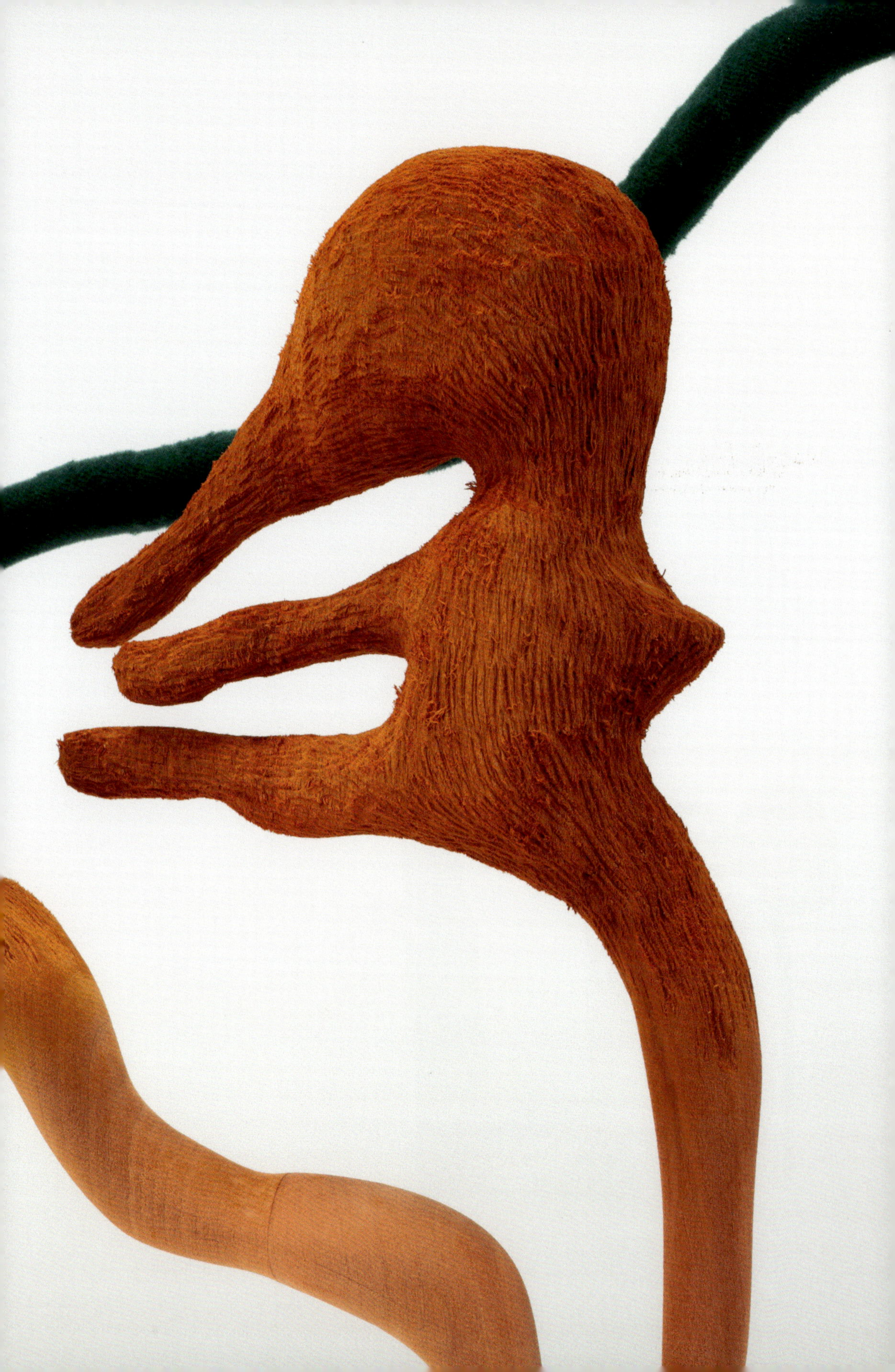

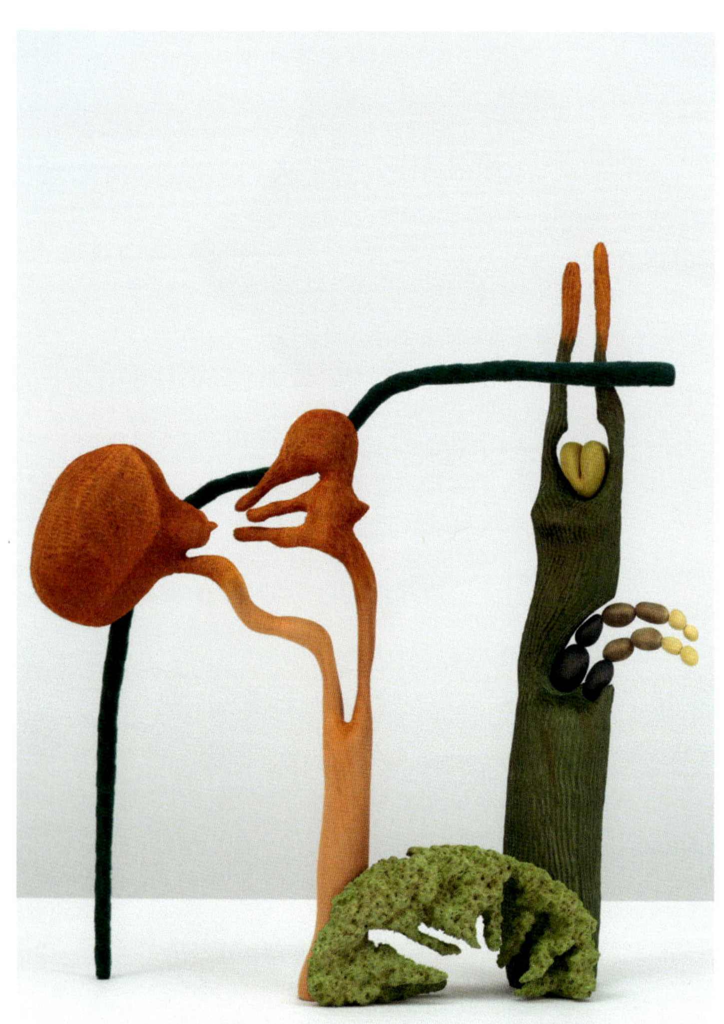

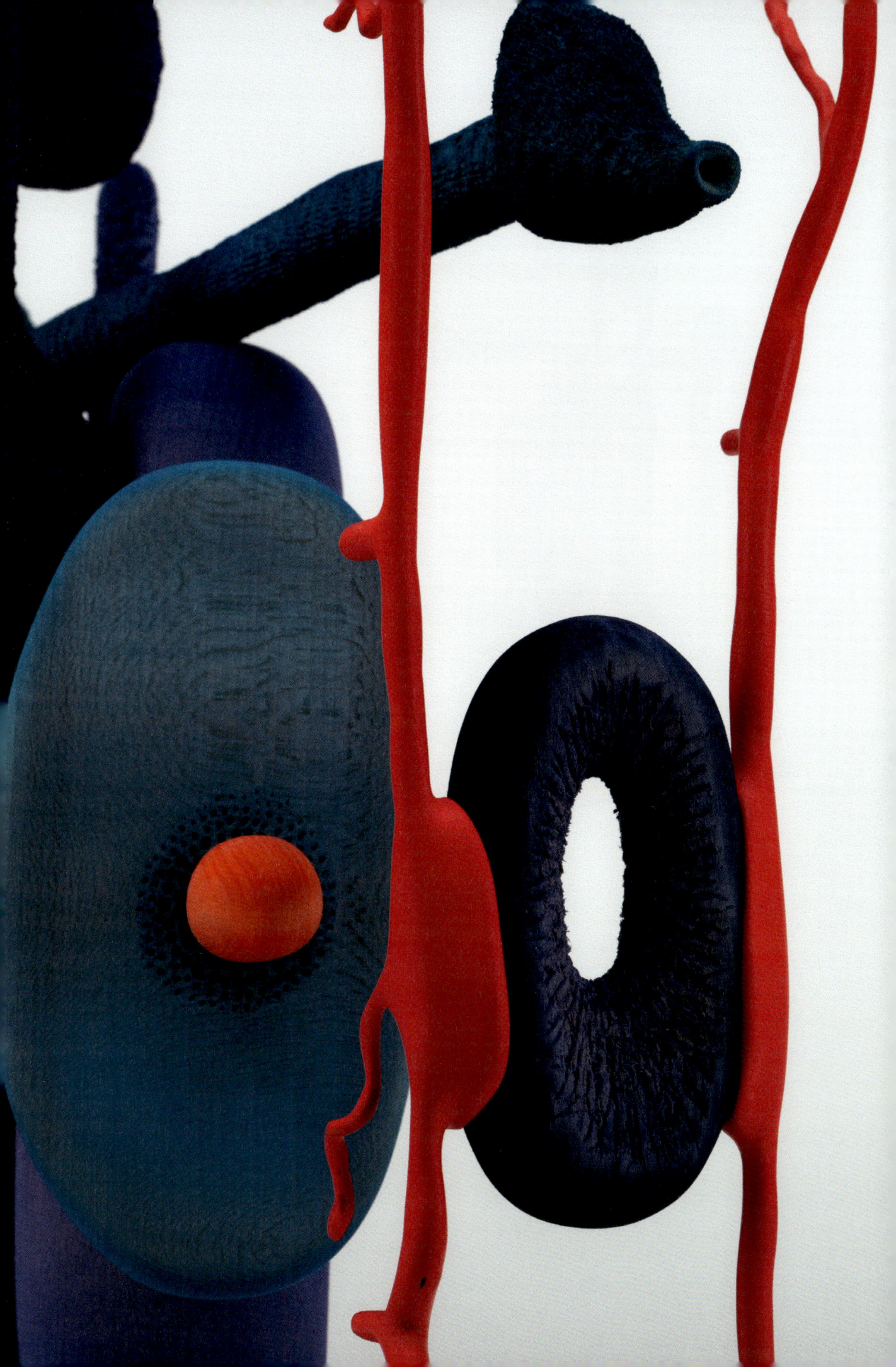

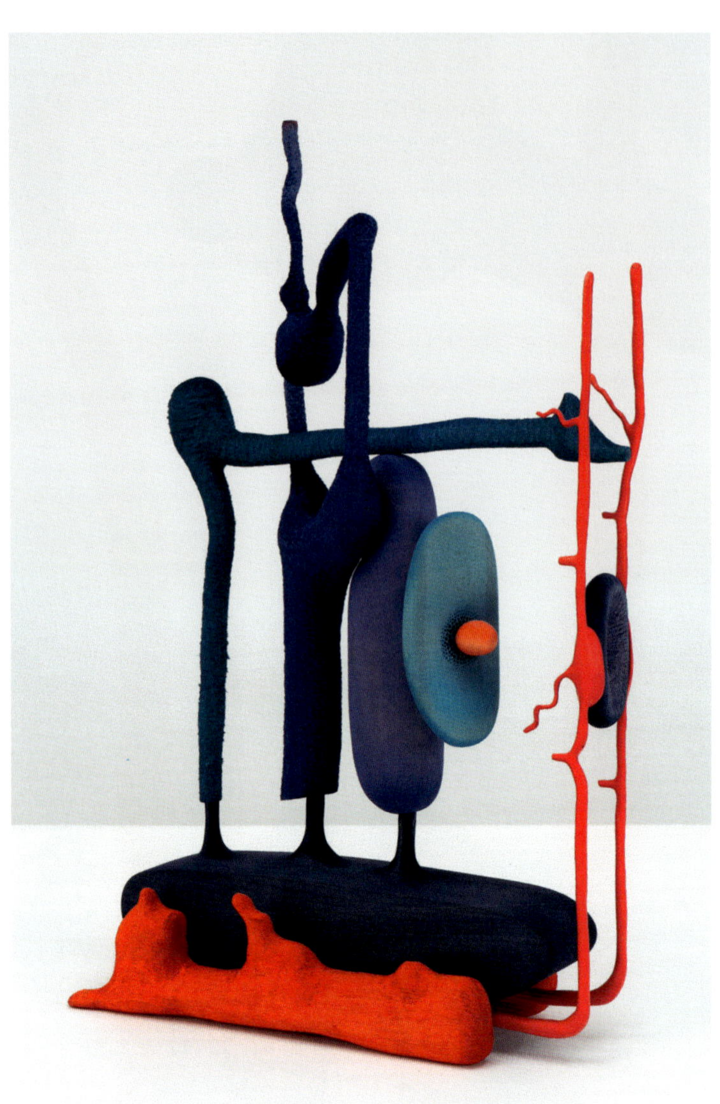

Brontes, Steropes, and Arges, 2023

Globules 2023
(detail)

174

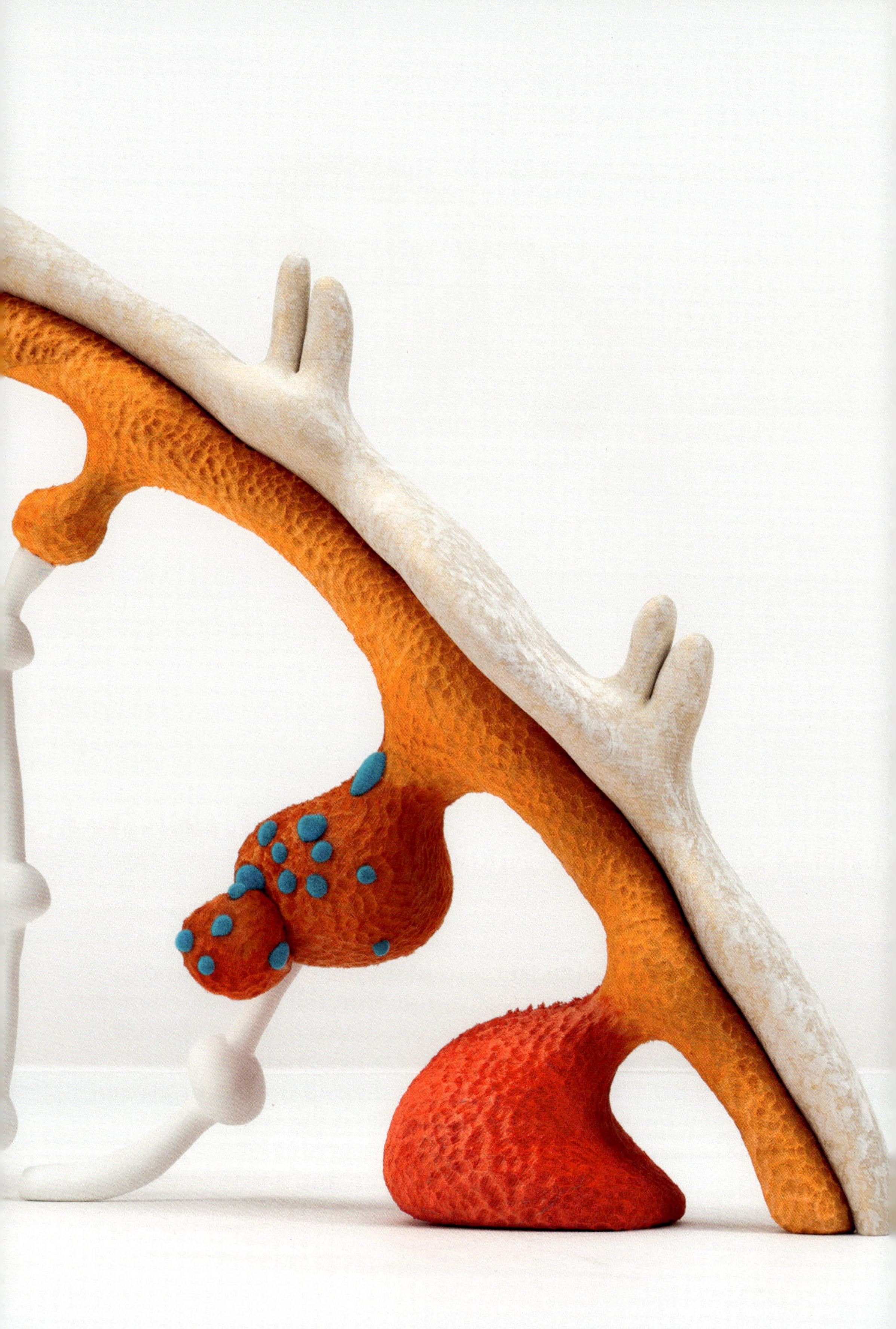

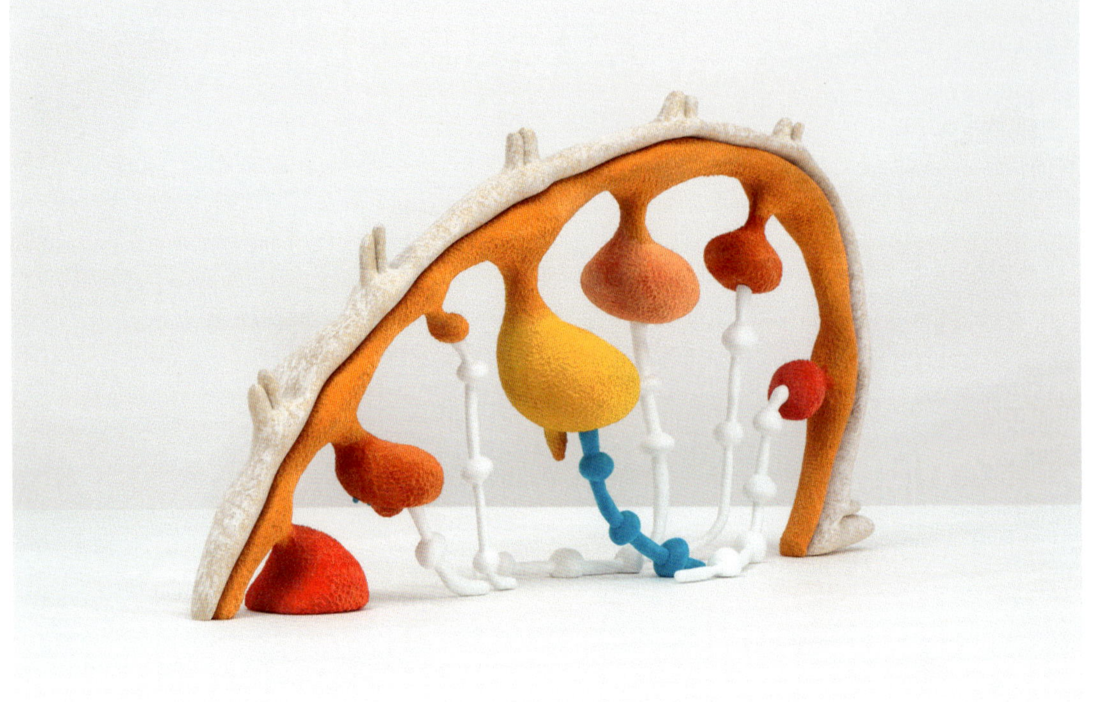

From fungus, I started to think of plant life in general and started to research all sorts of things that fell into my element of work, such as death, reproduction, disease, aging, sexual organs, orifices, peduncles, protuberances, mathematics, things of this sort. And I started to realize all these things that you think you invented, nature thought of them first. Beautiful textures and colors and divine geometries – just real brilliance of pattern, humor, theater, and a way in which nature embodies thoughts. MATTHEW RONAY

Third Instar,
2023

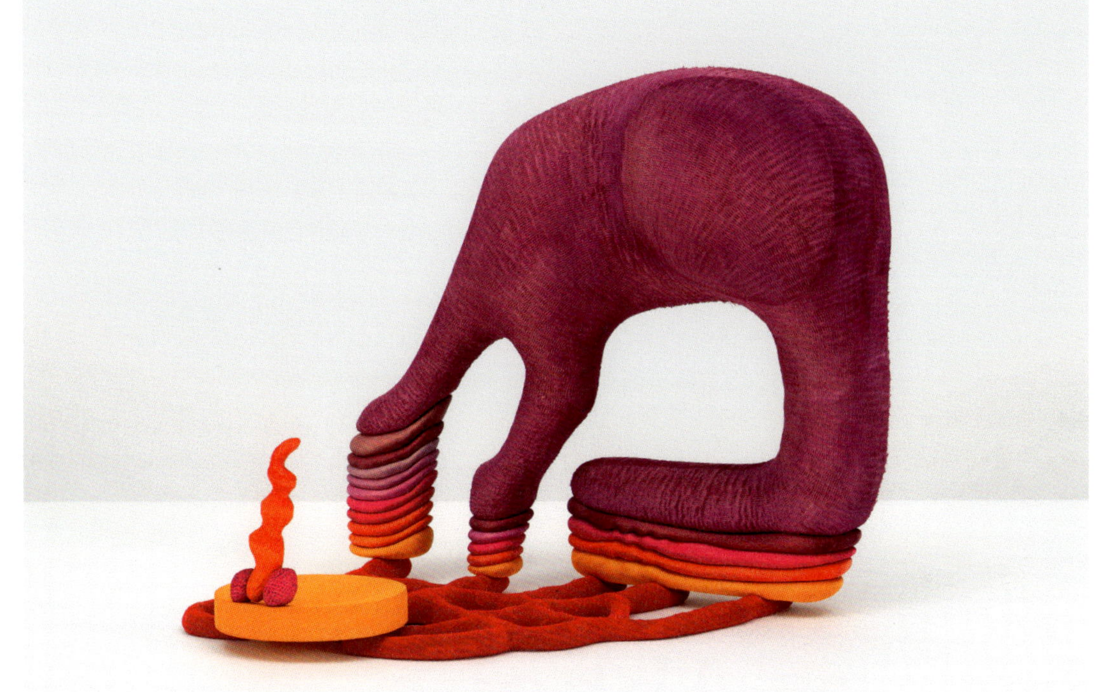

Teresa

Solar

Abboud

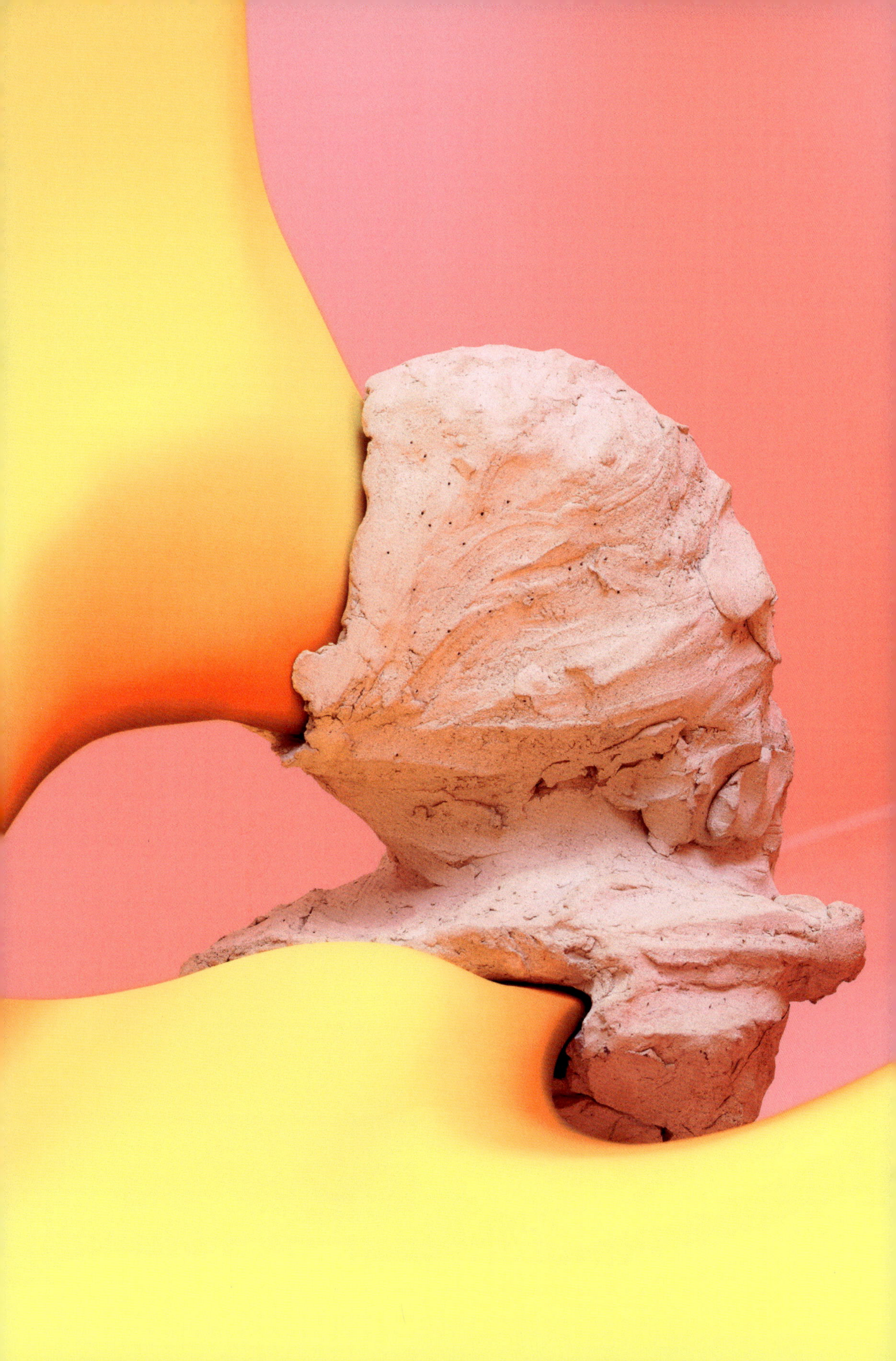

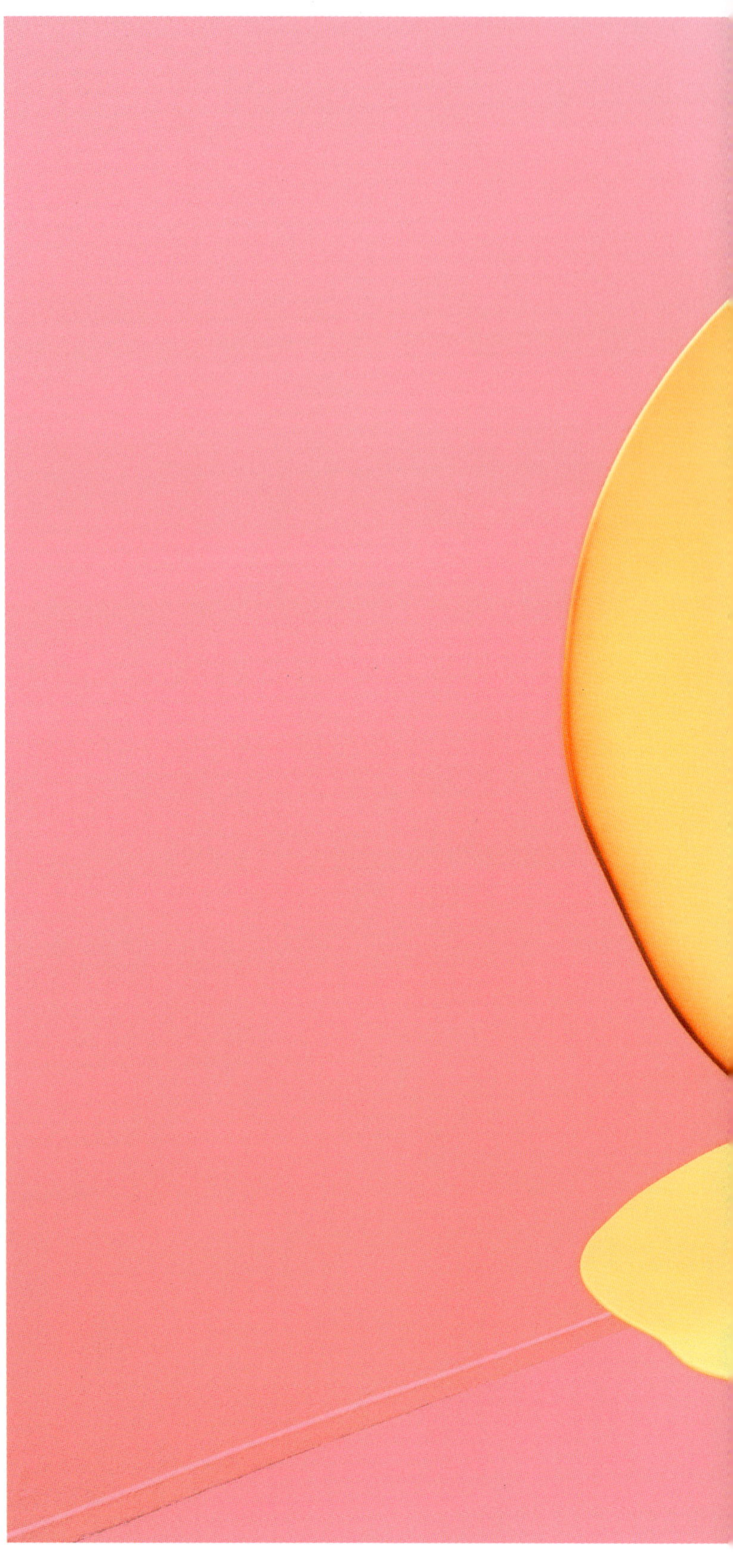

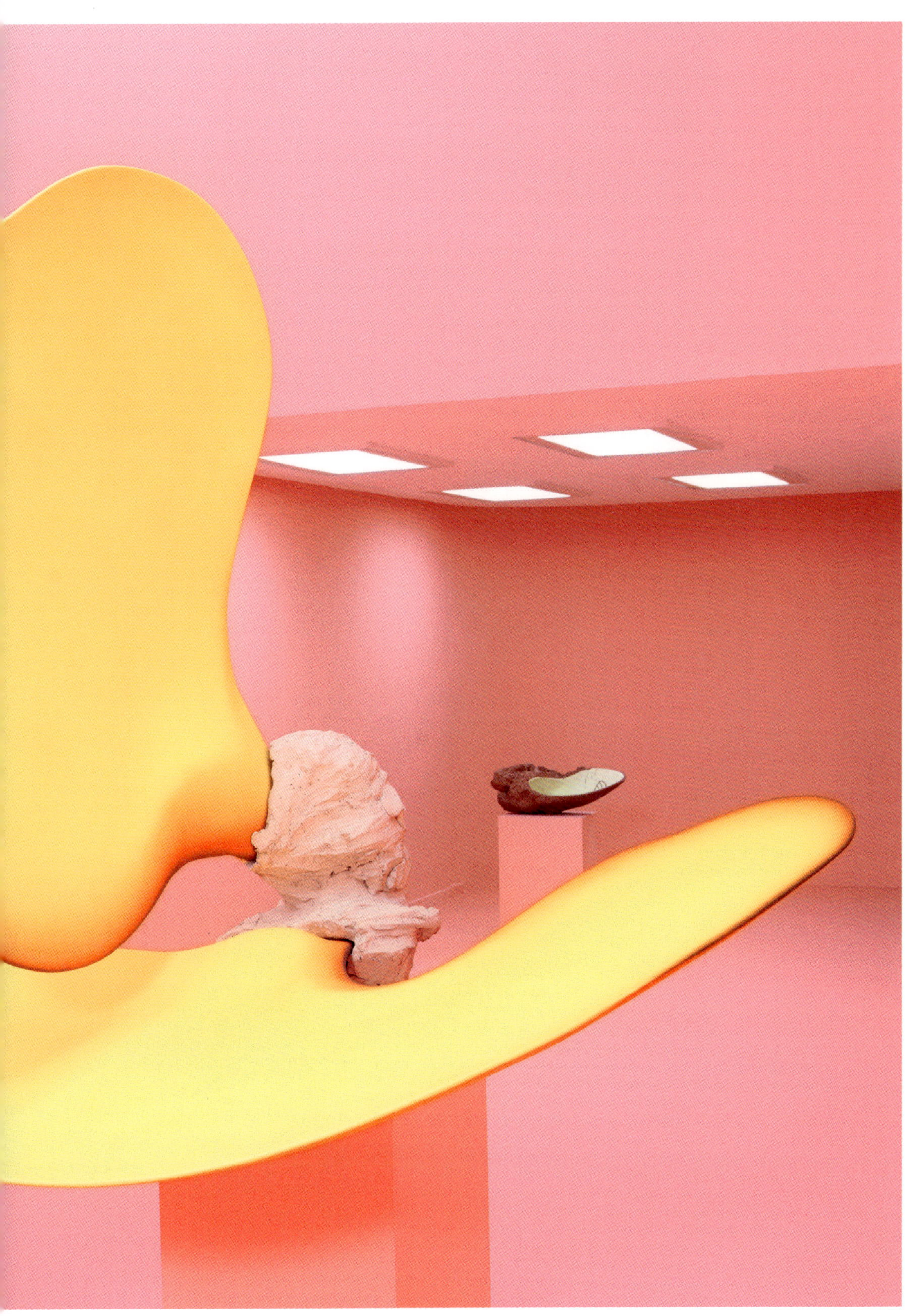

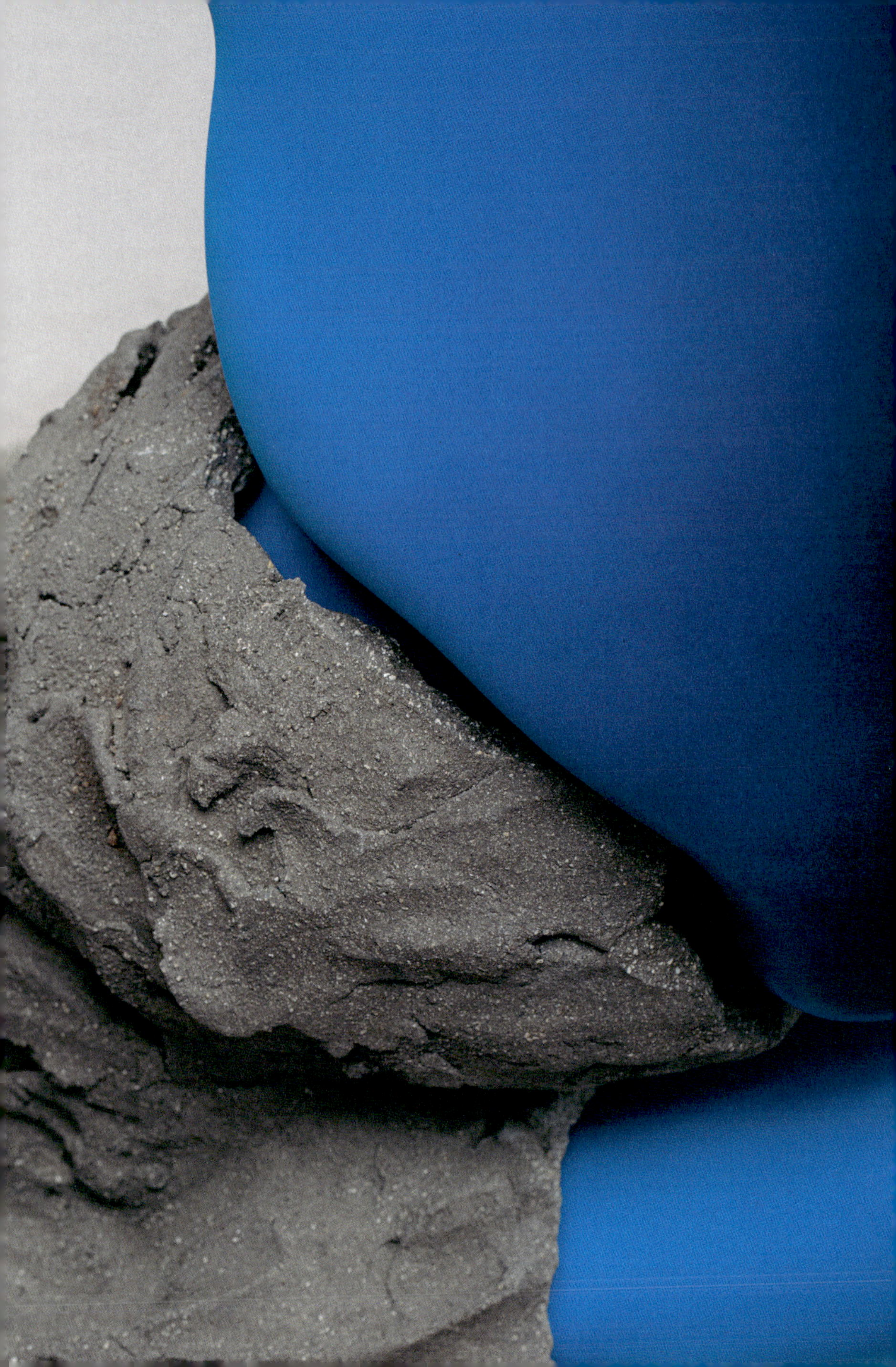

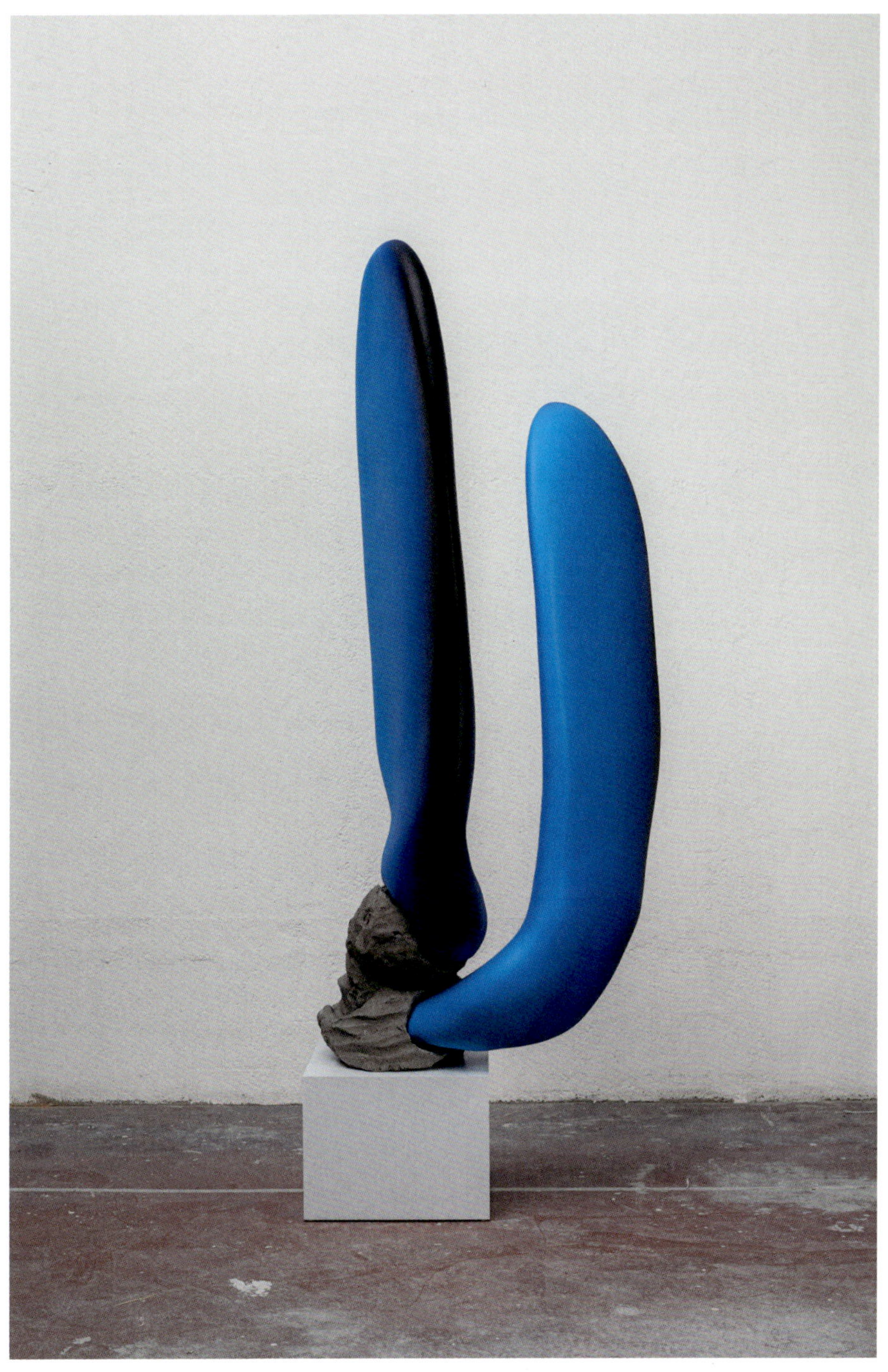

Tunnel Boring Machine,
2023

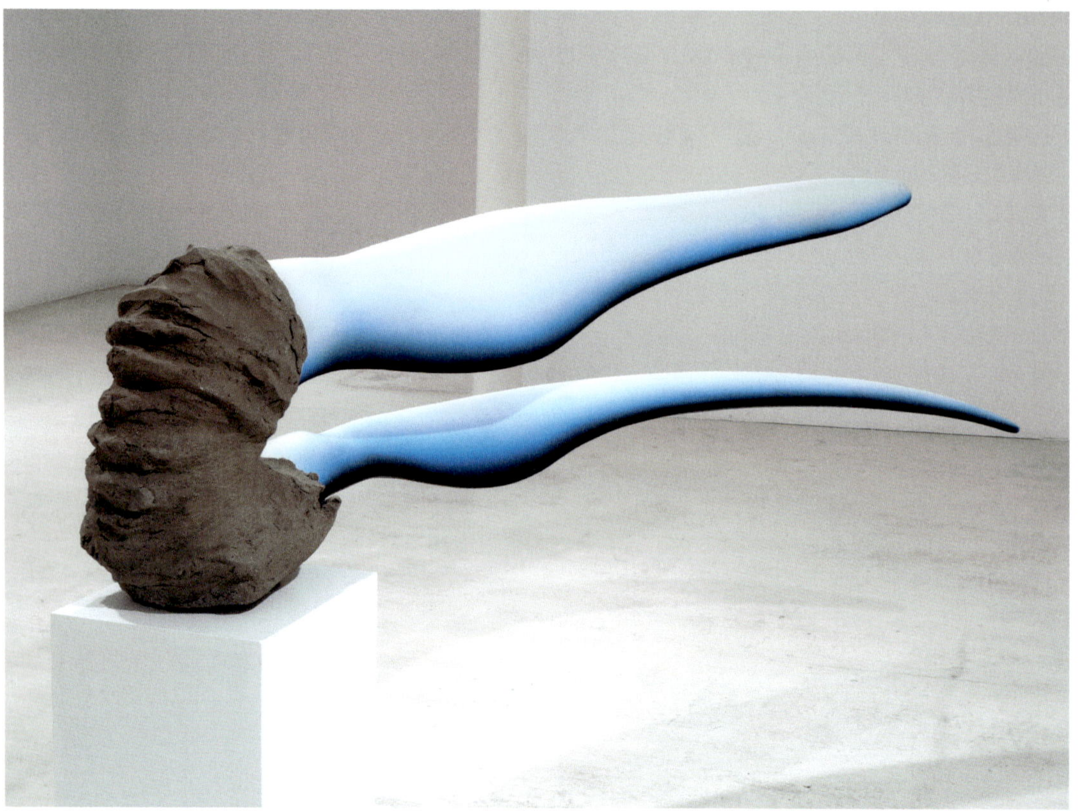

When I work with clay, I am always working with the idea of soil, the underground. It is a sort of macro representation of what lies beneath us and what in the end composes the underground. TERESA SOLAR ABBOUD

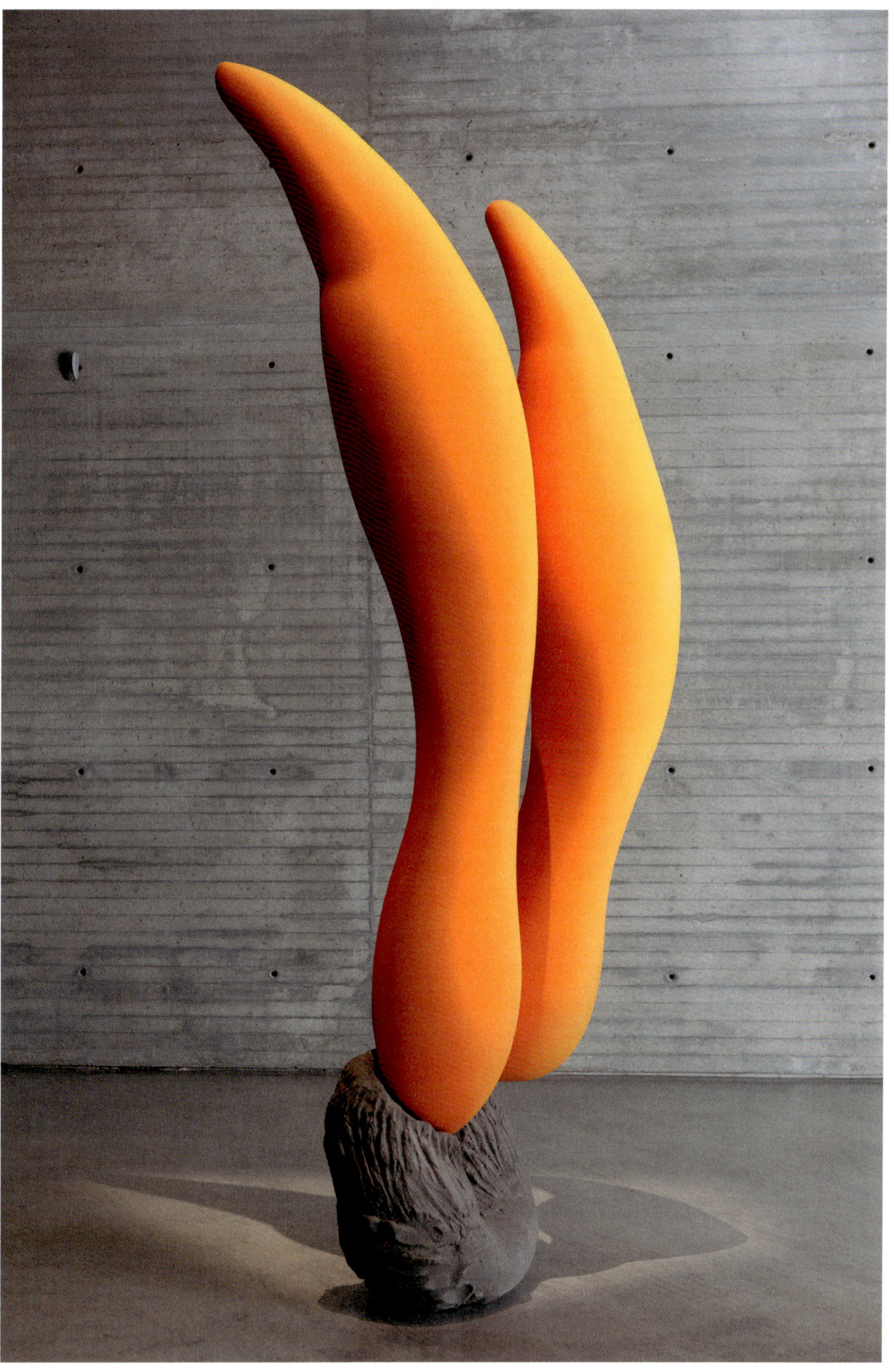

Franz

West

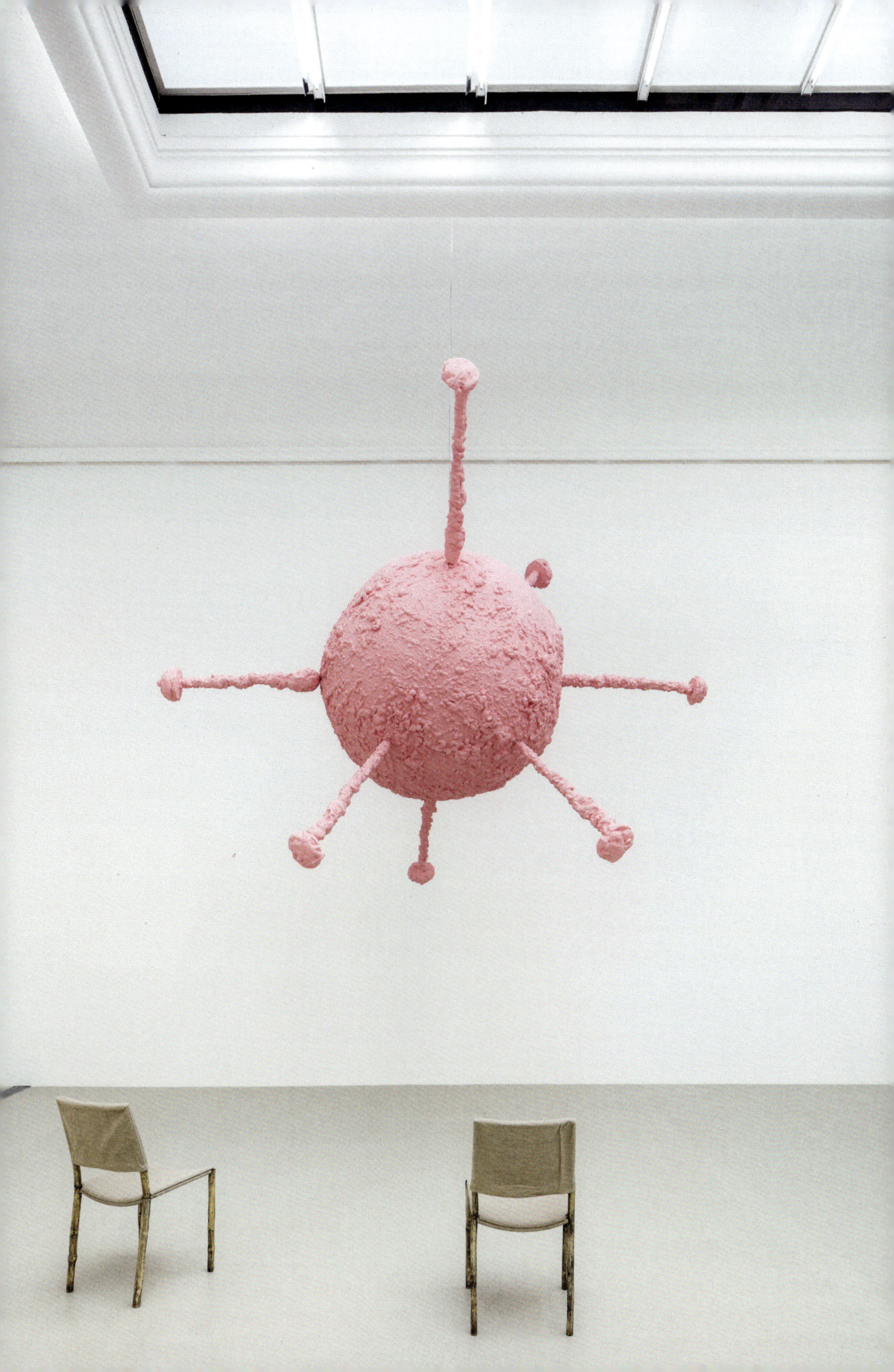

As a body, you stand or walk around the sculpture.
It's almost equivalent to your own corporeality,
to taking up space in one's own three-dimensionality
in a defined art space. As far as sculpture in the normal
sense is concerned, the viewer is more or less obliged
to engage in movement. There is something standing here
that you walk around, and perhaps the impression you
have of what is being presented also determines whether
the movement is quick or especially slow, depending
on whether you are really concentrating. FRANZ WEST

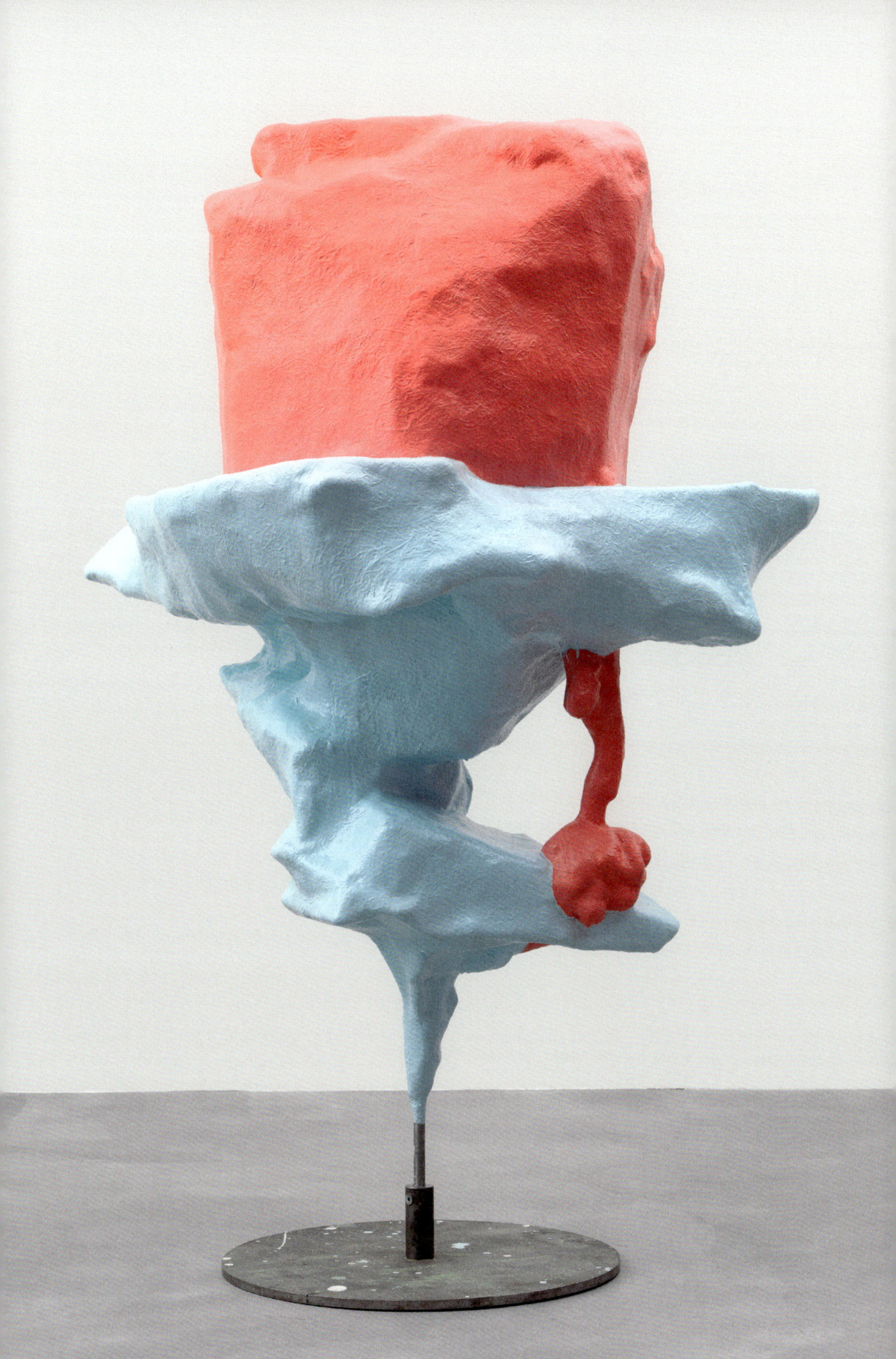

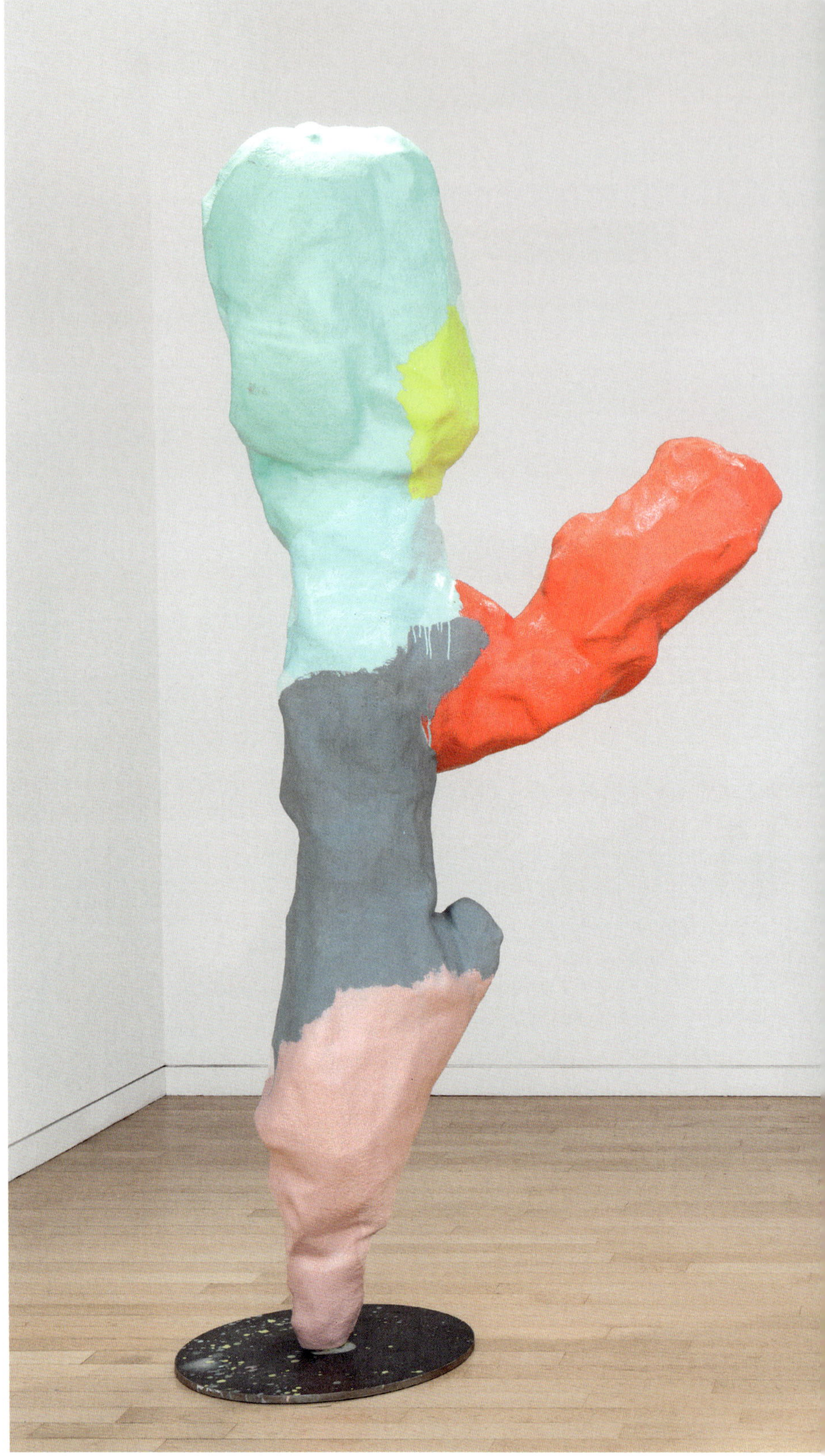

Kain naht Abel
(Kain approaching Abel), 2009

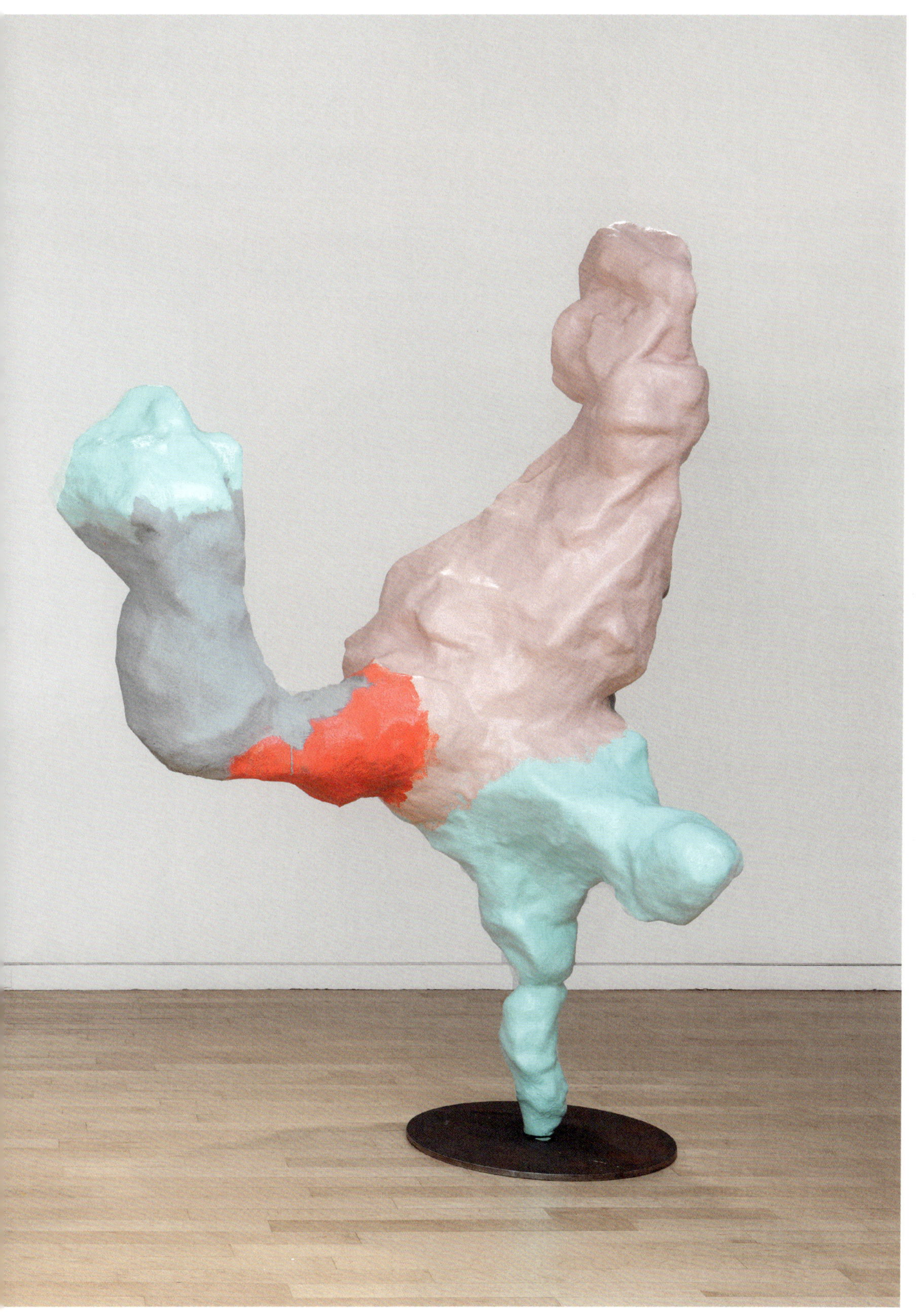

Ruth Asawa 194
Nairy Baghramian 196
Phyllida Barlow 198
Lynda Benglis 200
Michel Blazy 202
Paloma Bosquê 204
Olaf Brzeski 206
Choi Jeong Hwa 208
Tara Donovan 210
DRIFT 212
Eva Fàbregas 214
Holly Hendry 216
EJ Hill 218
Marguerite Humeau 220
Jean-Luc Moulène 222
Senga Nengudi 224
Ernesto Neto 226
Martin Puryear 228
Matthew Ronay 230
Teresa Solar Abboud 232
Franz West 234

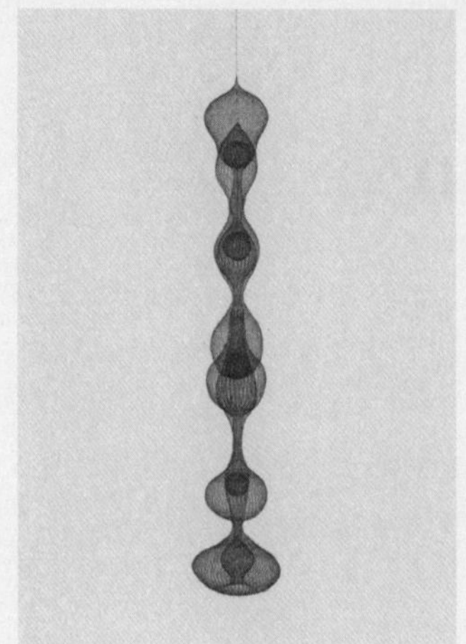

Untitled (S.065, Hanging Seven-Lobed, Multi-Layered Continuous Form within a Form with Spheres in the Second, Third, Fourth, and Sixth Lobes), c. 1960–63
Oxidised copper and brass wire
238.8×44.5×44.5

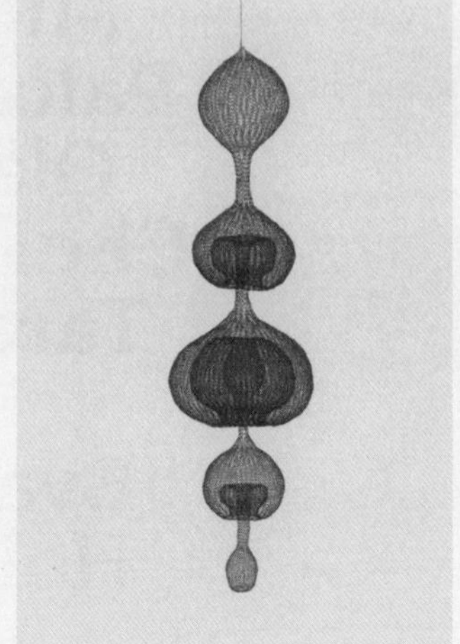

Untitled (S.142, Hanging Five-Lobed, Multi-Layered Continuous Form within a Foarm), 1990
Oxidised copper wire
137.2×35.6×35.6

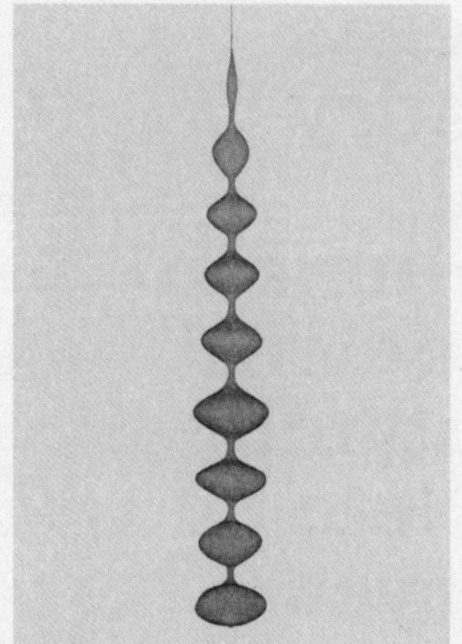

Untitled (S.154, Hanging Nine-Lobed, Single-Layered Continuous Form), c. 1958
Monel wire
281.9×38.1×38.1

The idea is to do it simply, and you end up with a shape. That shape comes out of working with the wire. You don't think ahead of time, *This is what I want.* You work it out as you go along. You make the line, a two-dimensional line, then you go into space, and you have a three-dimensional piece. It's like a drawing in space … The piece does not hide anything. You can show inside and outside, and inside and outside are connected. Everything is connected, continuous.[1]   R. A.

1   Ruth Asawa quoted in Jacqueline Hoefer, 'Ruth Asawa: A Working Life', in *The Sculpture of Ruth Asawa: Contours in the Air* (San Francisco and Oakland, CA: Fine Arts Museum of San Francisco/University of California Press, 2007), p. 36

Ruth Asawa

Born 1926 in Norwalk, California, USA
Died 2013 in San Francisco, USA

A variety of origin stories have been proposed for the looped wire sculptures Ruth Asawa first made in her early 20s and was still fashioning decades later. Asawa remembered sitting on the back of horse-drawn farm equipment in California as a child, drawing hourglass shapes with her toes in the dirt as they rolled along, shapes she felt resurfaced in the sculptures. She also recalled spending a summer in Mexico as a Black Mountain College student, where local craftsmen taught her how to create the looped wire baskets they used. Finally, it has been suggested the sculptures were influenced by the time she spent in an internment camp for Japanese Americans during the Second World War, where she saw adult internees weaving camouflage nets.

Whatever their inspiration, the sculptures are utterly original. Combining an organic simplicity with the pure geometry of the Bauhaus, they appear to float, defying gravity, their sinuous, biomorphic forms simultaneously solid and transparent, like drops of water or seed pods caught in sunlight. When lit, their shadows are almost as substantial as the works themselves. Their construction involved hours of repetitive toil that left Asawa's fingers bleeding, but was nevertheless something she could do at home, surrounded by her small children.

The three works included in the exhibition span 30 years. The earliest, *Untitled* (S.154) (c. 1958, p. 45), is the closest to the pure 'drawing in space' Asawa refers to in the quote opposite, its elegant lobes enclosing only emptiness. Yet *Untitled* (S.065) (c. 1960–63, p. 43) is already playing with perceptions of depth and solidity, its shapes perceived through and within other shapes, a dynamic still being explored in *Untitled* (S.142) (1990, p. 44). What Asawa sought, and appeared to achieve, was the impossible: to create forms that were 'inside and outside at the same time'.[2]   JAMES ATTLEE

2   Aiko Cuneo, 'Interview with Ruth Asawa' (20 October 2003), unpaginated. Ruth Asawa Papers, Department of Special Collections, Stanford University Libraries, Stanford, CA

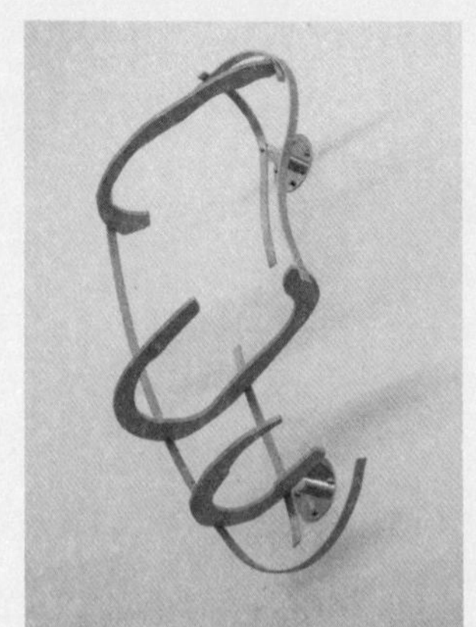

Chin Up (First Fitting A), 2016 (detail)
Waxed wood, polished
and lacquered aluminium
122×85×80

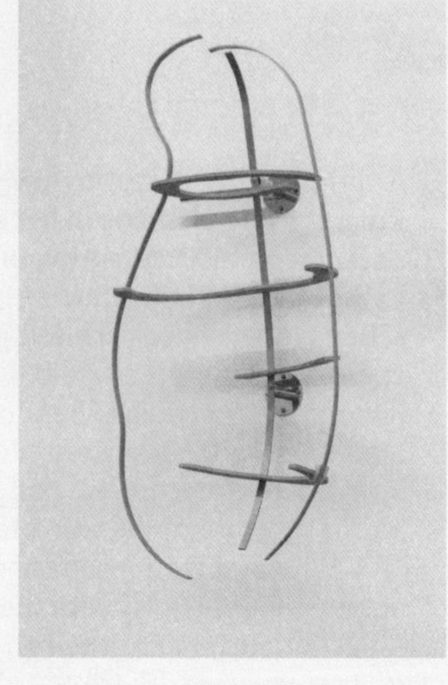

Chin Up (First Fitting C), 2016 (detail)
Waxed wood, polished
and lacquered aluminium
278×122×87

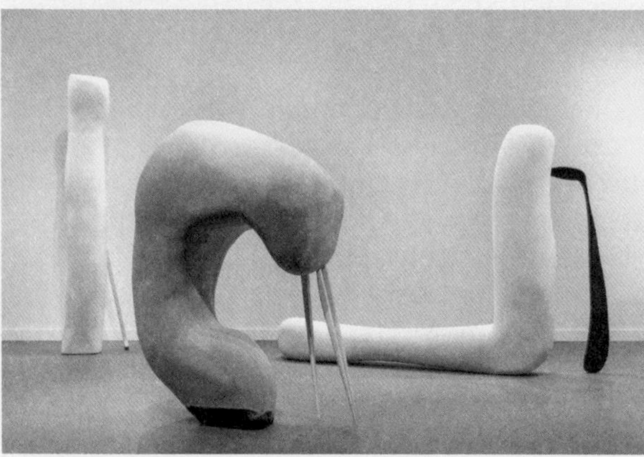

From left to right:
Stay Downers (Maverick); *Stay Downers
(Scallywag)*; *Stay Downers (Slowpoke)*, 2017
Polyurethane,
lacquered aluminium, silicone
Dimensions variable

My sculpture is aware of its performative aspects and potentials; it is able to move and make space[1] N. B.

1 Nairy Baghramian and Paulina Pobocha,
   'Nairy Baghramian: Ambivalent Abstraction.
   In Conversation with Paulina Pobocha', *Ocula*
   (28 August 2020), https://ocula.com/magazine
   /conversations/nairy-baghramian-on-ambivalent
   -abstraction/ (accessed 11 November 2023)

Nairy Baghramian

Born 1971 in Isfahan, Iran
Lives and works, since 1984,
in Berlin, Germany

Nairy Baghramian's sculpture embraces a range of processes and sites, and harnesses an associative approach to abstraction. Her description of her works as capable of movement could stem from Baghramian's background in theatre and dance; however, it also emerges from her critical questioning of how sculpture fits into the world. Baghramian's work connects recent histories of sculpture with wider modes of production including cooking and craft, fashion and cosmetics, design and commerce. She also examines how sculpture can engage with audiences, institutions and wider socio-political issues.

The series *Stay Downers* (2016–ongoing) reflects many of Baghramian's sculptural concerns. Within the series, the individual work *Stay Downers* (2017, pp. 56–57) comprises a grouping of cloud-like beings which occupy the gallery with anthropomorphic theatricality. Supported by various props, these suggestive forms assume a variety of crouched, leaning and rising postures. Their arrested motion alludes perhaps to the title of the work: the German word *Sitzengebliebene*, a colloquial expression for students required to repeat a year at school. Baghramian's embrace of wall and floor and engagement with issues of gravity and balance recall postminimalism, while the delectable pastel colour choices are reminiscent of mid-century design.

A sense of irresolution and provisionality inhabits *Chin Up (First Fitting)* (2016, pp. 51–55). Its skeletal forms have been assembled with the industrial precision more commonly seen in the worlds of fabrication and engineering, and the titular reference to a 'first fitting' invites the viewer to mentally complete them, asking us to reflect on issues of progress, economy and the role of the artist. Yet the works also evoke the body, both in the resemblance of these flowing frameworks to medical prostheses and orthodontic devices designed to guide and align our limbs, bones and teeth, and in the kidney-like shapes each work delineates.

Each of these pieces reflects on the relationships between sculpture, our bodies and the world. As Baghramian has explained: 'I am interested in the thin membrane that separates the inside from the outside in physical and social spaces. It's about inclusion or exclusion ... For me, the thin skin, the membrane, is often overlooked and underrepresented, but it is the thin, permeable, vulnerable skin that I value so much.'[2]   NATALIE RUDD

2   Bruna Roccasalva (ed.), *Nairy Baghramian: Misfits*, exh. cat., Gallerie d'Arte Moderna, Milan, 2022, p. 59

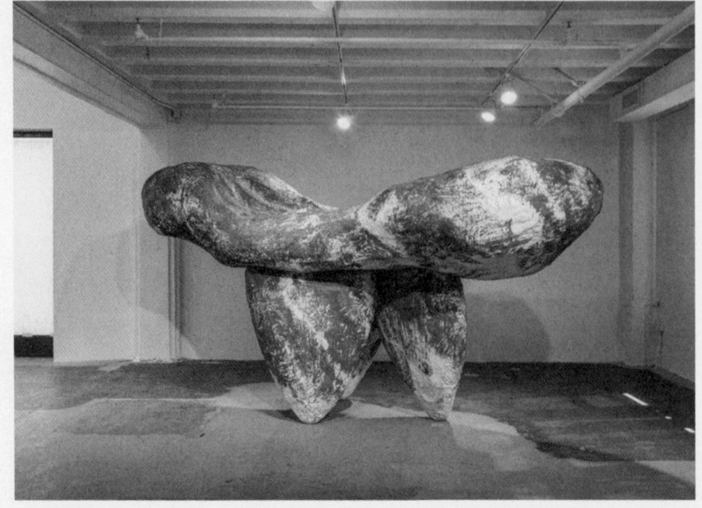

untitled: girl ii; 2019, 2019–20
Steel, timber, wire netting, polystyrene,
polyfoam board, scrim, plaster, paint, cement, PVA
250×410×200

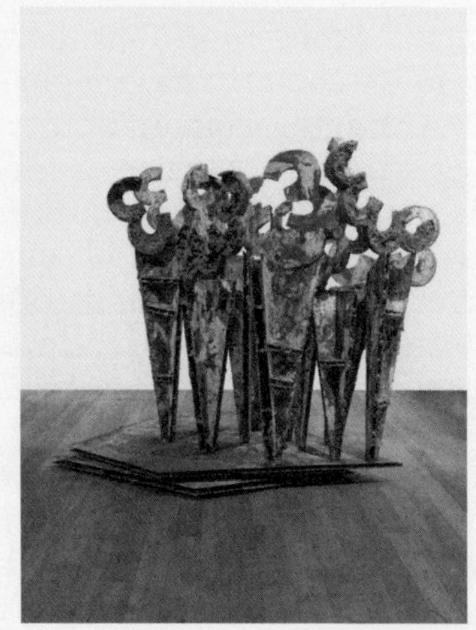

untitled: modernsculpture; 2022, 2022
Steel, filler, PVA, paint, polyurethane foam,
spray paint, sand, paint stripper
250×220×250

Maybe I don't think enough about beauty in my work because I'm so curious about other qualities, abstract qualities of time, weight, balance, rhythm; collapse and fatigue versus the more upright dynamic notions of maybe posture … the state that something might be in.[1] P. B.

1 'Phyllida Barlow: an artistic outsider who has finally come inside', *The Guardian* (28 April 2016), https://www.theguardian.com /artanddesign/2016/apr/28/phyllida-barlow -artist-success-2017-venice-biennale (accessed 6 November 2023)

Phyllida Barlow

Born 1944 in Newcastle upon Tyne, UK
Died 2023 in London, UK

Describing her abstract, sprawling, space-invading sculptural interventions as 'obstacles to be navigated, protagonists that I feel I'm encountering,'[2] Phyllida Barlow observed: 'They're actually looking at the flukes and the chances of how things encounter each other physically in the world.'[3] These epic, overwhelming structures which seem so awkward and precarious – built from cheap materials and often apparently slightly off-balance – challenged viewers to become active participants in their investigations of space. The complexities and improvisatory nature of their construction meant that not only the experience of the completed installations but also the act of their creation became performative; they were assembled with the help of assistants and the artist's role was like that of a theatrical director or an orchestral conductor.

Following a spate of creating vast space-filling installations both in the UK and abroad, including presentations at Tate Britain (2014) and the Venice Biennale (2017), Barlow's focus turned to the making of single objects which offer a very different, more reflective, visual and emotional experience. Unlike the ephemeral installations which spoke so urgently of urban environments and were events in themselves, the two autonomous works shown here imply a sense of precarious rootedness. *untitled: girl ii; 2019* (2019–20, pp. 59–61), a massive anthropomorphic boulder-like form with three hefty legs, and *untitled: modernsculpture; 2022* (2022, p. 63), inspired by the memory of an artwork glimpsed in Kyiv in 2012, suggest the space of landscape and things within it: a neolithic dolmen or a clump of trees. But these more contained sculptures also retain many of the qualities of Barlow's site-specific works: a predilection for low-grade materials that will 'do the job as efficiently and expediently as possible';[4] a sense of humour and absurdity verging on satire; a recognition that gravity, in the physical sense, is the most powerful issue. 'Oddly enough,' she once said, 'sculpture, despite its physicality, constantly disappears. You walk past it and it's gone. You come back to it and you discover it in a new way.'[5]   HELEN LUCKETT

2   Oliver Basciano, 'Phyllida Barlow', *ArtReview* (May 2010), https://artreview.com/feature-may-2010-phyllida-barlow/ (accessed 15 October 2023)

3   Ben Luke, 'Phyllida Barlow interview: "A cul-de-sac has the claustrophobia of suburbia"', *Evening Standard* (20 February 2019), https://www.standard.co.uk/culture/phyllida-barlow-interview-royal-academy-cul-de-sac-a4071436.html (accessed 15 October 2023)

4   Maggie Crosland/Patricia Smithen/Denis Stolyarov, 'Interview: Phyllida Barlow', Courtauld Institute (June 2017), https://courtauld.ac.uk/research/research-resources/publications/immeditations-postgraduate-journal/immediations-online/2017-2/interview-phyllida-barlow (accessed 14 October 2023)

5   Phyllida Barlow: 'An Age of Fallen Monuments', Louisiana Channel video interview (20 May 2014), www.youtube.com/watch?v=e86iiVjPDsY (accessed 1 November 2023)

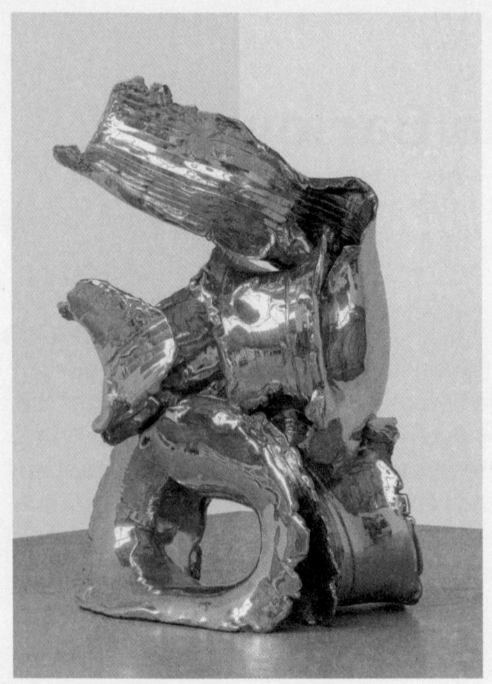

Power Tower, 2019
Everdur bronze (golden)
228.6×179.4×172.2

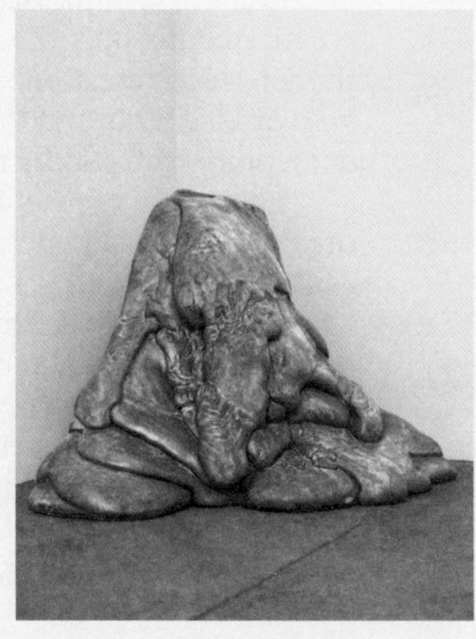

Quartered Meteor, 1969, cast 1975
Lead and steel on steel base
150×168×158

If you think about each one of my works as a body, that body is always in motion.[1] L. B.

1   Lynda Benglis/Andrew Bonacina,'Interview:
     Andrew Bonacina in conversation with
     Lynda Benglis', in Andrew Bonacina/Nora
     Lawrence/Bibiana Obler, *Lynda Benglis*
     (London: Phaidon, 2022), p. 11

200

Lynda Benglis

Born 1941 in Lake Charles, Louisiana, USA
Lives and works in New York and
Santa Fe, USA; Kastellorizo, Greece;
and Ahmedabad, India

In 1973, while teaching at CalArts in Los Angeles, Lynda Benglis took up scuba-diving, fascinated by the feeling of buoyancy and by the underwater forms she encountered. This anecdotal information makes sense of her sculptures, which often feel subject to otherworldly forces, even on solid ground. In the late 1960s and early '70s Benglis worked with liquid materials such as latex and polyurethane to create solid forms that played with sculptural assumptions of gravity and weightlessness. Her early latex floor pieces were flat spills of intermingling colours, reminiscent of an iridescent petrol leak or a run-off of melted ice cream. Polyurethane, a substance with the viscosity of lava, was piled up in layers and heaped in corners, before evolving into spectacular wall-mounted cascades.

Benglis later cast one of her polyurethane corner pieces, *King of Flot* (1969), in lead – a process that destroyed the original work. The resulting form, *Quartered Meteor* (1969, cast 1975, pp. 68–69), quite literally weighs a tonne, and occupies the corner of the gallery space as if it has struck the earth in a fiery fall from outer space. But a sense of fluidity belies its dead weight: the metal appears soft, even molten, as if – cornered – it has reached a temporary resting place, mid-flow, and might resume its liquidity once more. The artist specifies that the work be installed away from the wall, 'like a muffin coming out of its tin', humorously depreciating the acute difficulty of manoeuvring an enormous lump of lead with a baking metaphor that evokes the queasy prospect of ingesting the oversized excretory form.

Benglis's earliest experiments with knotted forms also occurred around this time. She made a series of wall-mounted sculptures in which she wrested tubes of wire mesh, covered with plaster-soaked cotton, into tangled submission. Over subsequent decades, Benglis has extended these formal experiments to glass and ceramics, continuing to test materials against the physical strength and technical skill of her own body. The resulting forms hold the charge of these exchanges, as well as a physical relationship to the artist's body through their scale and material resistance.

In *Power Tower* (2019, pp. 65–66), one of a recent series of large-scale bronze sculptures cast from digitally enlarged ceramics, the impossibility of a physical encounter between the artist's body and molten metal transposes the work into the realms of speculation and gesture. Dance-like twists and arcs refer to the physicality of the act of making, but also involve the spectator, whose body is stretched and morphed by the sculpture's reflective curves. Whereas Benglis's early sculptures contained the physicality of her encounters with materials, here the body is mobilised in the act of looking.   KATIE GUGGENHEIM

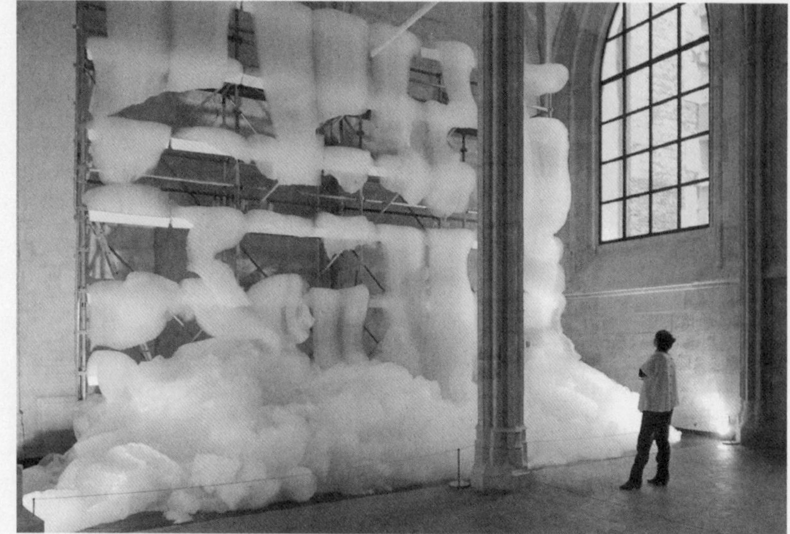

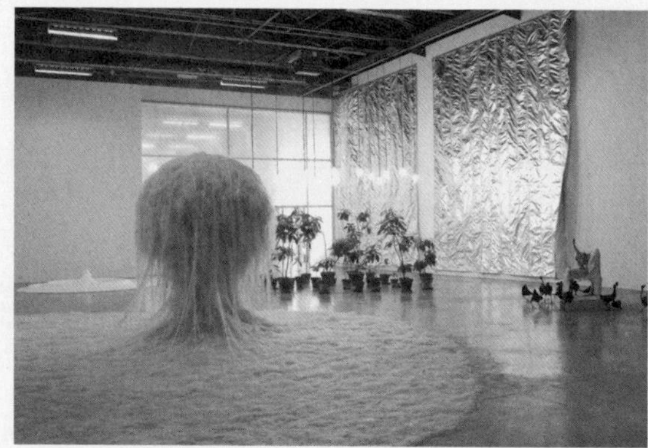

I consider my sculptures as living beings. My gesture
as a sculptor often consists of triggering a process that takes
shape on its own; I try to create the right conditions for
a material to perform. Soft materials interest me because
they are in movement, their form depends on themselves
and my degree of control is limited.[1]   M. B.

1   Michel Blazy on *Bouquet Final*,
    https://highlike.org/text/michel-blazy-2
    (accessed 19 September 2023)

Michel Blazy

Born 1966 in Monaco
Lives and works in Île Saint-Denis,
Paris, France

From the start of his career in the early 1990s, Michel Blazy has worked with ephemeral and perishable materials, creating paintings, sculptures and environments featuring the unremarkable stuff of daily life in a cycle of decay and regeneration. His frescoes, made with puréed vegetables, generate patterns as they putrefy; sculptures evolved from discarded trainers, laptops and jumpers sprout miniature gardens; floor pieces that begin as wastelands of instant mashed potato or beer-soaked carpets develop colourful oases of mould, or become festooned with the tracks of drunken snails. Chance and time are crucial agents in his work; he describes his own part in these acts of transformation as 'manipulations or gestures that do not belong to sculpture but to gardening, cooking and everyday life: cutting, folding, mixing, coating, tearing etc.'[2] In the case of *Patman 2* (2006, p. 74) he tipped an avalanche of soya noodles over a wooden frame, added food colouring and waited to see what happened. The result is a sort of supernatural vision – part atomic mushroom cloud, part living haystack – in a state of perpetual mutation.

Blazy refers to his artworks as 'experiments'; he gets to know them intimately whilst tending them and witnessing their reactions to different situations over time. In the mid-1990s, he began experimenting with foam, patiently observing what he calls 'the eccentric movement of matter'. Starting with simple ensembles – a bucket, a straw and some washing-up liquid that becomes a foaming fountain, or a bottle of frozen beer calculated to erupt at a certain moment – he moved on to more ambitious works including dumpsters which exude apparently solid clouds of froth. *Bouquet Final* (2012, pp. 71–73) takes this a stage further, creating an entire wall of foam which constantly produces baroque festoons and curls of lather, which grow, mutate and eventually disintegrate almost imperceptibly, like a cascade in suspended animation. Blazy cautions that these infinitesimal movements 'at the threshold of perception' take time to notice; this ultra-slow performance – a 'bouquet final' or 'final flourish' – is both unpredictable and a constant source of surprise.   HELEN LUCKETT

2   Lise Guéhenneux, 'A Meeting with Michel
Blazy', *Crash Magazine* (13 March 2020),
www.crash.fr/a-meeting-with-michel-blazy/
(accessed 14 September 2023)

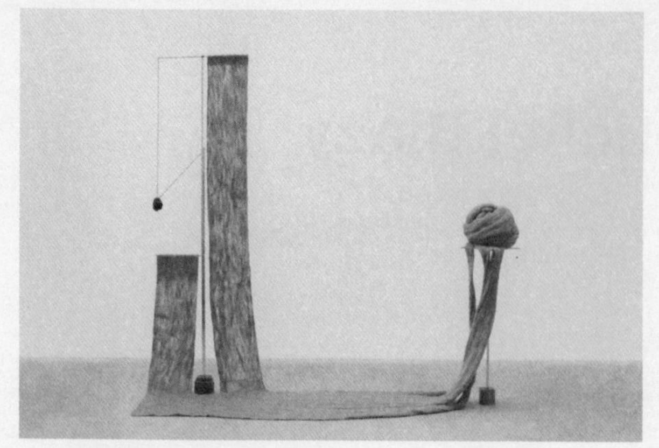

Two Stones, 2017
Lead sheet, brass rods, hand-felted wool
and beeswax with rosin
202×212×34

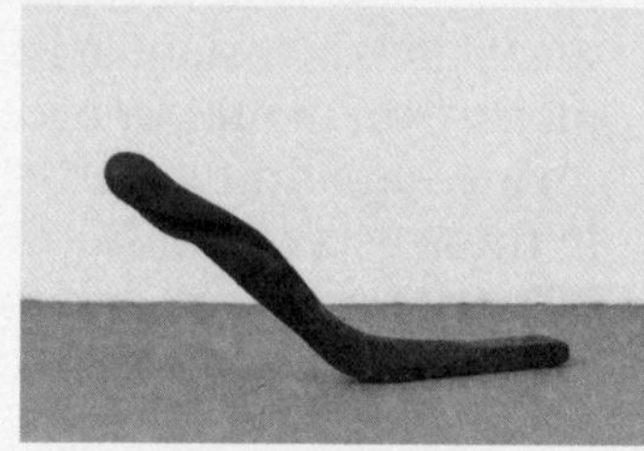

Snake, 2020
Cotton fibre, dental stone
and lead sheet
51×128×13

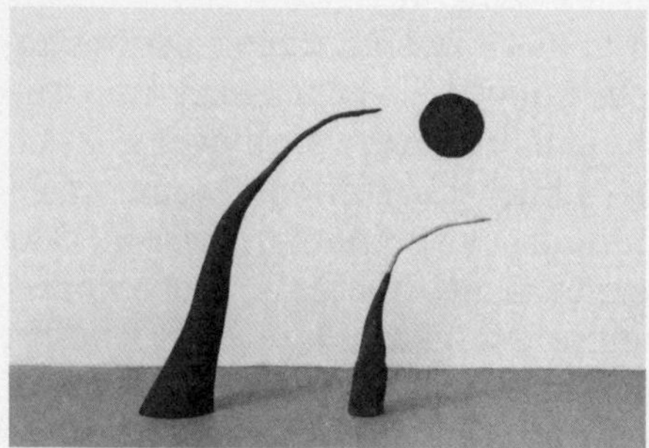

One Other Night, 2020
Cotton fibre, dental stone
and indian shellac
157×34×136; 110×22×78;
37×39×0.9

In the mechanics of tropical nature – my first experience of nature – things are in a constant state of transformation, everything decays very quickly and is born very quickly too. In this state, everything needs to be constantly remade, nothing remains unchanged. I am particularly interested in the state of things at the borderline of this transformation. A kind of 'in-between' moment.[1] P. B.

1   Conversation between Paloma Bosquê and
     Luiza Teixeira de Freitas, http://www.paloma
     bosque.com/files/entrevista-ltfen.pdf, p. 73

Paloma Bosquê

Born in 1983 in Garça, Brazil
Lives and works between
Brazil and Europe

Paloma Bosquê describes her artistic practice as a delicate and sincere negotiation with materials. In her sculptures and installations that explore weight, texture and balance, properties of juxtaposed materials are poetically brought together: wool, plaster and glass; lead sheet, brass, hand-felted wool and cast bronze; brass, wood, beeswax and rosin. 'My research revolves around materiality,' she has said, 'but more in a sense of how I can bring these things together and provide them with a body. And, once they have a body, how does that body relate to my own body? And, by extension, to everyone else's bodies.'[2]

Two Stones (2017, pp. 77–79) is a fragile yet playful experiment in texture and weight. A thin sheet of natural wool felt, delicately draped off brass rods and knotted, relies on a fine balance, rather than fixtures or fittings, to remain in equilibrium. A felt knot is lifted by brass rods into the centre line of the composition, and thus into association with the 'stone' made of beeswax and rosin. The two entities are caught in a still yet precarious moment where, somehow, they speak to each other, hence the title *Two Stones*. 'Conceptually, it interests me to bring bodies into relation with each other in a kind of negotiated equilibrium, usually at the limits of their fragility … So that's why my sculptures sometimes cause a certain discomfort, a physical sensation of fragility and/or instability.'[3] Bosquê's black sculptures of cotton fibre, dental stone, indian shellac, and lead sheet, *One Other Night* (2020, p. 81) and *Snake* (2020, p. 80), also appear to teeter on the threshold of transformation, as they seem to defy gravity or be caught in the act of moving slowly across the floor.   ANUSHA MISTRY

2   'Inside the Studio: Paloma Bosquê' (2020), https://mendeswooddm.com/artists/14-paloma-bosque/ (accessed October 2023)

3   Conversation between Paloma Bosquê and Luiza Teixeira de Freitas, http://www.palomabosque.com/files/entrevista-ltfen.pdf, p. 79

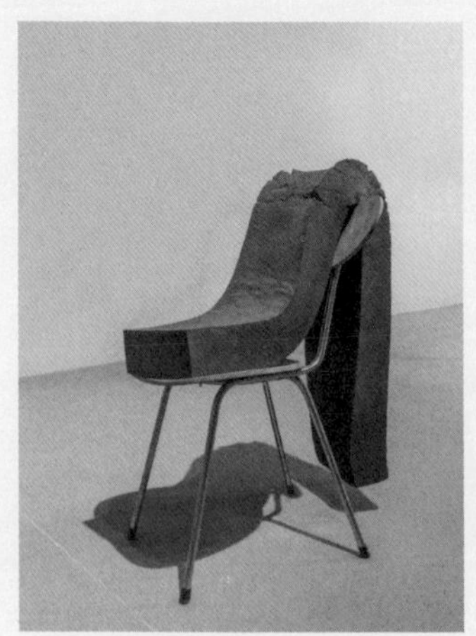

untitled (from Little Orphans series), 2009
Cast iron, chair
74×94×67

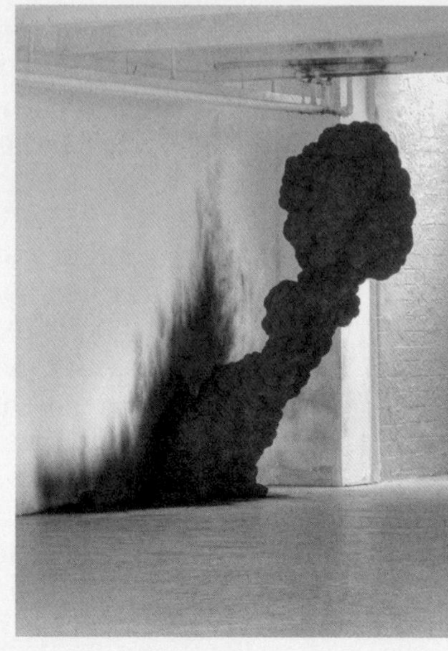

Dream – Spontaneous Combustion, 2008
Polyurethane resin, carbon fibre mat, black pigment, wood, steel
Dimensions variable, c. 145×85×78

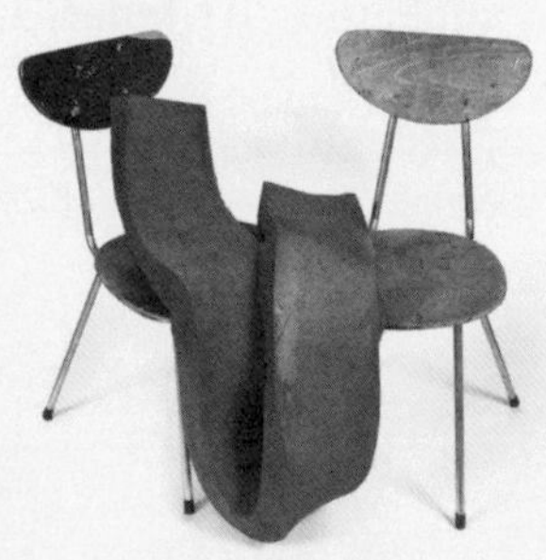

untitled (9), from the Little Orphans series, 2014, 2014
Cast iron, chairs
87×80×43

They creep slowly down. They are so tired of sitting on their socles that they're totally slacking.[1] O. B.

1   'Olaf Brzeski UNTITLED from the
LITTLE ORPHANS series' (12 July 2013),
www.youtube.com/watch?v=htas-TeHhfw
(accessed 8 November 2023)

Olaf Brzeski

Born 1975 in Wrocław, Poland
Lives and works in
Wrocław, Poland

Olaf Brzeski was, in his own words, 'educated in a 19th-century academic style, the French type'.[2] Perhaps inevitably, this prompted an emphatic and sometimes violent reaction in search of a different path – yet Brzeski's grounding in art history allows him to draw on and play with tradition with both irreverence and humour.

The works in the *Little Orphans* series (2009–14, pp. 84–87) resemble twentieth-century minimalist sculpture – the rusted metal constructions of Richard Serra, for instance, or the disciplined geometry of Donald Judd's wooden shapes. Brzeski's sculptures, however, seem to ooze, slug-like, off the chairs supporting them, beyond the constraints of the formal, as if escaping whatever unseen violence has dented a surface here or taken a bite out of a clean edge there. As well as shrugging off rigidity, these works have diminished in scale from the monumental to the domestic; instead of towering over plazas, they slump in scuffed chairs as if exhausted, finally submitting to gravity and time, elemental forces that affect art, artist and viewer alike.

Clouds and smoke recur in Brzeski's work, representing the untameable and unknowable. These elements first appeared in the *Art is Violence* series of ceramic sculptures (2006–07) as the solidified breath of monstrous heads. *Dream – Spontaneous Combustion* (2008, p. 83) takes us into a dark corner of European culture, linked to both the occult and divine retribution. Cases of spontaneous combustion, from the Middle Ages to the present day, all report a human body being completely consumed by fire, apparently from within, with little damage to the surroundings. The first recorded incident involved the Italian knight Vorstius, who died vomiting flames in 1471; the most recent case, examined in an Irish court, was in 2011.

Brzeski's interest in these stories began when he was cleaning a chimney, triggering a huge outpouring of soot that filled his studio space. He is intrigued by the notion of dreams or thoughts so incendiary they might cause a body to ignite, and by the creative and transformative nature of fire. In *Dream*, charred debris lies on the gallery floor beneath a flame-scorched wall; smoke and ash ascend, forming a cloud that hangs in the air – the embodiment of the hidden forces that have sparked the conflagration given brooding solidity through the nature-defying alchemy of art.   JAMES ATTLEE

2   'Open Zachęta: Olaf Brzeski – long version', Zachęta Narodowa Galeria Sztuki, Warsaw (13 January 2022), www.youtube.com/watch?v=MEqCAbtkKo4 (accessed 20 November 2023)

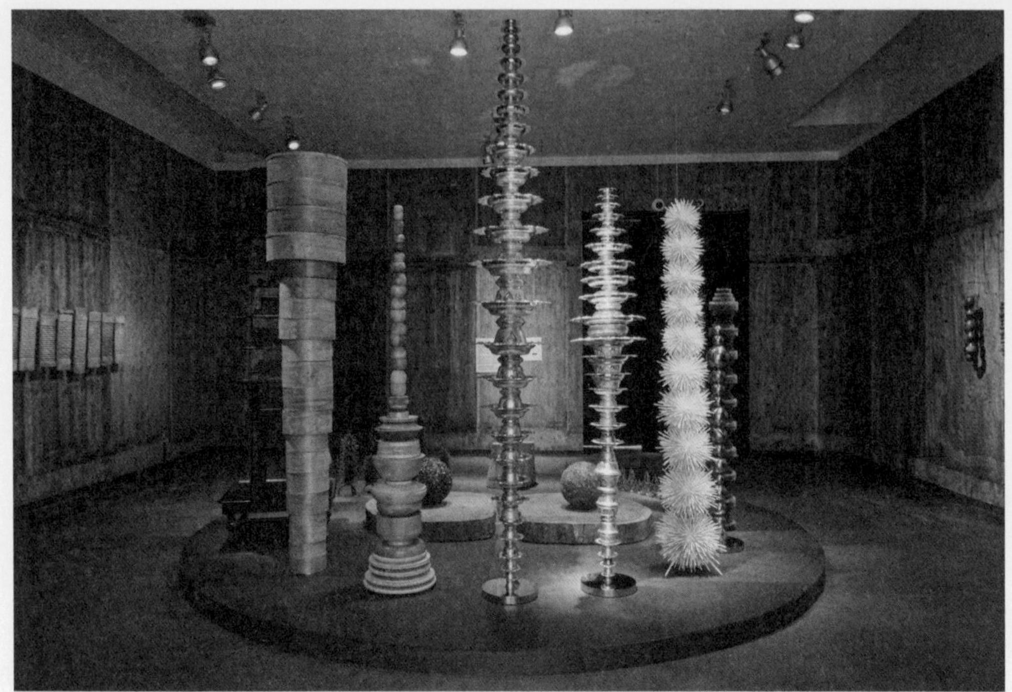

When you watch shopkeepers at the market stacking their wares, you can't help but gasp – not just because of the aesthetic beauty but because of the incredible skill, the years of practice you can feel. It's the beauty of the sublime, found in these countless piles of plastic.[1]   C. J. H.

1   Choi Jeong Hwa interviewed by Kim Min, 'Outsizing the Ordinary', Korea Foundation (20 September 2020), https://www.kf.or.kr /kfEng/na/ntt/selectDgtldetailView.do?dgtl Type=A&mi=2114&dgtlSn=6337&langTy=KOR (accessed 5 November 2023)

Choi Jeong Hwa

Born 1961 in Seoul, South Korea
Lives and works in Seoul, South Korea

As a student, walking to and from university in Seoul, Choi Jeong Hwa discovered that 'art was not taught in school but outside it'.[2] It was what he saw in alleyways, junkyards and traditional markets that fascinated him. Later, everyday life would become the focus of Choi's art and, from the early 1990s, plastic became his signature material. His earliest works consisted of vertiginous towers constructed from stacks of green and red plastic baskets: extraordinary balancing acts involving thousands of identical objects in which familiar household items suddenly became strangely unfamiliar. Choi uses this strategy of accumulation and repetition not only to delight and amaze but also to comment on the rampant consumerism that overtook his country during its rapid westernisation. Similarly, his gigantic inflatable flowers and fruit 'trees' ironically memorialise the natural flowers and trees that are now so rare in modern, industrialised Korea.

Having expanded his repertoire of objects to include other types of plastic products, from bottle caps and glittering beads to gloves and shoes and vintage bowls, with large installations such as *Alchemy* (2014–16) and *Blooming matrix* (2016–18) Choi turned to older items made from different materials collected at home and abroad over the past thirty years. Each work consists of a series of pagoda-like columns, which Choi refers to as 'stupas'. In his words: 'When you go to the mountains in Korea, you can find small stupas that native people make. These are built with time and effort ... A stupa is an altar standing on the ground [pointing] towards the sky.'[3] The playful stupas in *Blooming matrix* (2018, pp. 89–95) are built from rusty nails, saucepan handles, chicken feed trays, shells and stones, tangled wire, illuminated kitchenware, goat horns, and gas valve rings – the kind of outdated or worn-out things that once formed part of everyone's everyday life. Bearers of memory across time, space and cultures, these columns of discarded junk resemble natural forms. Choi describes each such assemblage as a 'holobiont' – a complex and interconnected system of organisms living in symbiosis with each other – a theme that encompasses all of his art.

HELEN LUCKETT

2   Choi Jeong Hwa, email to David Elliott (17 January 2013), quoted in D. Elliott, 'CHOIJEONGHWA: An Endless Cycle of Birth, Death and Rebirth', in *MMCA Hyundai Motor Series 2018: CHOIJEONGHWA — Blooming Matrix* (Seoul: MMCA National Museum of Modern and Contemporary Art, 2018)

3   Grace Ignacia See, 'An Interview with Choi Jeong Hwa', *The Artling* (18 December 2018), https://theartling.com/en/artzine/an-interview-with-choi-jeong-hwa (accessed 18 October 2023)

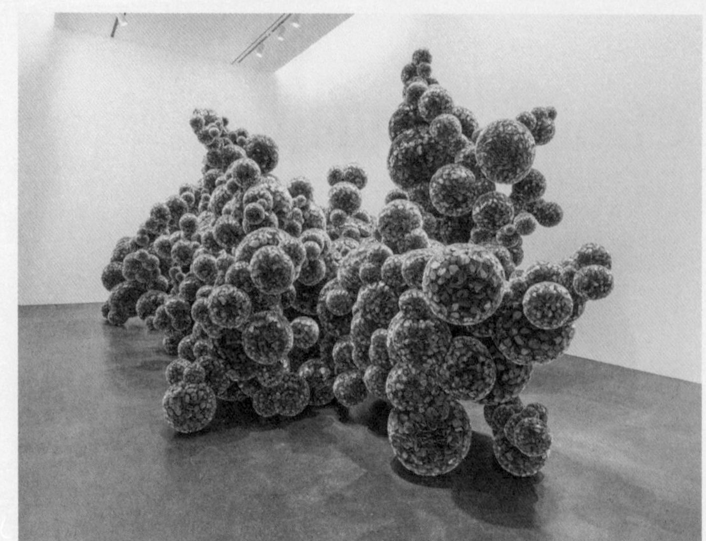

Untitled (Mylar), 2011
Mylar and hot glue
360×435×938

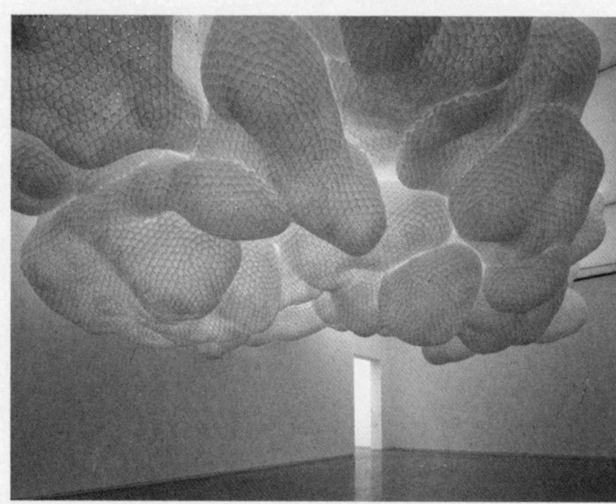

Untitled (Styrofoam cups), 2004/2008
Styrofoam cups, hot glue,
white thin rope, aluminum structure
Dimensions variable

Nature is my primary inspiration, so it is not surprising
that my work tends to mimic certain aspects such as cellular
and crystalline structures and growth patterns. I think my work
complicates this notion of 'synthetic' materials. After all, these
things are all made of earthbound ingredients so they have
a certain capacity to behave like organic materials and take
on structural possibilities found in nature.[1]   T. D.

1   Tara Donovan, 'Interview', in Jutta Mattern/
     Mette Marcus/Jean Rank Schelded (eds.),
     Tara Donovan (Humlebaek: Louisiana Museum
     of Modern Art, 2013), p. 17

Tara Donovan

Born 1969 in Flushing, New York, USA
Lives and works in New York City, USA

Since the late 1990s, Tara Donovan has created art that explores the unsuspected optical properties and phenomenological potential of accumulations of mass-produced objects and materials, including electric cables, sheets of polyester film, wooden toothpicks, steel pins, sticky tape, translucent drinking straws, Styrofoam cups and paper plates. For each project – free-standing sculptures, wall works or room-sized installations – she uses vast quantities of a single product, often chosen because of some chance discovery: the fleeting glimpse of an object's edge, an encounter with an unfamiliar material or 'a certain set of lighting conditions or a new way of combining or manipulating the material'.[2] After experimenting with it, 'like a scientist', she then develops basic rules for the work's repetitive, handmade production – stacking, folding, gluing, bundling and so on, according to the nature of the material. At this point, however, she has no set idea of what that work's final form will be, since 'it really grows out of a doing and making and a sense of play'.[3]

With site-responsive installations like *Untitled (Mylar)* (2011, pp. 97–100) and *Untitled (Styrofoam cups)* (2004/2008, pp. 102–03) – the first constructed from flat, circular sheets of Mylar (a metallic polyester film), folded, hot-glued and massed into spheres which are connected together, the other an accumulation of thousands of insulated foam cups which are also hot-glued, then clustered into billowing cloud-like forms suspended from the ceiling – two additional elements are crucial: the space that the works occupy and respond to, and the light that illuminates them. A third essential element is the viewer, whose presence and physical movement within the space activates a perceptual movement which unfolds on the surface of the work. And in leaving her works untitled, Donovan hopes that viewers will 'immerse themselves in a field of material' and 'detach their perception from the obvious materiality of the physical material', thereby allowing 'other associations to enter the fray'.[4]   HELEN LUCKETT

2   Ibid, p. 15
3   Lauren Christensen, 'Tara Donovan,
    a Sculptor Who Finds Beauty in the Mundane',
    New York Times (20 September 2018),
    https://www.nytimes.com/2018/09/20/books
    /tara-donovan-fieldwork.html (accessed
    25 October 2023)
4   Donovan 2017, pp. 18–19

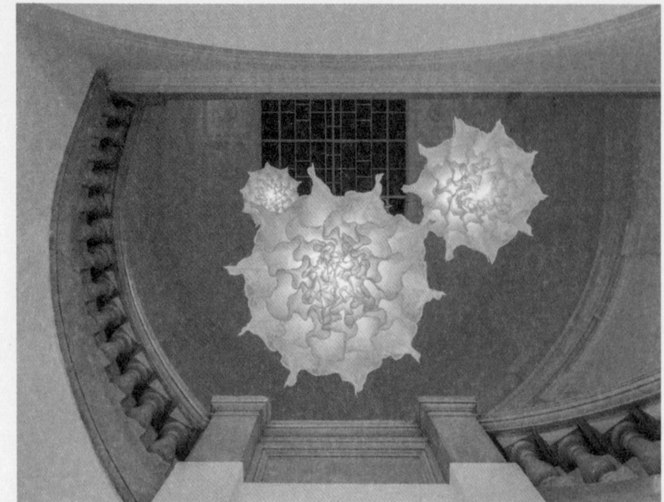

Shylight, 2006–2014
Aluminium, polished stainless steel,
silk, LEDs, robotics
Each part 365 × 480 × 500

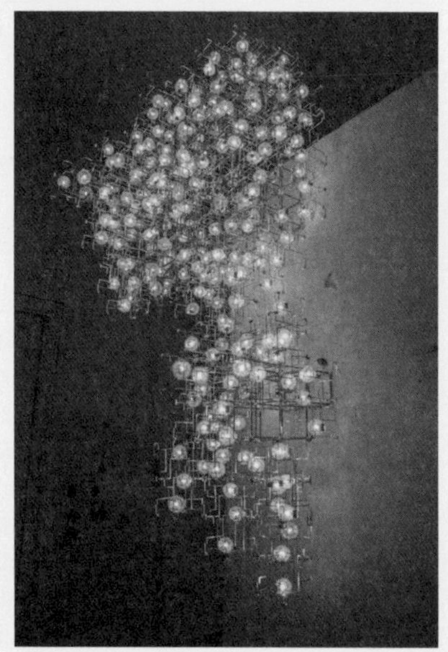

Fragile Future, 2000–ongoing
Phosphorus Bronze, LEDs, dandelion seeds
Dimensions variable

Shylight is a performative sculpture. When you enter the space it becomes a kind of dance that is performed in front of you.[1] DRIFT

1   'The Making of Shylight – Studio Drift',
      video (6 April 2016), https://www.youtube
      .com/watch?v=Kj71V6OrqPk (accessed
      24 September 2023)

DRIFT

Founded 2007 (as Studio Drift)
by Lonneke Gordijn (born 1980 in Alkmaar,
The Netherlands) and Ralph Nauta
(born 1978 in Swindon, UK)
Based in Amsterdam, The Netherlands

The story of DRIFT begins with a dandelion. The Dutch art collective's co-founders, Lonneke Gordijn and Ralph Nauta, who met as students at Eindhoven's Design Academy, first began working together when Nauta helped Gordijn with some technical aspects of her graduation project, which involved turning an actual dandelion 'clock' into a durable lamp. This work, for which Gordijn had taken apart a dandelion seedhead and painstakingly glued its individual filaments to a tiny LED light, became the inspiration for DRIFT's *Fragile Future* (2000–ongoing, pp. 102–03), a series of modular sculptures consisting of three-dimensional bronze electrical circuits connected to light-emitting dandelions: real seedheads, prepared as in Gordijn's prototype, that appear to float freely, producing an ethereal and mesmeric effect.

Driven by Gordijn's fascination with nature and Nauta's long-term interest in science fiction, DRIFT is committed to producing works combining natural processes with cutting-edge technology. They create experiential sculptures, interactive installations and performances involving light and movement, both inside art galleries, museums and theatres and, with the use of drones, outside in the open air. Asked to describe some of their sources of inspiration they list: 'Birds swarming, the proliferation of plants, a movement of a mass of clouds, how we encounter the world around us.'[2] *Flylight* 2009–ongoing), an indoor light installation that interacts with its surroundings and its audience, mimics the swooping and looping behaviour of a flock of birds in flight. The choreographic *Shylight* (2006–14, pp. 105–09), one version of which is permanently installed in Amsterdam's Rijksmuseum, is a performative installation of ascending and descending flower-like lights, programmed to open and close in the manner of flowers whose petals furl and unfurl in response to changes in light or climate. Describing themselves as 'future choreographers using the frequencies of nature to create experiential art',[3] DRIFT's hope is to awaken people to such rhythms and harmonies in our everyday natural environment.   HELEN LUCKETT

2   Adelina, 'DRIFT's Performative Installations that Connect to Nature', *Our Narratives* (23 March 2023), https://ournarratives.net/drifts-performative-installations-that-connect-to-nature (accessed 24 September 2023)

3   Veronica Simpson, 'Drift: Moments of Connection', *Studio International* (26 January 2022), https://www.studiointernational.com/studio-drift-moments-of-connection-review-museum-fur-kunst-gewerbe-hamburg (accessed 20 September 2023)

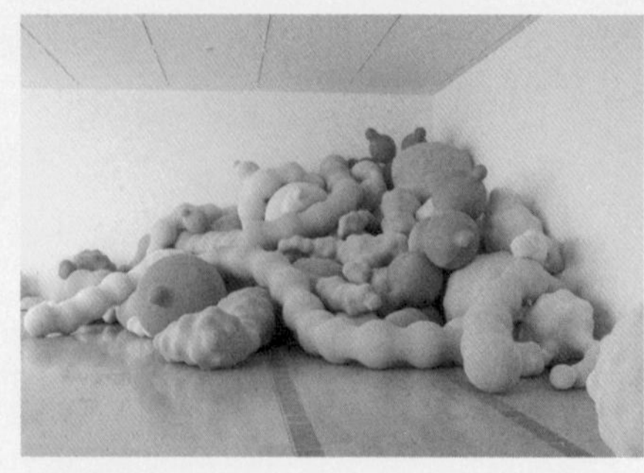

Oozing, 2023
Air, inflatable balls, Lycra
and robotics
Dimensions variable

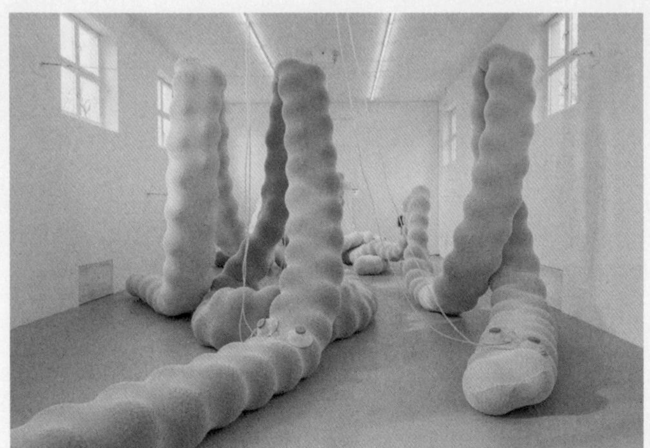

Pumping, 2019
Air, inflatable balls, Lycra, foam, Latex,
PVC and 8-channel sound installation
Dimensions variable

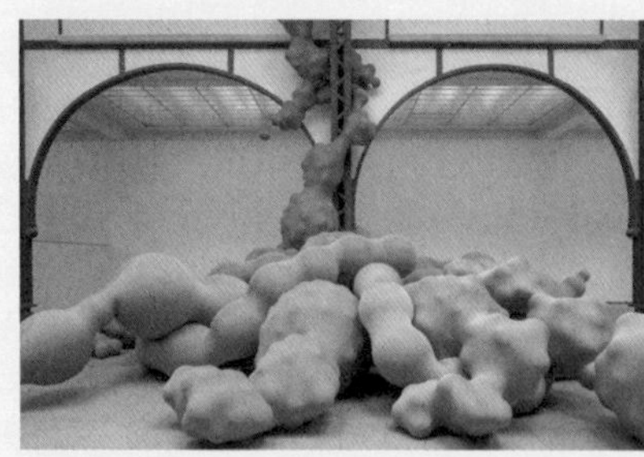

Devouring Lovers, 2023
Air, inflatable balls,
Lycra and robotics
Installation at Hamburger
Bahnhof, Berlin

My work belongs to the realm of the somatic, the experiential, the guttural and the unnameable. It aims to fully inhabit the world of the senses, invoking a pre-linguistic stage to imagine other possible bodies, other ways of feeling, caring and being in the world.[1] E. F.

1   Eva Fàbregas, artist statement,
     email to author (November 2023)

Eva Fàbregas

Born 1988 in Barcelona, Spain
Lives and works in Barcelona, Spain

Over the past decade, Eva Fàbregas has developed a unique sculptural language using both her studio practice and large site-specific interventions as spaces for playful explorations of materials, forms and themes. Throughout this artistic evolution, one concern has remained firmly at the forefront: the dissolution of the borders between the categories of living and being, of subject and object.

In Fàbregas's work, mundane consumer objects like inflatable balls are assembled and animated to conjure up outsized organs that mirror the viewer's own body, creating somatic encounters where traditional ontological hierarchies no longer apply. Take *Pumping* (2019, pp. 113–17), the large-scale installation that has been adapted to the architecture of the Hayward Gallery. These three thin sculptures, each 30 metres long, could be seen as giant worms or knotted innards: uncanny, in-dwelling stuff we might rather not see. But by showcasing the texture of the balls, which renders them familiar and identifiable, and by using a snazzy colour palette, Fàbregas flips the potential abjectness of her sculptures. She makes us want to feel them, lean on them, maybe even straddle their girth. This is very much the case, too, with *Oozing* (2023, pp. 118–19), another large-scale installation that viewers are actively invited to touch and hug. Here the colourful knot of sculptures has been taken to a more genital level of symbolic representation: a mass of intestines, breasts and penises, oozing apparatuses essential to bodily functions such as feeding, digesting and sexual reproduction.

The corporeal qualities of *Pumping*, however, are not limited to appearances. If you stop to observe it closely, you will notice that this is a piece that, in fact, moves. A string of conical subwoofers integrated into the sculpture emit a series of low and inaudible frequencies that animate the sculpture, making it breathe and vibrate. These loudspeakers have been lined with a perforated fabric like that of sticking plasters which, along with the transparent connecting tubes that protrude from them, gives them an air of wellness gadgets. When the work is seen in its full throbbing glory, though, the coupling of the speakers with the swollen balls recalls early electric breast pumps: the nipple, the breast flange and the cables criss-crossing them.

But the conceptual spark of *Pumping* wasn't quite linked to visions of motherly abundance. The idea first came to Fàbregas during a night out at Corsica Studios – a South London club famous for its top-notch sound system – where she felt sound throbbing and resonating within her own body. This seminal aspect of the work has been brought to the gallery via the lighting, with the sculpture inhabiting a dark cavernous space and its contours slowly coming into view beneath spotlights of changing colours.

LORENA MUÑOZ-ALONSO

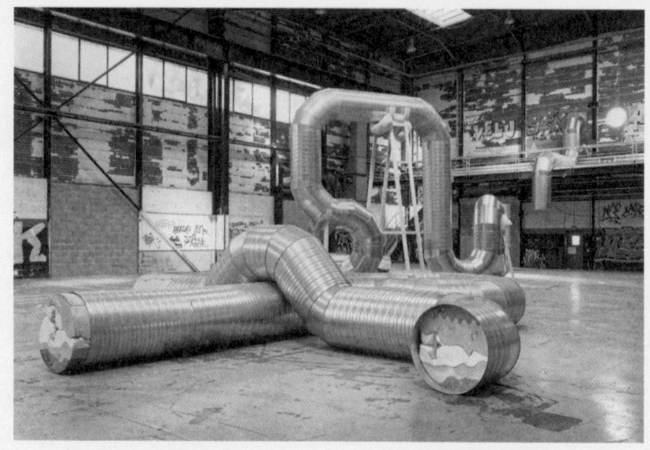

Deep Soil Thrombosis, 2019
Steel ducting, plaster, Jesmonite, foam, marble, concrete, aggregate, timber, fabric, stuffing
Dimensions variable

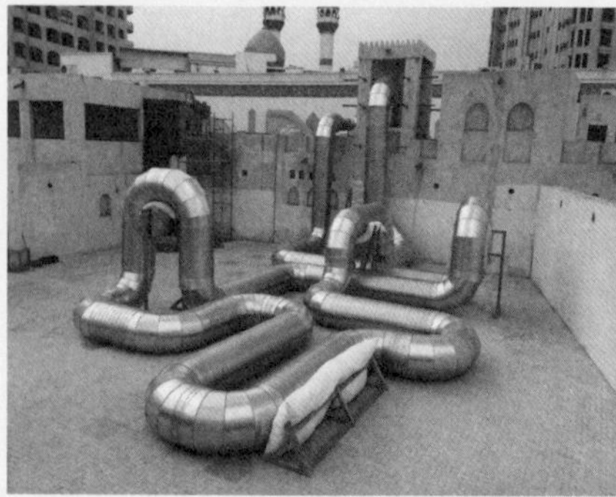

Homeostasis, 2014
Galvanised steel ducting, meranti wood, cushions, fan, air
Dimensions variable

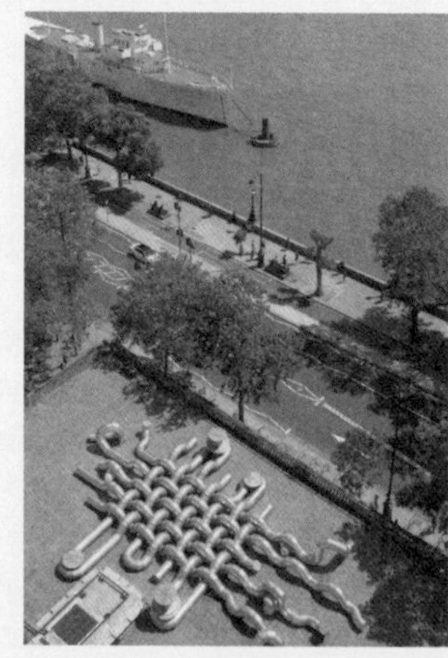

Slackwater, 2023
Steel ducting, car paint, wooden cable spools, Jesmonite cast fenders
Dimensions variable

I've always thought about my sculptures as twitching with life, whether it's a cartoon suggestion or a suggestion of bodily movement[1]   H. H.

1   Holly Hendry, video,
     https://www.stephenfriedman.com
     /artists/58-holly-hendry/
     (accessed 6 December 2023)

Holly Hendry

Born 1990 in London, UK
Lives and works in London, UK

In her sculptures and installations, Holly Hendry uses heavy-duty industrial materials – such as metal ducting, silicone, steel, bricks, sand, plaster and Jesmonite – to closely connect the anatomical and the architectural. Serpentine lengths of tubing flow in and out of buildings, snake across rooftops or lurk close to the ground, while densely packed matter, bulging membranes and congested production lines evoke digestive, respiratory and mechanical processes.

Hendry's sculptures materialise actions: extraction, decomposition and reconstitution; inflation, expansion and compression. She explains how, in her sculptures, 'outside and inside are totally interrelated' and that the work can 'open up new boundaries between internal and external'.[2] Here, the microscopic is remodelled earnestly, sometimes ridiculously, on a macro scale, while the cartoon nature of her imagery playfully challenges our ideas of flatness, fullness and space.

Homeostasis (p. 125), her first installation to use industrial ducting, was built in a public courtyard at the Sharjah Art Foundation in 2014. By attaching oversized galvanised steel ducting to its *barjeel* (wind towers) – structures designed for ventilation – the work effectively makes the building 'spill its guts'. In *Deep Soil Thrombosis* (2019, pp. 121–23), vast dissected pipes clogged with plaster, Jesmonite, foam, marble, concrete and aggregate speak as much to subterranean sewage systems as to anatomical drawings. *Slackwater* (2023, pp. 124, 127), a lattice of steel ducting, evokes the pattern on the surface of water when the incoming tide meets the flowing river.

Underneath the Hayward Gallery, a vast network of such ducts, pipes and tubes regulates air temperature and humidity, transforming the Thames-side building's concrete shell into a living, breathing site. Hendry's new commission, *Sottobosco* (2024), lies alongside the Hayward Gallery window, some of it succeeding in permeating into the galleries. The ducting appears to be growing and expanding, while glass water droplets evoke a sense of juiciness. Hendry's work brings succulence into the building's Brutalist exterior, making visible a feral ecosystem that architecture attempts to control, yet is inherently part of.   ANUSHA MISTRY

2   Holly Hendry discussing her work at the
De La Warr Pavilion, Bexhill, UK, video (2021),
https://www.dlwp.com/exhibition/holly-hendry
-invertebrate (accessed 6 December 2023)

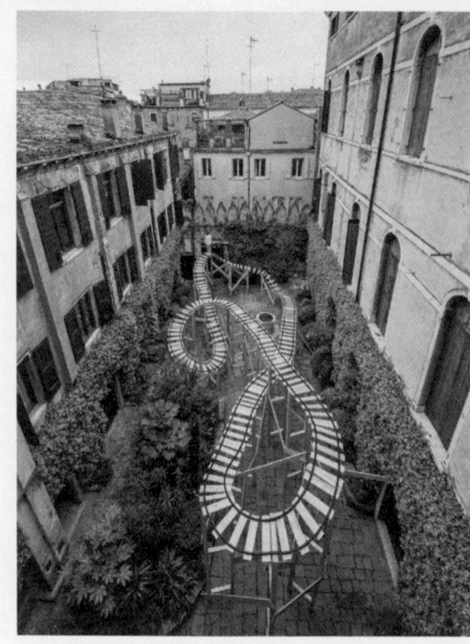

Pillar, 2017
Wood and PVC
Dimensions variable

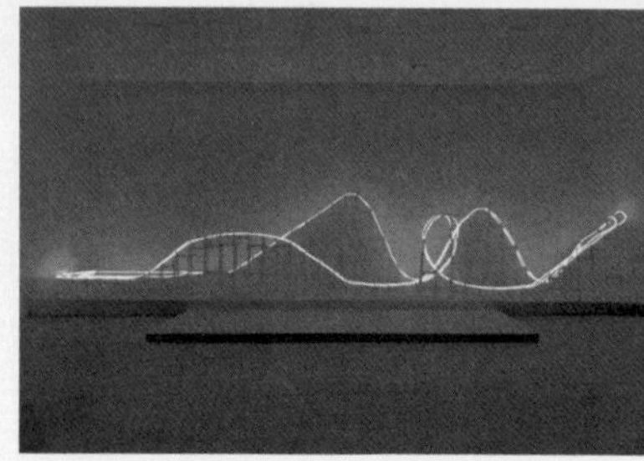

A Subsequent Offering, 2017
Wood and LED neon flex
1249.7×274.3×215.9

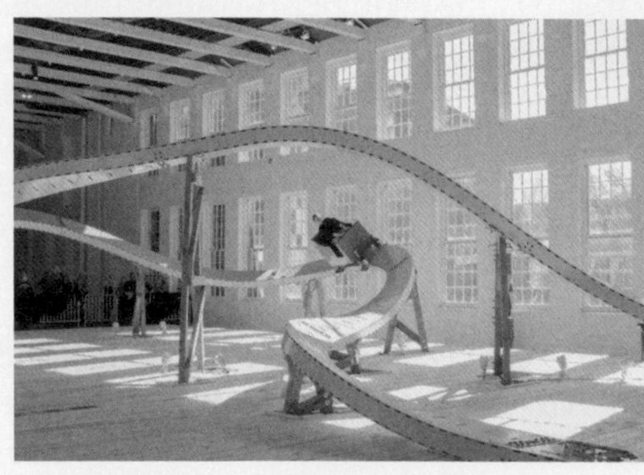

EJ Hill with Skyline
Attractions *Brava!*, 2022
Weld-free steel rollercoaster, enamel
spray paint, wood, and velvet
470×1100×2900

Thinking about rollercoasters, is one way for me
to communicate ideas that I have about struggle and
mortality and the impulse to go higher and faster
and test our physical and mental limits.[1]   EJ. H.

1   EJ Hill, video interview, 'Studio Museum
in Harlem Artist in Residence 2015–2016',
www.youtube.com/watch?v=SueEhngexhE
(accessed 11 December 2023)

EJ Hill

Born 1985 in Los Angeles, California, USA
Lives and works in Los Angeles, California, USA

EJ Hill's lifelong interest in rollercoasters first made itself felt in his work as an artist with *A Monumental Offering of Potential Energy* (2016). The gallery-scaled model is unrideable, but its steep banks, drops, twists and turns, traced in pink neon, evoke a rollercoaster's gravity and momentum, and the stomach-churning feelings of rapid acceleration, deceleration and rotation of a body subjected to external forces outside of its control. When Hill first exhibited the work, he completed the installation with his own live presence, lying still on a platform at the centre of the structure for up to nine hours a day, for three and a half months.

In rollercoaster physics, the potential energy that exists at the highest point of the track is converted into the kinetic energy that powers the ride. Popularly known as 'scream machines', rollercoasters are engineered to elicit extreme emotional responses, from the deathly terror provoked by the sensation of free-falling to the pure joy of being propelled at high speed. This collective simulation of near death is all over within a couple of minutes when the rollercoaster reliably returns its riders to the terra firma of the amusement park.

A similarly palpable energy is discernible in *A Subsequent Offering* (2017, pp. 130–31), a revised version of the original work in which Hill has left empty the platform that once held his body. Initially Hill installed a stage so that the rollercoaster could become a backdrop for live performance. Reanimated with communal experiences of music, comedy, and poetry, the work was offered up as a monument to the complexity of collective experience in the public expression of joy. Even in its vacant state, as it appears here, the work retains this potential: not only as a sculpture, but also as what Hill calls a 'performance relic'.

Hill has called the public expression of emotion afforded by rollercoaster rides 'a critical component of social equity'.[2] Yet this was historically almost completely denied to Black people in the US owing to anti-Black racism in the management of public leisure space: as the country moved towards desegregation in the 1960s, many amusement parks sought ways to restrict access to Black visitors, even to the degree of closing down.[3] The concept of leisure, and the public expression of emotions such as joy and terror, continue to be subject to the ongoing racism, homophobia and other forms of violence that undermine the taken-for-granted sense of safety in public space on which the rollercoaster's thrills rely.   KATIE GUGGENHEIM

2   Alexandra Foradas/Makayla Bailey, 'EJ Hill: Brake Run Helix' (North Adams, MA: MASS MoCA, 2022), p. 3, https://massmoca .org/wp-content/uploads/2022/11/EJHill _GalleryGuide_MECH.pdf (accessed 16 November 2023)

3   See Victoria W. Wolcott, *Race, Riots, and Roller Coasters: The Struggle Over Segregated Recreation in America* (Philadelphia: University of Pennsylvania, 2012)

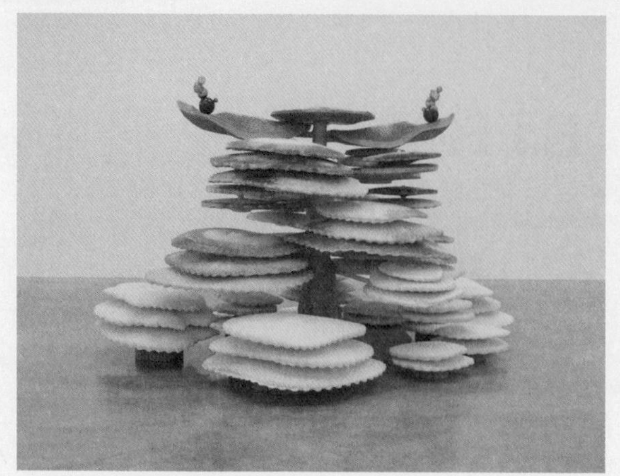

The Holder of Wasp Venom, 2023
Natural beeswax, microcrystalline wax, pigments,
150-year-old walnut (cause of death: unknown),
handblown glass and wasp venom
190×320×290

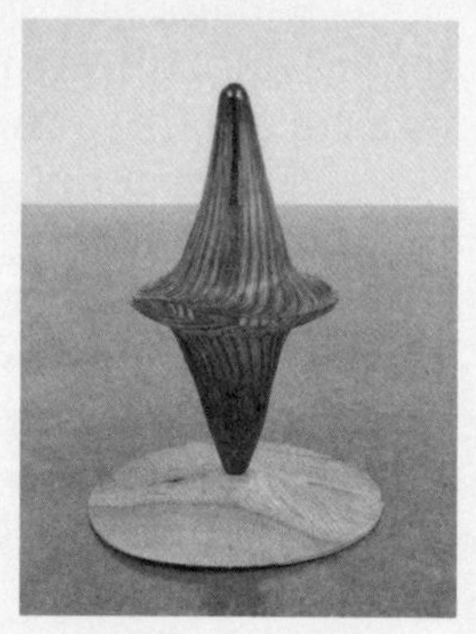

The Brewer, 2023
Handblown glass, 150-year-old
walnut (cause of death: unknown),
Bermondsey Street Bees raw
honey, 4,500-year-old yeast,
brewer's yeast, wasp venom and
culture of termite mushroom
(Termitomyces)
76×58×57

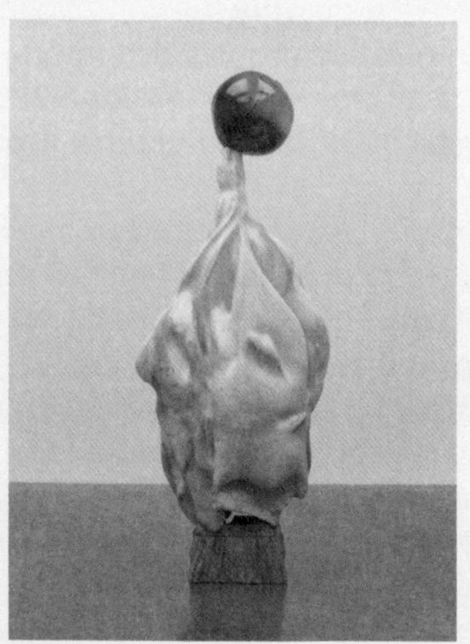

The Guardian of Ancient Yeast, 2023
Natural beeswax, microcrystalline wax, pigments,
150-year-old walnut (cause of death: unknown),
handblown glass and 4,500-year-old yeast
243×98×70

I don't make sculptures, I create beings that are alive … [for these pieces] I was really thinking of materials that … carry a strong history unto themselves: I worked with wax and with wood and ceramics … I conceived them as processes, so they are very much alive. They have their inner bloodflows, or heartbeats that you can hear when you get close to them.[1]   M. H.

1   Marguerite Humeau in conversation with
     Charlotte Burns, video, White Cube, London
     (12 May 2023), https://www.youtube.com
     /watch?v=vrBmZOyKI8E&ab_channel
     =WhiteCube (accessed 10 November 2023)

Marguerite Humeau

Born 1986 in Cholet, France
Lives and works in London, UK

Mining the worlds of speculative fiction and lost bodies of knowledge, Marguerite Humeau is best known for her large-scale sculptures of creatures suggestive both of prehistoric times and unknown futures. Her work brings us into contact with modes of existence across spaces and times with the aim to create 'an interconnected, resonant, and synchronised future'.[2] *FOXP2 (Biological Showroom)* (2016), for example, imagines an Earth on which elephants prevailed as the dominant species and explores the development of their consciousness through their rites of birth and death, while works such as *El Niño* and *La Niña* (both 2022) grapple with the subjects of migration, oceanic currents and climate change via a pod of foreboding marine sculptures that resemble alien whales beached in the gallery space.

The three pieces presented here are part of a recent body of work that continues this line of inquiry. Entitled *meys*, the series delves into fungi and fermenting processes, particularly those related to edible products such as yeast, positing them as the key to survival on a rapidly changing planet. Here, Humeau imagines a world in which we have become collective bodies. Her concerns on this topic crystallised during a trip to the Australian Outback, where she came face to face with the captivating world of mound-building termites. Always interested in the intricate nature of ecosystems, Humeau saw in the structures created by colonies of termites – mounds which can reach up to eight metres in height – the perfect embodiment of complex and collective architectures, and of the kind of intelligence that can allow a community to work together effectively to ensure its continuity. The towering *The Guardian of Ancient Yeast* (2023, pp. 139–41) is directly inspired by the spire-like form of the termite mounds, mirroring their organic, living qualities through the use of natural materials such as beeswax, 4,500-year-old yeast and 150-year-old walnut. *The Holder of Wasp Venom* (2023, pp. 135–37) is a mushroom-like tree, whose branches end in clusters of tiered honeycombs, flat like waterlilies. It too is made with a host of organic materials, evoking the intensive collective labour and ingenuity of the insect world. But an inorganic material is also key to the three *meys* pieces: glass, handblown in various dazzling shapes that derive from fungi structures, provides finishing touches to the first two sculptures, but reigns supreme in the third. Smaller in size, almost demure in comparison, *The Brewer* (2023, p. 138) takes the form of a vessel shaped like a spinning top. A brown, sticky liquid slides down its transparent grooves. It must be the remnants of the raw honey, brewer's yeast and culture of termite mushroom that Humeau lists as materials – maybe an elixir for collectiveness.   LORENA MUÑOZ-ALONSO

2   Email from the artist (6 December 2023)

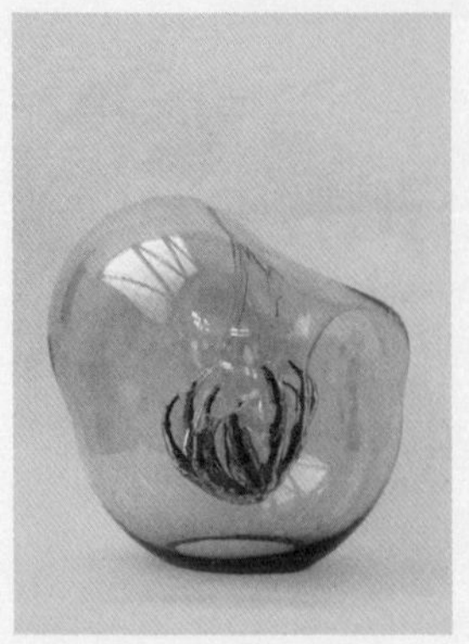

Plongement 1, Marseille 2023
Glass and bronze,
55×55×55

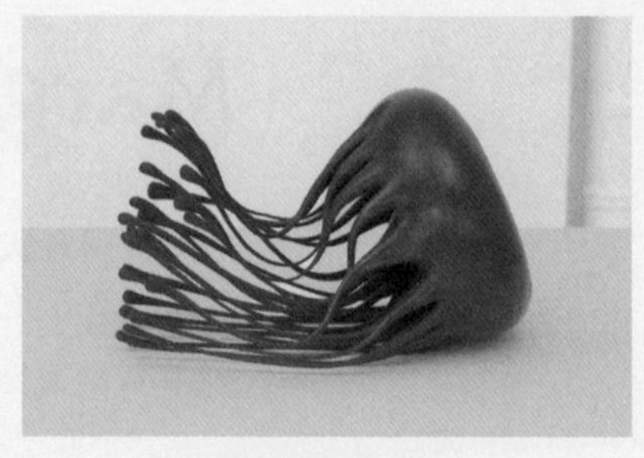

Méduse, Paris 2018
Bronze, blue patina,
27×29×45

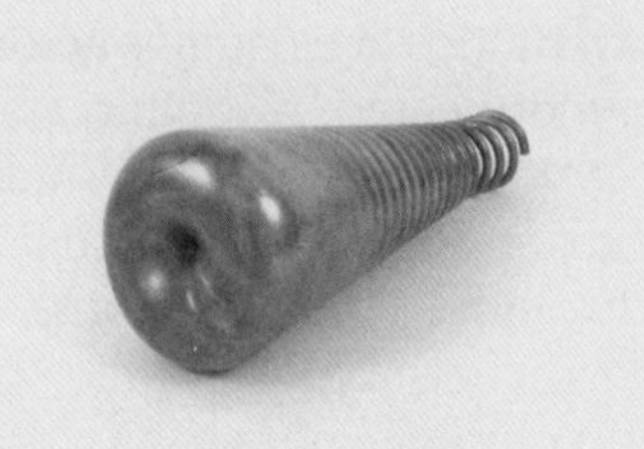

Ressort flou,
Le Buisson 2022
Bronze and silver patina
50×20×19.5

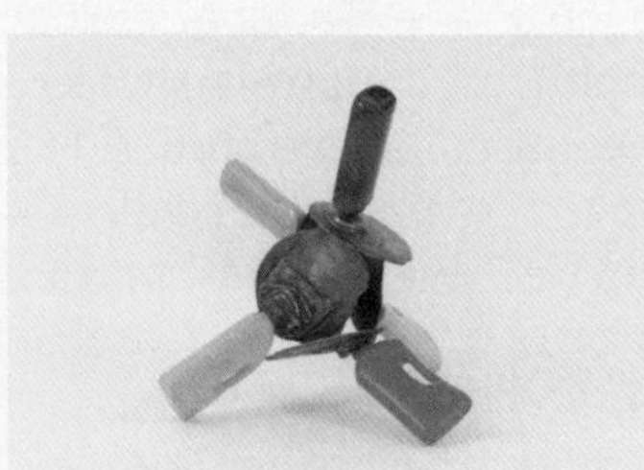

Vaisseaux Verseurs,
Le Buisson 2022
Plastic, plaster,
resin, bronze
63.5×57.1×59.7

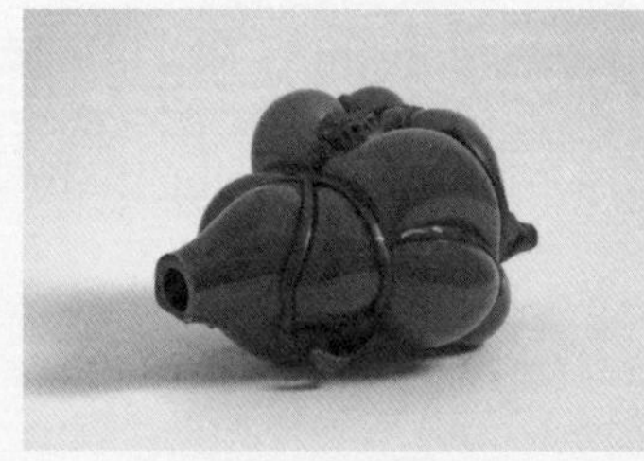

Parure 1, Marseille 2019
Bronze and glass
30×58×44

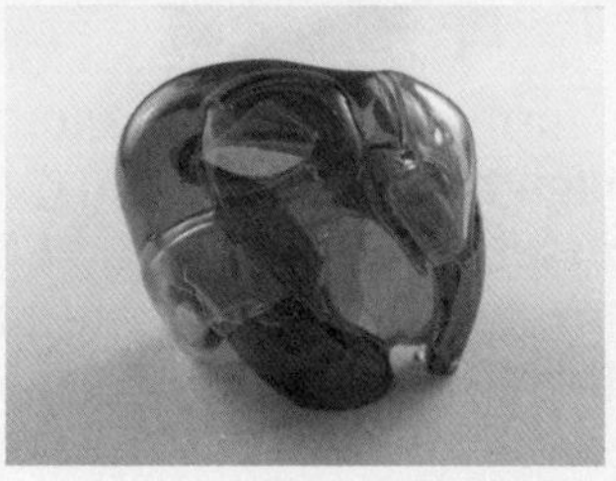

*Blown Knot 6$^3_2$
(Borromean) Varia 06*,
Marseille 2012
Glass, 31×23×25.5

My objects are surfaces, with no inside or outside, only holes.
Through the holes there are other surfaces.[1] J.-L. M.

1   Jo-ey Tang, '500 Words: Jean-Luc Moulène',
Artforum.com (4 November 2016),
www.artforum.com/columns/jean-luc-moulene
-discusses-his-exhibition-at-the-pompidou
-231389 (accessed 15 November 2023)

Jean-Luc Moulène

Born 1955 in Reims, France
Lives and works in Normandy, France

The objects Jean-Luc Moulène makes are the outcomes of industrial processes and of experiments with the laws of physics and mathematics; ideas modelled in physical form. Over the last decade he has regularly collaborated with the CIRVA glass centre in Marseille and the Fonderie de Coubertin near Paris to create a series of enigmatic works in glass and bronze.

The skeletal cast bronze structure inside *Plongement 1* (2023, p. 144) resembles two cupped hands. The crab-like object is caught mid-dive. It is simultaneously on the inside and outside of a bright blue blown glass vessel, reaching for the opening and threatening to turn the surface inside out in an endlessly morphing loop. In Mouléne's native French, 'plonger' means 'to dive', while the etymologically distinct 'plongement' is the mathematical term for a structure contained or embedded within another.

Parure 1 (2019, pp. 146–47) also includes a bone-like structure cast in bronze. Parts resembling segments of pelvis and spinal cord are arranged in a symmetrical net, like an exoskeletal skull, containing a bulging, blown glass form. 'Parure' is the formal term for a set of jewellery, usually comprising a necklace, earrings, bracelet and brooch – but here, like the gradual swelling of a finger around a long-worn wedding ring, the adornment restrains and deforms.

The Borromean knot, which comprises three intersecting rings, is the starting point for a series of blown glass objects that transpose the topological idea of the knot into physical form. The Borromean knot was used by the French psychoanalyst Jaques Lacan to represent human subjectivity as the interrelationship of the symbolic, the imaginary and the real. In Moulène's experiments, air inflates, deforms and collapses the glass, and interiors and exteriors become indistinguishable as colours and surfaces flow into one another.

Moulène considers his art analogous to a form of language, somewhere between the freedom of poetry and the structures of mathematics. His enigmatic objects are expositions of complex ideas realised with artisanal craftsmanship, by hand, and at a human scale that gives them an intuitive relationship to the organs of the human body – a heart, a brain, a stomach. Laid out on tables for public observation, Moulène's objects remind us that the infinite complexity of the universe is also contained within our own bodies and minds.   KATIE GUGGENHEIM

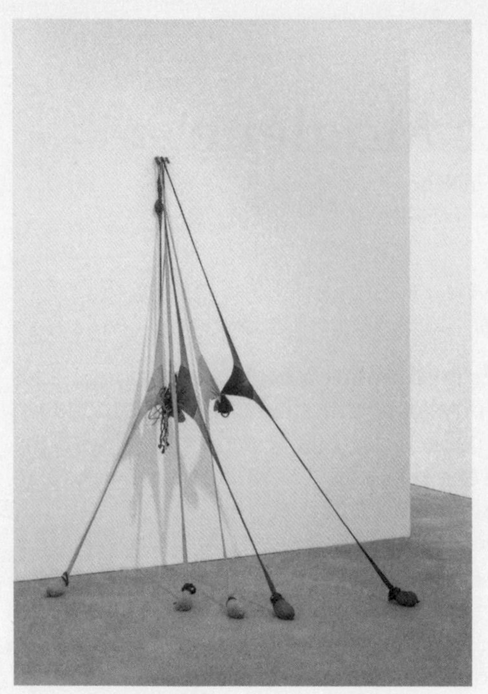

R.S.V.P. Reverie (Scribe), 2014
Nylon mesh, sand and found metals
231.1×137.2×170.2

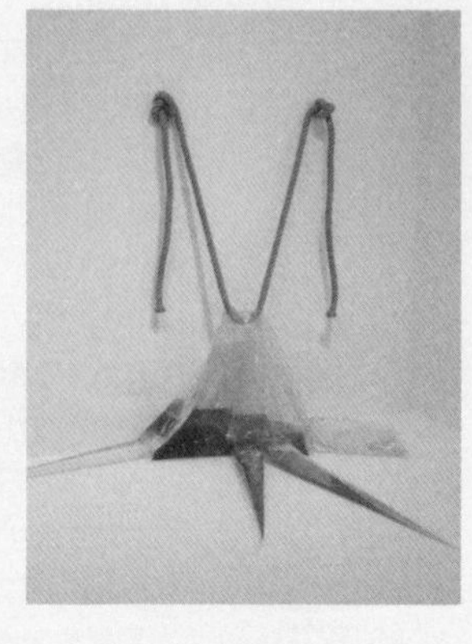

Water Composition I, 1969–70/2019
Vinyl, water, rope
146.1×177.8×221.7

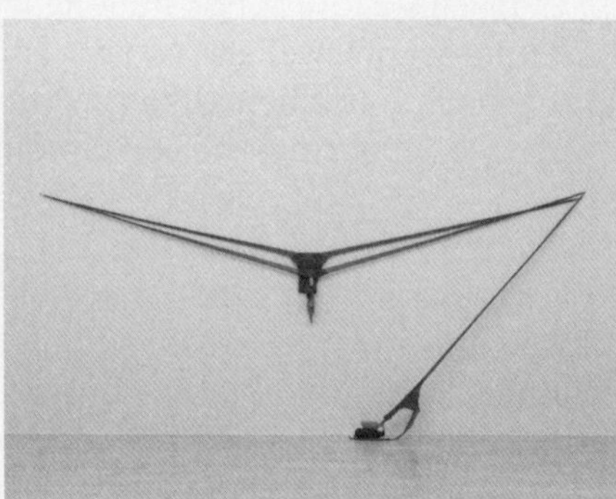

R.S.V.P. Reverie 'D', 2014
Nylon mesh, sand and copper
162.5×381×23

I am working with nylon mesh because it relates to the elasticity of the human body. From tender, tight beginnings to sagging end … the body can only stand so much push and pull until it gives way, never to resume its original shape.[1]   S. N.

1   Senga Nengudi, 'Statement on nylon
mesh works' (1977), Amistad Research Centre,
New Orleans, Senga Nengudi Papers,
1966–2017. Featured in *Senga Nengudi:
Topologies* (Philadelphia, PA: Philadelphia
Museum of Art, 2019), p. 156

Senga Nengudi

Born 1943 in Chicago, Illinois, USA
Lives and works in Colorado Springs,
Colorado, USA

Senga Nengudi has been creating work since the 1960s that evokes corporeality and embraces ephemerality. She often employs found materials that bear traces of their former use. The *R.S.V.P.* series (1976–ongoing) invites viewers to respond to clusters of nylon stockings that have been stuffed with sand, twisted, tied, knotted and stretched across the walls and floor of the gallery. Some early presentations were activated by performers – often Nengudi herself – who interacted with the sculptures, lifting and transposing their limbs, testing the tension of the nylon and negotiating the positionings of the weights and surrounding space.

More recently, Nengudi has reworked and reimagined works from the original series. In *R.S.V.P. Reverie (Scribe)* and *R.S.V.P. Reverie 'D'* (both 2014, pp. 151–53), stockings of various skin tones are pinned to the wall and weighted to the floor, making fine elongated lines. The artist has compared these stockings, stretched to their limits, to skin, whose elasticity accommodates our bodies' transformations, stretching to adapt to growth, motion, pregnancy or breastfeeding. 'After giving birth to my own son, I thought of black wet nurses suckling child after child … until their breasts rested on their knees, their energies drained'.[2] She notes how the strain on our bodies has a symbiotic relationship to the strain on our psyches: 'As human beings, we're fragile, yet we're so sturdy … there's a lot of tension simply existing as a human being and so I like to incorporate that energy of what it means to exist.'[3]

The *Water Composition* series (1970–), groupings of vinyl sacks filled with coloured fluid, similarly advocates motion and mutability in sculpture. Works range from the simple – *Water Composition I* 1969–70/2019, p. 155) – to the complex, in which multiple sacks of varying colours hang from the wall, lie on the floor or are draped on plinths. Early audiences were invited to touch the works and feel the coloured liquid responding to the pressure of their fingers. 'Water became this amazing material for me: it can be frozen solid or liquid; it seeks its own level. Water, more than any other natural element, has so many different forms. It is so powerful, healing, so nurturing but it can also drown you. When I began to put water into vinyl plastic forms, I was exploring that. The *Water Compositions* had to do with the body in the sense that they yielded to your touch. They produced a sensorial experience.'[4]   ANUSHA MISTRY

2   Ibid

3   Senga Nengudi, 'As human beings,
we're fragile yet we're so sturdy', Henry
Moore Foundation video (5 January 2023),
https://youtube/DutixbTscWM (accessed
5 October 2023)

4   Osei Bonsu, '"I Believe Deeply that the Best
Kind of Art is Public": An Interview with Senga
Nengudi', *Frieze*, No. 198 (October 2018),
www.frieze.com/article/i-believe-deeply-best
-kind-art-public-interview-senga-nengudi
(accessed 5 October 2023)

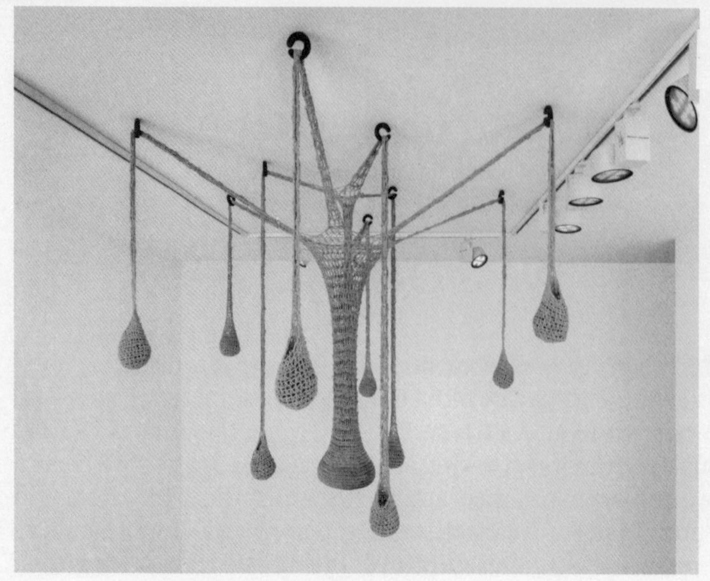

Iaia Kui Dau Arã Naia, 2021
Cotton string crochet dyed with spices
(turmeric, clove, cumin, pepper, ginger),
stones and wooden hooks
135×160×153

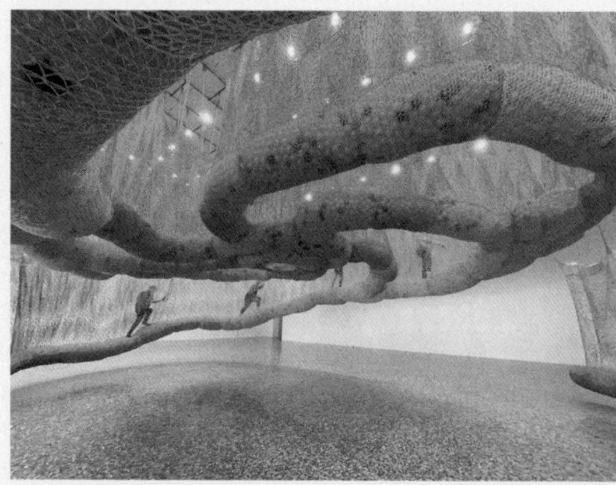

SunForceOceanLife, 2021
Crocheted textile and plastic balls
Dimensions variable

Art is a way of being in the world, it happens all the time, everywhere, invisible and inexplicable, an unnameable dream. Art spreads, pulsates, guides, blows, sings and dances life.[1] E. N.

1 Ernesto Neto, personal statement (13 December 2021), https://lugar -comum.com/f/bem-comum (accessed 15 November 2022). Author's translation from the Portuguese

Ernesto Neto

Born 1964 in Rio de Janeiro, Brazil
Lives and works in Rio de Janeiro, Brazil

Ernesto Neto's multisensory sculptures operate on the cusp of nature and culture, art and life. His biomorphic forms emerge from a process of stuffing natural and manmade substances – including sand, spices, shells and Styrofoam balls – into stretched polyamide fabric or crocheted textiles. The resulting organic structures, suspended from the ceiling or spread across the gallery floor, invite public interaction and evoke nature in all its microscopic and macroscopic delicacy. As Neto explains: 'I totally believe that nature is our teacher.'[2]

If Neto's interest in the gravitational suspension of soft, everyday materials links him to the discourses of postminimalism and arte povera, then his interest in the social potential of sculpture connects him to the participatory intentions of Brazilian neo-concretism. Neto's sculptures invite serious play.

Neto's large-scale work activates all the senses. The major 2021 installation *SunForceOceanLife* (pp. 161–63) invites gallery visitors to walk through a gigantic suspended spiral labyrinth. This intricately crocheted form recalls the traditional handicrafts of Brazil, which are often shared intergenerationally: as a child, Neto was taught to crochet by his grandmother. The crocheted walkway taken by the viewer is stuffed with small plastic balls which disrupt one's natural equilibrium and contribute to the sensation of floating, whole the work's spiralling orb structure and radiant colours celebrate the life-giving and spiritual energies of the sun and the sea.

Although the 2021 work *Iaia Kui Dau Arã Naia* (pp. 157–59) cannot be physically entered, everything inside of the work is a relationship and it still prompts an activation of the senses. Here a number of uterine protuberances in cotton string hang from the ceiling, each dangling limb stuffed and weighted with small stones and aromatic spices including cloves, cumin, pepper and ginger. Turmeric is used not just for its olfactory properties but also its brilliant gold colour, which sets the cotton string aglow. Again, the composition of the work evokes a natural phenomenon, in this case the physical attributes and resourceful endeavours of the spider as it weaves, hunts, eats and protects.   NATALIE RUDD

2   Hans Peter Wipplinger, 'Between Physics and Alchemy: Ernesto Neto's art as a sensuous, poetic metaphor for a life in flow', in Verena Gamper, Thomas Miessgang and Hans Peter Wipplinger, *Ernesto Neto* (Cologne: Verlag der Buchhandlung Walther König), p. 51

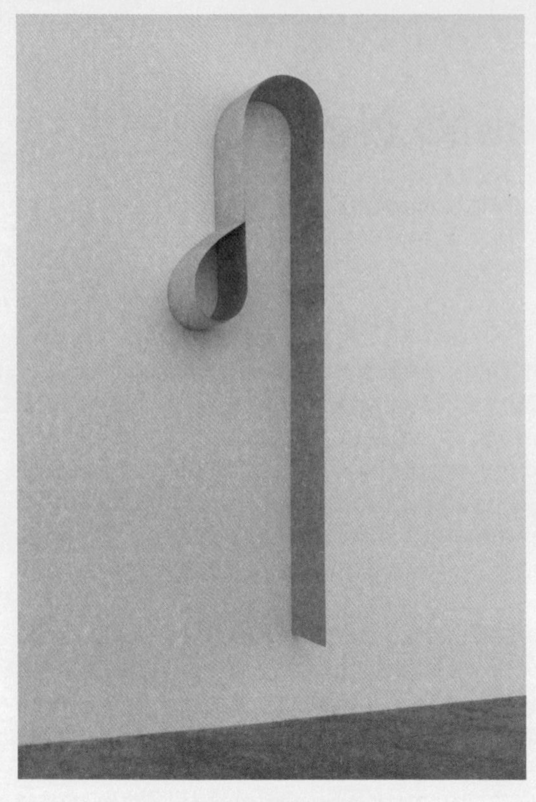

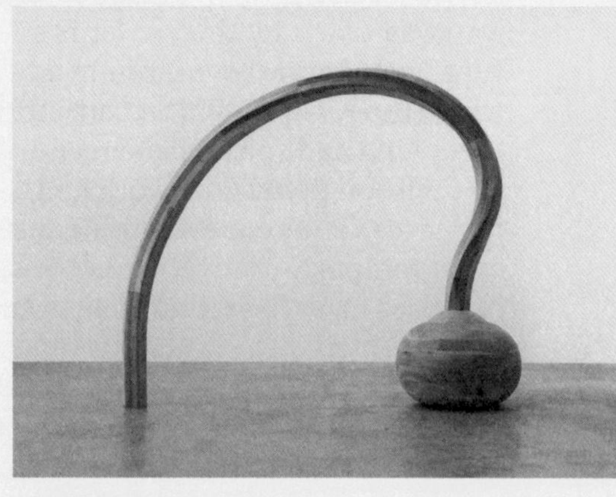

I never did minimalist art. I got real close. I looked at it, I tasted it, and I spat it out.[1] M. P.

1   Martin Puryear, quoted in John Yau, 'Martin Puryear's Open Questions' (23 January 2021), https://hyperallergic.com/615939 /martin-puryear-open-questions-matthew -marks-gallery/ (accessed 6 December 2023)

Martin Puryear

Born 1941 in Washington, D.C., USA
Lives and works in the Hudson Valley
region of New York, USA

In 2007, reflecting on 30 years of creating sculpture, Martin Puryear felt that 'it's obvious that my way of making art must seem anachronistic and out of sync with what is most vital in art today.'[2] The fact was that he still worked with his hands. His preferred medium was (and still is) wood; he grew up with wood and as a teenager he built guitars and canoes. He was exposed to West African craft techniques while volunteering in the Peace Corps in Sierra Leone, and Scandinavian design and woodworking alongside his printmaking studies at the Swedish Royal Academy of Art in Stockholm.

Later, talking about his abstract works, he remarked: 'I make these sculptures using methods that have been employed for hundreds of years to construct things that have had a practical use in the world.'[3]

Untitled (2015, pp. 165–66) and *Question* (2010, pp. 168–69) represent two distinct facets of Puryear's exploration of abstract form, and two examples of his virtuosity in crafting wood. The wall sculpture, *Untitled*, is essentially an illusionistic drawing in paper-thin wood: it forms a fluid, scrolling line; a ribbon seemingly made of some soft, gravity-responsive fabric, it is actually crafted from Alaskan yellow cedar. Free-standing but equally calligraphic in its way, *Question* is one of a series of sculptures based on the motif of the Phrygian 'liberty' cap, a revolutionary emblem of liberation from slavery and tyranny. As an African American acutely aware of his country's continuing history of racial inequality, Puryear often returns to this symbol, ironically traced in *Question* in the outline of the collapsed mark of interrogation. Of works such as *Untitled,* Puryear says that, though he prefers his works to be named, 'some things are just untitled; some things are just what they are.'[4]   HELEN LUCKETT

2   'In Conversation: Martin Puryear with David Levi Strauss', *Brooklyn Rail* (November 2007), https://brooklynrail.org/2007/11/art/martin -puryear-with-david-levi-strauss (accessed 20 September 2023)

3   Quoted in Michael Auping, 'Artisan', in *Martin Puryear* (New York: Museum of Modern Art, 2007), p. 62

4   Martin Puryear interviewed by Robert J. Powell, in *Martin Puryear* (New York: Museum of Modern Art, 2007), p. 107

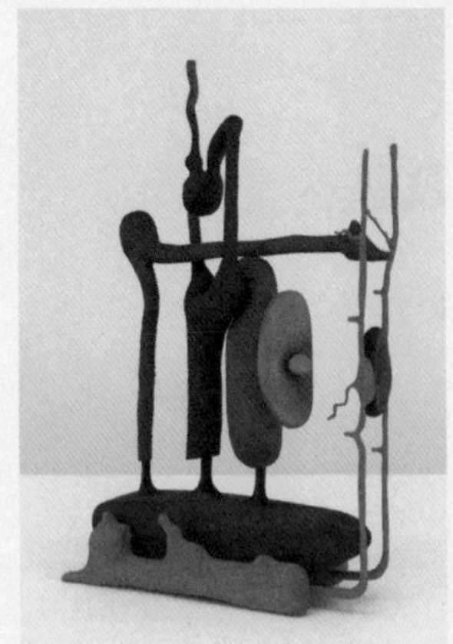

Brontes, Steropes, and Arges, 2023
Basswood, dye, primer, plastic, steel
71.8×49.53×18.42

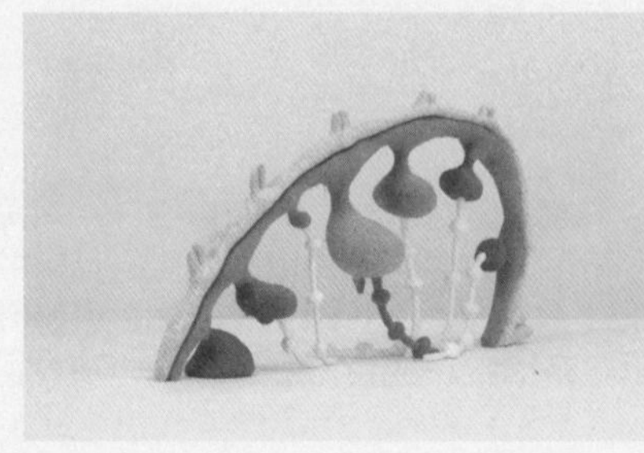

Globules, 2023
Basswood, dye,
shellac-based primer, flocking,
plastic, steel, HMA
34.3×69.9×14

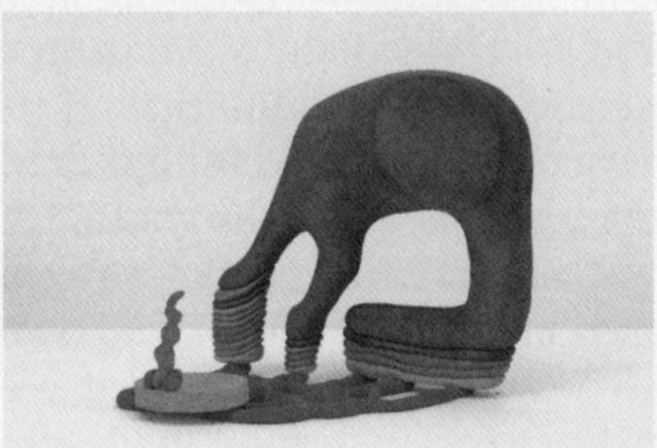

Third Instar, 2023
Basswood, dye,
flocking, plastic, steel
36.2×41.9×36.2

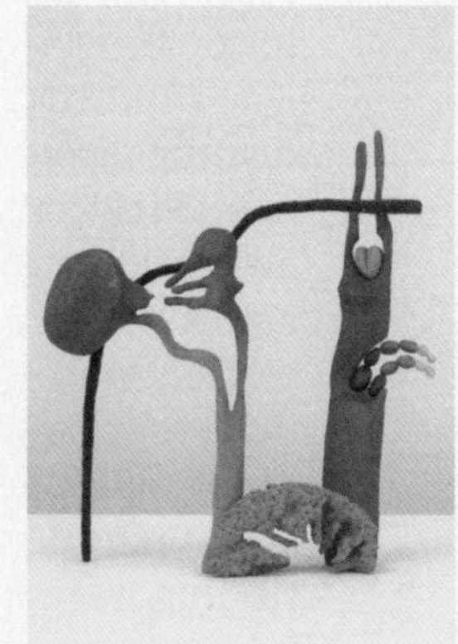

Crawl, 2023
Basswood, dye, flocking, plastic, steel
61.6×56.52×20

From fungus, I started to think of plant life in general and started to research all sorts of things that fell into my element of work, such as death, reproduction, disease, aging, sexual organs, orifices, peduncles, protuberances, mathematics, things of this sort. And I started to realize all these things that you think you invented, nature thought of them first. Beautiful textures and colors and divine geometries – just real brilliance of pattern, humor, theater, and a way in which nature embodies thoughts.[1]   M. R.

1   Matthew Ronay, 'Water-filled Space Suits
for our Skins', lecture delivered at the Nasher
Sculpture Center (20 December 2018),
www.nashersculpturecenter.org/read-watch
/articles/article/id/303 (accessed 5 October 2023)

Matthew Ronay

Born 1976 in Louisville, Kentucky, USA
Lives and works in Brooklyn, New York, USA

Matthew Ronay's sculptures are small in scale, inviting the viewer to get up close then ensnaring them with playful combinations of swirling biomorphic forms and snazzy colours. The works' physicality beckons for them to be touched, as if daring one to reach for their softness or stickiness. This squelchy quality belies a sturdy production process: Ronay always starts with black and white drawings, translating them into three-dimensionality by carving his designs in wood, before adding details in other materials such as plastic, flocking and dye.

In the last decade the American artist has developed a body of work based on a rich imagery that mines the fields of botany, anatomy and other biological shapes found in nature. What interests Ronay is the interconnectedness of forms, and how certain compositions and patterns reoccur in multiple contexts – from respiratory systems and neural networks to spiritualist drawings. He is also fascinated by how discrete elements are linked to form a whole, from the microscopic cells of a human body to the vast ecosystem of a forest. Hence, his display methodology relies on groupings: each sculpture can be seen and enjoyed in isolation, but it achieves its maximum force as part of an ensemble – as an element with a particular function within a group that has its own internal logic.

The works presented here are emblematic of Ronay's most salient themes. Take *Globules* (2023, pp. 175–76), which could be seen as an allegory of some obscure anatomical part, channelling the poetics of innards. Could it be a segment from the spinal cord of a small animal or a fragment of the gallbladder of a human? *Brontes, Steropes, and Arges* (2023, pp. 173–74) alludes to the three Cyclopes who forged Zeus's thunderbolts in Greek mythology: its vibrant red centrepiece could be the pupil in an elongated blue iris, embedded in a monstrous single eye. *Crawl* (2023, pp. 171–73), on the other hand, seems to be more interested in anthropomorphising vegetal elements like plants and moss. To the left, a strange double-headed stem seems to be screaming at itself, more brawl than crawl. To the right, a green trunk appears to be throwing up seed pods. The velvety reds and purples of *Third Instar* (2023, p. 177) evoke a melting elephant, Dalí-style, but the title refers to the most advanced stage in larval development, so perhaps what we are witnessing is the birth of a massive insect. Is it a surreal delight, the result of some idyllic foraging, or the stuff of body-horror nightmares? These are the riddles inherent in Ronay's work.   LORENA MUÑOZ-ALONSO

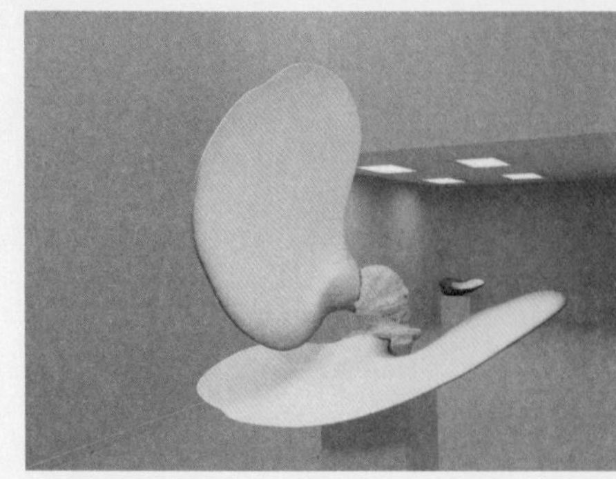

Tunnel Boring Machine, 2021
High temperature clay, resin, metal,
acrylic paint, matt acrylic varnish
173×150×124

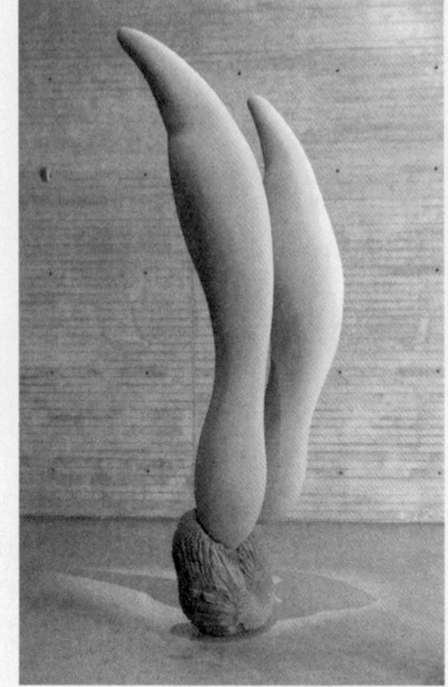

Tunnel Boring Machine, 2022
High temperature clay, resin, metal,
acrylic paint, matt acrylic varnish
320×75×115

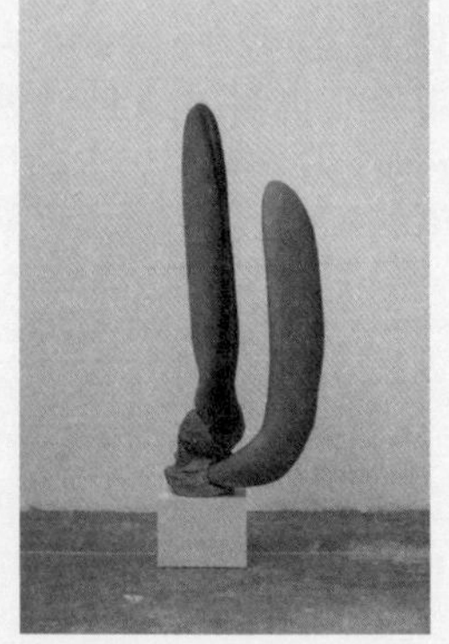

Tunnel Boring Machine, 2023
High temperature clay, resin, acrylic,
matt acrylic varnish, metal
207×72×50

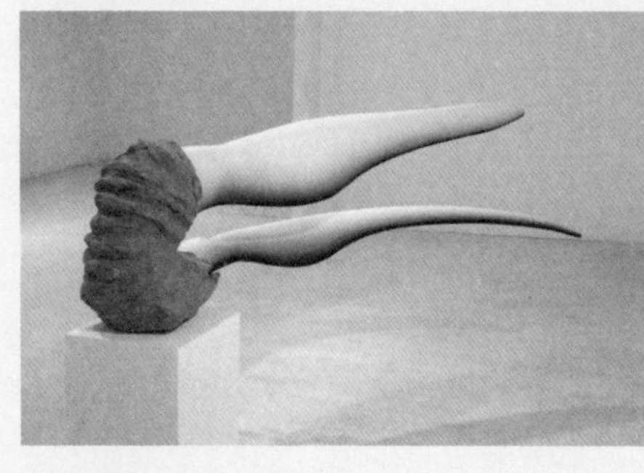

Tunnel Boring Machine, 2021
High temperature clay,
resin, metal, acrylic paint,
matt acrylic varnish
160×217×80

These works are a reimagination of the underground, with these vibrant, finely finished elements that ooze out from the pores of the rough clay. They are hybrids between biology, geology and engineering.[1]   T. S. A.

1   Teresa Solar Abboud, video discussing
    her participation in the 59th Venice Biennale
    (1 December 2022), www.youtube.com/watch?
    v=39iVMD3z-fY&ab_channel=BiennaleChannel
    (accessed 14 November 2023)

Teresa Solar Abboud

Born 1985 in Madrid, Spain
Lives and works in Madrid, Spain

Teresa Solar Abboud's artistic practice is rooted in the field of moving image, where her interest in set design first took hold. But as soon as the Spanish artist began experimenting with sculpture, she became absorbed by it, energised by the potentiality and physicality of the medium. Her *Tunnel Boring Machine* series, which she began in 2021, is the result of a synthesis of distinct themes and strands in her practice. The series combines her deep-seated interest in the sculptural qualities of theatrical spaces with a more recent curiosity about the subterranean realm as a site of enigmatic events and encounters. 'The sublime is traditionally associated with confronting the scale of the sea or the mountains,' the artist told me. 'But through my work with clay, and after becoming attuned to the material and its associations to the soil and the underground, I began to feel that the deepest earth could also be a locus of the sublime, as unknown and mysterious as the abyss of the ocean.'[2]

The *Tunnel Boring Machine* works displayed here (pp. 179–85) could perhaps be described as hybrid creatures. Organic traits and inorganic materials have coalesced into a cast of imposing yet alluring mythical characters. The creatures' propellers (or are they limbs, claws, fins?) suggest a slow and relentless rotating movement, as if they are at rest after tunnelling the earth up from geological strata, like fossils journeying in the twilight of deep time. Their limbs are held together by joints that function as bases or points of equilibrium. Made of clay, heavily texturised and neutrally hued, these joints conjure up something rocky or mineral, in marked contrast with the shiny finishes and industrial colours of the limbs (the highly artificial orange, blue and yellow), which are made of resin with a metal skeleton.

But as their title implies – and the tension inherent to their materials suggests – there is also a machinic dynamism to these creatures. They are not static objects, waiting passively to be exploited: they are daring, active agents that mimic and mirror the pervasive human logic of extraction and our tools, their futures hanging in the balance. In this sense, Solar's sculptures embody a feedback loop, a conversation of sorts between nature and culture.

LORENA MUÑOZ-ALONSO

2   Teresa Solar Abboud in conversation
with the author (September 2023)

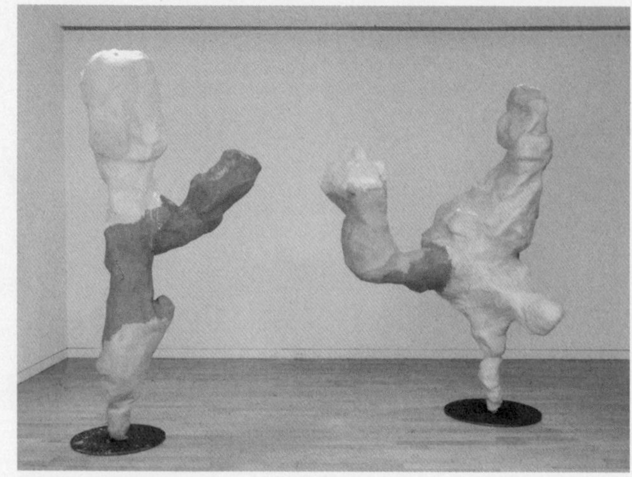

Kain naht Abel (Kain approaching Abel), 2009
Epoxy resin, lacquer, steel
241×196×108
247×132×77

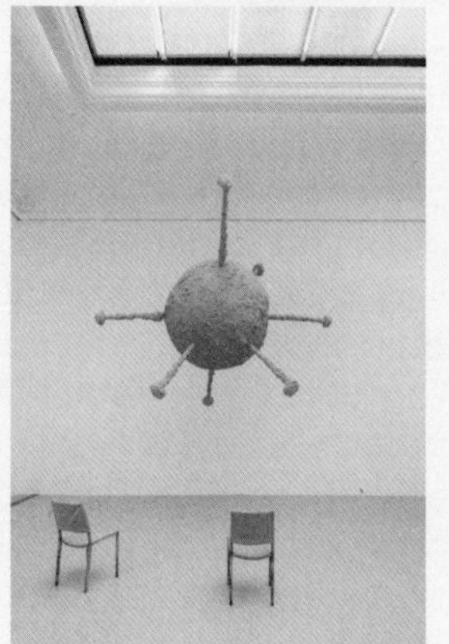

Epiphanie an Stühlen (Epiphany on Chairs), 2011
Sculpture: steel, polystyrene, gauze, dispersion
Ø 165; six arms, each 105×25×2
Chairs: steel, wood, bamboo, linen
Each c. 85×45×5

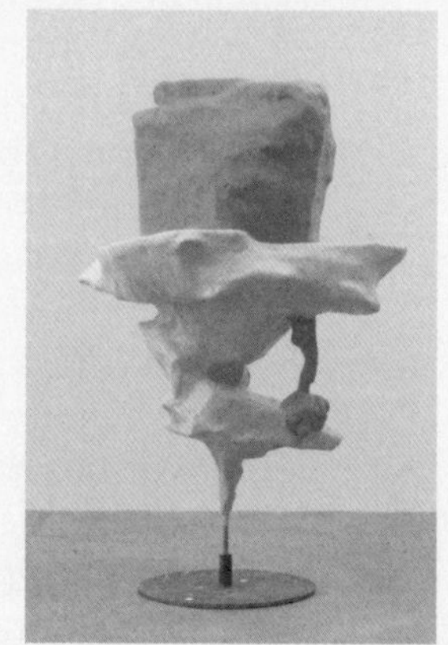

Untitled, 2007
Papier-mâché, styrofoam, epoxy resin,
synthetic resin varnish, metal
190×125×125

As a body, you stand or walk around the sculpture. It's almost equivalent to your own corporeality, to taking up space in one's own three-dimensionality in a defined art space. As far as sculpture in the normal sense is concerned, the viewer is more or less obliged to engage in movement. There is something standing here that you walk around, and perhaps the impression you have of what is being presented also determines whether the movement is quick or especially slow, depending on whether you are really concentrating.[1]　F. W.

1　Franz West cited in Robert Fleck/Bice Curiger/
Neal Benezra, *Franz West* (London: Phaidon,
1999), pp. 8–9

Franz West

Born 1947 in Vienna, Austria
Died 2012 in Vienna, Austria

Franz West's public journey as an artist began with his *Passstücke* (Adaptives), sculptures he made from the early 1970s until shortly before his death in 2012. Crudely fabricated from papier-mâché and scrap paper, they only function as West intended when they are picked up and interacted with by the audience, undermining the hallowed and protected status of the art object. His furniture sculptures exist to be used in a similar way: once seated, the observer becomes the observed, the boundary between audience and artwork broken down.

The title *Epiphanie an Stühlen (Epiphany on Chairs)* suggests that the chairs which form part of this 2011 work (p. 189) will propel those who use them to a state of revelation. But what is the object they will be contemplating as they sit? An organic sputnik, perhaps, or a vastly enlarged microbe escaped from a laboratory slide. It's the sculpture's colour that is most striking: candyfloss pink, the colour of women's underwear in the Vienna of West's youth and of the dentures his dentist mother left lying around the apartment. Don't trust the promises art makes or the paraphernalia around it, he seems to be telling us – it's all just voyeurism, prostheses, another fairground ride.

Catholic religious imagery alienated West as a child, yet *Kain naht Abel (Kain approaching Abel)* (2009, pp. 190–91) responds to one of the Bible's best known and most frequently depicted stories, the rivalry between brothers Cain and Abel that ended in Abel's murder and Cain's expulsion from Paradise. In West's hands, nothing is safe: didactic meaning evaporates and the story's protagonists shape-shift into grotesquely distorted blobs blotched with colour, seemingly scooped from the clay Cain tilled. The final outcome of the struggle between the forms hangs in the balance as, arrested in a moment of primal confrontation, the two hang frozen in an endless sparring match.

JAMES ATTLEE

List of Exhibited Works

Dimensions, where known,
are given in centimetres,
height × width × depth
The final selection of works
will be made during
the installation

RUTH ASAWA

· *Untitled* (S.154, Hanging
Nine-Lobed, Single-Layered
Continuous Form), c. 1958
  Monel wire
  281.9×38.1×38.1
  Private Collection

· *Untitled* (S.065, Hanging
Seven-Lobed, Multi-Layered
Continuous Form within
a Form with Spheres in the
Second, Third, Fourth,
and Sixth Lobes), c. 1960–63
  Oxidised copper
  and brass wire
  238.8×44.5×44.5
  Private Collection

· *Untitled* (S.142, Hanging
Five-Lobed, Multi-Layered
Continuous Form within
a Form), 1990
  Oxidised copper wire
  137.2×35.6×35.6
  Private Collection

NAIRY BAGHRAMIAN

· *Chin Up (First Fitting A)*,
2016
  Two parts; waxed wood,
  polished and lacquered
  aluminium
  122×85×80
  330×110×100
  Courtesy the Artist

· *Chin Up (First Fitting C)*,
2016
  Two parts; waxed wood,
  polished and lacquered
  aluminium
  160×450×80
  278×122×87
  Courtesy the Artist

PHYLLIDA BARLOW

· *untitled: girl ii; 2019*,
2019–20
  Steel, timber, wire netting,
  polystyrene, polyfoam
  board, scrim, plaster, paint,
  cement, PVA
  Overall: 250×410×200
  Courtesy of Hauser & Wirth

· *untitled: modernsculpture;
2022*, 2022
  Steel, filler, PVA, paint,
  polyurethane foam, spray
  paint, sand, paint stripper
  250×220×250
  Courtesy of Hauser & Wirth

LYNDA BENGLIS

· *Quartered Meteor*, 1969,
cast 1975
  Lead and steel
  on steel base
  150×168×158
  Tate: Presented by the
  American Fund for the
  Tate Gallery, partial
  purchase and partial gift
  of John Cheim and
  Howard Read 2010

· *Power Tower*, 2019
  Everdur bronze (golden)
  228.6×179.4×172.2
  Courtesy the Artist
  and Pace Gallery

MICHEL BLAZY

· *Bouquet Final*, 2012
  Bath foam, water,
  compressor unit, plastic
  tubes, troughs, scaffolding
  and EPDM rubber flooring
  500×500×120

PALOMA BOSQUÊ

· *Two Stones*, 2017
  Lead sheet, brass rods,
  hand felted wool
  and beeswax with rosin
  202×212×34
  Amitai Collection

OLAF BRZESKI

· *Dream – Spontaneous
Combustion*, 2008
  Polyurethane resin,
  carbon fibre mat, black
  pigment, wood, steel
  Dimensions variable,
  c. 145×85×78
  Collection of the Museum
  of Modern Art in Warsaw,
  courtesy of Joanna Sarwa

· *untitled (9), from the Little
Orphans series, 2014*, 2014
  Cast iron, chairs
  87×80×43
  Courtesy of the Artist
  and Raster Gallery

· *untitled (from Little Orphans
series)*, 2009
  Cast iron, chair
  74×94×67
  Private Collection
  Joanna Sarwa

CHOI JEONG HWA

· *Blooming matrix*, 2008
  Mixed media
  11 works from the series:
  227×92×92
  171×35×26
  183×60×60
  240×110×110
  217×73×73
  180×30×30
  20×17×71
  30×17×17
  180×30×30
  215×30×30
  175×30×30
  Courtesy the Artist
  and P21

TARA DONOVAN

· *Untitled (Mylar)*, 2011
  Mylar and hot glue
  360×435×938
  Courtesy of the Artist
  and Pace Gallery

DRIFT

· *Shylight*, 2006–2014
  Aluminium, polished
  stainless steel, silk,
  LEDs, robotics
  Eight parts, each
  365×480×500
  Courtesy the Artists
  and Pace Gallery

EVA FÀBREGAS

· *Pumping*, 2019
  Air, elastic fabric, sensory
  balls and 8-channel sound
  installation, including
  foam, latex, silicone
  tubing and 12 subwoofers
  Soundtrack produced
  by Equiknoxx. 8-channel
  mix by Chris Fitzpatrick.
  Sound installation
  developed with Sabel
  Gavaldon. Sound design
  developed with Carlos
  Ferreira. Commissioned
  and produced by
  Kunstverein München
  wih support from Acción
  Cultural Española
  Courtesy of the Artist and
  Kunstverein München

HOLLY HENDRY

· *Sottobosco*, 2024
  Steel ducting, stainless
  steel, blown glass, concrete
  canvas, Jesmonite, lead,
  timber, paint
  Courtesy of the Artist and
  Stephen Friedman Gallery,
  London and New York

EJ HILL

· *A Subsequent Offering*, 2017
  Wood and LED neon flex
  1249.7×274.3×215.9
  Courtesy of the Artist

MARGUERITE HUMEAU

· *The Guardian of Ancient Yeast*, 2023
  Natural beeswax, microcrystalline wax, pigments, 150-year-old walnut (cause of death: unknown), handblown glass, 4,500-year-old yeast
  243×98×70
  Original sound by Bendik Giske
  Courtesy of the Artist and White Cube

· *The Brewer*, 2023
  Handblown glass, 150-year-old walnut (cause of death: unknown), Bermondsey Street Bees raw honey, 4,500-year-old yeast, brewer's yeast, wasp venom and culture of termite mushroom (Termitomyces)
  76×58×57
  Original sound by Bendik Giske
  Courtesy of the Artist and White Cube

· *The Holder of Wasp Venom*, 2023
  Natural beeswax, microcrystalline wax, pigments, 150-year-old walnut (cause of death: unknown), handblown glass and wasp venom
  190×320×290
  Original sound by Bendik Giske
  Courtesy of the Artist and White Cube

JEAN-LUC MOULÈNE

· *Blown Knot 6 ³₂ (Borromean) Varia 06*, Marseille 2012
  Glass (CIRVA)
  31×23×25.5
  Private Collection, Derbyshire

· *Méduse*, Paris 2018
  Bronze (Fonderie de Coubertin), blue patina
  27×29×45
  Courtesy of the Artist and Galerie Greeta Meert

· *Parure 1*, Marseille 2019
  Bronze (Fonderie de Coubertin) and glass (CIRVA)
  30×58×44
  Private Collection

· *Ressort flou*, Le Buisson 2022
  Bronze and silver patina (Fonderie de Coubertin)
  50×20×19.5
  Courtesy the Artist, Paris and Thomas Dane Gallery

· *Vaisseaux verseurs*, Le Buisson 2022
  Plastic, plaster, resin, bronze (Fonderie de Coubertin)
  63.5×57.1×59.7
  Courtesy the Artist, Paris and Thomas Dane Gallery

· *Plongement 1*, Marseille 2023
  Glass (CIRVA), bronze (Fonderie de Coubertin)
  55×55×55
  Courtesy of T&C Collection, France

SENGA NENGUDI

· *Water Composition I*, 1969–70/2019
  Vinyl, water, rope
  146.1×177.8×221.7
  Dallas Museum of Art, TWO×TWO for AIDS and Art Fund
  Exhibition copy

· *R.S.V.P. Reverie 'D'*, 2014
  Nylon mesh, sand and copper
  162.5×381×23cm
  Städtische Galerie im Lenbachhaus und Kunstbau, München, eKiCo Collection.
  Exhibition copy

ERNESTO NETO

· *Iaia Kui Dau Arã Naia*, 2021
  Cotton string crochet dyed with spices (turmeric, clove, cumin, pepper, ginger), stones and wooden hooks
  135×160×153
  Collection Garance Primat

MARTIN PURYEAR

· *Untitled*, 2015
  Alaskan yellow cedar
  280×68×44
  Museum Voorlinden, Wassenaar, The Netherlands

MATTHEW RONAY

· *Brontes, Steropes, and Arges*, 2023
  Basswood, dye, primer, plastic, steel
  71.8×49.53×18.42
  Courtesy of the Artist and Casey Kaplan, New York

· *Crawl*, 2023
  Basswood, dye, flocking, plastic, steel
  61.6×56.52×20
  Courtesy of the Artist and Casey Kaplan, New York

· *Globules*, 2023
  Basswood, dye, shellac-based primer, flocking, plastic, steel, HMA
  34.3×69.9×14
  Courtesy of the Artist and Casey Kaplan, New York

· *Third Instar*, 2023
  Basswood, dye, flocking, plastic, steel
  36.2×41.9×36.2
  Courtesy of the Artist and Casey Kaplan, New York

TERESA SOLAR ABBOUD

· *Tunnel Boring Machine*, 2021
  High temperature clay, resin, metal, acrylic paint, matt acrylic varnish
  160×217×80
  TBA21 Thyssen-Bornemisza Art Contemporary Collection

· *Tunnel Boring Machine*, 2021
  High temperature clay, resin, metal, acrylic paint, matt acrylic varnish
  173×150×124
  Colección Fundación ARCO. Depósito Museo CA2M

· *Tunnel Boring Machine*, 2022
  High temperature clay, resin, metal, acrylic paint, matt acrylic varnish
  320×75×115
  Museo Nacional Centro de Arte Reina Sofía, Madrid. Long term loan from the Fundación Museo Reina Sofía, 2022. (Donated by TBA21 Thyssen-Bornemisza Art Contemporary)

FRANZ WEST

· *Kain naht Abel (Kain approaching Abel)*, 2009
  Epoxy resin, lacquer, steel
  241×196×108
  247×132×77
  Estate Franz West, Vienna

· *Epiphanie an Stühlen (Epiphany on Chairs)*, 2011
  Sculpture: steel, polystyrene, gauze, dispersion
  Chairs: steel, wood, bamboo, linen
  Sculpture: Ø 165, six arms: 105×25×25 each
  Chairs: approx. 85×45×55 each
  Estate Franz West, Vienna

Photographic Credits

All works of art copyright © the artists 2024 unless otherwise stated

ASAWA
All works © 2024 Ruth Asawa Lanier Inc./Artists Rights Society (ARS), New York. Courtesy David Zwirner
· p. 35: Photo by Imogen Cunningham © 2024 Imogen Cunningham Trust
· pp. 43–45: Photo Dan Bradica
· pp. 46–48: Photo Maris Hutchinson/EPW Studio

BAGHRAMIAN
Images courtesy of the artist, Marian Goodman Gallery, kurimanzutto, Mexico City / New York and Galerie Buchholz, Cologne
· pp. 51–55: Photo Timo Ohler
· pp. 56–57: Photo Alex Yudzon

BARLOW
All works © Phyllida Barlow, Courtesy Hauser & Wirth All images courtesy Hauser & Wirth
· pp. 59–61: Photo Zak Kelley

BENGLIS
All works © Lynda Benglis. Licensed by VAGA at ARS, NY and DACS, London 2023
· p. 24: Henry Groskinsky/ The LIFE Picture Collection/ Shutterstock
· pp. 65–66: Images courtesy of the Artist and Xavier Hufkens, Brussels; photo: HV-studio
· pp. 68–69: Images courtesy the artist, Pace Gallery and Thomas Dane Gallery; photo: Phoebe D'Heurle

BLAZY
Works © Michel Blazy, ADAGP 2023. Images courtesy the Artist and Art : Concept, Paris
· pp. 71–73: Photo Pauline Rymarski
· p. 74: Photo Marc Domage

BOSQUÊ
Images courtesy of the artist and Mendes Wood DM, São Paulo, Brussels, Paris, New York
· pp. 77–79: Photo Bruno Leão
· p. 80–81: Photo Ana Pigosso

BRZESKI
All images courtesy of Raster gallery, Warszawa, PL
· p. 8: The MAC, Belfast. Photo Simon Mills
· p. 83: EASTinternational 2009. © Norwich University of the Arts
· pp. 84–87: Photos Wojciech Pacewicz

CHOI
All images courtesy the Artist and P21

DONOVAN
All images courtesy Pace Gallery
· pp. 97, 98–99, 100: Photo Kerry Ryan McFate
· pp. 102–3: Photo Dennis Cowley

DRIFT
All images courtesy DRIFT
· pp. 104–7: Photo Ossip van Duivenbode
· p. 108: Photo Tomek Dersu Aaron
· p. 109: Photo courtesy of MK_G
· pp. 110–11: Photo courtesy of Carpenters Workshop Gallery

FÀBREGAS
All images courtesy bombon projects
· p. 118: Courtesy Fundación Botín
· p. 119: Photo Jacopo Laforgia

HENDRY
All images courtesy the artist and Stephen Friedman Gallery, London and New York
· pp. 121–23: Photo Mark Blower
· pp. 124, 127: Photo Hells Gibson

HILL
All images courtesy the artist
· p. 129: Photo Sergey Illin
· pp. 130–31: Photo Arlene Mejorado
· p. 132–33: Photo Kaelan Burkett

HUMEAU
All images © Marguerite Humeau and White Cube
· pp. 20, 135–37: © White Cube (Ollie Hammick)
· p. 138: © White Cube (David Westwood)
· pp. 139–41: © White Cube (Theo Christelis)

MOULÈNE
All works © Jean-Luc Moulène/ADAGP, 2024 All images courtesy the artist and Galerie Greta Meert except p. 145 courtesy the artist and Thomas Dane Gallery

NENGUDI
· p. 31: Courtesy of the artist and Thomas Erben Gallery, New York
· pp. 151, 153: Photo Timo Ohler
· p. 154: Photo courtesy Städtische Galerie im Lenbachhaus und Kunstbau München, Sammlung KiCo
· p. 155: Photo courtesy Dallas Museum of Art, TWO×TWO for AIDS and Art Fund 2021.24

NETO
· pp. 157–59: Courtesy Galerie Max Hetzler Berlin | Paris | London. Photo: Nicolas Brasseurpaul
· pp. 161–163: The Museum of Fine Arts, Houston, Museum purchase funded by the Caroline Wiess Law Accessions Endowment Fund, 2019.190. Photograph by Will Michels © The Museum of Fine Arts, Houston

PURYEAR
All images © Martin Puryear, Courtesy Matthew Marks Gallery

RONAY
All images courtesy the artist

SOLAR ABBOUD
All images courtesy of the artist and Travesía Cuatro, except p. 184 Courtesy Galería Joan Prats and Travesía Cuatro
· Cover, pp. 179–81: Photo Jhoeko
· pp. 182–83: Photo Pablo Gomez-Ogando
· p. 184: Photo Marta de Muga
· p. 185: Photo courtesy of TBA21, Museo Reina Sofia and Travesía Cuatro

WEST
All works © Archiv Franz West © Estate Franz West All images courtesy Franz West Privatstiftung

Author Biographies

JAMES ATTLEE
is a writer based in Oxford.
His previous publications
include *Isolarion: A Different
Oxford Journey* (2007),
*Guernica: Painting the End
of the World* (2017) and *Under
the Rainbow: Voices from
Lockdown* (2021).

KATIE GUGGENHEIM
is Assistant Curator
at the Hayward Gallery.

HELEN LUCKETT
is a writer based in London.
She has contributed to many
publications including
Women Artists (2020) and
*Dear Earth: Art and Hope
in a Time of Crisis* (2023).

ANUSHA MISTRY
is Curatorial Assistant
at the Hayward Gallery.

**LORENA
MUÑOZ-ALONSO**
is an art critic and writer
based in London, and
is currently finishing her
training to become a psycho-
analytic psychotherapist.

NATALIE RUDD
was Senior Curator
of the Arts Council Collection.
Her recent publications
include *Breaking the Mould:
Sculpture by Women*

since 1945 (2020) and
Contemporary Art
(2023). She is currently
a Midlands4Cities PhD
researcher at the University
of Birmingham studying
precariousness in sculpture.

RALPH RUGOFF
is Director of the
Hayward Gallery.

Acknowledgements

This exhibition has
been realised with the
collaboration of the
participating artists and
their representatives,
to whom we are greatly
indebted.

We are particularly grateful
to the following individuals
and organisations for their
collaboration and support:
· The Estate of Ruth Asawa:
  Henry Weverka
· Nairy Baghramian studio:
  Michel Ziegler
· Thomas Dane Gallery:
  Francois Chantala, Emma
  Da Costa, Olivia Rawnsley
· Tara Donovan studio:
  Claire Watkins
· DRIFT: Bram Prins
· Gagosian Gallery: Adele
  Minardi, Stefan Ratibor
· Galerie Greta Meert:
  Magali Wyns
· Hauser & Wirth: Florian
  Berktold, Elly Hawley
· Marguerite Humeau studio:
  Maudie Gibbons
· Casey Kaplan: Kaytlin
  Nodine
· Mendes Wood DM:
  Verônica Hornyansky
· Raster Gallery:
  Karolina Kowalska
· Sprüth Magers: Andreas
  Gegner, Hannes
  Schroeder-Finckh
· Travesía Cuatro:
  Andrea Celda
· Vita Nova, Choi Jeong Hwa
  studio: Sera Kang
· White Cube

SUPPORTERS

When Forms Come Alive is
generously supported by
the When Forms Come Alive
Exhibition Supporters
Group: Bianca and Stuart
Roden, Simon Morris and
Annalisa Burello, White
Cube, Sarah Cannon, Thomas
Dane Gallery, Gagosian,
Sprüth Magers and David
Zwirner Gallery. Additional
support has also kindly
been provided by the Henry
Moore Foundation, Hauser &
Wirth and Fluxus Art Projects.

LENDERS

· Amitai Collection
· Colección Fundación ARCO.
  Depósito Museo CA2M
· Collection Garance Primat
· Collection of the Museum
  of Modern Art in Warsaw,
  Courtesy of Joanna Sarwa
· Estate Franz West, Vienna
· Museo Nacional Centro
  de Arte Reina Sofía, Madrid.
  Long term loan from the
  Fundación Museo Reina
  Sofía, 2022. (Donated by
  TBA21 Thyssen-Bornemisza
  Art Contemporary)
· Museum Voorlinden,
  Wassenaar, The Netherlands
· Private Collection,
  Derbyshire
· Tate

And those who wish to
remain anonymous.

EXHIBITION
CREDITS

HAYWARD GALLERY
· Ralph Rugoff, Director
· Katie Guggenheim,
  Assistant Curator
· Anusha Mistry, Curatorial
  Assistant
· Mary Richards, Publisher
· Juliane Heynert, Installation
  Manager
· Archie Bell, Exhibition
  Senior Technician
· Matt Siwerski, Senior
  Technician for Eva
  Fàbregas's *Pumping*
· Charlotte Pearson, Senior
  Registrar
· Sophie Ridsdale-Smith,
  Assistant Registrar
· Kate Sullivan, Deputy
  Director, Visual Arts
· Alison Maun, Indemnity
  Coordinator
· Maya Baker, Hayward
  Gallery Coordinator
· Ananya Jain, Hayward
  Gallery Administrator
· Marcia Ceppo, Operations
  and Logistics Manager
· Jules Denton, Operations
  Administrator
· Nancy Bryan, Librarian
· Matt Arthurs, Philip Gardner,
  Chloe Windsor, Installation
  Technicians
· Leonie Warner, Senior
  Visitor Experience Manager
· Kate Ford, Daniel Pickard
  and Malini Stevenson,
  Duty Managers
· Additional exhibition
  research was conducted
  by Assistant Curator
  Suzanna Petot

SOUTHBANK CENTRE
We are grateful to all our
collaborators across
Southbank Centre, without
whom this exhibition
would not have been
possible. In particular,
we would like to acknowl-
edge the contributions
of our colleagues in
Southbank Centre's Creative
Engagement, Design,
Development, Digital, Health
and Safety, Marketing,
Press and Retail teams.

Published on the occasion
of the exhibition
*When Forms Come Alive:
Sixty Years of Restless Sculpture*
Hayward Gallery, London
7 February–6 May 2024

Curated by
Ralph Rugoff
Assistant Curator:
Katie Guggenheim
Curatorial Assistant:
Anusha Mistry

Exhibition supported by

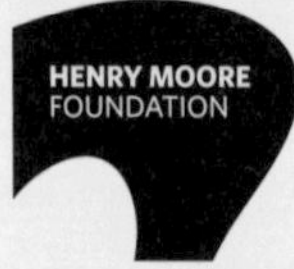

Published in 2024 by
Hayward Gallery Publishing
Southbank Centre
Belvedere Road
London SE1 8XX
www.southbankcentre.co.uk

Hayward Gallery Publisher:
Mary Richards
Copy-editor:
Neil Stewart
Picture Researcher:
Rosie Pickles

Catalogue designed by
In the shade of a tree
Typeset in
Tiempos (Klim Type)
New Spirit (Newlyn)
Printed in Belgium on papers
from sustainable forests
Arena Bulk white 100 gsm
Magno matt 135 gsm
Wibalin Natural white 500
120 gsm

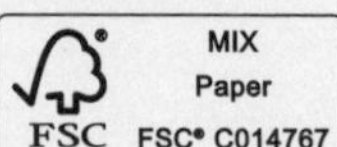

A catalogue record for this book
is available from the British
Library.
ISBN 978-1-85332-377-5

This catalogue is not intended
to be used for authentication
or related purposes. The Southbank
Board Limited accepts no
liability for any errors or
omissions that the catalogue
may inadvertently contain.

Distributed in North,
Central and South America by
ARTBOOK | D.A.P.
75 Broad Street, Suite 630
New York, NY 10004
tel: +1 212 627 1999
www.artbook.com

Distributed in the rest
of the world by
Thames & Hudson Ltd
181A High Holborn
London WC1V 7QX
www.thamesandhudson.com

Cover:
Teresa Solar Abboud,
Tunnel Boring Machine,
2021 (detail)

Endpapers:
Tara Donovan, *Untitled
(Mylar)*, 2011 (details)

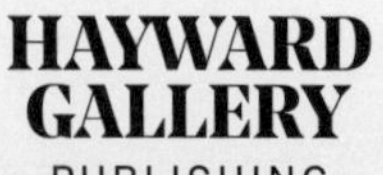
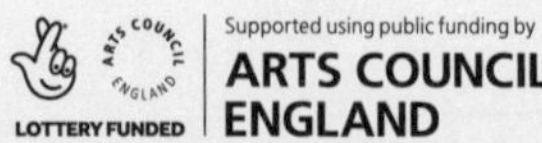

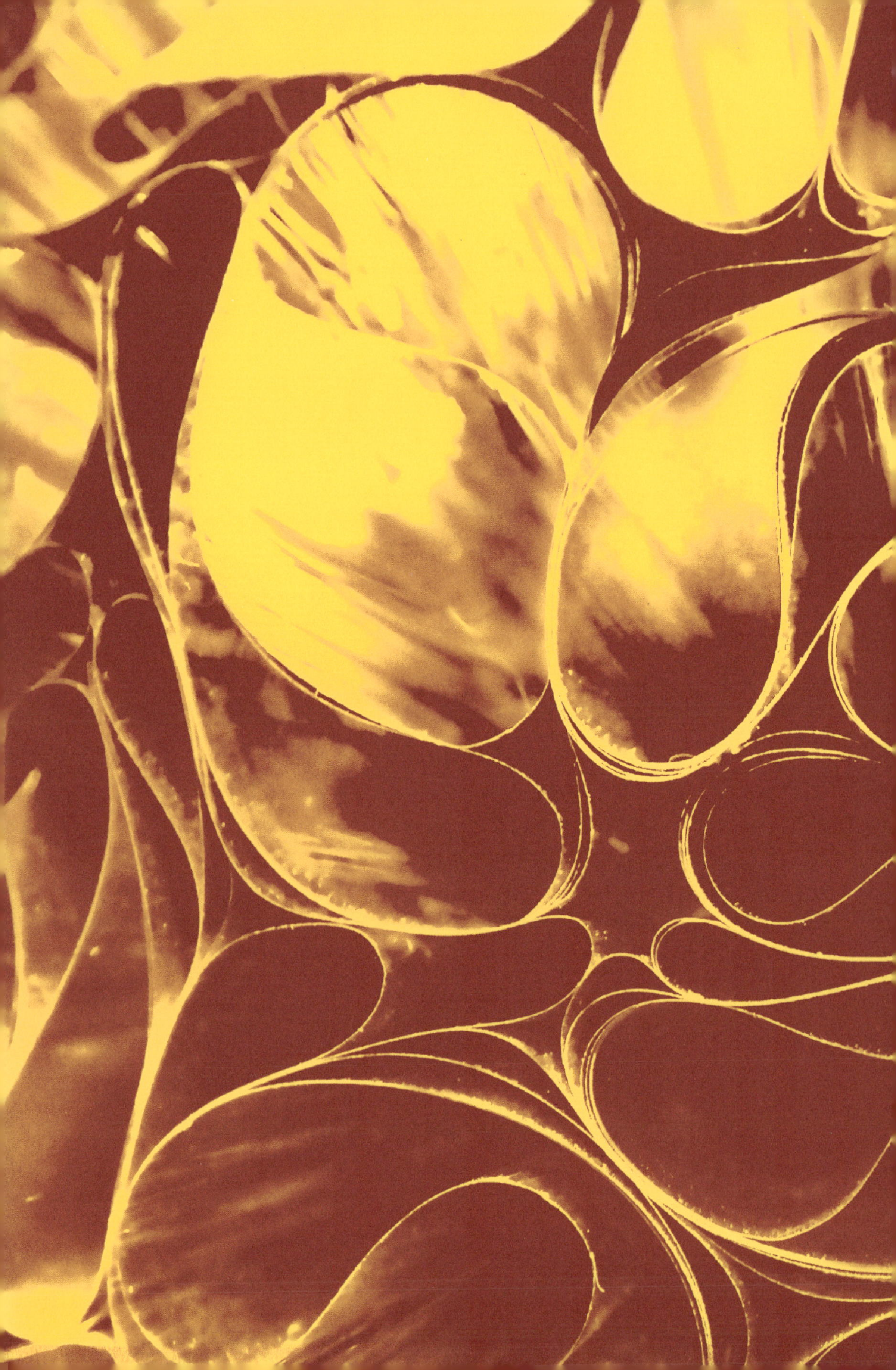